PENGUIN SPECIAL

THE NON-MEDICAL USE OF DRUGS

D0784190

THE
NON-MEDICAL USE
OF DRUGS

Interim Report
of the Canadian Government's
Commission of Inquiry

PENGUIN BOOKS

Penguin Books Ltd, Harmondsworth, Middlesex, England
Penguin Books Inc., 7110 Ambassador Road, Baltimore, Maryland 21207, U.S.A.
Penguin Books Australia Ltd, Ringwood, Victoria, Australia

—

First published by Information Canada 1970
Published in Penguin Books 1971

—

—

Made and printed in Great Britain by
Cox & Wyman Ltd,
London, Reading and Fakenham
Set in Linotype Times

The Honourable John Munro, P.C., M.P.,   April 6, 1970.
Minister of National Health and Welfare,
Brooke Claxton Building,
Tunney's Pasture,
Ottawa, Ontario.

Sir,

    The Commission of Inquiry Into the Non-Medical Use of Drugs, appointed by Order-in-Council P.C. 1969–1112 on May 29th of last year, has the honour to submit the attached Interim Report of its findings and recommendations.

    We would like to take this opportunity to express our gratitude to the many Canadians in all walks of life whose knowledge and views have been of great value to us during our inquiry to this date.

                          Respectfully yours,

                                      GERALD LE DAIN, CHAIRMAN

IAN L. CAMPBELL, MEMBER   HEINZ LEHMANN, MEMBER

J. PETER STEIN, MEMBER   MARIE-ANDREE BERTRAND, MEMBER

JAMES J. MOORE, EXECUTIVE-SECRETARY

CONTENTS

THE COMMISSION'S INTERPRETATION OF ITS TASK

The Background of the Commission's Appointment

1. The Commission of Inquiry into the Non-Medical Use of Drugs was appointed by the Government of Canada under Part I of the Inquiries Act on May 29, 1969, on the recommendation of the Honourable John Munro, Minister of National Health and Welfare.

2. The concern that gave rise to the appointment of the Commission is described in Order-in-Council P.C. 1969–1112, which authorized the appointment, in the following terms:

The Committee of the Privy Council have had before them a report from the Minister of National Health and Welfare, representing:
That there is growing concern in Canada about the non-medical use of certain drugs and substances, particularly, those having sedative, stimulant, tranquillizing or hallucinogenic properties, and the effect of such use on the individual and the social implications thereof;
That within recent years, there has developed also the practice of inhaling the fumes of certain solvents having an hallucinogenic effect, and resulting in serious physical damage and a number of deaths, such solvents being found in certain household substances. Despite warnings and considerable publicity, this practice has developed among young people and can be said to be related to the use of drugs for other than medical purposes;
That certain of these drugs and substances, including lysergic acid diethylamide, LSD, methamphetamines, commonly referred to as 'Speed', and certain others, have been made the subject of controlling or prohibiting legislation under the Food and Drugs Act, and cannabis, marijuana, has been a

13

substance, the possession of or trafficking in which has been prohibited under the Narcotic Control Act;

That notwithstanding these measures and the competent enforcement thereof by the R.C.M. Police and other enforcement bodies, the incidence of possession and use of these substances for non-medical purposes has increased and the need for an investigation as to the cause of such increasing use has become imperative.

During the year or so preceding the appointment of the Commission, members of parliament had called for an inquiry into the use of drugs. One member spoke of 'the galloping increase in the use of marijuana and the increasing number of young people tragically being paraded daily before the courts' and of 'the extreme urgency of dealing properly with these cases'. In announcing the Government's intention to appoint the Commission, the Minister of National Health and Welfare spoke of 'the grave concern felt by the Government at the expanding proportions of the use of drugs and related substances for non-medical purposes'.

The Commission's Terms of Reference

3. The Order-in-Council authorizing the appointment of the Commission sets out its terms of reference as follows:

That inquiry be made into and concerning the factors underlying or relating to the non-medical use of the drugs and substances above described and that for this purpose a Commission of Inquiry be established, constituted and with authority as hereinafter provided.

(a) to marshal from available sources, both in Canada and abroad, data and information comprising the present fund of knowledge concerning the non-medical use of sedative, stimulant, tranquillizing, hallucinogenic and other psychotropic drugs or substances;

(b) to report on the current state of medical knowledge respecting the effect of the drugs and substances referred to in (a);

14

(c) to inquire into and report on the motivation underlying the non-medical use referred to in (a);

(d) *to inquire into and report on the social, economic, educational and philosophical factors relating to the use for non-medical purposes of the drugs and substances referred to in (a)* and in particular, on the extent of the phenomenon, the social factors that had led to it, the age groups involved, and problems of communication; and

(e) *to inquire into and recommend with respect to the ways* or means by which the Federal Government can act, alone or in its relations with Government at other levels, in the reduction of the dimensions of the problems involved in such use.

The Implications of the Terms of Reference

4. While the Commission's terms of reference make specific mention of the sedative, stimulant, tranquillizing and hallucinogenic drugs, they also require inquiry concerning other psychotropic drugs and substances. *The Commission understands drug to mean any substance that by its chemical nature alters structure or function in the living organism. The psychotropic drugs are those drugs which alter sensation, mood, consciousness or other psychological or behavioural functions.* These concepts are further clarified in Chapter Two of this report. A number of classifications of psychotropic drugs have been brought to the Commission's attention. Chapter Two presents the classification that has been accepted by the Commission. It also contains a detailed account of the psychotropic properties and medical and non-medical uses of certain of the drugs causing the greatest public concern. It is clear to the Commission that it would not be appropriate to confine its attention to the so-called 'soft drugs' such as marijuana, hashish and LSD. The 'hard drugs' such as the opiate narcotics, of which heroin is an example, have marked psychotropic effects. The amphetamines or 'speed' drugs which are popularly considered as hard drugs appear to be increasing in their non-medical use. Moreover, both the structure of present Canadian drug laws

and the nature of the drug controversy make it impossible to consider the 'soft drugs' without reference to the amphetamines and the opiates. Indeed, the opiate narcotics have been and are an important reference point in establishing the public policy perspective for the non-medical use of many other drugs. The Commission believes that it has properly focused its primary attention in the initial phase of its inquiry on the non-medical use of drugs such as cannabis, LSD and amphetamines by young people. However, we have had a growing concern for the facts and implications of the use of drugs such as alcohol and tobacco by people of all ages. These two drugs, both of which are psychotropic, remain the most popular drugs in non-medical use among both young people and adults. Adults generally seem unwilling to accept the fact that alcohol and tobacco are drugs, and often find it difficult to view the non-medical drug use of youth with reference to and in the context of the socially acceptable use of drugs by adults.

5. Two broad categories in which the use of psychotropic drugs can be classified are: (a) medical and non-medical use, and (b) legal and illegal use. While the distinction between legal and illegal use is simple and derives directly from the law, it is difficult to find a satisfactory definition of medical and non-medical drug use. *Medical use of drugs is taken by the Commission to be use which is indicated for generally accepted medical reasons, whether under medical supervision or not; all drug use which is not indicated on generally accepted medical grounds is considered to be non-medical use.* Thus, the occasional use of aspirin to control the pain of an ordinary headache is considered to be medical use, while the dependent use of large quantities of barbiturates obtained through one or more prescriptions is not. Clearly, non-medical use is not to be equated with illegal use. The use of alcohol by adults is generally non-medical but it is legal, whereas the use of marijuana is both non-medical and illegal.

6. The Commission is invited to marshal the present fund of world knowledge concerning the non-medical use of psychotropic drugs and substances. Taken literally, this task is impossible with the time and resources available to the Commission. The world literature on all the psychotropic drugs and sub-

stances is very extensive. There are over 40,000 items on alcohol alone at Rutgers University, a major centre of alcohol studies. There are estimated to be over 2,000 items on cannabis. Experts in the field have testified to the extreme difficulty of keeping abreast of the literature, particularly because of its multi-disciplinary character. There are only a few sources of comprehensive information on this continent: the Addiction Research Foundation of Ontario is by far the best equipped in this country; the National Institute of Mental Health in the United States provides a computerized data retrieval service. In Geneva, the World Health Organization of the United Nations possesses extensive bibliographical resources.

Collecting the available data and information is only one stage. It is also necessary to establish and apply criteria of scientific validity to such data and information. In many instances, the Commission is obliged to rely heavily on the work of experts who have themselves sifted and critically evaluated the available literature. It must form its judgements on the basis of the materials which they have identified as most relevant and reliable. The Commission cannot carry out a comprehensive bibliographical work for the whole range of psychotropic drugs and substances. It must try to seize upon the essentials in the present fund of knowledge as they bear upon the areas of concern and the issues in this inquiry.

7. The Commission is required to report on the current state of medical knowledge concerning the effect of psychotropic drugs and substances. This it has attempted to do in an interim fashion, in Chapter Two, entitled 'The Drugs and Their Effects'. The effects contemplated by paragraph (b) in the terms of reference are presumably the physiological and psychological ones, including their behavioural manifestations. The term 'medical' is rather too narrow as a reference to the expertise which is involved in the determination of drug effects since these are a complex result of many factors, including the expectation of the user and the social setting in which the drug is taken. In its interim brief to the Commission, the Canadian Medical Association stressed the multi-disciplinary character of the study required for a proper understanding of non-medical drug use. We have, therefore, interpreted the word 'medical' to refer broadly

17

to all scientific knowledge concerning the effects of drug use. The language of paragraph (*b*) of the terms of reference suggests that it was not intended that the Commission would itself undertake original research into the effects of non-medical drug use. Although we do not exclude the possibility of some clinical or experimental work, particularly with respect to the effect of certain drugs on psychomotor functions, it is our opinion that with the time and resources at our disposal, and having regard to the research currently being conducted by such organizations as the Addiction Research Foundation and the National Institute of Mental Health, we should confine ourselves to carrying out a critical review of the existing knowledge and ongoing research, as well as attempting to identify research priorities and the role which the federal government can play in relation to research.

8. The remaining paragraphs in the terms of reference deal with the extent and the causes of non-medical drug use. They reflect a broad concern to understand the reasons for the increase in such use. They invite the Commission to attempt to place this phenomenon in a proper social and philosophic context. We cannot help feeling that this is one of the most important aspects of our task: one on which there is a compelling need for an understanding of current Canadian attitudes. This is implied by the allusion in paragraph (*d*) of the terms of reference to 'problems of communication'. To understand the factors underlying non-medical drug use and the problems for which government action may be indicated, it is necessary to consider not only the effects, extent, and causes of such use, but the range of social response and attitude which such use has elicited from government, other institutions and individuals. For non-medical drug use and the social response to it are interacting and mutually conditioning phenomena.

Methods of Inquiry

9. The Commission has used a variety of methods of inquiry. Because of the profound social significance of the non-medical drug use phenomenon and of the importance of personal and public attitudes to it, the Commission decided early to conduct

public hearings in all of the provinces. It has attached particular important to these hearings. They have been used to foster the widest possible public discussion. In order to encourage the participation of young people, it was decided to hold some of the public hearings in more informal settings than may have been customary for such commissions in the past. In addition to the public hearings, the Commissioners have collectively and individually held numerous private hearings, have consulted with experts in several fields related to non-medical drug use, and have read extensively in the scientific and legal literature. The Commission has also received many communications, written and oral, from Canadians in all walks of life.

10. At the beginning of September, 1969, the Commission wrote to over 750 individuals and organizations inviting them to submit briefs or to make oral submissions. In particular, the Commission solicited briefs from: federal and provincial government departments; law enforcement authorities; educational institutions and associations; members of university faculties and departments; medical and pharmaceutical institutions and associations; addiction research foundations; street clinics and other innovative services; correctional and welfare organizations; bar associations; youth organizations; student organizations; and a wide variety of other organizations and individuals having an evident concern or point of contact with the phenomenon of non-medical drug use in Canada. The Commission received a gratifying response to this invitation, and despite the relatively short time available in some cases for the preparation of briefs, individuals and organizations made a very commendable effort to prepare submissions for the public hearings which began in the middle of October.

11. A list of the organizations and individuals who have been identified with submissions to the Commission in the initial phase of this inquiry is contained in Appendix A to this report. Fifty-five organizations have been represented at the public hearings at which they have submitted written briefs; twenty have been represented by oral submissions; forty-five have made written submissions to the Commission without appearing at a public hearing. Thirty-two individuals have sub-

mitted written briefs and 45 others have made oral submissions at public hearings. In addition, there have been numerous oral submissions and interventions by members of the public who have attended the hearings. The Commission has also received several hundred letters from individuals, and a selection of these letters or excerpts from them is included in the Report as Appendix B. We emphasize that this selection is not intended to convey the weight of opinion in this correspondence, but simply to reflect something of the range of response.

12. In the initial phase of this inquiry, the Commission has held public hearings in the following centres: Toronto – October 16, 17 and 18; Vancouver – October 30 and 31; Victoria – November 1; Montreal – November 6, 7 and 8; Winnipeg – November 13 and 14; Ottawa – December 12 and 13; Halifax – January 29 and 30; St John's – January 31; Fredericton – February 19; Moncton – February 20; Sackville – February 20, and Charlottetown – February 21; Kingston – March 5.

A special word may be appropriate concerning the nature of the public hearings. They have been conducted in a rather informal manner. There has been a considerable degree of audience participation. People have felt free to comment on formal submissions, and there has been a great deal of informal exchange among persons attending the hearings. On the whole, response to this style of hearing has been favourable, although there has been some criticism from one or two organizations who have expressed the opinion that we should not have permitted questions and critical comments from members of the public. Because of the nature of the phenomenon which it is required to investigate, the Commission is convinced that it has been essential to attempt to establish a true public forum for discussion of the issues. Most organizations have reacted favourably to this kind of inquiry. In addition to the more traditional settings of hotels and public buildings, the Commission has held public hearings at universities and from time to time in coffee houses that have become centres of the new youth culture.

Informal hearings have been held in the following universities: York University; the University of Toronto; the University of British Columbia; the University of Montreal; McGill University; Sir George Williams University; the University of Manitoba; the University of Winnipeg; the University of Ottawa; Carleton University; Dalhousie University; Memorial University; the University of New Brunswick; the University of Moncton; Mount Allison University; the University of Prince Edward Island; and in the following coffee houses: 'The Penny Farthing' in Yorkville, Toronto; 'The Bistro' in Vancouver, and the 'Back Door' in Montreal.

The hearings in these more informal settings have given the Commission direct and vivid contact with the opinions and attitudes of young people in Canada. All the Commission hearings have been recorded on tape, and in addition there has been a stenographic record. In many ways it is a matter of regret that an audio-visual record could not have been made, but the nature of the subject matter is such that the Commission felt obliged to protect individuals appearing before it from undue publicity. The media have cooperated with the Commission in respecting its request that members of the public should not be photographed while making submissions. In many cases, the submissions have been of a highly personal nature, and the hearings would have been much inhibited if they had been photographed. At the same time, the Commission has been intensely aware of the fact that it was listening to an unusual social commentary. Opinions and feelings have poured forth in the hearings with great spontaneity, particularly in the more informal settings. The Commission has been deeply impressed, and on several occasions, moved by the testimony which it has heard. It has been struck by the depth of feeling which this phenomenon and the social response to it have aroused. As a result of the initial phase of its inquiry, the Commission is more than ever convinced that the proper response to the non-medical use of psychotropic drugs is a question which must be worked out by the people of Canada, examining it and talking it over together. It goes to the roots of our society and touches the values underlying our whole approach to life. It is not a matter which can be confined to the discrete consultation of experts, although experts obviously have their role, and a very important one, to play.

13. A word should be said about the protection of witnesses. The terms of reference of the Commission empower it to take testimony in such manner as to safeguard the anonymity of witnesses. The Order-in-Council authorizing the appointment of the Commission provides:

> That the said Commissioners may, if they deem the same expedient, cause a record to be made of the evidence which shall be given or produced before them, or any part of that evidence, as to the matters to be inquired into and reported upon and may direct that the oral evidence of witnesses before them, or any such witness, shall be taken in shorthand by a shorthand writer, approved and sworn by the said Commissioners or one of them, and may direct that the oral evidence of any such witness may be so given and recorded, whether under oath or otherwise, without a disclosure of the identity of that witness, and that any evidence so recorded shall be certified by the person or persons taking the same in shorthand, as correct.

The notices which the Commission has published of its hearings have given prominence to this readiness to take evidence given privately and anonymously, and many witnesses have availed themselves of this opportunity. The Commission has also received a number of anonymous submissions through the mail. At the same time, concern has been expressed from time to time that the public hearings might be used for law enforcement purposes. As a result of an understanding at the outset of this inquiry with the officers of the R.C.M.P., the Commission has been able to assure the public that its hearings would not be exploited for law enforcement purposes. It has every reason to believe that this understanding has been respected. Although there have been rumours from time to time that law enforcement personnel have taken advantage of the hearings for purposes of investigation, no evidence of this has been brought to the attention of the Commission, despite public statements by the Chairman that any such instances should be reported to him.

The Commission has been very impressed by the candour with which people of all ages have come forward and spoken from a depth of conviction and feeling about the phenomenon of non-medical drug usage and its relation to other aspects of social and cultural change today.

14. Altogether, it is estimated that nearly 12,000 Canadians have attended the hearings up to the end of February. The Commissioners have travelled some 17,000 miles, and in the months ahead they will continue to move back and forth across the country until every province and major city have been visited, as well as many of the smaller communities.

15. The Commission has had the benefit of a wide range of advice from experts in the field of non-medical drug use. It is only possible here to mention some of those who were particularly helpful.

The Commission has had several sessions with officers of the R.C.M.P. and has received the fullest cooperation from the Force in its attempt to understand the lessons of law enforcement in this field. In addition to the public submission of the Force, each Division prepared a brief, and the Commission has had the advantage of private hearings with officers from each Division. Moreover, research consultants of the Commission have been permitted to observe law enforcement by the Force at first hand. The Commission has also received a number of written communications from the Force in addition to its formal submissions. We can not speak too highly of the cooperation that we have received from the R.C.M.P., who went to particular trouble, on relatively short notice in the initial stages of the inquiry, to give the Commission the benefit of their experience. Whatever view one may take of law enforcement policy in this controversial field, we feel obliged to record our respect for the highly professional manner in which the R.C.M.P. have sought to perform their duty in relation to this inquiry. We look forward to their continued cooperation as we deepen our study of the problems of law enforcement and the administration of justice in the field of non-medical drug use.

The Commission has also received a great deal of valuable assistance from addiction foundations, notably the Addiction Research Foundation of Ontario, the Narcotic Addiction Foundation of British Columbia, and OPTAT (Office de la Prévention et du Traitement de l'Alcoolisme et des Autres Toxicomanies). From the outset of its inquiry the Commission has had the benefit of frequent consultation with members of the Ontario Foundation, and the Commission's research staff have made extensive use of the bibliographical and documentary resources of the Foundation.

The Commission has also consulted with many other experts, in Canada and the United States. It plans to consult with many more, including experts outside North America, in the ensuing year. For the present, it would like to make special mention of the assistance which it has received from Dr J. Robertson Unwin, Dr Lionel Solursh and Mr Wilfred Clement, whose intimate knowledge of the Canadian drug scene from a scientific, yet deeply human perspective, has made their observations and advice invaluable. The Commission should also record its indebtedness for advice received in the early stages of the inquiry from Dr Helen Nowlis of the University of Rochester; Samuel Pearlman of the City University of New York; Dr Daniel Glaser of the New York State Narcotic Addiction Control Commission; members of the National Institute of Mental Health, and Department of Justice in the United States.

The Role of the Interim Report

16. We have had some difficulty in determining what should be the role of our interim report. In particular, we have been somewhat perplexed as to how far we are justified in coming to conclusions and making recommendations at this time. But we are required by our terms of reference to render an interim report, and we assume that something more is expected than a simple report of progress. We believe that what is expected, at the very least, is a report which conveys our initial understanding of the subject matter of the inquiry and makes such recommendations as we feel are urgent and for which we believe we have a sufficient basis at this time. We hope it will serve to put the phenomenon of non-medical drug use in some perspective, to identify the issues, and to provide the basis for further consideration and discussion by the people of Canada.

Further, by identifying certain attitudes, hypotheses, and tentative opinions, the interim report will serve, we hope, as a sounding board, eliciting further evidence and opinion, and indicating to us wherein our definition of the issues and our preliminary opinions may require revision.

17. The function of the final report will be to complete the picture begun by the interim report and to report upon the system of social response which we recommend for the phenomenon of non-medical drug use. The inquiry between the interim report and the final report will test the definitions of issues and the hypotheses reflected in the interim report, add necessary information with respect to the effects, the extent, and the causes of non-medical drug use, as well as the role played by the various aspects of social control and response, and lay the foundation for specific recommendations concerning these various aspects. The interim report is primarily concerned with a statement of the issues and applicable principles, and the final report is to be concerned with the detailed application of these principles to the development of a satisfactory system of social response.

We recognize, however, that the urgency of some of the problems involved in non-medical drug use and the time required to develop adequate resources to cope with them may indicate the appropriateness of certain recommendations at this time. This is particularly true with respect to preparations and organization for which considerable lead time is required. In such cases it may be sufficient to indicate the general direction which certain responses should take, leaving it to further study and consultation in the ensuing year to settle matters of detail.

18. Chapter Two on the effect of the drugs is offered at this time for two reasons. First, we have been profoundly impressed by repeated assertions of the need for more reliable information, and we hope that this chapter will serve a useful purpose as material for drug education. Secondly, we feel that it is an indispensable basis for the development of public understanding of the issues. In effect, in Chapter Two we disclose our initial assumptions concerning the effects of the drugs. Our

object is to identify the body of reliable and generally accepted knowledge, and to determine where the important uncertainties and gaps exist. We certainly concur in the impression which others have conveyed of a field of knowledge bedevilled by controversy, conflicting professional opinion, and uncertainty. Some observers question whether it is possible, in view of the intense feelings on this subject, ever to come to agreement on what should be accepted as scientifically known. Erich Goode in his article, 'Marijuana and the Politics of Reality', observes that 'the multitude of results from the many marijuana reports forms a sea of ambiguity into which nearly any message may be read'. He makes the point that whether a particular drug effect is good or bad depends on one's subjective point of view – the implications of the effect in terms of one's own system of values. Goode sees no possible reconciliation of these 'differential *evaluations* of the same "objective" consequences', and he concludes that 'the essential meaning of the marijuana issue is the meaning which each individual brings to it'. The Addiction Research Foundation of Ontario makes the same point in its preliminary submission to the Commission. It puts the matter this way:

> However, after all possible information has been acquired and verified scientifically, the final steps in the formulation of legislation or governmental policy will be based upon value judgements. Even the classification of the effects of drug use as 'beneficial' or 'adverse' is a process of evaluation with respect to subjective standards.

The response to non-medical drug use is profoundly a matter of attitudes. At the same time we must make every effort to ascertain what should be accepted as scientific knowledge of the 'objective' effects. It is intolerable that the process of subjective evaluation should take place in ignorance of the objective facts. All the same, we would do well to heed Goode's caution that there is an inevitable tendency to select and emphasize those views of 'objective' facts which support our own subjective evaluation. And as Goode points out, with special reference to the La Guardia Report on marijuana, the various findings can be used to support conflicting points of view. Are we to conclude that the task is hopeless? We think not. We can certainly make progress by attempting to identify what should be accepted scientifically concerning the 'objective' effects, by pointing out the important areas of scientific controversy or lack of scientific knowledge, and by making explicit the value judgements underlying the conflicting views as to how the effects should be subjectively characterized. We believe it is helpful to clarify the issues of the debate.

Staff and Research

19. The members of the Commission and their staff are listed in Appendix C. The Commission is carrying out its task with a small nucleus of full-time staff and with research consultants on a part-time basis for special aspects of its study. The Commission's Research Associates, Dr Charles Farmilo and Dr Ralph D. Miller, are concentrating on psychopharmacological research into the effects of the drugs. Dr Miller is the author, with the assistance of Dr Farmilo, of Chapter Two on 'The Drugs and Their Effects'. Research that has been commissioned so far includes survey research to determine the extent and patterns of non-medical drug use in Canada, as well as Canadian perceptions of and attitudes towards this phenomenon, and legal studies, both doctrinal and empirical, of the various problems involved in the regulation of non-medical drug use. The section of Chapter Five dealing with the law is based in part on preliminary work by Professor Paul Weiler and John Hogarth.

Research is only part of the work that is involved in an inquiry of this kind. Special mention should be made of the administrative staff who have had to work under particular pressure because of the requirement of an interim report, impinging concurrently with the organization and conduct of the public hearings. We would like to express our appreciation of the work of Mr James J. Moore, Executive-Secretary of the Commission, who has had the general direction of operations and who has also participated in the writing of the report; Mr Jack Macbeth, who has been of great assistance in the organization of hearings and the preparation of the report; Mrs

Vivian Luscombe who has supervised the secretarial staff of the Commission; Mr C. William Doylend, the Ottawa Office Manager, and other members of the administrative, secretarial and research staff.

CHAPTER TWO

THE DRUGS AND THEIR EFFECTS

INTRODUCTION

20. The primary purpose of this chapter is to review in preliminary fashion the current scientific knowledge of certain psychotropic drugs used non-medically in Canada. In addition, this section will introduce a few basic concepts which may be helpful to the understanding of some of the potentials and limitations of the scientific method as applied to the study of human behaviour and drugs.* Psychopharmacology, the branch of science specifically concerned with these issues, can be defined as the study of the interaction of drugs with ongoing psychological and behavioural activity.

A certain amount of the current controversy and lack of communication regarding the 'drug problem' has been attributed to the multitude of meanings that the term 'drug' has to different people, and to the often arbitrary way in which our society defines, and endeavours to solve, the problems arising from man's persistent use of chemical substances to alter his existence. To some people the word 'drug' means a medicine used in the prevention, diagnosis, or treatment of an abnormal or pathological condition. In other situations, it is often used to refer only to illegal or socially disapproved substances. Some individuals employ the word in a manner suggesting dependence or addiction, regardless of whether it refers to some chemical substance or to other preoccupations such as television, music, books, or sports and games. Some consider alcohol, tea and coffee as drugs, while to others these are simply normal beverages not to be confused with the more foreign and unfamiliar substances viewed as drugs. Furthermore, the terms 'drug' and 'narcotic' are given special meanings in legal areas.

* A glossary of technical terms, as used in this report, is presented at the end of this volume.

Even scientists frequently disagree as to the precise definition of the term 'drug'.

Modell[164] has suggested a comprehensive pharmacological definition of drugs which the Commission has adopted. As noted in Chapter One, a *drug* is considered to be *any substance that by its chemical nature alters structure or function in the living organism.* Modell observed that:

> Drug action is therefore a general biological phenomenon ... pharmacologic effects are exerted by foods, vitamins, hormones, microbial metabolites, plants, snake venoms, stings, products of decay, air pollutants, pesticides, minerals, synthetic chemicals, virtually all foreign materials (very few are completely inert) and many materials normally in the body.

While this interpretation may be too broad for certain practical purposes, it provides some perspective into the ubiquitous nature of our internal and external chemical environment, and the complexity of the question of human drug use. The Commission's primary concern is focused on the use and effects of drugs taken for their *psychotropic* or *psychoactive* properties as defined by their capacity to *alter sensation, mood, consciousness or other psychological or behavioural functions.*

21. The use of psychoactive drugs seems to be an almost universal phenomenon and has apparently occurred throughout recorded history, in almost all societies. Some scholars have suggested that this use of drugs may have been among the earliest behavioural characteristics distinguishing man from the other animals. Blum, in the United States *Task Force Report* (1967), has stated:[27]

> Mind-altering drug use is common to mankind. Such drugs have been employed for millennia in almost all cultures. In our work we have been able to identify only a few societies in the world today where no mind-altering drugs are used; these are small and isolated cultures. Our own society puts great stress on mind-altering drugs as desirable products which are used in many acceptable ways (under medical supervision, as part of the family home remedies, in self-medication, in social use [alcohol, tea parties, coffee klatches, etc.] and in

private use [cigarettes, etc.]). In terms of drug use, the rarest or most abnormal form of behaviour is not to take any mind-altering drugs at all. . . . If one is to use the term 'drug user', it applies to nearly all of us.

The Role of Science

22. It has been suggested that the potential role of science in the solution of the 'drug problem' is to provide information to better enable individuals and society to make informed and discriminating decisions regarding the availability and use of particular drugs. Unfortunately, considerable disparity often exists between the need for such information and the capacity of science to acquire and communicate it.

Helen Nowlis has noted:[172]

There are many reasons why the 'facts' invoked in non-scientific discussions of drugs are often not facts at all. They may be second or third-hand quotations of statements attributed to scientists. There is a readiness on the part of many to accept as 'scientific fact' any statement made by, or attributed to, someone labelled as scientist, whether it is a statement based on research, on uncontrolled observation, or merely on personal opinion.

While science may be able to serve as a useful guideline and source of information, science itself is not a policy-making process, but merely a practical system designed to explore and test notions of a certain abstract nature. Even though the aim of science is to maximize objectivity, the interpretation and application of scientific data is usually a subjective venture regardless of the controls maintained in the formal analyses. The practical use of such information in the social sphere often entails economic, legal, philosophical and moral issues which are not amenable to scientific analysis as we know it today.

Even though considerable progress has been made in advancing our knowledge of biology, science has provided only a minimal understanding of the essential nature of psychological and behavioural functions and their relationship to underlying physiological processes. Consequently, psychopharmacology

31

today must be content with exploring the interaction of chemicals (often with certain identified physical characteristics) with a largely unknown human psychobiological system of enormous complexity.

The Classification of Drugs

23. Drug classifications based on a variety of different considerations have been developed and there appears to be little general agreement as to the optimal scheme for ordering the universe of biologically active substances. For example, drugs might be organized according to chemical structure, clinical-therapeutic use, potential health hazards, liability to non-medical use, public availability and legality, effects on specific neural or other physiological systems, or influence on certain psychological and behavioural processes. The classification systems developed from these different approaches may show considerable overlap, although there are often striking incongruities. For example, some drugs which appear very similar in chemical structure may be quite different in pharmacological activity and vice-versa. The most useful organization depends on the intended use of the classifications.

Since our major concern here is with the effects of psychologically active substances, our interim drug classification system is based primarily on general psychological and pharmacological considerations. In Table I eight major classes are presented along with some examples of drugs from each group. While the categories are not considered to be exhaustive, the general system is applicable to the majority of drugs used for their psychological effects. Since the effects of drugs depend on a vast number of psychological and physiological components, many of which seem unpredictable, these categories are to some extent based on a typical reaction by an average subject to a common dose. Large variations in any of various factors can greatly alter the effects and may reduce the reliability of the descriptions.

TABLE ONE

CLASSIFICATION OF MAJOR PSYCHOACTIVE DRUGS

I – *Sedatives and Hypnotics*[a]
>   Barbiturates – e.g.,
>> Verpnal* (barbital)
>> Seconal* (secobarbital)
>> Nembutal* (pentobarbital)
>
>   Minor tranquillizers – e.g.,
>> Librium* (chlordiazepoxide)
>> Valium* (diazepam)
>> Doriden* (glutethimide)
>> Miltown* (meprobamate)
>
>   Others – e.g.,
>> bromides, alcohol (ethanol), paraldehyde,
>> chloral hydrate, antihistamines (e.g., Gravol*),
>> anticholinergics (e.g., datura stramonium, atropine, scopolamine [Sominex* and Compoz*])

II – *Stimulants*[a]
>   Amphetamines – e.g.,
>> Benzedrine* (amphetamine)
>> Dexedrine* (dextroamphetamine)
>> Methedrine* (methamphetamine)
>
>   Others – e.g.,
>> Ritalin* (methylphenidate), Meratran* (pipradol),
>> Preludin* (phenmetrazine), cocaine, ephedrine,
>> caffeine (coffee, tea and cola drinks),
>> nicotine (tobacco), khat

III – *Psychedelics and Hallucinogens*[b]
>> LSD (lysergic acid diethylamide-25, lysergide)
>> Cannabis (marijuana, hashish)
>> THC (tetrahydrocannabinol)
>> Mescaline (peyote)
>> Psilocybin
>> DMT (dimethyltryptamine)
>> DET (diethyltryptamine)
>> DOM (STP, dimethoxymethamphetamine)
>> MDA (methylenedioxyamphetamine)
>> MMDA (methoxymethylenedioxyamphetamine)

      LBJ (methylpiperidylbenzilate)
      PCP (Sernyl*, phencyclidine)

IV – *Opiate Narcotics*[a]
      Opium (e.g., Paregoric*, Pantopon*)
      Heroin (diacetylmorphine)
      Morphine
      Codeine (methoxymorphine)
      Synthetics – e.g.,
        Deremol* (pethidine)
        Alvodine* (piminodine)
        Dolophine* (methadone)

V – *Volatile Solvents*[b]
      Sources: Glue, gasoline, paint thinner, nail polish, nail polish remover, lighter and cleaning fluid, spray cans, etc.
      Active agents: Toluene, acetone, benzene, naphtha, trichloroethylene, ether, chloroform, amyl nitrite, nitrous oxide, freon, etc.

VI – *Non-Narcotic Analgesics*[a]
      Aspirin* (acetylsalicylic acid)
      Phenacetin* (acetophenetidin)

VII – *Clinical Anti-Depressants*[c]
      Monoamine oxidase (MAO) inhibitors – e.g.,
        Nardil* (Phenezine)
      Tricyclics – e.g.,
        Tofranil* (Imipramine)

VIII – *Major Tranquillizers*[c]
      Phenothiazines – e.g.,
        Largactil* (chlorpromazine)
      Rauwolfia alkaloids (snake root) – e.g.,
        Serpasil* (reserpine)
      Butyrophenones – e.g.,
        Haldol* (haloperidol)
      Thioxanthenes – e.g.,
        Taractan* (chlorprothixene)

[a] Used medically and non-medically.
[b] Little or no medical use.
[c] Wide medical use, and little or no non-medical use.
* Registered Trade Name.

24. The *sedatives* and *hypnotics* (e.g., alcohol, barbiturates, 'sleeping pills' and minor tranquillizers) generally decrease central nervous system (CNS) arousal (although some psychological stimulation may result at low doses). Most of these drugs are used medically to reduce anxiety and tension, to produce general sedation and, at higher doses, sleep. The anticholinergic substances (e.g., belladonna alkaloids) are often used as sedatives at low doses although larger amounts may produce excitation and delirium.

25. The *stimulants* (e.g., amphetamines or 'speed', 'diet' and 'pep pills', caffeine, and cocaine) generally suppress appetite, increase activity, alertness, tension and general CNS arousal, and, at higher doses, block sleep. Tobacco (nicotine and coal tars) is usually considered a physiological stimulant although a variety of other effects are not uncommon.

26. The third group includes drugs described as *psychedelic* (mind-manifesting), *hallucinogenic* (hallucination-producing), *psychotomimetic* (psychosis–imitating), *illusinogenic* (illusion-producing), and *psychodysleptic* (mind-disrupting). While these terms refer to somewhat overlapping effects alleged to occur with the drugs in this class, the various labels emphasize different characteristics which are neither synonymous nor necessarily mutually exclusive. Probably none are entirely adequate as descriptive terms. These drugs may produce profound alteration in sensation, mood and consciousness at doses which result in comparatively light physiological activity. LSD and marijuana are examples from this group. The medical value of these drugs is the subject of considerable current controversy.

27. The drugs in the fourth category have traditionally been referred to as narcotics or opiates, and are derivatives of, or pharmacologically related to, products of the opium plant. The best known examples are heroin, morphine and codeine. The word 'narcotic' has been used inconsistently in scientific as well as lay language and has been the subject of considerable disagreement in legal matters (for example, marijuana, cocaine, and other non-opiates are frequently controlled under laws regulating narcotics, in spite of the fact that they are phar-

macologically different from this group). The use of the term 'opiates' is generally more specific, although its application has not always been limited to these drugs. Consequently, the specific term *opiate narcotics* is suggested to reduce ambiguity. These drugs are used medically mainly for their pain-relieving effects.

28. The fifth group is an aggregate of chemically diverse substances perhaps best described on a physical basis as *volatile solvents*. They are usually inhaled and include the vapour of such common materials as glue, gasoline and lacquer thinner. Some of these drugs have been called *deliriants* although delirium is only one of many potential effects and is clearly not restricted to these substances. Many are quite similar in effect to the sedative group and might be considered in a sub-class of that category. Others may have slight psychedelic or hallucinogenic effects. Most of these substances have no known medical use although several have been employed as clinical anaesthetics.

29. The *non-narcotic analgesics* (e.g., Aspirin* and Phenacetin*) are primarily used to reduce aching pain and to lower fever. In some instances they may also serve as mild sedatives.

30. The *clinical anti-depressants* (e.g., Tofranil* and Nardil*) are used medically to improve mood in severely depressed patients. These drugs are rarely used for non-medical purposes since they have little effect on normal mood states.

31. The final group, the *major tranquillizers*, are primarily used to reduce the symptoms of severe psychosis (e.g., schizophrenia). Largactil* and reserpine are examples. While these have initiated a widespread revolution in chemo-therapy in psychiatry, they are rarely involved in non-medical use.

Psychological Considerations

32. The general effect of most drugs is greatly influenced by a variety of psychological and environmental factors. Unique

* Throughout this chapter an asterisk indicates a registered drug trade name.

qualities of an individual's personality, his past history of drug experience, his attitudes towards the drug, his expectations of its effects and his motivation for taking it are extremely important and in some instances may completely obscure the typical pharmacological response to a drug. These factors are often referred to collectively as the person's mental 'set'. The 'setting' or total environment in which the drug is taken may also be a factor of major significance.

A few drinks of alcohol may produce drowsiness and fatigue in some situations, while the same individual under different circumstances may be psychologically stimulated and aroused by the same dose. It appears that the set and setting may be of greater significance with the psychedelic-hallucinogenic substances than with the other drugs, and it has been suggested that psychological factors may often be the primary components in determining the quality or character of the psychedelic drug experience.

The so-called *placebo effect* is a striking example of the importance of set and setting in determining the drug response. A placebo, in this context, refers to a pharmacologically inactive substance which elicits a significant reaction, entirely because of what the individual expects or desires to happen. In certain individuals in some settings a placebo substance may have surprisingly powerful consequences. The placebo effect is specific to the individual and the setting, and not to any chemical properties of the substance involved. Therefore, in spite of an apparent 'drug effect', the placebo is not considered a drug since it does not alter function 'by its chemical nature'.

Placebos have been reported in therapeutic situations to significantly relieve such symptoms as headache and a variety of other pains, hay fever, colds, seasickness, neuroses, and a number of gastro-intestinal complaints.[97] Some scientists have suggested that the bulk of medical history may actually have been a history of the placebo, since many 'effective cures' of the past have been shown to be without relevant direct pharmacological action, and are today of no value as therapeutic agents.

To control for the influence of such psychological factors in drug research, testing is usually done under at least two conditions: an assessment is made using the actual drug of interest, and a separate measurement is taken after a placebo is given under identical circumstances. By comparing these two conditions some of the effects of set and setting can often be controlled and the actual drug effect uncovered.

Pharmacological Considerations

33. In studying how drugs affect the body, pharmacologists generally divide the analysis into several processes:

1. *Administration:* how does the drug enter the body?
2. *Absorption:* how does the drug get from the site of administration into the physiological system of the body?
3. *Distribution:* how is the drug distributed to various areas in the body?
4. *Action:* how and where does the drug produce what effects?
5. *Physiological Fate:* how is the drug inactivated, metabolized, and/or eliminated from the body?

Different routes or modes of administration can have considerable influence on the latency, duration, intensity and the general nature of the drug effect. Many drugs are well absorbed from the stomach and intestines after ingestion while others are poorly taken up or may be destroyed by the gastric juices. Certain drugs may be injected, with a hypodermic syringe for example, just under the skin (subcutaneous or S.C.), into the muscle (intramuscular or I.M.), or into a blood vein (intravenous or I.V.). The effects are generally most rapid and intense after intravenous injection and, consequently, this mode of administration can be quite dangerous in inexperienced hands. In addition, certain volatile substances can be rapidly and efficiently absorbed from the lungs by inhalation.

34. The action of a drug is in many cases terminated by chemical changes which it undergoes in the body. Certain organs (often the liver) metabolize or 'break down' the original substance into other chemicals which are usually (but not always) less active and more easily eliminated from the body.

Some drugs may be excreted unchanged in the urine, faeces or breath. Action is not always terminated by excretion, however, and the effects of some drugs greatly outlast the actual presence of the chemical in the body. Numerous physiological factors alter absorption, distribution, action and fate, and must therefore be taken into consideration in the study of drug effects.

The details of cellular physiology are largely unknown and with rare exceptions there is little information as to the mechanism by which any particular drug changes the activity of the nervous system. At the simplest level, it appears that a drug alters the functioning of the living cell by entering into some sort of chemical combination with substances already present. Even if this molecular process were well understood, it would not provide a straightforward basis for predicting the overall effects of the drug on a group of interacting cells, or, at higher level, on the total nervous system (comprising billions of cells) and associated psychological and behavioural processes.

35. *The importance of dose.* One of the basic principles of pharmacology is that specific statements about drug effects can not be made without consideration of the quantity or dose of the drug involved. With all drugs, the response differs both in the intensity and the character of the reaction, according to the amount of the drug administered. The relation between the dose and the intensity of an effect is often referred to by scientists as the *dose-response* or *dose-effect relationship*.

Although the magnitude of the effects of some drugs may increase in a rather uniform (monotonic) fashion as dose is increased, other drugs, particularly the sedatives, may show a *bi-phasic response* and actually produce behaviourally opposite effects at some doses compared to others. Low doses of alcohol may, in certain instances, be somewhat stimulating, while higher doses generally have a strong sedating effect. Scopolamine (a belladonna alkaloid) may produce sedation at low doses, and excitation, delirium and hallucinations with larger quantities. Very toxic doses of this drug can again produce sedation, coma and even death.

For every drug there is a dose low enough so as to produce no noticeable reaction, and at the opposite extreme, some degree of toxicity or poisoning can be produced by any substance if enough is taken. The concept of a poison, in fact, really refers to the quantity of a drug which exceeds the body's capacity to cope with it without damage. No drug can be designated either safe, beneficial, or harmful without consideration of the dose likely to be consumed. Chlorine, for example, which is present in most urban drinking water in concentration so low as to have little or no pharmacological effect on humans, is intended to poison harmful bacteria. The same substance, highly concentrated in gaseous form, was developed during World War I as an extremly potent respiratory poison. Even the concept of a psychotropic drug implies some notion of the range of doses likely to be consumed, since almost any drug can, in high quantities, affect psychological function. In many instances, however, considerable physical toxicity or poisoning develops before significant psychological effects occur.

It is usually essential to study a drug's effect over a range of doses in order to obtain an adequate understanding of the nature of the response. It is also important to consider doses which have some relevance to existing or potential patterns of use if social implications are to be inferred from experimental findings.

36. *The importance of time.* Another important pharmacological concept is the *time-response relationship* or the relation between the time which has elapsed since administration and the effect produced. Such a temporal analysis may be restricted to immediate or short-term (acute) effects of a single dose, or on the other extreme, may involve the long-term effects of persistently repeated (chronic) use of a drug.

The intensity and often the character or quality of the overall drug effect may change substantially within a short period of time. For example, the main intoxicating effects of a large dose of alcohol generally reach a peak in less than an hour, then gradually taper off. An initially stimulating effect may later change to one of sedation. With some drugs, an initial state of tension or anxiety may later turn into one of relaxation and sense of well-being, or vice-versa, as a function of time.

It may also be important with some drugs to consider the

long-term consequences of chronic use. Usually such effects can not be readily predicted from what is known of the immediate response. For instance, while there is little doubt that the smoking of a few tobacco cigarettes has no lasting detrimental effect on lung or cardiac function, there is increasing scientific evidence that long-term heavy use of this substance has serious consequences. As another example, the clinical picture of the chronic alcoholic involves psychological and physiological disturbances which do not develop with moderate drinking. In simple terms, it is essential to ask: 'How much?'; 'How often?'; and 'For how long?' (as well as 'By whom?') when discussing the long-term reaction to repeated drug use.

37. *Main effects and side effects*. It is highly unlikely that any drug has only a single action on a particular behavioural or physiological function. Most drugs can produce an almost unlimited number of effects on the body, each with a somewhat unique dose-response and time-response relationship. The relative strength of the different responses to a drug generally varies with the amount taken, and a particular effect which is prominent at one dosage level may be quite secondary at another.

In a therapeutic or clinical setting, one is usually interested in a single or perhaps a small number of the many possible effects. Those which are desired are generally considered 'main effects' whilst the other unwanted but concurrent drug responses are labelled 'side effects'. This distinction between main and side effects is a relative one and depends on the purpose or the anticipated use of the drug. A response which is considered unnecessary or undesirable in one application may, in fact, be the main or desired effect in another. For example, in the clinical treatment of severe pain, the analgesic (pain-reducing) properties of morphine are considered the main effects, and the psychological euphoria and the intestinal constipation also produced are undesirable side effects. To the 'street addict', however, the euphoric properties are the main effects, and the analgesic and constipating effects may be irrelevant or undesired. Certain opiate compounds such as paregoric are used in treatment of diarrhoea and, in this instance, the constipating effect of the drug is desired and the other responses are con-

sidered side effects. It is universal that drugs have undesirable
and toxic side effects if the dose is sufficiently increased.

38. *Drug interaction*. Even in cases where the individual
effects of different drugs are well known and reliable, if several substances are taken at the same time, the interaction may
produce a response which is quite unpredictable on the basis of
the knowledge of the individual drugs alone. Less commonly, a
particular interaction effect may be anticipated. If the drugs
normally have similar properties, they may often have an additive effect if taken together, resulting in a general increase in
responses similar to that produced by a larger single dose of
either one. There are also instances in which one drug may
potentiate the action of another, and the two together produce a
greater effect than would be expected by merely adding the individual reactions. Furthermore, some drugs have antagonistic
effects, and one may counteract or inhibit certain normal responses to the other.

Tolerance and Dependence

38a. *Tolerance is said to develop when the response to the
same dose of a drug decreases with repeated use.* With most
tolerance-producing drugs, effects of original intensity can be
retained, to a certain extent, if the dose is increased. The extent
of tolerance, and the rate at which it is acquired, depend on the
drug, the individual using it, and the magnitude and frequency
of administration. The body does not lose sensitivity to all
aspects of the reaction to a particular drug with equal rapidity,
or to the same degree. Some of the effects of a drug may 'drop
out' sooner than others with repeated use. Tolerance to the
effects which are reinforcing or rewarding drug use (i.e., 'main
effects') is usually reflected by a tendency for users to increase
dose. Most aspects of tolerance dissipate with abstinence from
the drug.

A moderate degree of tolerance to most effects of alcohol and
barbiturates develops and a heavy drinker may be able to consume two to three times the alcohol tolerated by a novice. Little
tolerance develops to the lethal toxicity of these drugs, however,

and a heavy user of sedatives is just as susceptible to death by overdose as is a non-tolerant individual. Opiate narcotics, such as morphine, are capable of producing profound tolerance, and heavy users have been known to take up to ten times the amount which would normally produce death. By contrast, no noticeable tolerance develops to cocaine (a short-acting stimulant).

The exact mechanisms by which the body adapts, or becomes tolerant, to different drug effects are not completely understood, although several processes have been suggested. Certain drugs (e.g., barbiturates) stimulate the body's production of the metabolic enzymes which inactivate them. In addition, there is evidence that a considerable degree of central nervous system (CNS) tolerance may develop to certain drugs independent of changes in the rate of absorption, metabolism or excretion. An individual tolerant to alcohol, for example, can be relatively unaffected by a large dose even though the resulting high level of alcohol in his blood may accurately reflect the magnitude of his intake. It is uncertain as to whether this represents some general molecular adaptation to the drug at the level of the individual nerve cell, or perhaps a specific response by the central nervous system to counteract the sedating effects and maintain normal function. Learning factors often appear to play an important role in changing the individual's response to a drug after experience with it. Effects which initially may be strange or frightening may later be accepted without reaction or concern, or perhaps, even be desired. There is evidence that people may learn to control some drug effects, or otherwise come to function normally in the presence of certain responses which might originally have been distracting, or otherwise disrupting of behaviour.

A phenomenon often referred to as 'reverse tolerance' has been noted with some drugs (notably the psychedelics) in which the desired effects may be achieved with smaller doses after experience with the drug. Both learning and pharmacological mechanisms have been suggested to underly this process.

In many instances, after an individual becomes tolerant to the effects of one drug, he will also show tolerance to others with similar action. This is called *cross-tolerance*. For example, a heavy drinker will normally show a reduced response to barbiturates, tranquillizers and anaesthetics, as well as to alcohol.

39. *Physical dependence is a physiological state of adaptation to a drug, normally following the development of tolerance, which results in a characteristic set of withdrawal symptoms (often called the 'abstinence syndrome'), when administration of the drug is stopped.* These symptoms may be of an intense nature after persistent heavy use, and with some sedatives and opiate narcotics, may include tremors, vomiting, delirium, cramps and, in severe cases with some drugs, convulsions and death. There are generally no overt signs of physical dependence if the drug level is kept high enough to avoid the withdrawal syndrome. In a sense, the body comes to depend on the drug for 'normal' functioning after adapting to its presence, and when the drug is absent, considerable disruption of essential physiological processes occurs until readjustment develops. The withdrawal syndrome may also be elicited without abstinence, by the administration of a substance which specifically antagonizes or blocks certain effects of the original drug.

Withdrawal symptoms can be prevented or promptly relieved by the administration of a sufficient quantity of the original drug or one with similar pharmacological activity. The latter case, in which different drugs can be used interchangeably in preventing withdrawal symptoms, is called *cross-dependence*. As an example, barbiturates and tranquillizers can be used in treating the abstinence syndrome associated with chronic alcoholism.

Often the recovery phase associated with different drugs is characterized by a rebound phenomenon dominated by activity opposite to that produced by the drug. For instance, withdrawal from the sedatives generally results in symptoms of acute and toxic hyperactivation and physiological arousal, while the pattern following intense stimulant (e.g. 'speed') use usually involves sedation, depression and sleep.

Although physical dependence can develop with such common drugs as alcohol and barbiturates, it is not a factor in the drug-taking behaviour of the vast majority of regular users. In the few individuals who become physically dependent on these particular drugs, serious social, personal and physiological consequences of drug use usually precede the physical dependence. Therefore, although physical dependence is a serious medical problem in a minority of sedative users, the abstinence syndrome itself is not the cause of major public health problems. The potent opiate narcotics, by contrast, tend to produce very pronounced tolerance and physical dependence early in the history of regular use. These features then soon become an integral part of the particular drug problem presented by the opiate narcotics. However, with these and other drugs, psychological factors in the dependence are often more significant in the long run.

40. *Psychological dependence* (also often called behavioural, psychic or emotional dependence, and habituation) is a much more elusive concept and is difficult to define in a satisfactory manner. A World Health Organization paper[69] defines psychic dependence thus: 'In this situation there is a feeling of satisfaction and a psychic drive that require periodic or continuous administration of the drug to produce a desired effect or to avoid discomfort.' A major problem with this definition is the difficulty in operationally defining and objectively identifying the characteristics of the dependence in a practical situation.

By contrast, some scientists[224] have identified behavioural dependence as repeated self-administration of a drug. This approach seems far too broad for most purposes since it only indicates that the drug is in some way reinforcing or rewarding to the user, and merely restates the observation that he takes the drug.

Extreme instances of psychological dependence are easier to identify and may be characterized by an intense craving for, or compulsion to continue the use of, a drug with obvious behavioural manifestations. In many instances, psychological aspects may be considerably more important than physical dependence in maintaining chronic drug use. The major problem with opiate dependence is not the physical aspects, since withdrawal can be successfully achieved in a few weeks, but the great likelihood that the individual will later return to chronic use due to psychological dependence.

In most instances of even regular non-medical use of drugs, such intense psychological dependence probably does not occur. However, more subtle psychological and social factors usually have persisting effects in maintaining the behaviour of drug consumption.

In talking about dependency in any context, whether dealing with drugs or not, it would seem useful to specify what it is that is being depended upon and for what reasons, and to identify the consequences of its presence or its absence. The significance of dependency changes considerably if the entity is relied upon, for example, for the maintenance of life (e.g., insulin for the diabetic) or for the escape from an unpleasant or intolerable situation (e.g., privacy), or perhaps for a feeling of well-being or satisfaction with life. In one sense psychological dependence may be said to exist with respect to anything which is part of one's preferred way of life. In our society, this kind of dependency occurs regularly with respect to such things as television, music, books, religion, sex, money, favourite foods, certain drugs, hobbies, sports or games and, often, other persons. Some degree of psychological dependence is, in this sense, a general and normal psychological condition.

A statement in the preliminary brief of the Addiction Research Foundation of Ontario reflects the complexity of interpreting the question of dependency:[4]

> It should be recognized, however, that dependence is not necessarily bad in itself, either for the individual or for society. The question to be evaluated, therefore, is not whether dependence can occur, but whether dependence in a given case results in physical, psychological or social harm.

41. *The concept of addiction.* The term 'addiction' has had a variety of meanings, and a consensus as to the proper definition seems unlikely, even in scientific circles. Often it has been used interchangeably with dependence (psychological and/or physiological), while at other times it appears to be synonymous with the term 'drug abuse'. The classical model of the addiction-producing drug was based on the opiate narcotics, and has traditionally required the presence of tolerance, and physical and

psychological dependence. However, this approach has not been generally satisfactory since only a few commonly used drugs (e.g., alcohol and other sedatives), in addition to the opiates, seem to fit the model at all. It is clearly inappropriate for many other drugs which can cause serious dependency problems. For example, amphetamines can produce considerable tolerance and strong psychological dependence with little or no physical dependence, and cocaine can produce psychological dependence without tolerance or physical dependence. Furthermore, in certain medical applications, morphine has been reported to produce tolerance and physical dependence without a significant psychological component.

Recognizing the problems with the concept of addiction, the World Health Organization (WHO) proposed the following:[69]

> It has become impossible in practice, and is scientifically unsound, to maintain a single definition for all forms of drug addiction and/or habituation. A feature common to these conditions as well as to drug abuse in general is dependence, psychic or physical or both, of the individual on a chemical agent. Therefore, better understanding should be attained by substitution of the term drug dependence of this or that type, according to the agent or class of agents involved. . . . It must be emphasized that drug dependence is a general term that has been selected for its applicability to all types of drug abuse and thus carries no connotation of the degree of risk to public health or need for any or a particular type of drug control.

The WHO committee presented short descriptions of various different types of drug dependence which may occur in some individuals and situations. The list identifies drug dependence of the morphine type, the barbiturate – alcohol type, the cocaine type, the cannabis (marijuana) type, the amphetamine type, the khat type, and the hallucinogen (LSD) type. Details of these various kinds of drug dependence are discussed separately later in this chapter.

For reasons analogous to those presented above, it is further suggested here that the term *dependent* rather than the ambiguous description 'addict' be used to refer to an individual who has developed drug dependence of either the physical or psychological forms.

Scientific Methods

42. *The role of statistics.* Statistics can be helpful in collecting and handling numerical or quantified information, interpreting data, and making inferences or generalizations from it. The simplest use of statistics is to describe or summarize certain abstract characteristics of a group or sample. For example, the average height of players on a basketball team provides a shorthand description of the group. The numerical mean is a common index of the average. Considerably more information could be communicated if some idea of the variability of heights within the team were known. The range of measures, for example, is a crude index of the variance of 'spread' in the distribution within a group.

A second function of statistics is to provide a system for inference about some population on the basis of a smaller group or sample selected from that population. For example, the mean I.Q. of a group of 50 students randomly selected from a school with 500 individuals might provide a reasonable estimate of the average intelligence of the entire student population of that school. The success of such generalization or extrapolation depends on the relative size of the sample and the accuracy or fidelity with which the group studied represents the overall population of interest. Any bias in sampling which reduces the similarity between the selected group and the population to which the results are to be generalized reduces the validity of such extrapolation.

Statistics may also assist in distinguishing between the differences in measurements resulting from random variation and the variance due to the factor which is being studied. By obtaining an estimate of the natural variability in a population, it may be possible to distinguish, with some confidence, between a 'real effect' associated with a particular condition or treatment, and the difference which might be expected by chance alone. The phrase 'statistically significant' is used to indicate an effect considered significantly greater than that likely due to chance.

However, statistical techniques alone can only indicate an association between different variables and can not actually identify cause and effect. Such causal inferences must be based on an overall consideration of the research design. In many laboratory experiments, the stimulus and its response may be readily identified, but in less tightly controlled social studies (e.g., surveys) and clinical observations, it is often very difficult or impossible to positively identify the causal variable in a complex pattern of associations among different characteristics of the sample. For example, the demonstration that persons who are heavy users of tranquillizers also tend to be regular alcohol drinkers does not necessarily indicate that one causes the other. It may well be that a third factor (e.g., the desire to avoid or escape anxiety and tension) may be responsible for both behaviours. Interpretation of the data generally requires considerations beyond that involved in the statistical analysis.

43. *Experimental methods.* Details of research design would not be appropriate here, although some simple notions as to elementary requirements for adequate experimental techniques in psychopharmacology may be worthwhile. A major goal of scientific research is to eliminate or control all factors, other than those to be studied, which can influence or bias measurement.

As discussed above, the subjects of the study must be sufficiently similar to the general population of ultimate interest to allow generalization from the data. Extrapolation from one animal species to another, from one human society to another, or from one social group to another is often quite tenuous and must be viewed with extreme caution. Variables such as age, sex, and social class often exert considerable influence on psychological measures, and must be taken into careful consideration.

Unless there is some reason why a particular dose level is of singular significance, more than one dose should be studied. If the purpose of the experiment is to allow inferences of a general social nature, then the dose, mode of administration and the general circumstances of the study must be relevant to the pattern of use in the general population.

In order to determine the effect of a particular treatment, it is necessary to have a reference or control condition for comparison, which has been treated identically to the experimental condition except for the factor under analysis. These data may be obtained from a separate group of control subjects, which is sufficiently similar to the experimental group, or from the same subjects studied at a different time. Due to the great variation between individuals in response to drugs, the latter approach is often most efficient, although it is sometimes inappropriate or impractical. Using subjects as their own controls requires special statistical techniques for handling the data, since repeated experience in the situation will affect the subject's subsequent performance through such mechanisms as general adaptation, practice and other learning variables, and often fatigue.

Care must be taken to control or eliminate the possible effects of the subject's and researcher's expectations and biases. Since set and setting play an important role in determining drug effects, an inactive placebo substance should be tested in a control situation under conditions which are identical to those present when the drug is studied. Sometimes, however, if the subject has had previous experience with the experimental drug, he may soon realize whether he was given the active drug or an inactive substance despite his initial lack of information, and consequently the placebo control may not be complete. An experimental design in which the subject is not informed as to which treatment is being investigated is called a *single-blind* study.

Since the scientist's bias and expectations can also influence the subject's performance and the interpretation of his behaviour (as well as the later data analysis), the validity of the measurements can often be further increased if the researcher is also unaware of which treatment condition is in effect at the time of the experiment. A study in which neither the subject nor the researcher knows which of the experimental treatment variables are operating is called a *double-blind* design. There are certain circumstances where a double-blind is inappropriate or impossible, although it is often the most efficient way to acquire specific information about drug effects in an experimental situation.

A Review of Selected Drugs

44. The remainder of this chapter is devoted to a short critical review of the scientific literature pertaining to the effects of certain psychoactive drugs. Barbiturates, alcohol, minor tranquillizers, amphetamines, LSD, cannabis, opiate narcotics, and volatile solvents are discussed. In these interim reviews an attempt has been made to concentrate on human psychopharmacological studies rather than on animal experiments or general social reports. Although original scientific sources were sought and used as often as possible, it was frequently necessary at this interim stage to rely on reviews prepared by others.

There has been no attempt to be exhaustive in the references presented in the text. These citations often indicate a typical example chosen from among numerous sources which would have been appropriate. The bibliography at the end of this chapter contains a broader representation of some of the materials used in preparing the summaries.

BARBITURATES

45. The term 'barbiturate' generally refers to drugs which are derivatives of barbituric acid. Barbital, the first drug of this class to be synthesized, was introduced into medicine in Germany in 1903. Barbiturates rapidly gained a wide usage as tranquillizers, sedatives and hypnotics (sleep inducers) which continues to this day. In the past half-century, over 2,000 different barbiturates have been synthesized, although less than a dozen make up the bulk of current use. Among these are amobarbital (Amytal*), pentobarbital (Nembutal*), phenobarbital (Luminal*), and secobarbital (Seconal*). These drugs are frequently referred to as 'barbs', 'nemmies', 'goof balls', 'yellow jackets', 'red devils', 'downers' or 'sleeping pills'.

The barbiturates are often classified by the duration of their sedative or hypnotic action at a standard dose. Since the similarities among these drugs exceed the differences, they will be discussed in general terms as a group.

46. Barbiturates are among the most widely used psychoactive drugs (medically and non-medically) in our society, and are the toxic agents in thousands of accidental or intentional deaths annually in North America. In addition, the barbiturates have considerable potential for producing psychological and physiological dependence, and are probably second only to alcohol in frequency of drug-induced debilitation in modern society. While a considerable body of research exists into the many medical applications of these drugs, there has been relatively little careful investigation of non-medical use.

Although the medical and non-medical use of barbiturates appears to be widespread across age groups and social class, the chronic use of these drugs, as with alcohol, seems to be primarily an adult practice. Good epidemiological data in this area are not available. Since prescription control is only partially effective and possession of these drugs for personal use without medical authorization is not a criminal offence and, perhaps, because the users do not appear to form any homogeneous, cohesive or easily recognized minority, the usual medical and law enforcement statistics are of little assistance in assessing the extent of non-medical use.

47. It has been frequently said that in Canada, the supply of barbiturates lawfully manufactured or imported greatly exceeds the requirements of legitimate medical use. It appears that many current non-medical users were initiated into barbiturate use for medical reasons. Numerous medical users develop dependence and continue use long after the original medical purpose or prescription is absent, and there are indications that most chronic barbiturate users obtain the drugs through legitimate channels.[98] Since many physicians do not adequately maintain or monitor prescription records, a patient may be able to arrange an increase in the frequency and/or quantity of drug prescribed. In addition, many chronic barbiturate (and other prescription drug) users obtain 'legitimate' prescriptions from a number of different doctors simultaneously, without the physicians' awareness.[79] Because of

these patterns, the distinction between medical and non-medical use of barbiturates is often particularly difficult. Essentially all of the medical and non-medical barbiturate supply in Canada is legitimately and professionally manufactured; 'home-made' versions have not been identified.

Medical Use

48. Barbiturates are commonly used in medical practice today and it would seem likely that many households have had first-hand experience with them. Most of the medical uses are based on the sedative, hypnotic, and anti-convulsant effects of the drugs. Barbiturates are widely prescribed where a general depression of nervous system activity is desired. In low doses, they are widely used as day-time sedatives or tranquillizers. The hypnotic effect of these drugs is familiar to thousands of Canadians who use barbiturates in higher dose in the form of the common sleeping pill. Barbiturates are also often administered alone, and in conjunction with other drugs, as anaesthetics in surgical and related medical situations; but they are poor analgesics if used alone. The anti-convulsant effects of certain barbiturates have been very important in the treatment of acute convulsions associated with drug dependence withdrawal symptoms, various neurological disorders (including epilepsy), and poisoning due to the overdose of such stimulants as strychnine, nicotine and cocaine.

Other medical applications include diagnosis and attempted therapy of certain psychiatric disorders. In these instances the drug is usually administered intravenously in a dose adjusted to keep the patient in a semi-conscious state in which inhibitions are reduced and various suppressed and emotionally charged material may be released. This procedure is essentially that used in the so-called 'truth serum' application in criminal investigations. This effect, then, is really just a carefully monitored dose-response to ordinary short-acting barbiturates and, while this procedure frequently results in information different from that communicated normally, there is little evidence that it really exposes the 'truth' as such.

49. In crystalline form, barbiturates are odourless, white or yellow powders, with a slightly bitter taste. They are available as powders, elixirs, injections, suppositories, capsules or tablets (both in sustained and delayed release forms). They are frequently marketed for medical use in mixtures with other drugs, such as other sedatives or tranquillizers, analgesics, belladonna alkaloids (e.g., atropine or scopolamine), various stimulants (e.g., amphetamine or caffeine), vitamins and various gastrointestinal agents.

Barbiturates are usually administered orally for both medical and non-medical purposes and are readily and efficiently absorbed by the stomach, small intestine, and rectum. Absorption is more rapid on an empty stomach than if the drug is taken immediately after eating. Both intramuscular and intravenous injections are also effective, but they are more prone to physiological complication and are generally avoided except for special purposes. While most chronic dependent users take barbiturates orally, those who are experienced with self-injections (e.g., opiate narcotic or amphetamine dependents) may use the intravenous route.

After absorption into the bloodstream, barbiturates are initially distributed rather uniformly throughout the body, with the latency of the psychological response being partly a function of the facility of the particular drug in entering the brain. The body eliminates barbiturate activity in several ways. Most barbiturates are broken down or metabolized in the liver into relatively inactive substances which are excreted by the kidney in the urine, along with various quantities of the unaltered drug. Temporary binding of drug molecules by plasma and tissue protein soon after distribution, plus the affinity of certain barbiturates for body tissue fats, may further shorten the initial central nervous system (CNS) effects (and possibly prolong other more subtle reactions). The preceding factors of metabolism, excretion, and distribution are largely responsible for the differences in potency and duration of action among the different barbiturates. Acute and chronic barbiturate use can be identified from blood and urine samples. [198]

50. Many of the psychological and behavioural effects of hypnotic doses of barbiturates are quite similar to the alcohol inebriation syndrome and consequently do not need much elaboration. While the drug user may be able to discriminate between the alcohol and barbiturate states subjectively, it is extremely difficult to tell the difference from the user's behaviour.

Although high doses invariably produce behavioural sedation, drowsiness, and sleep, the effects of smaller quantities may be quite unpredictable. As with alcohol and other sedatives, barbiturates may initially produce behavioural excitation, stimulation and lack of inhibition (especially at low doses), rather than sedation, depending on the situation and the individual. In certain persons, sedation is not produced until a considerable quantity has been administered, whereas other psychological and behavioural effects may be quite pronounced. The user may become happy, pleasant, euphoric or 'mellow' on one extreme, or possibly hostile, suspicious, aggressive and violent on the other. Emotional depression, self-pity, and withdrawal are also not uncommon, and barbiturate-related suicides are frequently reported. Although low-dose effects are often erratic, moderate to high doses generally slow down reaction time, impair complicated mental functions, and produce a lessening of inhibition, a reduction in emotional control, and an impairment of physical co-ordination as well as a variety of other effects resembling alcohol inebriation. Acute toxic psychoses are rare. The extreme variability in response, even within the same individual over a short period of time, is illustrated by Wikler's report.[243]

After intravenous injection of 0.25 to 1.0gm of amobarbital, a subject may fall asleep if he lies in bed undisturbed, yet he may be awake and voluble if interviewed by a psychiatrist, or he may exhibit ataxia on attempting to walk back to his bed, but he may 'sober up' promptly when instructed to pose for a motion picture demonstration of ataxia.

51. Frequent mention is made of a phenomenon called 'drug automatism', associated with toxic barbiturate overdose, although, many observers have expressed doubts as to its significance. In this situation, the individual, in a drug-induced state of confusion or stupor, is said to administer additional doses of the drug without being fully aware of the previous administration.[148]

52. Although it appears certain that driving skills would be diminished by barbiturate intoxication, little direct investigation has been conducted. Related behavioural studies do suggest such an effect. Low therapeutic doses may not reduce driving ability, however, if the drug is not taken in conjunction with other sedatives such as alcohol.[72]

53. On the basis of existing evidence – it would appear that the long-term psychological effects of moderate barbiturate use are negligible for most users. Some of the complications of chronic high-dose use will be dealt with later.

Physiological Effects

54. The short-term effect of moderate to high doses of barbiturates is a general depression of neural and muscular activity. As with psychological and behavioural effects, the response to low dose is much more variable. Initially, the electroencephalogram (EEG) may suggest cortical activation, although this pattern is usually soon replaced by signs of drowsiness or sleep. The sleep induced by hypnotic doses generally resembles normal sleep with the exception of a marked reduction in the rapid eye movement (REM) stage, the significance of which is only beginning to be understood. Drowsiness or 'hangover' symptoms may follow acute intoxication or drug-induced sleep. Although the sedative action of the barbiturates has frequently been attributed to their effects on the reticular activating system of the brain, little is known of the specific details, and this action might occur through a variety of different pharmacological mechanisms.

A variety of other transient or temporary physiological changes may occur with moderate barbiturate use; the majority of these apparently reflect a general 'slowing down' of physiological activity (in the respiratory, cardiovascular and other systems) normally occurring with behavioural sedation, and are of little clinical significance. After even chronic non-medical use there is generally a fairly complete recovery of psychological and physiological capabilities following withdrawal – instances of permanent psychological or neurological disorder, or of irreversible liver or kidney damage are rarely reported. This is a rather surprising picture in light of the vast number of disabilities attributed to chronic alcoholism and the general pharmacological similarities between alcohol and the barbiturates. It may be significant to note here that persons physically dependent on barbiturates seem to be more likely to maintain a reasonable state of nutrition than do chronic alcoholics.

The toxic or poisoned state induced by barbiturate over-dose is characterized by coma, a general shock syndrome (e.g., weak rapid pulse, low blood pressure and cold sweaty skin) and may result in death due to respiratory arrest, cardiovascular collapse or kidney failure. If the over-dose is not fatal, a temporary jaundice due to impaired liver function is likely to follow and skin reactions may result. Some of these responses will also occur to normal doses in individuals allergic to or abnormally sensitive to the barbiturates. Because of the well documented additive or potentiating effects (as well as cross-tolerance) among the sedatives, users of related drugs, such as alcohol, must be especially attentive to dose levels.

Tolerance and Dependence

55. Tolerance to some of the effects of barbiturates can be demonstrated, although the degree and rate of tolerance acquisition varies considerably with the dose, frequency of administration and the individual. The potential for tolerance is much lower with barbiturates than with the opiate narcotics, and appears to level off at a maximum of 1.0 – 2.5gm. per day. (A normal sleep-inducing dose might be around 0.1 – 0.3gm.) While this loss of drug sensitivity is quite general and applies to both sedative and mood effects, no tolerance appears to develop to

the lethal toxicity level since chronic users are as susceptible to fatal over-doses as are initiates. In other words, the safety margin decreases with increased tolerance. Several mechanisms operate in producing tolerance. Barbiturates stimulate the body's production of the metabolic enzymes which inactivate the drug. Also, some insensitivity to the depressant effects appears which might reflect a general neurological adaptation. Certain learning processes are also probably involved in changing the character of the response upon repeated administrations. Most aspects of tolerance disappear after a few weeks of abstinence from the drug.

Although barbiturates were not recognized as 'addictive' drugs for decades after their general medical acceptance and usage, in chronic users, physical dependence may develop along with tolerance. Barbiturate dependence is in some respects similar to opiate narcotic dependence, although barbiturate (and alcohol) withdrawal symptoms are frequently more severe and are more likely to result in death. The abstinence syndrome following withdrawal of the drug in chronic heavy users may begin with a reduction in intoxication and an apparent improvement in condition. Within a few hours, however, general physical weakness, dizziness, anxiety, tremors, hyperactivity, nausea, abdominal cramps and vomiting may occur. These may be followed after one-and-one-half to five days by muscle spasms and grand mal (epileptic) seizures. Between the third and seventh day, delusions and hallucinations may appear; this psychosis may last for days or even months although recovery usually occurs within a week or two. Death during the convulsive phase occasionally occurs. [111, 89]

56. The full picture of barbiturate withdrawal only appears after heavy chronic use, and the effects of abstinence following more moderate consumption are considerably less severe, and may manifest only a few of the classic symptoms. Many regular users of therapeutic doses develop neither significant tolerance nor physical dependence. As is the case with alcohol and opiate narcotics, babies born of mothers physically dependent on barbiturates are also physically dependent on the same drugs.

Psychological dependence also occurs in some users, and

anxious or tense individuals may become dependent on even small doses in order to function in a manner which they consider satisfactory. Many persons depend upon the hypnotic effects of the barbiturates and can not sleep without a pill. In other individuals, the drug may be depended upon for a variety of subjective effects which the user considers essential to his well-being. The problem of psychological and behavioural dependence on barbiturates has not been adequately explored, however, and remains in the area of clinical impression and conjecture.

Barbiturates and Other Drugs

57. Because of the many similarities between barbiturates and other sedatives, they are often used interchangeably. A certain amount of cross-tolerance exists among these drugs, and chronic users of barbiturates are generally quite resistant to many of the effects of alcohol, minor tranquillizers and volatile anaesthetics, as well. This cross-tolerance, however, does not appear to affect the lethal dose, and large quantities of alcohol and barbiturates taken simultaneously (acting in an additive fashion) may produce a toxic or fatal reaction. In addition, the sedative drugs have the capacity to be substituted for each other in diminishing withdrawal symptoms, and barbiturates are frequently used therapeutically to reduce the severity of withdrawal in alcoholics. Since the sedatives show this cross-dependence, individuals dependent on one may turn to other sedatives if the supply of the preferred drug is restricted. Consequently, chronic barbiturate dependents are usually heavy alcohol users as well. Such multiple users often refer to the barbiturate intoxication as a 'dry drunk'. Barbiturates have the advantage of producing inebriation without the obvious odour of alcohol.

The relationship between barbiturates and the opiate narcotics is more complicated. These drugs may not show significant cross-tolerance, although barbiturates can be useful in the treatment of opiate narcotic withdrawal symptoms and may effectively reduce the unpleasantness of the abstinence syndrome. The drugs do interact in some sort of complementary way since barbiturates are frequently used by opiate narcotic dependents to strengthen or reinforce a weak heroin dose or as a substitute in an emergency. Many opiate users, however, avoid barbiturates and consider the barbiturate-dependent person to be at the bottom of the 'addict' community, together with the alcoholics.

58.   Barbiturates are often used in conjunction with amphetamines. Dexamyl*, for example, is a combination of dextroamphetamine and amobarbital which supposedly produces stimulation without certain of the irritation or tension-producing effects of the amphetamines. More important clinically, is the frequently noted alternating cycle of sedation and stimulation which many medical and non-medical drug users demonstrate. A stimulant may be used to overcome the drowsy hangover the day after a hypnotic dose of barbiturate. By evening, another sedative dose may be necessary to overcome the insomnia potentiated by the day's amphetamine. This continuing cycle is apparently not at all uncommon among otherwise socially respectable drug users. A somewhat related pattern has been demonstrated by some amphetamine-injecting 'speed freaks' who use barbiturates to terminate the stimulant effect or produce sleep after a 'high' of several days' duration.

ALCOHOL

59. Alcohol is one of the most widely used psychoactive drugs known to man; it has apparently been with us since the dawn of civilization. Breweries flourished in Egypt almost six thousand years ago and there is evidence that Stone Age prehistoric man made alcoholic beverages long before that.[223] The use of alcohol has appeared in varying degrees in most societies throughout recorded history and has traditionally played an important symbolic as well as pharmacological role in many social, religious and medical practices and customs. Just as the use of alcohol has been almost universal, so, apparently, has its misuse. Consequently, some degree of opposition to 'drink' appears to have arisen in all indulging cultures,

although attempts to eradicate its use have met with a uniform lack of success.

What is this drug which has been hailed as the 'water of life' and 'nectar of the gods' by some, and damned by others as 'second only to war' as a source of human problems? Made up of three common elements, carbon, hydrogen and oxygen, ethyl alcohol (C_2H_5OH) is a colourless, inflammable and volatile liquid. The word 'alcohol' by itself is usually taken to mean ethyl alcohol or *ethanol* (common beverage alcohol), although there is a vast number of other substances in the aliphatic alcohol family, many of which are highly toxic in even low doses.

Although the technique of producing alcoholic beverages by fermenting fruit, grain, vegetables, and other food-stuffs has hardly been a secret over the past few thousand years, the exact process by which the drug is generated was first illuminated by Louis Pasteur in the middle of the nineteenth century. His investigations revealed that alcohol was produced by a single-celled microscopic plant, one of the yeast fungi, which by a metabolic form of combustion breaks down certain sugars, releasing carbon dioxide (CO_2) with ethyl alcohol as a by-product. This production of CO_2 is responsible for the 'head' on a glass of beer, and the 'popping' of champagne corks, as well as the leavening effects of yeast in the rising of bread. Since yeast cannot digest starch, mash from cereal grains such as barley, rye, corn and rice must be malted (i.e., converted to maltose sugar) prior to fermentation in the production of beer, gin and whisky.

60. Fermentation normally continues until the sugar supply is exhausted. However, as the amount of alcohol in the fermenting solution increases, the metabolic activity of the yeast is slowed until it is finally killed when the alcohol level reaches about 14%, thus setting a limit on the maximum strength of natural (undistilled) beverages. The distillation process of boiling off and isolating the more volatile alcohol from the other fluids (mostly water) allows a further increase in ethanol concentration. Although this technique was used in Middle Eastern cultures centuries earlier, the production of 'spirits' by dis-

tillation has been known in Europe for less than seven hundred years. Today, ethanol can be produced synthetically.

In Canada, beer usually contains about 5% alcohol by volume, natural wine 7% to 14%, fortified wine up to 20% and spirits or liquor (distilled) approximately 40% alcohol. In other words, a 12 oz. bottle of beer or 3 to 4 oz. of wine contain about as much alcohol as $1\frac{1}{2}$ oz. of whisky.

61. The notion of alcohol 'proof' originated centuries ago from a crude but effective analytic technique designed to assess the strength of spirits. If gun powder soaked with the beverage exploded on ignition, this was taken as 'proof' that the liquor was more than half alcohol. 'Proof spirit' in the United Kingdom and Canadian system contains about 57% alcohol, while in the United States proof is calculated as twice the per cent by volume (e.g., 80% proof whisky is 40% alcohol).[80]

Canada has experimented with alcohol prohibition in varying ways since 1878. Although there are currently some 'dry' localities, alcohol is generally legally available across the country. An interesting bit of drug history is connected with alcohol law: over 300 years ago the prohibition of liquor sales to Indians was Canada's first alcohol regulation. Some such discriminatory policies are only now being eliminated.[32]

62. There was a 15-year period of prohibition in the United States, ending in 1934. The failure of that programme has been attributed to the unworkable form of the laws, inadequate enforcement, corruption among public authorities and, perhaps most importantly, a general lack of public support. During that period, the elimination of legitimate alcohol outlets resulted in home breweries and distilleries, 'bootleg' liquor or toxic substitutes, and smuggling, and created an economic vacuum rapidly filled by organized crime. Many authorities feel that this multi-million-dollar illicit market provided the initial capital for the construction of a network of syndicated criminal and quasi-legal business empires which have considerable economic and political strength in North America today.

Alcohol is now used by more than three-quarters of the Canadian population over the age of 15. Although most of it is undoubtedly consumed primarily for its pharmacological properties, there is a significant aspect of alcohol usage which is, in some respects, independent of its immediate drug effects. There are many longstanding customs, traditions and superstitions which pervade alcohol use in the Western world. Because it has become an integral part of our culture, the set and setting surrounding alcohol use is substantially different from that associated with other drugs in Canada.

63. Alcohol may have special meanings in various social contexts. Alcohol use is often symbolically and pharmacologically associated with the acknowledgement of birth, death, marriage and other contracts, adulthood, friendship, and, to some, it may imply virility and masculinity. Although it is employed in some religious ceremonies, many individuals have moral apprehensions about alcohol and may approach its use with feelings of ambivalence and guilt. Some reject it outright on grounds of principle, while still others feel that moderate use is morally acceptable. In many social circles abstinence is frowned upon and 'teetotallers' are looked upon with suspicion. On the other hand, it is obvious that considerable alcohol intoxication is tolerated, condoned and even encouraged in many situations in North American society. When one considers the fact that these various attitudes are ultimately tied to, or interact with, the diverse pharmacological potentials of alcohol in determining the overall drug effect, the complexity of the psychopharmacology of the drug in North America becomes apparent. Because its use is so ingrained at all levels of society, there is a tendency for many Canadians not to even consider alcohol a drug.

In a wider context, Jaffe, in *The Pharmacological Basis of Therapeutics* observes:[111]

The large role that the production and consumption of alcoholic beverages plays in the economic and social life in Western society should not permit us to minimize the fact that alcoholism is a more significant problem than all other forms of drug abuse combined.

64. Alcohol is currently recognized as an official drug in the British and U.S. Pharmacopeias, although the various alcoholic beverages, as such, are no longer listed for medical use. Alcohol has been cited over the past few thousand years as a cure for nearly every ailment or disease. Most of the medical benefits were probably more imagined than real, and many of alcohol's legitimate pharmacological functions have now been filled by more effective drugs, although it still plays a useful role in medicine.

Alcohol is often used as a preservative, solvent, and vehicle for other drugs, and is contained in tinctures, elixirs, spirits and many medicinal syrups. It is used to cleanse, disinfect and harden the skin, to cool it during fever, to decrease sweating (and is included in many antiperspirant deodorants), to reduce bed sores, to treat fainting, to temporarily or permanently block nerves by injection, and to stimulate appetite and digestion. In concentrations around 70%, alcohol is an effective antibacterial agent, although it is not satisfactory for disinfecting open wounds since it damages the raw tissue.[186]

Alcohol is still sometimes recommended as a tranquillizer, sedative, or hypnotic and may also serve as a mild mood stimulant for some individuals. It is no longer considered a safe surgical anaesthetic, since the dose necessary to produce unconsciousness is often dangerously close to the fatal level. However, the drug does produce mild analgesia (pain reduction) at lower doses. Alcohol is still used in the lay and folk medicine to 'treat' the common cold, although its benefits, if any, are probably limited to an improvement in mood and increased relaxation and rest.

Administration, Absorption, Distribution and Physiological Fate

65. Alcohol is usually taken orally and is rapidly and completely absorbed in the gastro-intestinal tract. Some absorption takes place in the stomach although diffusion into the blood stream is most rapid from the upper intestine and, conse-

quently, the quicker the alcohol passes through the stomach the shorter the latency of its action. Food eaten before or with alcohol tends to decrease the drug effect by slowing stomach emptying, and a meal before drinking alcohol may reduce the peak alcohol level in the blood by almost one-half compared to that attained by drinking on an empty stomach. Once absorbed, alcohol is distributed quite uniformly in all bodily fluids, easily enters the brain, and in pregnant women crosses the placental barrier into the foetus. Alcohol temporarily diffuses into fat tissue and consequently, a lean muscular individual will normally experience a greater pharmacological effect with a given dose than will a person with much body fat.

Approximately 95% of the alcohol in the body is broken down by oxidation in the liver and the rest is excreted unchanged, primarily in the urine and breath. While certain alcoholic beverages, such as beer, contain some protein and carbohydrates, alcohol itself provides only calories when metabolized and has little general food value. Depending on the form of alcoholic beverage and possible mixers, an ordinary drink may contain 90 to 150 calories or more. The rate of disappearance of alcohol from the body is quite constant within individuals at a given time, and the average 150 lb. man can metabolize about 9 ml. (0.3 oz) of alcohol per hour.

A convenient index of the quantity of the drug in the body is the *blood alcohol level*, represented in per cent by weight. Since the amount of alcohol excreted in the breath bears a fixed relationship to that in the blood, it is possible to accurately estimate the blood alcohol level from expired air. This principle is utilized in the *Breathalyzer* tests now employed in the enforcement of driving laws.

Short-Term Effects

66. Alcohol exerts its more significant effects through the central nervous system, usually producing a general sedation or depression of neural activity over a wide dosage range, although in certain circumstances, considerable behavioural and psychological arousal may result. Little is known as to the specific mechanism by which alcohol produces its psycho-

pharmacological action. As with most drugs, alcohol effects, especially those resulting from low or moderate amounts, depend to a large extent on the individual and the situation in which the drinking occurs. A drink or two may produce drowsiness and lethargy in some instances, while the same quantity might lead to increased activity and psychological stimulation in another individual, or in the same person in different circumstances. Furthermore, a dose which is initially stimulating may later produce sedation.

In many social settings, alcohol seems to result in a lessening of inhibition and a feeling of well being, sociability and camaraderie in most individuals. For many people alcohol relieves tension and anxiety – the common notion that one 'needs a drink' when worried, irritated or upset, reflects a general acknowledgement of this function. Although alcohol usually elevates mood at first, a general lack of emotional control, including anxiety, withdrawal, self-pity and depression may occur later. Alcohol has been frequently cited as an important contributing factor in many suicides.

Hostility and aggression are not at all uncommon in some drinkers, and fights and other forms of violent antisocial behaviour are often reported to accompany bouts of heavy drinking. It appears that some criminals fortify their courage by drinking prior to a sortie and alcohol intoxication reportedly plays a significant role in a large proportion of the violent crimes (murder, rape and assault against persons and property) in North America.[18]

67. Alcohol does not have a specific aphrodisiac (sex stimulating) effect *per se*, although the emotionality and general lessening of inhibitions often induced may lead to an increase in sexual activity and other normally restricted behaviour. An increase in desire or opportunity may be neglected by acute sexual impotence, however.

Although delusions, illusions and amnesic 'black outs' may occur in some individuals, acute alcohol psychosis (pathological intoxication) in normally moderate drinkers is rare. Even so, many persons might sympathize with the Roman philosopher Seneca who, almost 2,000 years ago, observed that, 'Drunkenness is nothing but a condition of insanity purposely assumed'.[197]

In moderate amounts (e.g., a few drinks) alcohol may increase or decrease heart rate, produce a 'flushing' or dilation of small blood vessels in the skin (giving a sensation of warmth), lower body temperature, stimulate appetite and the secretion of saliva and gastric juices, increase urination, produce a slowing of the electroencephalogram (EEG), increase reaction time, reduce muscular co-ordination. In addition, alcohol generally reduces performance on tests of a wide variety of psychological functions. Tests requiring a high degree of attention, concentration or vigilance are particularly sensitive to alcohol effects, and impairment is usually most pronounced on complex and recently learned tasks. In a few situations, however, a small amount of alcohol may actually improve performance. In high doses, alcohol produces drunkenness, disorientation and confusion, slurred speech, blurred vision, inadequate muscular control, and often induces nausea and vomiting. As an increasing quantity is ingested, there occurs a depression of respiration, general anesthesia and unconsciousness and, rarely, death due to respiratory arrest and circulatory failure. Acute alcohol intoxication is often followed by pronounced 'hangover' symptoms characterized by nausea, weakness, dizziness, poor co-ordination and a variety of aches and pains. Some authorities consider this post-inebriation phase a form of acute withdrawal syndrome.

68. Effects of alcohol on driving ability are well known – even moderate amounts produce serious impairment in many individuals. A recent study of alcohol involvement in fatal motor vehicle accidents in three Canadian provinces presented findings similar to those reported regularly across North America.[37] It has commonly been observed that alcohol is a factor in a large proportion of all fatal traffic accidents. Approximately 70% of drivers killed in single vehicle accidents and 50% of drivers killed in multi-vehicle collisions had been drinking. Among all driver fatalities, alcohol was detected in the blood of 60 to 70 per cent of those considered responsible for their own deaths. Furthermore, more than half of the pedestrians killed in

traffic accidents had recently been drinking, and there are numerous reports that alcohol is a contributing factor in a great number of industrial accidents as well. A large proportion of the people involved in such accidents are chronic alcoholics, although the majority are apparently 'social' drinkers.

The intensity of the acute effects of alcohol can, to a certain extent, be predicted from the amount of alcohol in the blood, although the relationship between the quantity of alcohol present and the central nervous system (CNS) response may vary considerably from individual to individual. Recent Federal legislation prohibits driving with blood alcohol level greater than 0.08%. Depending on the person, this concentration may be produced by three or four ordinary drinks, if consumed in a short time. While certain individuals might be capable of driving satisfactorily with this much alcohol, most persons are probably impaired by even lower quantities. Although the *Breathalyzer* can be used to assess acute alcohol intoxication, there are no simple methods of detecting a 'hangover', and there are indications that this post-inebriation phase also has severe effects on psychomotor performance.

Long-Term Effects

69. Many authorities differentiate between 'low risk' (moderate) and 'high risk' (heavy) drinking in discussing the long-term effects of alcohol. For most otherwise normal individuals, moderate drinking over a prolonged period of time may produce little significant psychological or physiological change. High risk or heavy drinking (e.g., five or six or more drinks a day) may lead to a variety of disorders, however, many of which are subsumed under the general term 'alcoholism'.

There is considerable disagreement among authorities as to the proper delineation of the concept of alcoholism – definitions may be as general as 'a family of disorders accompanying chronic heavy drinking' with various social and economic complications, or may contain more restrictive specifications of physical dependency or psychological and physiological harm. Jellinek has described five different types of alcoholics which differ in degree and kind of psychological, behavioural and physiological involvement.[112] In some areas of North America, at least two per cent to five per cent of alcohol users become alcoholics and many more would be considered problem drinkers.

70. No group of drug-dependent persons presents a sorrier picture of psychological and physiological pathology than that of the 'skid row' derelict alcoholics. Frequently observed in these individuals and many other alcoholics are disorders of the digestive tract, cardiovascular system, lungs, kidney, pancreas and the nervous system, with sleep disturbance and various kinds of irreversible neurological damage and cerebral atrophy. Considerable attention has been focused on liver disorders in heavy drinkers, and it is well established that alcohol is a major contributing or causal factor in liver cirrhosis. Alcoholics may develop specific psychotic syndromes, permanently impaired memory, epilepsy, chronic incoordination, sexual impotence, loss of appetite and a variety of nutritional disorders which may result in an increased susceptibility to other diseases and infections.[111]

In the past, these and numerous other disorders were thought to be a direct result of alcohol toxicity, but now many of these pathologies are considered to be of secondary origin – often a function of chronic dietary deficiencies, poor personal care and other aspects of the general life style which may accompany alcoholism. The diet of certain alcoholics may consist of 40-50% alcohol, with periods of weeks or even months of nothing else, and thus may be dangerously low in proteins, vitamins, minerals and other essential foodstuffs. Proper diet and medical care may be able to prevent or alleviate many, but not all, of the problems associated with chronic alcoholism.[182]

Only a minority of alcoholics are 'down and out' derelicts, and there are many alcohol-dependent persons in all levels of society who function in varying degrees of effectiveness in spite of the handicap. Psychological and physiological disorders in these individuals vary considerably as a function of general life style, drinking patterns and perhaps certain inherited characteristics. Many heavy drinkers show little functional impairment.

71. Tolerance to most of the effects of alcohol develops with frequent use, although it does not occur as rapidly or to the same degree as with the opiate narcotics. The rate of acquisition and extent of tolerance depends on the pattern of use, and regular heavy drinkers may be able to consume two or three times as much alcohol as a novice. In Western culture, some symbolic masculinity frequently accompanies the development of tolerance and the ability to 'hold one's liquor'.

Most intermittent or moderate drinkers show little tendency to increase dose, although regular heavy drinkers may, in order to obtain the desired psychological effects, ingest quantities which lead to chronic alcohol toxicity symptoms. In addition to the probable neurophysiological and metabolic mechanisms involved in tolerance, learning to function under the influence of alcohol may further reduce some of the acute behavioural effects of intoxication in regular users. Little or no tolerance develops to the lethal dose, however, and acute alcohol poisoning is a noted cause of death in alcoholics, although nausea, vomiting and unconsciousness usually prevent self-administration of a fatal overdose. In some alcoholics, tolerance later seems to decline and a special response or oversensitivity to certain effects of alcohol develops. In such individuals even a single drink may produce profound loss of control and initiate unrestricted further indulgence.

72. Physical dependence on alcohol occurs in some long-term heavy drinkers after the development of tolerance. Although alcoholic hallucinosis, delirium tremens ('DT's'), and convulsions ('rum fits') were noted and studied in the nineteenth century, until recently there was a lack of consensus as to whether these symptoms were essentially the direct result of acute or chronic alcohol toxicity, secondary nutritional deficiences, or part of a physical dependence withdrawal syndrome.

Isbell *et al*[108] and Mendelson *et al*[156] have clearly demonstrated that even when diet is controlled, a characteristic severe abstinence syndrome can occur after only a few weeks of continual heavy drinking. The quantities of alcohol ingested in these studies were much greater than those normally consumed, however, and with the usual drinking patterns, such physiological dependence does not occur until after 3 to 15 or more years of heavy consumption. Some heavy drinkers never become physically dependent on alcohol.[112]

73. The overall picture of the alcohol withdrawal syndrome is generally similar to that noted earlier for barbiturates. Nausea, anxiety, severe agitation, confusion, tremors, and sweating are followed by cramps, vomiting and illusions and hallucinations. After several days, delirium tremens may develop and convulsions, exhaustion and cardiovascular collapse may occur. The delirium tremens stage is fatal in about 10% of cases. Major recovery in those surviving usually occurs within a week, although certain psychological symptoms may continue for a longer period.[234]

Psychological dependence on alcohol seems to occur in many individuals, and such dependence appears to be generally accepted in contemporary North America. A great number of people regularly turn to alcohol for relief or aid prior to or after facing a stressful situation, to escape worries, troubles or boredom, to relax and enjoy a party, or even to sleep, and many feel they do not function as well in certain situations without a drink or two. There would appear to be a strong psychological component in the drinking behaviour of the developing alcoholic, as is exemplified in the usually compulsive nature of his drinking and his frequent inability to control his use of alcohol in spite of obvious consequences.

Alcohol and Other Drugs

74. A certain degree of cross-tolerance and cross-dependence occurs among the sedative drugs. Heavy alcohol users are normally resistant to the effects of barbiturates, minor tranquillizers, volatile solvents and anaesthetics, as well as alcohol, although the cross-tolerance does not significantly affect the lethal dose. Consequently, many over-dose deaths occur due to the mixing of these drugs in chronic users. Barbiturates and minor tranquillizers effectively block alcohol withdrawal symptoms and are frequently used in treating alcoholics in the acute phase of abstinence. Alcoholics are often heavy users of other

sedative drugs as well and may switch from one to another, if it is convenient or necessary. The use of high toxic alcohols, such as methyl or 'wood' alcohol, and even automobile anti-freeze, has been reported in derelict alcoholics. In addition, persons dependent on opiate narcotics generally have a history of heavy alcohol consumption.

75. Certain drugs, such as disulfiram (Antabuse*) or Temposil*, which may have little direct pharmacological activity themselves, have the capacity to inhibit certain stages of alcohol metabolism in the body and can thereby produce a highly unpleasant toxic reaction known as the *acetaldehyde syndrome* when used in conjunction with alcohol. Such drugs have been used in the treatment of problem drinkers.

Amphetamines, caffeine and other stimulants may reduce the drowsiness often associated with inebriation, although they can not fully compensate for most of the effects of alcohol intoxication.

MINOR TRANQUILLIZERS

76. The term '*minor* tranquillizers' was introduced into the scientific literature in the 1950s to distinguish the medicines prescribed to reduce anxiety and tension from the *major* tranquillizers, like reserpine and chlorpromazine, which are employed (as antipsychotic drugs) in the treatment of severe mental illness such as schizophrenia. Another phrase, often used interchangeably with the words 'minor tranquillizers' is *anxiolytic sedatives*. This class of drugs may be defined as substances which reduce anxiety, tension and agitation without other significant effects on cognition or perceptual processes.

It seems safe to say that the optimal anxiolytic sedative, which effectively separates anxiety-reducing properties from those producing undesired psychological side effects does not yet exist. There are a variety of drugs of several chemical classes which approximate these criteria, however: bromides, paraldehyde, chloral hydrate; the newer minor tranquillizers such as meprobamate (Miltown*), diazepam (Valium*), and chlordiazepoxide (Librium*) and assorted other compounds (e.g., ethchlorvynol, glutethimide) which do not fall into a neat chemical classification. Alcohol and barbiturates are also often considered with the anxiolytic sedatives, although we will keep them separate in the following discussions since they have already been covered in previous sections of this report.

77. Most minor tranquillizers fall between alcohol and barbiturates in sedative action at a therapeutic dose. The disparate classes of chemicals have generally similar physiological action and will be treated as a group, with individual differences sometimes characterized. The minor tranquillizers have tended to replace barbiturates as day-time sedatives in recent years. These drugs and other sedatives are commonly referred to as 'downers' in the drug argot.

In Canada and the U.S.A., well over $500 million is spent each year on sedative drugs, to treat a wide variety of symptoms falling under the category of anxiety.[181] Although there are no statistics available to us at this time on the Canadian imports, exports, manufacture, production or sale of minor tranquillizers, many observers feel that the supply greatly exceeds medical needs. The distribution route which the drugs follow after production is not known, and a considerable percentage may be diverted for non-medical use. Clandestine manufacture of minor tranquillizers does not appear to occur and all such drugs initially start into the market as lawful materials. As described in the section on barbiturates, patients may be able to procure large quantities of these drugs through legitimate prescription channels.

78. In the U.S., production figures for tranquillizers exceed those for 'sleeping pills', 'pep pills', and opiate narcotics combined.[77] In addition,[178]

In 1965 in the U.S.A., some 58 million new prescriptions and 108 million refills were written for psychotropes (sedatives, tranquillizers and stimulants) and these 166 million prescriptions accounted for 14% of the total prescriptions of all kinds written in the United States.

79. Minor tranquillizers are so widely prescribed that the American Medical Association warned doctors about over-prescription and outlined ways in which the 'misuse of seda-

tives' by 'the prolonged and unsupervised administration of (tranquillizers) for symptomatic relief often without adequate diagnosis or knowledge of the patient's past experience with medications, or attitudes towards drugs' is aggravated.[8] Evidence in these recent U.S. surveys indicates that the minor tranquillizers and other sedatives are more commonly used than the stimulants among respondents above age 20.

The minor tranquillizers, along with barbiturates, tobacco, and alcohol, are among the most widely used drugs in North American society, and are the toxic agents in a large number of poisoning cases. Since chronic tranquillizer dependence may be quite frequent, and may involve considerable impairment, the public's relative indifference to the hazards of tranquillizer pill-popping is quite alarming. As in the case of alcohol and barbiturates, much research on medical use has been done, but little investigation of non-medical use of tranquillizers has been carried out.

Medical Use

80. Minor tranquillizers are widely used in medical practice today, and are mainly prescribed for patients suffering from anxiety, tension, behavioural excitement and insomnia. They are also used in the treatment of lower back pain, convulsive disorders and withdrawal symptoms of opiate narcotic and alcohol dependence.

Some clinicians feel that chemotherapy of anxiety is a secondary approach (although frequently the most expedient) and that the minor tranquillizers should be used primarily to relieve immediate distress, and to aid the patient only until other treatment procedures become effective.

Administration, Absorption, Distribution and Physiological Fate

81. Minor tranquillizers are usually administered orally as elixirs or tablets, but are also sometimes injected, for both medical and non-medical purposes. They are generally rapidly absorbed by the stomach, intestine and rectum, and the absorp-

tion is most rapid with an empty stomach. Once absorbed, the drugs are distributed quite uniformly throughout the body, with the latency of response dependent on the particular chemical class. Some are metabolized, or otherwise chemically altered (usually in the liver), and excreted into the urine, while others are eliminated unchanged. The factors of distribution, metabolism, and excretion, are primarily responsible for differences in potency and duration of action of the different minor tranquillizers. The detection of some acute and chronic tranquillizer use is not easy, and the methods of detection of the metabolites in urine are highly sophisticated and expensive.

Psychological Effects

82. Many of the psychological effects of minor tranquillizers are similar to those observed with alcohol and barbiturates. As with these other sedatives, psychological and behavioural responses to low doses of minor tranquillizers are quite variable. There may be a sedation in some instances and, in others, an increase in activity. Studies reveal that complex interactions between the type of drug and the level of anxiety occur, even within the same pharmacological group; the drugs may impair or improve performance, depending on dose and the degree of anxiety present.[131]

Normal doses usually provide relaxation, a feeling of well-being and perhaps some loss of inhibition. With excessive use of these drugs the following effects may be observed: disorientation, confusion, memory impairment, trance-like episodes, double vision, personality alterations, rage reactions and other symptoms resembling those of drunkenness. Such manifestations are difficult to differentiate from the inebriation caused by barbiturates and alcohol.

83. It appears that driving skills may not be impaired at clinical doses, so long as the user is not already drowsy or has not taken other sedatives such as alcohol. At higher doses, driving skills are more likely to be seriously impaired. One report states that the accident rate in a group of drivers using prescribed doses of Librium* was 10 times the general accident rate for

New York State, but it is not clear whether the accident rate among these drivers who 'needed' a tranquillizer, was so high because of, or in spite of, the drug they were taking.[167] In Canada it is an offence to drive under the influence of drugs, and the penalties are similar to those for drunken driving, although convictions involving tranquillizers are rarely reported.

Physiological Effects

84. The response to moderate and high doses of minor tranquillizers is a general depression of nervous and muscular activity and several other bodily functions. Compared with other sedatives, the newer minor tranquillizers may have less inhibitory effect on the parts of the brain which are responsible for arousal and motor control and may have greater muscle relaxant effects. The minor tranquillizers affect the levels of some neurohumors in the brain which may be involved in the tension-anxiety states. However, the exact mechanism by which these drugs produce their effects is unknown.

Side effects observed with these drugs include drowsiness, ataxia, lethargy, skin rashes, nausea, diminished sex interest, menstrual and ovulatory irregularities, blood abnormalities and increased sensitivity to alcohol. High doses may depress respiration, produce unconsciousness and coma and can produce death. There is no clear evidence of permanent irreversible damage to neurological or other physiological processes even with long-term non-medical use. The fact that chronic users of minor tranquillizers maintain a reasonable diet and are not reported to suffer from malnutrition, may account for some of the differences between the chronic effects of tranquillizer use and alcoholism.

Tolerance and Dependence

85. Tolerance usually develops to most of the effects of the minor tranquillizers on repeated use and the dose must often be increased in order to obtain the desired effects. No tolerance develops to the lethal toxicity, however, and chronic users must be especially attentive to the quantities consumed. With one or

two exceptions, these drugs have been reported to produce both psychological and physiological dependence, resembling that seen with alcohol and the barbiturates.

The clinical descriptions of the abstinence syndrome, reported to follow abrupt withdrawal, after excessive dosages of the minor tranquillizers, indicate a marked similarity to one another and to alcohol and barbiturates. The syndrome may be characterized by anxiety, apprehension, tremulousness, muscle twitches, insomnia, headache, fever, loss of appetite, nausea, vomit, abdominal cramps, sweating, tachycardia, fainting, hyperactive reflexes, convulsions, and uncontrolled urination and defecation. In addition, delirious states can occur with motor agitation, hallucinations, delusions, disorientation and confusion. The abstinence syndrome can be very serious, and deaths have been attributed to withdrawal of meprobamate (Miltown*) and methyprylon (Noludar*).[72]

Minor Tranquillizers and Other Drugs

86. Cross-tolerance and cross-dependence exist among the minor tranquillizers and with other sedative drugs. This cross-tolerance does not appear to affect the lethal dose and, consequently, alcohol or barbiturates taken simultaneously with large quantities of minor tranquillizers may act additively and produce toxic or fatal reactions. Heavy users of these drugs may switch among the sedatives, if necessary or convenient, and alcoholics often use barbiturates and tranquillizers to sustain inebriation. Individuals dependent on opiate narcotics often also use large quantities of minor tranquillizers.

AMPHETAMINES

87. Amphetamines are synthetic amines which are in many ways similar to the body's own adrenalin (epinephrine). These drugs generally evoke an arousal or activating response not unlike one's normal reaction to emergency or stress. Amphetamines were first synthesized in the early part of the century and entered medical use by the 1930s. Although a variety of related drugs and mixtures currently exist, the most common

77

amphetamine substances are amphetamine (Benzedrine*), dextroamphetamine (Dexedrine*), and methamphetamine (Methedrine* or Desoxyn*), with Benzedrine* being the least potent. Generally, if the dose is adjusted, the psychological effects of these various drugs are similar and, consequently, they will be discussed as a group. Other drugs with somewhat similar pharmacological properties are phenmetrazine (Preludin*), methylphenidate (Ritalin*) and pipradol (Meratran*). Common slang terms for amphetamines include: 'speed', 'crystal', 'meth', 'bennies', 'dexies', 'A', 'uppers', 'pep pills', 'diet pills', 'jolly beans', 'truck drivers', 'co-pilots', 'eye openers', 'wake-ups', 'hearts' and 'footballs'.

The stimulating effects of the amphetamines were widely used by soldiers during World War II to counteract fatigue. Since then, they have been commonly used both medically and non-medically by vehicle drivers on long trips, night-shift workers, fatigued housewives, students studying for exams and others who must meet deadlines, athletes for increasing performance, and others for general stimulation, pleasure or fun.

88. In the 1940s, much of the wartime stockpile was dumped on the world market and in many countries amphetamines were available on a non-prescription 'over the counter' basis. Widespread use followed in most industrialized areas with numerous unpleasant consequences. Use reached epidemic proportions, for example, in Japan in the 1950s – a country which had never had a previous serious drug problem.[34] Since this time, amphetamines have been quite uniformly put under governmental control and in some countries (e.g., Sweden) are currently prohibited from medical and non-medical applications. Although the popularity of both medical and non-medical use of these drugs spread rapidly in all age groups and social classes in North America after the war, heavy use was apparently largely confined to delinquents and to members of the criminal-addict population of a few decades ago. The drug was usually taken orally, sometimes injected by heroin addicts, or sniffed. In many instances it was used interchangeably with cocaine (a short-acting but powerful stimulant). Frequent use was made of 'dis-

mantled' Benzedrine inhalers, which were on the unrestricted legal market at that time.

More recently, major concern has developed in many circles for a relatively new amphetamine phenomenon – that of massive doses used intravenously by persons often referred to as 'speed freaks'. Although this practice has been most frequently noted among youthful multi-drug-taking individuals, considerable opposition to such use of amphetamines has developed within the 'hip' community. The 'speed trip' is in many respects the antithesis of the experience sought with the psychedelic drugs. Instead of the orientation towards the 'consciousness expansion', personal insight, and aesthetic and religious awareness often attributed to the psychedelic drug experience by users, the speed phenomenon is usually characterized by action, power, arrogance and physical pleasure ('kicks'), and regularly leads to suspicion, paranoia, hostility and often aggression. In addition to these undesirable personality changes, which render 'speed freaks' highly unpopular in the community, such individuals generally present a picture of chronic ill-health unparalleled among youthful drug users.

89. The message received by the Commission at public and private hearings, and in written communications with youthful drug users has been mostly negative towards 'speed'. Many experienced illicit drug users consider amphetamines extremely dangerous and undesirable, and have expressed surprisingly hostile attitudes towards these drugs in no uncertain terms. Recently, numerous persons well known to youth, who have had considerable influence on drug attitudes during the past decade (e.g., John Lennon and the Beatles, Frank Zappa and the Mothers of Invention, Timothy Leary, and Donovan), have made public statements against the use of 'speed' and related drugs.

Many physicians have suggested that the supply of amphetamines legitimately imported and manufactured in Canada greatly exceeds medical need. As with other prescription drugs which are widely used, such as the barbiturates and tranquillizers, the distinction between medical and non-medical use is not always easily made.

90. As early as 1935, amphetamines (in doses from 20-200 mg) were found to be a specific treatment for narcolepsy, an uncommon illness which is characterized by sudden attacks of sleep and weakness. Since the 1940s, amphetamines (in doses of 10-50 mg) have been used in the treatment of overactive children who showed disorders of attention and impairment of learning capacity. In the last few years, several investigators have again published results of clinical trials which revealed that amphetamines and methylphenidate were among the most effective treatments for these childhood disorders.

Psychiatrists have frequently used intravenous injections of methedrine (in doses of 15-30mg) for diagnostic purposes. Administered in this fashion, the drug induces a state of excitation, elation and increased talkativeness, during which a previously inhibited patient might reveal information and symptoms which may be considered important for the understanding of his disorder. He might also express, more freely, previously suppressed emotions. It has been observed that some patients with a borderline psychosis show typical psychotic symptoms more clearly following an injection of amphetamines.

At one time, these drugs were used in the treatment of alcoholism and opiate narcotic dependency, but this practice was abandoned because amphetamines often produce dependency when taken for longer than two or three weeks. Since alcoholism is a chronic condition, some alcoholics who took this treatment for long periods of time became dependent on amphetamines and alcohol.

91. Early hopes that amphetamines would prove to be an effective general treatment for severe depression were soon disappointed. Although these drugs are powerful stimulants and increase a depressed person's activity, they may also make him more anxious and agitated, deprive him of sleep, and may fail to elevate his mood or to reverse the fundamental depressive process. In some individuals, these drugs have been effective in relieving mild depression and chronic fatigue, however.

Amphetamines, and some related drugs, have a strong suppressive effect on appetite. Most so-called 'diet pills' contain amphetamines or similar preparations. However, the appetite-suppressing action of amphetamines usually disappears after about two weeks, together with the pleasant stimulating effects, unless the dose is continuously increased.

Amphetamines have also been occasionally used to treat petit mal epilepsy, parkinsonism, pregnancy nausea, asthma, nasal congestion and sedative poisoning. Many observers feel that because of the risk of dependency and undesirable personality change with amphetamines, even the medical use of these substances should be severely restricted.

Administration, Absorption, Distribution and Physiological Fate

92. Amphetamines are available in a variety of tablets, capsules (both in immediate and delayed release forms), elixirs, injections and, until recently, inhalers. These drugs also appear in powder ('crystal') form on the black market. Amphetamines are available commercially combined with such drugs as barbiturates (e.g., Dexamyl*) and other sedatives, atropine, caffeine, vitamins and minerals, thyroid extract, and, on the illicit market, amphetamines are reportedly sometimes added to LSD. One of the most esoteric pharmaceutical combinations has been described as follows:[133] 'This is a multi-coated tablet of pentobarbital on the outside to induce sleep rapidly, phenobarbital under a delayed dissolving coating to extend the sleep, and under another coating, an amphetamine to awaken the patient in the morning.'

Amphetamines are usually administered orally and are readily absorbed from the gastro-intestinal tract. Occasionally both intramuscular and intravenous injections are used medically. In the past, an amphetamine-base inhaler was also available. Non-medical users may employ any of these administration routes, including sniffing 'crystal', although chronic 'speed freaks' prefer intravenous injections.

About half of the amphetamine which enters the body is excreted unchanged in the urine, the remainder being previously deactivated or chemically altered in the liver prior to elimination. Although excretion is generally rather rapid, traces of the drug can be found in the urine up to a week after withdrawal. Because of the considerable proportion excreted unchanged, certain individuals have been known to extract and reuse crystals obtained from the urine. (This general practice of 'reclaiming' excreted drugs is not new and such procedures have been recorded for centuries.)

Effects

93. Both the psychological and physiological response to amphetamines vary profoundly with dose, and the effects of intravenous injections of massive quantities may differ greatly in character from, and bear little resemblance to, responses to low doses administered orally. These effects vary continuously over the full dosage range, but for clarification in the following discussions, the use of moderate quantities of amphetamines will be separated from the discussion of the practice of high-dose intravenous injection.

94. *Moderate-dose effects.* At typical therapeutic doses (e.g., 5-30 mg), amphetamines produce electrophysiological signs of central nervous system (CNS) activation along with a variety of adrenalin-like peripheral (sympathomimetic) effects such as increased blood pressure, pulse-rate and blood sugar, slight dilation of some blood vessels and constriction of others, widening of the pupils, increased respiration rate, depression of appetite and some relaxation of smooth muscle. Such effects might last 3-4 hours.

The psychological response varies considerably among individuals, but might typically include increased wakefulness, alertness, and vigilance, improvement in concentration and a feeling of clearer thinking, greater responsiveness to environmental stimuli, decreased fatigue and boredom, elevation of mood, mild euphoria, a feeling of sociability, increased initiative and energy, and increased verbal and other behavioural activity. There may be an improvement in some simple mental tasks, and athletic performance may be increased. In general, improved functioning is most likely to occur when prior performance was at a subnormal state due to drowsiness, fatigue or boredom.

On the other hand, a moderate dose of amphetamines in different individuals (or perhaps even in the same individual at different times) might produce irritation, restlessness, insomnia, blurred vision, tremor, nausea, headache, inability to concentrate, dizziness, heart palpitation, confusion, anxiety, chest pains, chilliness, diarrhoea or constipation, and other adverse symptoms. In cases of higher dose or hypersensitivity, delirium, panic, aggression, psychosis, hallucinations and cardiovascular abnormalities may occur in some individuals. Although deaths are rare, some have been reported among athletes.[15]

95. After continued administration of moderate doses, recovery may be associated with fatigue, drowsiness and, not infrequently, emotional depression. The increased energy and alertness elicited by the drug merely postpones the need for rest and clearly provides no long-term substitute for it. Many regular users of stimulants rely on the drug for energy when fatigued and often do not get proper rest for long periods of time.

The amphetamine toxic psychosis may be indistinguishable from schizophrenia.[56] While this syndrome is generally associated with high-dose use, many of the symptoms have been observed with the use of more moderate amounts. There does not appear to be any irreversible physiological damage associated with long-term use of moderate doses of amphetamines although temporary disorders do occur.

96. *Tolerance and dependence with moderate doses.* Tolerance to the various drug effects develops at different rates and to different degrees – some responses 'drop out' in chronic use sooner than others. The tendency to increase dose depends upon which of the potential drug effects is rewarding or reinforcing drug use. Many individuals, for instance, who use amphetamines to control narcolepsy, may reach a stabilized dose and show very little need for increased quantity over a period of years. On the other hand, those using the drug to control appetite generally increase their dose. Many psychological effects, such as the mood-elevating response, may show a considerable sensitivity to tolerance, and individuals who either began using the drug to obtain these effects, or who acquired the taste for

them after initially using amphetamines for other purposes, generally show a marked tendency to increase dose over time. Tolerance to some of the toxic properties occurs, and certain chronic users administer thousands of milligrams intravenously in a day, while even a fraction of that quantity would be extremely toxic in a non-tolerant user. As with other drugs, the rate of development of tolerance to the different pharmacological effects depends on the doses used, the frequency of administration and various individual factors. No suggestion of physiological dependence on amphetamines occurs with moderate doses; but psychological dependence on even low doses is frequently reported, and is considered a major hazard in both medical and non-medical amphetamine use.

97. *High-dose effects*. The chronic high-dose intravenous amphetamine syndrome has recently been described by several authors.[124, 71] The cycle or pattern of use usually begins with several days of repeated injections (usually of Methedrine*), gradually increasing in magnitude and frequency. Some users may 'shoot' or 'crank' up to several thousand milligrams in a single day. Initially the user may feel energetic, talkative, enthusiastic, happy, confident and powerful, and may initiate and complete highly ambitious tasks. He does not sleep and usually eats very little. After the first few days, however, toxic unpleasant symptoms become stronger, especially as the dose is increased. These toxic effects may be similar to those described earlier for lower doses, but appear in amplified form. Some symptoms commonly reported at this stage are: confused and disorganized patterns of thought and behaviour, compulsive repetition of meaningless acts, irritability, self-consciousness, suspiciousness, fear, and hallucinations and delusions which may take on the characteristics of a paranoid psychosis. Aggressive and anti-social behaviour may occur at this time. Severe chest pains, abdominal pain mimicking appendicitis and fainting have also been reported.[207]

Towards the end of the 'run' (usually less than a week), the toxic symptoms dominate; the drug is discontinued, fatigue sets in, and prolonged sleep follows, sometimes lasting several days. Upon awakening, the user is usually lethargic, often emotionally depressed and ravenously hungry. The user may overcome these effects with another injection – thus initiating the cycle anew. Runs are often separated by days or weeks, however, at a time. In certain instances, 'down' drugs, such as barbiturates or tranquillizers, or even opiate narcotics may be used to 'crash' or terminate a run which has become intolerable or otherwise unpleasant.

98. The immediate effects of the intravenous injection of amphetamines are a sudden, overwhelming pleasurable 'rush' or 'flash' which has been described by users as 'an instant total body orgasm'. This effect is qualitatively different from the warm, drifting sensation associated with the opiate narcotics, but is reported to be initially similar to the 'splash' produced by intravenous cocaine.[124] Some users claim that the immediate pleasure of the injection is the prime motivation for the drug use and that other effects are secondary.

Some individuals report that sexual activity is prolonged, and may continue for hours. When orgasm finally comes it may be more pleasurable than normal, although, on the other hand, some describe an inability to reach a climax. While only a minority of users report increased sexual activity, some people give this reason as a primary one for taking the drug.[124, 23]

Some investigators have reported that many users claim that they take the drug for euphoria or 'kicks', or because it enables them to be more confident and active. In addition, there are reports of 'needle freaks', in whom the use of the hypodermic syringe has special rewarding connotations.

99. The clinical picture of the chronic 'speed freak' is a distressing one indeed. Continued use of massive doses of amphetamines often leads to considerable weight loss, sores and non-healing ulcers, brittle fingernails, tooth grinding, chronic chest infections, liver disease, a variety of hypertensive disorders, and in some cases, cerebral haemorrhage.[124] The extent to which these effects are the direct result of the drug or the secondary consequences of poor eating habits, over-exertion and improper rest is unclear. Further complications may be caused by unsterile injections, including hepatitis and a variety of other infections.[47] Although some users feel that certain of

their mental abilities have been impaired by amphetamine use, no clear picture of permanent brain damage has been demonstrated.

100. Heavy use of amphetamines frequently precipitates a psychosis which is indistinguishable from paranoid schizophrenia. In addition, several investigators contend that schizophrenics, and others with borderline psychotic conditions, are more likely to use the drug intravenously than are other individuals. In one study, 41% of those requiring hospital admission for treatment of amphetamine disorders were thought to be schizophrenic before taking the drug.[100] However, there is still no reliable information on what proportion of users develop psychoses and what the predisposing factors actually are. The majority of acute psychotic reactions occur towards the end of a run, and such symptoms are usually dissipated by a few days rest.

'Speed freaks' are generally unpopular within the multi-drug-taking community and are often shunned. Consequently, these individuals may live together in 'flash houses' totally occupied by amphetamine users. Frequent 'hassles', aggression and violence have been reported in such dwellings. Heavy users are generally unable to hold a steady job because of the drug habit and often have a parasitic relationship with the rest of the illicit drug-using community. There are reports that many users support themselves through petty crime.[184, 23]

101. *High-dose dependency.* The question of physical dependence on amphetamines depends on the definition of the withdrawal symptoms necessary to meet the criterion. While it is clear that withdrawing amphetamine from chronic users does not produce the dramatic, physically painful and often dangerous abstinence syndrome associated with alcohol, barbiturates, or opiate narcotics, many investigators feel that the fatigue, prolonged sleep, brain wave (EEG) changes, voracious appetite, cardiovascular abnormalities, occasional gastro-intestinal cramps, lethargy and, often, severe emotional depression following the 'speed binge' constitute a physiological reaction analogous to the more dramatic withdrawal seen with depressant drugs.[56, 207]

The tendency for tolerance-producing drugs to manifest a 'rebound' type of physiological and psychological pattern upon withdrawal has been given considerable attention; amphetamine abstinence in chronic users is generally characterized by a profound sedation, and depression of mood and physiological function, while drugs such as the sedatives and the opiate narcotics (all of which produce sleep in high doses) generally exhibit a withdrawal syndrome of severe and toxic overstimulation (in some instances to the point of convulsions).

The fact that amphetamines have, if any, a physically rather benign withdrawal syndrome, clearly indicates that a profound physical dependence is not a necessary component in an overall severe drug dependency situation. Subjective psychological factors seem to have considerably greater motivational importance in many instances – especially with chronic high-dose amphetamine use.

102. *Speed Kills*. In recent years, the slogan 'Speed Kills' has received much attention, and the idea appears to play a significant role in the attitude that some users and non-users have towards the drug. One commonly hears the view that once you're 'on speed' you have only two to five years left to live. Some chronic 'speed freaks' incorporate this notion into the identity they present to others and the image they entertain of themselves. Many observers contend that the chronic use of intravenous amphetamines reflects a thinly disguised suicidal tendency, as well as an attention and sympathy gaining device. 'Hello, I'm Philbert Desanex; I'm a speed freak and I'm going to be dead by fall', is only a slightly exaggerated caricature of the image purposefully projected by some of these individuals.

103. What is the evidence, in fact, that 'Speed Kills' in the literal direct physical sense? Fatalities due to acute overdose are rarely reported. We have no reliable knowledge of the extent of intravenous amphetamine use, and although we hear many dire predictions, there is no good information on the long-term prognosis or outcome of such use. It would certainly appear, however, that chronic adherence to this practice is most detrimental to the individual and, often, to those with whom he interacts.

Although there is no clear evidence that the life expectancy of 'speed freaks' is lower than others living under similar circumstances, many investigators suspect this to be so. While there are few cases in the literature of death directly attributed to chronic amphetamine use, Clement, Solursh and Van Ast[47] '. . . have recently become aware of a number of cases of death on the streets (of Toronto) apparently related to high-dose amphetamine abuse. At autopsy, however, pathological evidence of death directly due to amphetamines is rare in such cases'. After a thorough review of the literature, Cox and Smart of the Addiction Research Foundation reported: 'Currently there is no evidence available on mortality rates among speed users and it is not certain that speed itself is a lethal drug. There is no evidence to support or deny that "Speed Kills".'[60]

The slogan was originally borrowed from a highway traffic campaign of the last decade and it has been suggested that, originally, in adopting this phrase, drug users were referring to the 'death' of the personality, the 'spirit', or the freedom of the individual when he becomes dependent on amphetamines, rather than to physical mortality.

Amphetamines and Other Drugs

104. As noted earlier, amphetamines are frequently used in conjunction, or in alternation, with a variety of depressant drugs such as barbiturates, alcohol and even heroin. The barbiturate and amphetamine up-down cycle has been described in both youthful and 'respectable' adult users at a variety of doses. Amphetamines intensify, prolong or otherwise alter the effects of LSD and it is reported that the two drugs are sometimes mixed. In addition, it would appear that the majority of youthful speed users have also had experience with a variety of psychedelic and other illicit drugs. Persons dependent on the opiate narcotics also frequently make use of stimulants such as cocaine and amphetamine – either as mixtures of drugs or used separately on different occasions. It is interesting to note that STP (DOM) and the newer MDA, both extremely potent psychedelic-hallucinogenic drugs, are chemically closely related to amphetamine.

105. One of the most remarkable and controversial drugs known today is d-lysergic acid diethylamide-25, better known as LSD or simply 'acid'. LSD is capable of producing profound and unusual psychological changes in almost infinitesimal doses, with relatively little general physiological effect and, along with other related drugs, has exerted noticeable influence in a variety of aesthetic, scientific, philosophic, religious and social areas over the past two decades. LSD is often considered the prototype of the drug class we have labelled Psychedelic-Hallucinogens, although there are a great number of less potent synthetic and naturally occurring substances with somewhat similar psychopharmacological properties. To date, almost 3,000 articles on LSD have been published in scientific journals, although many of these reports do not meet adequate scientific standards.

106. LSD was developed in 1938 by Hofmann and Stoll, in Switzerland, as part of a research programme investigating potential therapeutic uses of certain ergot compounds. LSD is a semi-synthetic derivative of lysergic acid, an ergot alkaloid produced by a parasitic fungus, or 'rust', sometimes found on rye or other grains. Closely related substances are also produced in the seeds of certain varieties of morning glory. Most ergot alkaloids are not particularly psychoactive, although some may have a variety of powerful, and often toxic, physiological actions, and have been used for centuries for medical purposes.

107. Since LSD appeared to be relatively uninteresting, physiologically, in animal studies, it received little attention until Hofmann unwittingly ingested a minute quantity some years after its original synthesis. He subsequently described his experience as follows:[102]

In the afternoon of 16 April 1943, when I was working on this problem, I was seized by a peculiar sensation of vertigo and restlessness. Objects, as well as the shape of my associates in the laboratory, appeared to undergo optical change. I was unable to concentrate on my work. In a dreamlike state I left for home, where an irresistible urge to lie down overcame me. I drew the curtains and immediately fell into a peculiar state similar to drunkenness, characterized by an exaggerated imagination. With my eyes closed, fantastic pictures of extraordinary plasticity and intensive colour seemed to surge towards me. After two hours this state gradually wore off.

To confirm his suspicion that LSD was responsible for this effect, Hofmann investigated further:

However, I decided to get to the root of the matter by taking a definite quantity of the compound in question. Being a cautious man, I started my experiment by taking 0.25 mg of d-lysergic acid diethylamide tartrate, thinking that such an extremely small dose would surely be harmless, and bearing in mind that the natural ergot alkaloids produce toxic symptoms in man only with doses exceeding several milligrams. After 40 minutes I noted the following symptoms in my laboratory journal: slight giddiness, restlessness, difficulty in concentration, visual disturbances, laughing.

And later:

I lost all count of time. I noticed with dismay that my environment was undergoing progressive changes. My visual field wavered and everything appeared deformed as in a faulty mirror. Space and time became more and more disorganized and I was overcome by a fear that I was going out of my mind. The worst part of it being that I was clearly aware of my condition. My power of observation was unimpaired. ... Occasionally I felt as if I were out of my body. I thought I had died. My ego seemed suspended somewhere in space, from where I saw my dead body lying on the sofa. ... It was particularly striking how acoustic perceptions, such as the noise of water gushing from a tap or the spoken word, were transformed into optical illusions. I then fell asleep and awakened the next morning somewhat tired but otherwise feeling perfectly well.

108. Since various aspects of the experience were thought to resemble symptoms of naturally occurring schizophrenia, many

investigators became interested in using LSD as a tool for producing an artificial or 'model psychosis' in the laboratory. The possibility of gaining insight into psychiatric disorders by the study of the LSD-induced state stimulated considerable activity in medical and scientific communities, and the terms *psychotomimetic* (psychosis-mimicking) and *psychotogenic* (psychosis-producing) were coined. The subsequent discovery that the LSD experience is, in fact, generally different from natural psychoses has lessened interest in this aspect of its use. The descriptive label *hallucinogenic* (hallucination-producing) has gained wide acceptance, in spite of the fact that true hallucinations do not commonly occur with LSD. The term *illusinogenic* (illusion-producing) is probably more appropriate.

In the 1950s the exploration of LSD as an aid to psychotherapy began. Much of the early work, in Canada, investigating the use of LSD in the treatment of alcoholics, was conducted under the direction of Dr A. Hoffer at the University of Saskatchewan. In 1957, after reviewing the various descriptive names given LSD and related drugs, Dr H. Osmond, then Superintendent of the Saskatchewan Hospital, suggested the terms *psycholytic* (mind-releasing) or *psychedelic* (mind-manifesting) as more appropriate general labels.[174] For various reasons the latter has gained world-wide usage, although its common application has strayed considerably from its original context, and it may now denote general styles of art, fashion and music which are, in some sense, felt to reflect, enhance, or substitute for the psychedelic drug experience.

109. While LSD has had a rather short, and somewhat stormy history, numerous naturally occurring substances with apparently similar psychological effects have been used in the Western Hemisphere for centuries. Perhaps the most widely known are mescaline, from the peyote cactus (lophophora williamsii), psilocybin, one of the active principles in 'sacred mushrooms' (teonanactl), and the Mexican morning-glory 'ololiuqui' (Rivea Corymbosa). In addition, DMT (dimethyltryptamine) and the related DET (diethyltryptamine) are found in special snuffs used for centuries by certain South American Indians. Some of these botanical substances were considered divine by

the ancient Aztecs and played an important role in religious ceremonies long before the Spanish invaded the land. In spite of the Conquistadors' attempts to destroy the culture and its historical and religious underpinnings, the sacramental use of peyote spread to the Mexican Indians and, later, in the nineteenth century to certain North American tribes. Today, peyote is used in religious ceremonies by the Native American Church which has over 200,000 Indian members in Canada and the United States.

110. Until recently, psychedelic drugs received little general public attention, even though some had been intensively explored over the past century by various writers, scientists and 'adventurers'. Based on his mescaline experimentation, Aldous Huxley[106] presented, in his twin volumes *The Doors of Perception* and *Heaven and Hell*, one of the most lucid and perceptive analyses of some of the possible personal, philosophical and social implications of the psychedelic experience.

Non-medical interest in LSD and related drugs began to grow during the 1950s, although such use was apparently largely restricted to a few professional, academic, and artistic experimenters. The drug gained continental notoriety in the early 1960s as a result of experimentation by two Harvard University psychology professors, Drs Alpert and Leary, who invited other 'explorers' to 'Turn on, tune in, and drop out' of the existing social institutions. Their unorthodox religious orientation to the LSD experience is presented in *The Psychedelic Experience*[128] (a manual based on the *Tibetan Book of the Dead*), which became one of the 'bibles' of the psychedelic drug movement. Another significant influence, with considerably less religious orientation was writer Ken Kesey's group, the adventures of which are well documented in *The Electric Kool-Aid Acid Test*.[247]

111. Since 1963, the Canadian Government has controlled the medical and scientific use of LSD, and in 1969 the possession of LSD without governmental authorization was made a criminal offence. Regulation of the legal supply of LSD has apparently had little effect on 'street' use, however, since essentially all of the drug so used has come from clandestine lab-

oratories. Although the constituent chemicals are not readily available and some sophisticated apparatus is necessary for its proper synethesis, LSD can be produced by individuals without extensive training in chemistry. Since it is odourless, colourless and tasteless in solution, and active in almost invisible quantities, effective legal control of its transportation, distribution and use has been extremely difficult.

In recent years, several new synthetic drugs with effects similar to LSD have appeared on the black market. These include MDA (alphamethyl-3,4-methylene – dioxyphenethylamine), STP or DOM (2,5-dimethoxy-4-methyl-amphetamine), and PCP or Sernyl* (phencyclidine).

Medical Use

112. There is currently no widely accepted medical use of LSD, although it may be employed experimentally for therapeutic purposes. There have been numerous impressive reports of LSD successes in the treatment of alcoholics, opiate narcotic dependents, criminals and various psychiatric patients.[101, 129] LSD has also been used with patients dying of cancer, to alleviate their anxiety and pain, and to help them adjust to the prospects of death.[176] Many of these leads have not been followed up with adequate scientific investigation, however, and several recent controlled studies have not substantiated the claim that LSD adds to the effectiveness of conventional psychotherapy.[205]

113. Two basic forms of psychological treatment with LSD have developed: *psycholytic* therapy, which uses small or moderate doses on repeated occasions, sometimes over a period of several months; and *psychedelic* therapy which calls for higher doses and a more profound acute effect and is, as a rule, given only once or twice. While some investigators claim that LSD, itself, is more effective than psychotherapy, others claim that its usefulness is mainly limited to the removal of therapeutic 'blocks' which may occur at times in the course of psychotherapy, and still others feel that LSD has no useful contribution to make to psychiatric treatment. Most clinicians who

have had experience with this form of therapy, stress the need for a careful selection of patients and for special qualities and experience in the therapist.

More sophisticated scientific investigations of possible therapeutic uses of LSD are now underway and may help clarify some of these issues. It seems justified to say at this time, however, that the general medical effectiveness of LSD has not yet been adequately demonstrated. It may well be another decade before definitive evidence will be available.

Administration, Absorption, Distribution and Physiological Fate

114. LSD is usually taken orally, and may be sniffed in powdered form or injected in solution. While it is available in ordinary capsules or tablets, LSD is often impregnated in such innocuous substances as sugar cubes, candies, biscuits, and cloth or blotter sections for oral use. It is well absorbed from the gastro-intestinal tract, is distributed in the blood and easily diffuses into the brain, and in pregnant females crosses the placental barrier into the foetus. Although only a tiny portion actually reaches the central nervous system, LSD is one of the most potent biologically active substances known and, in some individuals, exerts a noticeable psychological effect with quantities as low as 20 to 30 micrograms (millionths of a gram). Customary doses are usually around 200 mcg and some individuals have taken up to several thousand micrograms.

Taken orally, LSD effects usually occur within an hour but may be much faster; response to intramuscular injection usually appears within ten minutes; and if the intravenous route is used, the latency may be only a few minutes or less. The duration of the action depends to a certain extent on the amount taken, and with a customary dose, major effects usually last 8-12 hours or more with gradual recovery over a similar period. Essentially all of the LSD in the body is metabolized into an inactive substance in the liver and excreted.

115. The psychological effects of LSD are not readily predictable, and are determined to a considerable degree by various personality factors in the individual, his past history and experiences, his attitudes, expectations, and motivations, the general setting in which the drug is taken, persons accompanying the 'trip' and external events occurring during the experience. While the psychological response is to some extent dose-related, certain effects appear to be relatively independent of dose over a considerable range. Increased quantities often seem to affect the duration more than the intensity or quality of the 'trip'.

116. Subjective psychological effects of LSD are extremely difficult to describe and many scientists are quite pessimistic about the possibility of presenting an objective list of responses which in any way communicates the essence of the experience. The intensely personal nature of the effects further limits description and generalization. Pahnke and Richards[177] have described several major types of psychological experience which have been reported with psychedelic drugs. The outline presented below is based on, but is not identical to, that proposed by these researchers. While the list is certainly not exhaustive and does not describe necessarily discrete or non-overlapping categories, it provides a convenient basis for the discussion of LSD effects. It should be noted that not all of the experiences listed happen in all sessions or in all individuals, although several may occur in varying degrees, in sequence or simultaneously, within a 'trip'.

117. First is the *psychotic adverse reaction*, or 'freak-out' which may be characterized by an intense negative experience of fear or nightmarish terror to the point of panic, complete loss of emotional control, paranoid delusions, hallucinations, catatonic features, and, perhaps, profound depression and sense of meaninglessness. Such states are usually acute, although prolonged reactions have been noted.

118. Second is the *non-psychotic adverse reaction* in which the person may experience varying degrees of tension, anxiety

and fear, unpleasant illusions, depression and despair. Inappropriate or disordered social behaviour may occur. This kind of reaction may differ from the first in the intensity of the experience and in the degree of control and 'reality contact' expressed by the individual. Such unpleasant experiences are commonly labelled 'bad trips' or 'bummers'.

119. Third is the *psychodynamic psychedelic experience* characterized by a dramatic emergence into consciousness of material which had previously been unconscious or suppressed. Strong emotional feelings can accompany what may be experienced subjectively as a reliving of incidents from the past or a symbolic portrayal of important conflicts. Such effects are often sought in LSD psychotherapy.

120. Fourth is the *cognitive psychedelic experience* characterized by an impression of astonishingly lucid thought. Problems may be seen from a novel perspective and the interrelationships of many levels of meaning and dimensions may be sensed simultaneously. The relationship between this experience and naturally occurring insight and creativity has been the subject of considerable interest and speculation.

121. Fifth is the *aesthetic psychedelic experience* characterized by a change and intensification of all sensory impressions, with vision often most affected. Fascinating alteration in sensation and perception may occur; *synaesthesia* or crossing-over of sensory modalities may be produced (music and other sounds may be 'seen'); objects such as flowers or stones may appear to pulsate or 'become alive'; ordinary things may seem imbued with great beauty; music may take on an incredible emotional power; and visions of beautiful colours, intricate geometric patterns, architectural forms, landscapes and 'almost anything imaginable' may occur.

122. The sixth type of psychedelic experience has been called by such names as *psychedelic-peak*, *cosmic*, *transcendental,* or *mystical*. Some of the psychological phenomena which are said to characterize this experience, are: a sense of unity or 'cosmic oneness' with the universe; a feeling of transcendence of time and space; a deeply felt positive mood of joy, blessedness, love,

and peace; a sense of sacredness, awe and wonder; a feeling of profound theological or religious awareness; a feeling of insight into reality at an intuitive, nonrational level; an awareness of things which seem logically contradictory and paradoxical; and a belief that the experience is beyond words, non-verbal and impossible to describe. The full peak experience, in its entirety, does not occur in the majority of individuals, is usually transient, and does not last for long in its full intensity, although it may have persisting effects on attitudes and behaviour.

123. With few exceptions, little general information can be given as to the relative frequency of occurrence of these various types of psychedelic drug reaction, since the response is largely determined by such variable factors as the particular individual involved, his set and the setting. As is often the case in science, techniques designed to measure the effects of LSD may greatly influence or distort the phenomenon under study. Savage[193] has pointed out that unless the LSD experience takes place '. . . in a secure setting, with sufficient emotional support where S (the subject) feels safe to encounter the bizarre and often powerful manifestations of his own mind unharassed by tests, interpretations, and the coldly precise scientific analytic attitudes, the only result can be confusion and paranoia'.

Reports of 'objective' study of LSD's subjective effects vary considerably in content and often appear to be as much a function of the individual scientist's conceptual orientation and experimental methods as they are of the subjects and the drug itself. Some researchers report that LSD experiences in their subjects are definitely unpleasant and anxiety-ridden, and that subsequent sessions are uniformly avoided, while other scientists claim that anxiety is infrequent and that subjects generally enjoy the sessions and are eager to participate further.[228] Experiences in non-supervised and indiscriminate settings are undoubtedly even more variable.

124. It is generally reported that LSD has deleterious effects on performance in tests requiring a high degree of attention, concentration or motivation. It is often difficult to get meaningful data from such measurements, since subjects frequently become engrossed in the subjective aspects of the drug experi-

ence and lose interest in the tasks presented by the investigators. Psychological tests are often seen as absurd or irrelevant by the subjects. Performance on standard tests of intelligence, learning, memory and other cognitive functions, as well as certain psychomotor tasks generally show impairment and sometimes lack of change and, rarely, improvement.[205] Certain types of conduct by some persons under the influence of LSD indicate gross impairment of judgement. Recall of events occurring during the drug experience is generally good, however. Effects on driving skills have not been systematically investigated, although available related data, and reports by users, as well as certain eye witness accounts, suggest that driving ability is usually drastically reduced by the acute effects of LSD. There is no evidence that the drug has been a significant factor in automobile accidents, however.

True hallucinations, where false sensory signals are believed to be physically real, are rarely reported, although pseudo-hallucinations and other perceptual distortions and illusions are frequently noted. One of the most uniformly cited and significant subjective effects is the alteration of ordinary temporal perception, or time-sense. Moments may seem like hours, and time may seem to be transcended. Pleasant experiences may extend indefinitely or, on the other hand, bad trips can become an interminable horror.

125. Current arguments as to whether LSD is truly 'consciousness-expanding' as its proponents contend or 'consciousness-constricting' as its opponents assert, will probably not be resolved by science in the near future, since it seems unlikely that such hypotheses can be put to adequate empirical test given the current state of technology.

Contentions are often made that LSD can elicit new levels of spontaneity, insight, problem-solving and creativity.[214] These claims are very difficult to assess, since the effects described are often highly subjective and personal, and are hardly amenable to empirical validation. The problems of studying creativity in the laboratory are considerable, and little is known of the basic psychology of such cognitive processes. A generally agreed upon definition of the concept of creativity has eluded investigators so far, and few meaningful tests are available. Studies of the effects of psychedelic drugs on allegedly creativity-related behaviours have produced inconsistent results. Often performance does not reflect the subjective impressions of the drug experience. Although sophisticated scientific investigation in this area is only just beginning, it is already obvious that LSD will not perform the miracle of turning an uninspired and untalented individual into a creative genius. The question of more subtle effects on creative activity in certain individuals must be answered by future research.

126. Most authorities agree that LSD does not have a specific aphrodisiac or sex-drive stimulating effect. Some users indicate an enhanced appreciation of sexual experience, while many others report a total disinterest in sex while on a 'trip'. Some increase in sexual behaviour may occur as a result of a lessening of inhibitions and an increase in emotionality, tactile appreciation, and interpersonal contact. LSD has been used in the treatment of sexual disorders of psychological origin (e.g. frigidity and impotence) although its general usefulness has not been clearly demonstrated in this area.

127. An LSD-induced 'bad trip' may range from a mildly negative or ambivalent experience to an episode of intense terror and nightmarish panic. Such adverse reactions often seem to focus on the fear of death, fear of permanent insanity, basic sexual conflicts, and fear of legal repercussions in illicit users, or may be precipitated by an objective 'hassle' or problem of real or imagined significance. Under the influence of LSD, it is often difficult to cope with immediate problems which arise, and emotional vulnerability may be increased. 'Bad trips' seem to occur most often when the individual is poorly prepared, alone, or in an otherwise unprotected or unsupervised setting. While an experienced 'guide' or therapist can often help prevent or alleviate negative reactions, this is no guarantee against an unpleasant experience. Neither are earlier positive experiences – severe 'bad trips' have been noted in individuals who had previous long histories of unequivocally pleasant psychedelic experiences. Certain tranquillizers can be of assistance in reducing the unpleasantness of the experience, often by ter-

minating the drug effect, although many observers feel that non-chemical, personal supportive guidance is most important in treating negative reactions.

Although most negative LSD experiences appear to be of short duration, prolonged psychotic episodes lasting months or even years have been elicited by LSD.[50] Many investigators contend that such extreme experiences occur only in individuals already predisposed to psychotic reaction, and are simply precipitated by the stress of a 'bad trip'. On the other hand, numerous examples have occurred in persons without obvious prior pathology, and it would appear that there is no satisfactory method for predicting who might suffer a serious adverse reaction.

128. Prolonged psychoses are quite rare in clinical or experimental settings, even when psychiatric patients are used as subjects. Cohen[49] surveyed 44 investigators who had given LSD or mescaline to approximately 5,000 persons a total of about 25,000 times, and found that psychotic reactions lasting over 48 hours occurred in 0.18 per cent of the psychiatric patients studied and 0.08 per cent of the experimental subjects. There were four suicides in the patients, all occurring months after the LSD experience, and none among the experimental subjects. Whether these deaths can be attributed to LSD use is not certain. Similar incidents of adverse reaction under controlled circumstances have been reported by others and the use of LSD in medically supervised settings has been considered by many investigators to be comparatively safe from a psychiatric point of view.[65, 132]

These findings do not provide a satisfactory basis for estimating the effects of illicit use, however, since set, setting, purity and quantity of drug, and consequently, the quality of the trip, are all apt to be quite different in these situations. The frequency of bad trips among street LSD users is unknown, although many such cases have come to the attention of medical authorities and certainly cannot be considered uncommon. Solursh[213] reports that in one series of street users studied retrospectively, 'freak-outs' occurred in 24 of 601 'acid trips'. Furthermore, impressionistic accounts from individuals in close contact with the 'drug-scene' suggest that the incidence of 'bad trips' is steadily increasing. Ungerleider[229] studied 70 individuals who required hospitalization in a Los Angeles medical centre after illicit LSD use. One-third of these admissions were diagnosed psychotic and two-thirds were hospitalized for more than a month.

129. Usually neither the therapist nor the patient is certain as to the identity, purity or quantity of the drug involved in 'street' cases, and records are further complicated by the fact that there is considerable discrepancy among reporters as to what exactly constitutes an adverse reaction. Furthermore, it would appear that many 'bad trips' are treated by friends and never come to the attention of the medical authorities. In addition to personal support and assistance in these situations, tranquillizers (and niacinamide) are available legally and on the black market for such emergencies. Even if some accurate estimate could be made of the number of negative reactions occurring, it would not be possible to assess the relative significance of the figures, since we have little idea as to the overall frequency of illicit LSD use in the general population.

130. Illicit users of LSD commonly voice the opinion that bad trips are caused by bad drugs and that 'pure acid' is relatively free from adverse reactions. These claims are rarely based on chemical analysis, and although contaminants and other drugs reported to appear in black market LSD can undoubtedly affect the experience, it is uncertain what proportion of the negative reactions can be accounted for by contaminants. It is certain that well-documented 'freak-outs' have occurred with clinically pure LSD.

131. Although suicide may be rare among illicit as well as medically supervised LSD users, a few cases have been documented. Attempts at self-mutilation have also been reported on rare occasions. Accidental deaths are somewhat more common and a number of cases of fatality or serious injury have been noted as a result of a loss of critical judgement or attentional processes. For example, some individuals have jumped from buildings or trees apparently under the delusion that they could

fly or were indestructible. Stories of numerous persons who had become permanently blind while staring at the sun during LSD trips were generated by a state official in the United States and widely circulated in the public media. These reports were subsequently shown to be a hoax and no such cases are on record.[170'b']

132. Although fear, panic and aggression may result from a 'freak-out', homicides associated with LSD use are rare and only a few have been documented. Reports of violence occurring while under the influence of LSD have generally not been supported,[78] although there may be some significant exceptions. The majority of non-drug arrests associated with LSD use seem to be in the order of 'disturbance of the peace' offences and there is little evidence that LSD plays a significant role in major crimes.

Recurrence of certain aspects of LSD experiences ('flashbacks' or 'echoes') of varying duration and intensity have been reported over periods ranging from a few months to more than a year after last (or only) LSD use.[189] The quality of these experiences, which usually last only a few minutes or less, may depend on as many factors as the original trip. They may be triggered or precipitated by seemingly irrelevant stimuli or events, by other drugs, or may appear spontaneously. We have no good information as to the frequency of these recurrences, although they appear to occur most often in heavy users and could clearly be unpleasant or dangerous in certain circumstances.

133. The possible religious significance of psychedelic drug experiences has been the subject of heated controversy for centuries. While many authorities have pointed out basic similarities between drug-induced feelings of transcendental or mystical awareness and the *satori* or *kensho* of Zen Buddhism, the *samadhi* of Hinduism or the *beatific vision* of Christianity, others have been outraged by the suggestion that such 'instant mysticism' could be produced chemically. It is quite apparent, however, that a considerable degree of religiosity has pervaded the psychedelic drug movement of the 1960s and has played a major role in the use of such drugs in other cultures.

The major theoretical positions and scientific research in this area have been reviewed by several investigators[208, 147] and these reports provide experimental support for the notion that drug-evoked experiences may have religious significance for certain individuals. Perhaps the most rigorous scientific evidence comes from Pahnke's[175] controlled psilocybin experiment with seminary graduate students conducted in the setting of a Good Friday religious service. He notes that: 'Those subjects who received psilocybin experienced phenomena which were indistinguishable from, if not identical with, the categories defined by our typology of mysticism.' The religious aspects of the psychedelic experience apparently depend a great deal on the individual, his values and expectations, and the setting involved, and do not normally occur with great intensity in most persons or in most situations. Masters and Houston[147] report that 6 out of 206 of their subjects attained a mystical experience, while other researchers report no such events and still others, a much higher incidence. Differences in semantic meaning, definition and criteria may account for part of these discrepancies. The 'objective validity' of drug-elicited religious experiences, however, is by nature untestable in the scientific sense, and the area will doubtless remain in a storm of controversy.

134. Numerous claims have been made by various LSD users, psychotherapists and scientists that LSD can produce long-lasting beneficial effects on personality and behaviour. On the other hand, many observers feel that chronic use of LSD may result in a lessening of work output and a deterioration of social behaviour, a general 'amotivational syndrome' in some individuals. Both types of allegation are difficult to evaluate, since few adequately controlled investigations have been done on the long-term effects of either medically supervised or non-medical LSD use.

Physiological Effects

135. LSD exerts its most significant physiological effects on and through the central nervous system, although the exact

mechanism by which this occurs is not yet known. As a result of its potent general arousal or activation capacity, LSD may produce a variety of autonomic nervous system (sympathomimetic) actions, considered to be of little clinical significance at normal doses. Commonly reported are: widened pupils, increased heart rate and blood pressure, sweating, increased body temperature, chills, increased blood sugar level, 'goose pimples', flushing of the facial skin, increased urination, headache, and rarely nausea and vomiting. It generally increases the activation of the brain (as indicated by the EEG), produces alertness, blocks sleep, decreases appetite, may induce tremors and reduce coordination, changes respiration patterns, and facilitates certain simple reflexes.[138] In a few instances convulsions have occured. LSD has remarkably low physiological toxicity and, to date, no human deaths have been reported due to overdose. Although the evidence is not clear, psychological indications of minor brain damage may be present in chronic heavy users of LSD.[152]

136. In the past few years, considerable controversy and sensational publicity has arisen around the possibility that LSD may affect hereditary transmission through chromosomal alterations, produce changes in white blood cells resembling leukemia and adversely affect the developing human foetus.[48] Relevant studies involving test-tube preparations of human live animal and insect experiments, and examinations of illicit LSD users, have been contradictory to date and provide no clear answers to these important questions.[105] The relationship between *in vitro* (test-tube) and *in vivo* (living organism) effects is rarely straightforward, and generalizations from one species to another are difficult. Furthermore, studying the users of 'street' drugs gives little information regarding specific compounds, since such individuals may use a variety of drugs and neither the investigator nor the subject can be sure of the purity, quantity or identity of substances obtained from the illicit market. In the few controlled studies in which chromosomes were examined in humans before and after clinically supervised administration of known doses of pure LSD, little evidence of significant change was noted.[225] [58] The effects of prolonged

regular use of LSD have not been carefully investigated, however, and the presence or absence of alterations under such conditions can not be completely predicted on the basis of present information.

Research in this area is complicated by the fact that temporary or permanent chromosome breakage is not an uncommon response to a variety of non-drug experiences, and can be produced by nuclear radioactivity, many pollutants, X-rays, fever and a number of virus infections. Furthermore, there is evidence that such frequently used drugs as caffeine and aspirin may cause chromosome breaks in certain cells.[122] It should be noted that chromosome damage *per se* does not necessarily affect either the individual or his offspring, although the possibility must be considered.

137. High doses of LSD administered at certain times early in pregnancy have been shown to produce deformities in the offspring of some animal species and not others. No unequivocal evidence of such teratogenic LSD effects in humans has been reported, although there have been a few widely publicized instances of abnormalities in babies born of mothers who had used LSD. Whether such anomalies occur more frequently in LSD users than in the normal population is uncertain. Most investigators feel that the possibility of chromosome or foetal damage in humans forbids the use of LSD for either medical or non-medical purposes, by women who are either pregnant or expect to become so in the near future.

Tolerance and Dependence

138. Tolerance to the psychological and physiological effects of LSD develops on repeated use, although the form of psychological tolerance is unusual in several respects. Tolerance to most drugs can be overcome and effects of full intensity obtained by simply increasing dosage. With LSD, often a period of three or four days or longer must separate 'trips' if the full effects are to be obtained, regardless of dose. A second unusual quality of LSD tolerance is the rapidity with which it develops and dissipates. A reduction in effects may occur after only one

or two consecutive administrations. Furthermore, when LSD is used intermittently many users report a 'reverse' tolerance, or increased sensitivity to the drug and may, after experience, use less to achieve the desired effects. These factors suggest that the pharmacological mechanism underlying LSD tolerance may be quite different from those seen with most other psychoactive drugs.

139. Physical dependence does not develop to LSD, even in cases in which the drug has been used more than two hundred times in a single year.[51] Psychological dependence has been reported to occur in certain individuals who become preoccupied with the drug experience and feel emotionally depressed and unsatisfied without it. Normally, however, LSD use is intermittent and periods of weeks or months may separate 'trips' in even 'confirmed' users.

LSD and Other Drugs

140. It appears that many LSD users will also experiment with other psychedelic drugs. Cross-tolerance occurs among some of these substances and an individual who has recently taken LSD will generally show reduced response to mescaline and psilocybin, but not to cannabis or phencyclidine (PCP). It should be noted that mescaline and psilocybin are rarely found in Canada and no such black market samples have been verified by chemical analysis.

Other drugs, such as atropine or amphetamines, are reported to be sometimes added to LSD to intensify, prolong or otherwise alter the experience. Strychnine (a stimulant once commonly used in medical practice) is rumoured to have also been employed for such effects. In spite of such stories, black market products purported to contain mixtures of LSD and other drugs have rarely been found on analysis to be as represented. Such combinations appear to be infrequent in Canada. Unsuccessful attempts at LSD synthesis may produce a variety of other ergot alkaloids with possibly unpleasant or dangerous pharmacological properties in high doses. Samples of such concoctions have been obtained from black market sources.[144]

Chlorpromazine (Largactil*), a major tranquillizer, usually

blocks LSD effects, although in rare instances it paradoxically potentiates the original drug response. In addition, certain sedatives and niacinamide (nicotinamide) may also reduce some of the effects of LSD.

CANNABIS

141. *Cannabis sativa* is an herbaceous annual plant which readily grows untended in temperate climates in many areas of the world, including Canada. Although there are several varieties (i.e., indica, americana, and africana) most botanists consider these to be members of the same species. Indian hemp, as this plant is sometimes known, has separate male and female forms and may grow to 10 to 12 feet under favourable conditions.

The first detailed description of cannabis available today appeared in a medicinal book prepared by the Chinese Emperor Shen Nung around 2737 B.C. Since then, cannabis has been known in the East by such descriptions as 'the heavenly guide', 'poor man's heaven', 'soother of grief' and, in a more moralistic tone, 'the liberator of sin'.[223] A United Nations' report 20 years ago estimated that 200 million people in the world used the drug for medical, religious or recreational purposes.

142. What is commonly referred to as marijuana ('grass', 'pot', 'weed', 'tea', 'boo' or 'Mary Jane') in North America is usually made up of crushed cannabis leaves, flowers, and often twigs, and may vary considerably in potency from one sample to another. Similar preparations are known as *bhang* and the more potent *ganja* in India, *kif* in Morocco and *dagga* in Africa, while the relatively pure resin is called *hashish* ('hash') in the West and much of the Middle East, and *charas* in India. Hashish is usually prepared by pressing or scraping the sticky amber resin from the plant, and may be more than five times as potent on a weight basis as high quality marijuana. In addition to these common forms, concentrated cannabis extract is available in some countries in an alcohol solution (tincture of Cannabis) designed for medical purposes (e.g., British Pharmacopoeia).

The various forms of the drug are frequently listed under the general term cannabis since they differ primarily in the degree of potency. It must be stressed, however, that differences in the preparation, quantities involved, mode of administration and patterns of use are also important determinants of effect, and it is often essential that these factors be identified in the examination of individual reports.

143. In many societies, *cannabis sativa* has been a highly valued crop. The trunk fibres of the woody plant are used in the production of hemp rope and twine; the seeds are a source of a product similar to linseed oil and, until recently, were also commonly used as bird food; the pharmacological properties of the leaves, flowers and resin have been used for thousands of years, for both medical and non-medical purposes.

Cannabis was apparently brought to the Western hemisphere in the sixteenth century by the Spaniards and was an important fibre and seed crop centuries later in the British colonies of North America. A portion of George Washington's Mount Vernon plantation was dedicated to the cultivation of hemp and it was reported that, 'Virginia awarded bounties for hemp culture and manufacture, and imposed penalties on those who did not produce it.'[31] Although there are conflicting opinions, it would appear that the psychotropic properties of cannabis may have been little known to the colonial farmers at that time.[12, 120] Hemp was again cultivated in North America during World War II after the major supply lines from the East were cut off. These plants were apparently selected for high fibre content and low pharmacological activity.

144. When grown under optimal conditions, almost all parts of both male and female plants may be potentially psychoactive. The female has traditionally been considered the more efficient producer of the resin responsible for the pharmacological effects, although recent studies question this conclusion.[235] Female flowers, prior to pollination, contain the greatest concentration of resin and, consequently, the flowering tops are highly valued and are frequently prepared separately from the remainder of the plant. The potency is further affected by the climate and soil conditions, certain genetic factors, and the time and method of harvesting and preparation.

145. In recent years, the chemistry of cannabis has come under careful investigation. Although numerous cannabinols were considered potential candidates in the search for the active principles of cannabis, it appears that certain forms of tetra-hydrocannabinol (THC) are the most potent psychoactive constituents. Several of these have recently been isolated and synthesized.[155] It would be incorrect to say, however, that *the* active ingredient in cannabis has been established, since much basic psychopharmacological work remains to be done in this area. Several related synthetics (Synhexyl* or Pyrahexyl*) have also been investigated. Although there are continual reports of THC being sold on the illicit market, samples alleged to be THC have invariably been found to be some other drug.

146. Frequent cases of cannabis use first came to the regular attention of government and public health officials in North America after World War I, although earlier references to such use exist. This increase was correlated with an influx of Mexican workers into the Southern United States, and subsequent use was apparently largely confined to ethnic minority groups, with a high proportion of urban-dwelling Afro- and Spanish-Americans among the known users. In addition, cannabis use was often noted among musicians and others in the fields of entertainment and creative arts. In the last decade, however, the use of cannabis has spread to quite a different segment of the population and appears to be most prevalent among, although by no means restricted to, middle-class youth of high school and college age. In spite of the risk of severe penalties, estimates based on a variety of sources suggest that eight to 20 million North Americans have at least tried cannabis.[250] These figures must be considered tenuous however, since there is no satisfactory way to assess their validity.

147. Recently the controversy surrounding this drug has reached epidemic proportions. Usually reliable authorities have publicly taken diametrically opposed positions regarding cannabis, not only on moral and social policy issues, but on the supposedly 'hard' scientific facts as well. Although the current world literature on cannabis numbers some 2,000 publications, few of these papers meet modern standards of scientific inves-

tigation. They are often ill-documented and ambiguous, emotion-laden and incredibly biased, and can, in general, be relied upon for very little valid information. Scientific expertise in the area of cannabis is limited by the simple fact that there is little clearly-established scientific information available, and preconceived notions often dominate the interpretation of ambiguous data. The resulting confusion is exemplified by current legislation in many parts of the world, including Canada and the United States, which classifies cannabis with the opiate narcotics, even though these drugs are pharmacologically different.

This rather sorry state of affairs can be attributed to several factors. To begin with, governmental restrictions on the medical and scientific use of cannabis in North America have been so strict over the past few decades that the majority of would-be researchers have found it more attractive to work in other areas. Secondly, since the widespread use of cannabis in North America is a relatively new phenomenon, it has not, in the past, been considered a particularly high priority research area from a public health standpoint. In addition, until recently, there was little possibility of standardizing the cannabis substances being studied, since little was known about the relevant aspects of cannabis chemistry. Consequently, there was little basis for comparing reports, and generalizations were limited. To date, no authorized experimental research of cannabis effects on humans is being conducted in Canada.

The observations collected during centuries of relatively unrestricted cannabis use in regions of the East have rarely been scientifically documented because most of what we consider modern science has been, until recently, basically a Western phenomenon. Furthermore, profound cultural, moral and legal differences complicate the problem of extrapolating from reports of Eastern usage to the North American scene.

While there has been a concerted effort, in the following discussions of cannabis effects, to concentrate attention on fairly well documented topics and to avoid areas where the evidence is especially weak, the scanty nature of our current scientific knowledge of cannabis necessitates a cautious and tentative approach to this interim review.

148. There is no currently accepted medical use of cannabis in North America outside of an experimental context. Although cannabis has been reported to produce an array of possibly useful medical effects, these have either not been adequately investigated, or can be replaced by using other more readily available and convenient drugs. The natural product's variability in potency and instability over time are among the factors which have led to its disfavour in Western 20th century medicine. However, recent advances in isolation and synthesis of certain active principles of cannabis have prompted a second look at some of the potentially therapeutic aspects of the drug.[159]

Cannabis has been used in the past, is presently used in some cultures, or is currently under clinical investigation, for its alleged anxiety-reducing, tranquillizing, mood-elevating, appetite stimulating, analgesic (pain reducing) and anti-bacterial effects. It has also been used to reduce fatigue or insomnia (sleeplessness), to ease opiate narcotic withdrawal, and as an aid to psychotherapy in applications analogous to *psycholytic* LSD therapy or as a clinical anti-depressant. In addition, cannabis has often been employed in the past, and is currently used illicitly in North America, to reduce the secondary symptoms and suffering caused by the flu and the common cold. These various alleged therapeutic properties of cannabis have not been adequately studied in a scientific context, and their general medical potential remains a matter of conjecture.

Administration, Absorption, Distribution and Physiological Fate

149. Marijuana is usually smoked in hand-rolled cigarettes known as 'joints', 'J's', 'sticks' or 'reefers', the butt of which is often called a 'roach'. Normally one or two joints is sufficient to produce a mild 'high', although this varies considerably according to individual factors and the potency of the sample. Hashish may vary in colour from very light to dark-brown and ranges from a hard waxy substance to a crumbly, powdery con-

sistency. Small pieces of hashish may be placed on the tip of a burning tobacco cigarette and the smoke inhaled off the top. Ordinary pipes, water pipes (hookahs) and a variety of specially made instruments are also employed in the smoking of hashish and marijuana.

In the Middle East and Far East cannabis is often mixed with such substances as *datura stramonium* (Jimson weed), tobacco, *nux vomica*, and opium, which further complicates the interpretation of reports from these areas.[107] Samples of cannabis obtained in Canada generally do not contain other drugs, although they may be 'cut' with relatively inert substances.[143] There have been no analytical reports to support rumours that heroin or other opiate narcotics have been found in cannabis in this country.

150. Cannabis smoke is usually inhaled deep into the lungs and held there for an extended time, in order to increase absorption. The onset of psychological effects is almost immediate with the smoking of more potent forms of cannabis, and the peak effects usually occur within the first quarter-hour following inhalation. Major effects usually last several hours while milder ones may endure for half a day longer.

Absorption by the gastro-intestinal tract is effective, although relatively slow. Since the resin is fairly soluble in hot water, cannabis is often used in making tea or other beverages – mild *bhang* drinks, for example, are common in India. In some countries hashish is incorporated into buttered candies called *majoon*, or other foods. The effects of cannabis taken orally usually begin after an hour or so, and gradually reach a peak within several hours, then slowly decline. Very high doses may produce some effects lasting more than a day, although the drug is not ordinarily used in such large quantities in North America. The effects of oral administration are often noticeably different from those of inhalation. It is uncertain whether this is due to chemical changes from the heat in the smoked material, effects of the digestive juices or other metabolic enzymes after oral administration, or differences in rapidity and efficiency of absorption and distribution in the two methods. On a weight basis, however, smoking seems to be the most effective mode of administration. The speed of acquisition, the duration of effects, and the recovery from the cannabis 'high' depends on the rate, quantity, and mode of administration, in addition to various psychological and physiological characteristics of the user.

151. While considerable progress is being made in this area, little is known at the present time regarding the metabolism, excretion, and mechanism of action of cannabis. There is evidence that some metabolites of THC are psychoactive. Techniques are being developed which are designed to measure cannabis products in the urine, blood and saliva, and substantial breakthroughs are expected in these areas in the near future.

Effects of Cannabis

152. Although the literature is brimming with impressionistic reports of the effects of cannabis, only a small number of these meet even the most rudimentary scientific standards. A review of those effects which have been unequivocally established and scientifically documented would be a scant summary indeed. In spite of strong disagreement among extremists on many points in the cannabis controversy, major governmental reports by independent commissions of various backgrounds over three-quarters of a century have come to some surprisingly similar conclusions regarding the use of cannabis. Such reports include the British *Indian Hemp Drugs Commission Report* (1893–4),[107] Mayor La Guardia's Report on *The Marijuana Problem in The City of New York* (1944),[149] the United States President's Commission on *Law Enforcement and Administration of Justice: Task Force on Narcotics and Drug Abuse* (1967),[220] and the *Cannabis* report (1968), by the British Advisory Committee on Drug Dependence, prepared under the chairmanship of the Baroness Wootton of Abinger.[5]

In many areas in which formal scientific data are not available, we shall have to rely on expert opinion, and in such instances reference will be made to some of the observations presented in these aforementioned governmental reports. A general overview of the effects of cannabis will be followed by a more detailed examination of certain selected scientific studies. Primary concern will be given to recent publications.

153. *Physiological Effects.* The short-term physiological effects of cannabis are usually slight and apparently have little clinical significance. The following effects have been established in adequately controlled studies: increase in heart rate, swelling of the minor conjunctival blood vessels in the membranes around the eye, and minor unspecific changes in the electro-encephalogram (EEG). Also commonly noted, but less well documented, are: a slight drying of the eyes and nasal passages, initially stimulated salivation followed by dryness of the mouth, throat irritation and coughing during smoking, and increased urination. Less commonly, nausea, vomiting, diarrhoea or constipation are reported. These gastro-intestinal disturbances rarely occur with smoked cannabis, although nausea is not uncommon when large quantities are taken orally. Changes in blood sugar level and blood pressure have been inconsistently reported. Appetite is usually stimulated. Contrary to popular belief, there is little evidence of pupil dilation. In some individuals, incoordination, ataxia and tremors have been observed and chest pains, dizziness and fainting have occasionally been noted, usually at high doses. Physiological hangover effects have been described but are rare, even after considerable intoxication.

154. Cannabis has little acute physiological toxicity – sleep is the usual somatic consequence of over-dose. No deaths due directly to smoking or eating of cannabis have been documented and no reliable information exists regarding the lethal dose in humans. One fatality, however, was reportedly caused by distention of the bowel during a prolonged bout of gross over-eating under the acute influence of cannabis.[134]

155. There is little reliable information on the long-term effects of cannabis use. There are numerous reports from Eastern countries of chronic ill-health among very heavy long-term users of hashish. Most commonly reported are minor respiratory and gastro-intestinal ailments. These studies rarely provide a control group of comparable non-users for a reference standard, and clinical findings are usually confounded with a

variety of social, economic and cultural factors which are not easily untangled. Consequently, much important work remains to be done in this area. The British *Cannabis* report (1968) states:[5]

> Having reviewed all the material available to us, we find ourselves in agreement with the conclusion reached by the Indian Hemp Drugs Commission appointed by the Government of India (1893-1894) and the New York Mayor's Committee on Marihuana (1944), that the long-term consumption of cannabis in *moderate* doses has no harmful effects.

156. Some observers have suggested that chronic smoking of cannabis might produce carcinogenic effects similar to those now attributed to the smoking of tobacco, although no evidence exists to support this view at this time. A meaningful comparison is difficult to make since the quantity of leaf consumed by the average cigarette smoker in North America is many times the amount of cannabis smoked by even heavy users. The present pattern of use by regular cannabis smokers in North America is more analogous to intermittent alcohol use (e.g., once or twice a week), than to the picture of chronic daily use presented by ordinary tobacco dependence. However, the deep inhalation technique usually used with cannabis might add respiratory complications.

157. Recently, there have been conflicting reports that large quantities of cannabis extract, injected into pregnant females of certain strains of rodents, may cause abnormalities in the offspring.[85] These disparate results can not be simply extrapolated to humans and at this time there is no scientific evidence that cannabis adversely affects human chromosomes or causes deformed children.

158. *Psychological Effects.* The psychological effects of cannabis vary greatly with a number of factors and are often difficult to predict. The dose, type of preparation, and rate and mode of administration can greatly influence the response, even if the effective doses and peak responses are made comparable. Furthermore, the psychological effects depend to a considerable degree on the personality of the user, his past experience with

cannabis or other drugs, his attitudes, and the setting in which the drug is used.

Although 'hash' may be many times more potent than marijuana, the effects of these two forms of cannabis, as usually used in North America, are often indistinguishable. It has been reported that most experienced individuals smoke to attain a certain effect or level of 'high', and adjust the dose according to the potency of the substance used. 'Grass' and 'hash' are generally used interchangeably and great variations in potency of different samples are accommodated by the experienced user through a 'titration' of dose – i.e., intake is stopped when the smoker reaches a personally comfortable level of intoxication. Such precision is generally not possible with oral use, however, due to the long delay in action, and a 'non-optimal' effect is therefore much more likely to occur with this practice. In some Eastern countries, different social norms have evolved around the different forms of cannabis, and the pattern of drug use associated with bhang drinks may be quite different from that seen in regular hashish users. Long-term heavy cannabis users invariably prefer the more potent ganja or hashish.[45, 107]

It is often difficult to find descriptions of the psychological effects of marijuana that are free from value judgements. Many effects seem to take on good or bad connotations depending on the circumstances in which they occur, the personal attitudes of the individual undergoing the experience, and the orientation of the observer who is recording them. Moreover, since many of the significant psychological effects are intensely personal, the laboratory scientist often has little opportunity to make objective measurements, and must rely on subjective, introspective reports, communicated verbally through a language system which is frequently inadequate.

159. Cannabis is one of the least potent of the psychedelic drugs, and some might object to its being classified with LSD and similar substances. It is often suggested that marijuana is a mild intoxicant, more like alcohol.[82] There is evidence, however, that high doses of cannabis in some individuals may produce effects similar, in some respects, to an attenuated LSD experience. While such effects are rarely reported, many milder

aspects of the psychedelic experience regularly occur with a cannabis 'high'. The outline of potential reactions to psychedelic drugs presented in the section on LSD include: *psychotic and non-psychotic adverse reactions, psychodynamic, cognitive, aesthetic, and psychedelic-peak (transcendental) or religious experiences*. While analogous experiences may occur in varying degrees with cannabis, the quality of the effects is reportedly different, the intensity considerably lower, and the overall reponse more controllable than with the more powerful psychedelic drugs. It would be incorrect to say that cannabis in moderate dose actually produces a mild LSD experience; the effects of these two drugs are physiologically, behaviourally and subjectively quite distinct. Furthermore, since no cross-tolerance occurs between LSD and THC the mechanism of action of these two drugs is thought to be different.[109]

160. A cannabis 'high' typically involves several phases. The initial effects are often somewhat stimulating and, in some individuals, may elicit mild tension or anxiety which usually is replaced by a pleasant feeling of well-being. The later effects usually tend to make the user introspective and tranquil. Rapid mood changes often occur. A period of enormous hilarity may be followed by a contemplative silence.

Psychological effects which are typically reported by users include: happiness, increased conviviality, a feeling of enhanced interpersonal rapport and communication, heightened sensitivity to humour, free play of the imagination, unusual cognitive and ideational associations, a sense of extra-ordinary reality, a tendency to notice aspects of the environment of which one is normally unaware, enhanced visual imagery, an altered sense of time in which minutes may seem like hours, changes in visually perceived spatial relations, enrichment of sensory experiences (subjective aspects of sound and taste perception are often particularly enhanced), increased personal understanding and religious insight, mild excitement and energy (or just the opposite), increased or decreased behavioural activity, increased or decreased verbal fluency and talkativeness, lessening of inhibitions, and at higher doses, a tendency to lose or digress from one's train of thought. Feelings of enhanced

117

spontaneity and creativity are often described, although an actual increase in creativity is difficult to establish scientifically. While most experts agree that cannabis has little specific aphrodisiac (sex stimulating) effect, many users report increased enjoyment of sex and other intimate human contact while under the influence of the drug.[93, 161]

Less pleasant experiences may occur in different individuals, or possibly in the same individuals at different times. Some of these reactions may include: fear and anxiety, depression, irritability, nausea, headache, backache, dizziness, a dulling of attention, confusion, lethargy, and a sensation of heaviness, weakness and drowsiness. Disorientation, delusions, suspiciousness and paranoia, and in some cases, panic, loss of control, and acute psychotic states have been reported. Schwarz[196] has compiled an extensive catalogue of reports of adverse symptoms which have been attributed to cannabis in the world literature.

161. The possibility of psychiatric disorders associated with cannabis use has received considerable attention. Although there are some well documented examples of very intense and nightmarish short-term reactions (usually among inexperienced users in unpleasant situations and with high doses), these cases seem to be relatively rare and generally show a rapid recovery. Although many regular users have had an experience with cannabis which was in some way unpleasant, 'freak-outs' are apparently rare. Ungerleider[230] has reported 1,887 'adverse reactions' to marijuana in the Los Angeles area. These data are difficult to interpret since no clear definition of adverse reaction is provided and no follow-ups were made. By contrast, Unwin in Montreal reports:[233]

I have seen only three adverse reactions in the past two years; all following the smoking of large amounts of hashish and all occurring in individuals with a previous history of psychiatric treatment for psychiatric or borderline conditions.

The few cases of prolonged psychosis which have been reported have usually been attributed to an earlier personality predisposition, although this hypothesis is not always easy to substantiate. Earlier notions of a specific 'cannabis psychosis'

118

have generally been abandoned since there is little evidence of such a distinct psychiatric entity. Smith[206] in San Francisco, reports that he has never observed 'cannabis psychosis' in over 35,000 marijuana users seen at the Haight-Ashbury clinic. But a recent psychiatric report described several psychotic reactions occurring in American soldiers in Vietnam, who had used cannabis.[218] The psychiatrist believed that the psychotic episodes may have been related to cannabis use. This emphasizes the need for caution before any generalizations about the evidence of psychiatric complication with cannabis use are made – particularly in individuals who have consumed large doses of potent material under conditions of increased physical and psychological stress. Such general conditions are, of course, by no means restricted to military operations.

162. There have been a few reports of 'flash-backs' or spontaneous recurrences of certain cannabis effects some time after the last use of the drug, although such events are apparently quite rare. In addition, cannabis has also been reported to have precipitated LSD recurrences in some heavy users of LSD.[123]

Only a few adequate laboratory investigations have been made of the effects of cannabis on normal psychological functioning. Most of the data indicate little change under the conditions tested, although reports of both impaired and improved performance have been made. Because of the perceptual, cognitive and psycho-motor effects often attributed to cannabis, it seems reasonable to expect that in high doses the drug would impair automobile driving. Many regular users feel this is so and avoid driving, while others content that they are more careful and are probably better drivers when slightly 'high'.[93] There is no available evidence that cannabis has been a significant factor in traffic accidents. The one study testing cannabis effects on driving skills found little impairment to be caused by a 'mild social high'.[61] Some of the studies pertinent to these topics will be discussed in more detail at the end of this section.

163. A study by Suchman[217] suggests a close association between the use of marijuana in some young people and adher-

ence to what is termed the 'hang-loose' ethic. Central to this notion is the questioning of such traditional patterns of behaviour and belief as conventional religion, marriage, pre-marital chastity and the accumulation of wealth. Subscribers to this ethic apparently do not necessarily reject the *mores* of the established order, but are strongly critical of them. In this study, the stronger the student embraced the ethic the more favourable he was towards marijuana use. Smoking marijuana was highly associated with 'non-conformist' behaviour such as participating in mass protests and was more likely to be reported by those students who were dissatisfied with the education they were receiving. The 'hang-loose' ethic, while it may represent antagonism to the conventional world, does not appear to create apathy and withdrawal. The investigator suggests that the smoking of marijuana is part of the behaviour associated with this ethic rather than the cause of it.

A somewhat different view is suggested by McGlothlin and West[154] on the basis of clinical observation. They have described an 'amotivational syndrome' in some heavy marijuana users in North America. It is suggested that such use of marijuana may contribute to some characteristic personality changes including apathy, loss of effectiveness, diminished capacity or willingness to carry out complex long-term plans, endure frustration, follow routines or successfully master new material. The interpretation of these observations is complicated by the fact that such individuals are usually involved with other drugs as well as cannabis.

164. Several Eastern studies have suggested that chronic high-dose use of the more potent preparations of cannabis may have detrimental effects on the individual. One of the most comprehensive reports was that of the Chopras in 1939.[45] An eight-year study was carried out on a sample of 1,238 cannabis users. With regard to moderate doses, users of relatively mild bhang reported a general feeling of well-being, relief from worry and sharpened appetite. Heavy users were often found to suffer from several adverse symptoms. In some instances, cannabis use was seen as an attempt at self-medication in response to these disorders rather than as the cause.

The researchers report that among the *ganja* and *charas* users, a small percentage suffered from serious psychiatric disorder, and minor emotional problems, including impairment of judgement and memory, were observed in the majority of these subjects. According to the authors, a significant proportion of the group had pre-existing neurotic tendencies which may have contributed to their problem of drug use. Heavy users were often observed to show marked inactivity, apathy and self-neglect. The majority of those who took small doses of any of the cannabis preparations felt that the overall consequences of their drug habit were nil or beneficial, while the majority of those who chronically took heavy doses, thought the practice harmful. These subjective judgements were generally consistent with the clinical observations reported.

165. This and other reports from Eastern countries are difficult to interpret and apply to the Western situation. To begin with, no equivalent data are presented from a comparable control group of non-users of similar social and economic background (although some comparisons among users are possible) and there is no means of estimating the representativeness of the sample studied. In addition, there are many social and economic factors which complicate cross-cultural comparisons. The use of cannabis has a different meaning in Eastern cultures – where a long history and tradition surrounds its use – than it does in the West, where it is a relatively recent phenomenon. Often, concepts of normalcy and deviancy differ considerably from one culture to another. In addition, the Eastern cannabis user generally consumes larger quantities of more potent forms with greater frequency than does the Western user.

166. Although the possession of cannabis is a crime, and in obtaining it an individual must normally come in contact with other individuals committing drug offences, there is no scientific evidence that cannabis itself is responsible for the commission of other forms of criminal behaviour. Chopra and Chopra[45] suggest that cannabis use may, in fact, actually reduce the occurrence of crime and aggression by decreasing general activity. While criminals may be more likely to use cannabis than other individuals, few crimes committed under the influence of mari-

juana have been documented, and a causal relationship between the drug use and other illegal behaviour has not been established. It may well be that an individual who is inclined to commit one illegal act (e.g., a drug offence), may also be more likely than average to transgress in other areas as well. Some observers feel that the lessening of inhibitions often reported with cannabis use might, in certain delinquent individuals, increase the likelihood of asocial behaviour. In a 1967 judgement, rendered by Judge G. Joseph Tauro, Chief Justice of the Supreme Court of Massachusetts, in the Boston trial of two men (Leis and Weiss) accused of trafficking cannabis, the following statement appears:[54]

In my opinion, a proper inference may be drawn from the evidence, that there is a relationship between the use of marijuana and the incidence of crime and anti-social behaviour.

The brief presented to the Commission by the Royal Canadian Mounted Police dealt at considerable length with the alleged association of illegal drug use and criminal behaviour in Canada. This evidence is discussed later in the report.

The British *Cannabis* report (1968) states that:[5]

In the United Kingdom the taking of cannabis has not so far been regarded, even by the severest critics, as a direct cause of serious crime.... The evidence of a link with violent crime is far stronger with alcohol than with the smoking of cannabis.

167. *Tolerance and Dependence.* While gross tolerance to the major effects of cannabis does not seem to occur in humans, there are many more subtle aspects of this situation which have yet to be clarified. Although there is little tendency for intermittent users to increas dose, certain cannabis effects may be modified by repeated experiences with the drug. Many investigators have pointed out that in some individuals there appears to be a 'reverse' tolerance – i.e., smaller doses may produce the desired effects after the user has become familiar with the drug. Many individuals experienced little or no effect the first time they smoked cannabis. Whether this is due to initially poor

smoking technique, some learning or psychological adaptation process, or perhaps some more molecular pharmacological sensitization, is uncertain. On the other hand, a few individuals appear to be extremely sensitive to the effects of cannabis at the beginning and may initially report intense, ornate, and perhaps frightening experiences which are rarely, if ever, equalled in subsequent administrations.

168. Investigators have reported that regular users learn to direct or control some of the psychological and behavioural effects while subjectively 'high' and may be able to perform certain functions better than non-users given the same dose. This would suggest that some sort of differential selective adaptation or tolerance may develop to some of the initially 'uncontrollable' effects. Users remain sensitive to the rewarding effects of the drug since there is generally no marked inclination for them to increase dosage. Some users report that if they stay 'high' for several days in a row the drug experience loses much of its freshness and clarity and, consequently, they prefer intermittent use.

There are reports of chronic, heavy users from the East who consume what would seem to be rather large quantities by Western standards.[24, 30] Whether this reflects some degree of tolerance with heavy use in these users or differences in desired effects or general drug-using norms, is not known.

169. Physical dependence to cannabis has not been demonstrated and it would appear that there are normally no adverse physiological effects or withdrawal symptoms occurring with abstinence from the drug, even in regular users. On the other hand, there have been several reports from the Far East and Middle East, of irritability, mild discomfort, and certain behavioural symptoms occurring after withdrawal of the drug in chronic heavy users.[24] It must be kept in mind that these cases are not clearly documented and that the purity of the substances involved is not certain. Since hashish is smoked with large quantities of tobacco and other drugs in many Eastern countries, these mixtures could be responsible for the minor withdrawal symptoms reported.

170. No controlled research has been done into the effects of discontinuing cannabis administration after unusually high doses of the unadulterated substance have been given over a prolonged length of time. While such an extreme situation may appear to be of little social significance, it should be noted that physical dependence on the sedatives (alcohol, barbiturates and tranquillizers) usually occurs in only a small minority of users who take abnormally large quantities of the drug for extended periods of time.

171. The presence or absence of psychological dependence in a given situation, of course, depends on one's definition of the term. While many cannabis users in North America seem to take the drug once or twice a week, in a social context similar to that in which alcohol is normally consumed, and readily abstain for weeks or months with no ill effects, there is a small minority of users who smoke it daily and whose regular routine and sense of well-being is disrupted if they are unable to obtain the drug. Most users apparently find the drug pleasant and desirable, and often will go out of their way to acquire it – even at the risk of criminal penalty. However, the craving and urgency associated with opiate narcotic or sedative (or tobacco) dependence do not seem to occur. There are reports from the East that considerable psychological dependence has occurred in a minority of individuals in whom the use of the drug has become a major component of their existence.[107]

Cannabis and other Drugs

172. The majority of cannabis users studied in North America have had experience with a variety of other psychoactive drugs, alcohol and tobacco being the most frequently mentioned. As might be expected, most of those who smoke cannabis first acquired a regular tobacco habit.

A link between tobacco smoking and marijuana use has been suggested by Rowell, who worked closely with the United States Bureau of Narcotics in the 1930s:[191]

Slowly, insidiously, for over three hundred years, Lady Nicotine was setting the stage for a grand climax. The long years of tobacco using were but an introduction and training for marijuana use. Tobacco, which was first smoked in a pipe, then as a cigar, and at last as a cigarette, demanded more and more of itself until its supposed pleasures palled, and some of the tobacco victims looked about for something stronger. Tobacco was no longer potent enough.

173. The relationship between cannabis and alcohol use has been the subject of much controversy. Many marijuana users claim that they have drastically reduced their consumption of alcohol, or quit it, since using cannabis. They often suggest that cannabis may be a cure for society's alcohol ills. The considerable hostility towards and rejection of alcohol expressed by many cannabis-using youth, however, is clearly not reflected in the majority of cannabis users. In general, survey studies find that those who use alcohol are more likely than 'teetotallers' to use cannabis, and most cannabis users still use alcohol. We have no information as to what effect cannabis has on an individual's drinking behaviour and overall alcohol intake. It is not clear whether cannabis tends to replace alcohol as an intoxicant in the user population, or whether the use of these drugs is additive without significant interaction, or if the use of one of these drugs potentiates the use of the other. It appears that, if used simultaneously, the alcohol effects dominate and many of the psychedelic aspects of cannabis are suppressed. For this reason, many cannabis users refuse to mix the drugs even if they may enjoy one separately.

The question of comparing benefits and ills of alcohol and cannabis has become a popular and engaging endeavour. Due to the profoundly different social connotations and patterns of use, as well as scientific knowledge of these drugs, such a comparison must be made on limited and tenuous grounds.

174. In the United States, the majority of persons studied who had been dependent on opiate narcotics, had previous experience with cannabis (and were usually heavy users of alcohol). In Canada this has less often been the pattern, and it appears that heavy use of sedatives (alcohol and barbiturates) rather than cannabis has most frequently preceded heroin use.[246,215]

It has been suggested that the Canadian pattern is becoming more similar to the United States experience.

On this topic, the *United States Task Force Report* (1967) concludes:[220]

> The charge that marijuana 'leads to the use of addicting drugs' need to be critically examined. There is evidence that a majority of the heroin users who come to the attention of public authorities have, in fact, had some prior experience with marijuana. But this does not mean that one leads to the other in the sense that marijuana has an intrinsic quality that creates a heroin liability. There are too many marijuana users who do not graduate to heroin, and too many heroin addicts with no known prior marijuana use, to support such a theory. Moreover there is no scientific basis for such a theory.
>
> The most reasonable hypothesis here is that some people who are predisposed to marijuana are also predisposed to heroin use. It may also be the case, that through the use of marijuana a person forms the personal associations that later expose him to heroin.

With a similar orientation, the British *Cannabis* report (1968) states:[5] '. . . we have concluded that a risk of progression to heroin from cannabis is not a reason for retaining the control over this drug (cannabis).'

175. Many heavy users of cannabis reportedly also experiment with a variety of other drugs, including amphetamines as well as psychedelic substances. Again, marijuana is often the first drug (other than alcohol and tobacco) taken by youthful multi-drug users. The role of cannabis in the 'progression' to other drugs has not been adequately studied and it is unclear whether it plays a predisposing role, or is often used earlier simply because of its wider availability and social acceptance.

176. While no cross-tolerance occurs between cannabis and the other psychedelic drugs or the stimulants, considerable mention has been made of 'multi-drug' psychological dependence in which individuals may seem to depend on a variety of drugs in general, rather than on any particular chemical substance.

177. *Initiation of Cannabis Use.* Cannabis users are usually 'turned on' for the first time by friends and associates who have had previous experience with the drug. There is little evidence of aggressive 'pushers' being responsible for the initiation of cannabis smoking, although many individuals have reported considerable peer-group pressure to try it. The distribution or trafficking of cannabis is largely carried out in the same social manner, and is usually handed from friend to friend, although there are some individuals whose motivation for trafficking is primarily commercial. Some of the marijuana in Canada is 'home-grown' but most apparently comes from Mexico and the southern United States.

Some Cannabis Studies of Current Significance

178. I. In 1939, after consulting with the New York Academy of Medicine, Mayor La Guardia of New York appointed a special scientific committee to investigate the effects of marijuana, both in the community and under laboratory conditions. The final report entitled *The Marijuana Problem in the City of New York: Sociological, Medical, Psychological and Pharmacological Studies*[149] was published in 1944, and is still one of the most widely quoted and comprehensive studies of cannabis.

The report provoked considerable controversy, and although it has been generally well received by the scientific community, certain other individuals were quite vociferous in expressing their dismay at the committee's conclusions. O. J. Kalant[120] of the Addiction Research Foundation, has prepared a careful critical analysis of the Mayor's report. She observed that: 'Judged from a purely scientific standpoint this study deserves neither the extravagant praise nor the vicious attacks to which it has been submitted.'

179. The field work for the sociological study was under-taken by six specially trained police officers. The squad 'lived' in the environment in which marijuana smoking or peddling was suspected. They frequented poolrooms, bars and grills, dance halls, subways, public toilets, parks and docks. On the basis of

their observations, the following conclusions were drawn: The distribution and use was centred in Harlem. While the cost of marijuana was low and therefore within range of most persons, the sale and distribution was not under the control of any single organized group. The consensus among users was that the drug created a definite feeling of adequacy. The practice of smoking marijuana did not lead to addiction in the medical sense of the word, did not lead to morphine or heroin or cocaine addiction, and no effort was made to create a market for opiate narcotics by stimulating the practice of marijuana smoking. Marijuana was not the determining factor in the commission of major crimes, nor was it the cause of juvenile delinquency. Finally, 'the publicity concerning the catastrophic effects of marijuana smoking in New York City is unfounded.'

180. The clinical studies were conducted with an experimental group of 77 persons – 72 of whom were inmates of various New York Prisons. Forty-eight of these subjects had used marijuana previously and some had been heavy users of opiate narcotics. Both orally ingested cannabis concentrate and ordinary marijuana cigarettes were administered in various quantities.

A feeling of euphoria, occasionally interrupted by unpleasant sensations, was the usual response to cannabis. Also noted were other common aspects of a marijuana 'high', such as laughter and relaxation. No signs of aggression occurred, although some indications of anti-social feelings were expressed. Dizziness, a light floating sensation, dryness of the throat, thirst, an increase in appetite (particularly for sweets), unsteadiness and a feeling of heaviness of the extremities, were among the common somatic symptoms noted. Nausea and vomiting occasionally occurred with oral ingestion. Most effects seemed to increase with dose and were often more pronounced on those who had not previously used cannabis.

181. There were 9 cases of psychotic reaction in the prisoners studied. In 6 instances, acute or short-term adverse reactions characterized by '... mental confusion and excitement of delirious nature with periods of laughter and anxiety' occurred. Three cases of 'true' psychosis appeared to be associated with

128

the experiment. 'The precise role of marijuana in the psychotic states of the three unstable persons is not clear.' In the first subject ... 'the psychotic episode was probably related to epilepsy.' 'In the case of the second and third subjects, the fact that they were sent back to prison to complete their sentences must be considered an important, if not the main factor in bringing on the psychosis.' None of the nine individuals had been a regular user of cannabis. The researchers pointed out, however, that marijuana can bring on a true psychotic state under certain circumstances in predisposed individuals.

182. The most consistent physiological effects reported were: a temporary increase in heart rate, an inconsistent increase in blood pressure, an increase in frequency of urination, dilated pupils, and a moderate increase in blood sugar level and basal metabolism. Other organic and systematic functions were unchanged. It should be pointed out that the tests reported were not conducted under controlled double-blind conditions, and some of these findings have not been confirmed in later controlled studies.

183. Simple psychomotor functions were only affected slightly by large doses, and negligibly or not at all by small doses of marijuana. More complex functions, hand steadiness, static equilibrium, and complex reaction time were impaired by both dose levels. Generally, non-users were more affected by the marijuana than those with previous marijuana experience. Strength of grip, speed of tapping, auditory acuity, 'musical ability' and estimation of short time intervals and linear distances were unchanged. Placebos were not generally used in this section and the details of the statistical analysis were not presented.

184. In the section on Intellectual Functioning, a variety of psychological tests designed to measure aspects of intelligence, learning, memory and performance were administered. Two doses of oral concentrate were used in most instances. The author concludes that marijuana ingestion '... has a transitory adverse effect on mental functioning', with the greatest impairment at high dose on tasks involving complex functions. No

statistical analysis was done to distinguish drug effects from random variation, however, and again, no controlled double-blind design was used. Furthermore, the author's conclusions are not always consistent with the evidence which, for example, suggests some improvement in verbal abilities and certain other functions after marijuana ingestion. These data are not discussed. The author notes that 'indulgence in marijuana does not appear to result in mental deterioration'.

Kalant has noted with respect to this section:[120]

In summary, the results seem to bear out the conclusion that big enough doses of marijuana impair a variety of mental functions, while small doses may improve some of them. These conclusions are only tentative, because the author presents no statistical treatment of the data.

185. The 'Emotional and General Personality Structure' of varying numbers of users and non-users were studied before and after several doses of cannabis. The effects of low dose were generally pleasant and favourably received by the subjects, while the high dose seemed more likely to produce anxiety, distress, and a sense of insecurity. The committee concluded:

Under the influence of marijuana the basic personality structure of the individual does not change, but some of the more superficial aspects of his behaviour show alteration. The new feeling of self confidence induced by the drug expresses itself primarily through oral rather than through physical activity. There is some indication of a diminution in physical activity. The disinhibition which results from the use of marijuana releases what is latent in the individual's thoughts and emotions, but does not evoke responses which would be totally alien to him in his undrugged state.

186. A comparison between users and non-users as regards the possibility of physical and mental deterioration as a consequence of marijuana use was made on 48 users, some of whom had been smoking regularly for two to seventeen years. The investigators concluded that:

There is definite evidence in this study that the marijuana users were not inferior in intelligence to the general population and that they had suffered no mental or physical deterioration as a result of their use of the drug.

187. The therapeutic use of cannabis in the treatment of opiate narcotic addicts was explored in 56 patients. Tentative conclusions suggest improved appetite and mood, less severe symptoms and a generally improved clinical picture during withdrawal. Again no control group was studied.

The Committee reported:

> From the study as a whole, it is concluded that marijuana is not a drug of addiction, comparable to morphine, and that if tolerance is acquired, this is of a very limited degree. . . . The habit depends on the pleasurable effects that the drug produces.

These views were based largely on interviews with hundreds of users, the sociological studies and the laboratory investigations. Some observers have pointed out that these conclusions may not apply to the conditions of heavy chronic use sometimes reported in Eastern countries.

188. Some individuals have criticized the research for often using high doses of little social relevance – the authors admit that users, if left to their own devices, tend to approximate the lower doses used in the experiment. Other investigators feel that more chronic users of higher doses should have been studied for the investigation of long-term effects including tolerance and dependence.

189. In summary, although the La Guardia report remains one of the more significant contributions to the cannabis literature, the conclusions must be qualified in accordance with the numerous weaknesses in the experimental methodology: blind and placebo controls were absent and statistical analyses often lacking, reporting was occasionally biased when the data were ambiguous, sample selection may not have been adequate for certain conclusions in the sociological study, and the almost

complete use of prison inmates as subjects in the clinical studies and hospital ward setting may further restrict generalizations.

190. II. Isbell *et al*[109] investigated the effects of various doses of smoked and orally ingested tetrahydrocannabinol (Δ^9 THC) in a group of former opiate narcotic addicts who had also had experience with marijuana. The drug was compared to an inactive placebo control in a single-blind design (i.e., the researchers, but not the subjects, knew which samples were being tested).

191. Regardless of dose and route of administration, THC caused no significant change in pupillary size, respiration rate, blood pressure, or knee-jerk reflex threshold. Heart pulse rate was consistently elevated, and swelling of the conjunctival blood vessels in the membrane around the eyes occurred after the higher doses. In both physiological and psychological measures, THC (at a standard dose) was found to be two to three times as potent when smoked as when taken orally.

192. Patients identified the drug as being similar to marijuana and some suggested that it was something like LSD or cocaine as well. Euphoria was consistently noted and no mention was made in the report of unpleasant adverse reactions. Psychological changes included '. . . alterations in sense of time and in visual and auditory perception (usually described as keener).' With higher doses, both smoked and orally ingested, '. . . marked distortion in visual and auditory perception, depersonalization, derealization and hallucinations, both auditory and optical, occurred in most patients. Δ^9 – THC, therefore is a psychotomimetic drug and its psychotomimetic effects are dependent on dose.' Such occurrences may also appear in some individuals as 'idiosyncratic' reactions at lower doses. It had been noted that the symptoms which Isbell has labelled 'psychotomimetic' might be called 'psychedelic' by scientists with a different orientation.

193. The application of these findings to marijuana use as it occurs in North America is unclear. Some observers, in both lay and scientific circles, have interpreted this report as an indication of the dangers of marijuana, while other scientists ques-

tion the relevance of these findings in relation to the 'real world' of marijuana usage.[251]

194. III. In 1968, Weil, Zinberg and Nelsen[239, 240] reported the first adequately controlled experiment on cannabis effects in humans. The primary section of the study is concerned with effects on nine subjects who were inexperienced with cannabis. The researchers gave two different doses of marijuana (0.5 and 1.0gm of 0.9% THC) and an inactive placebo substance in a controlled 'double-blind' situation – i.e., neither the subjects nor the researchers knew at the time of the experiment which dose of cannabis or placebo was administered. This procedure greatly reduces the influence of expectations and bias on the part of both subjects and researchers. In addition to the naïve subjects, eight chronic marijuana users (who normally smoked daily or every other day) were tested with the high dose only. No placebo was used with these subjects since the authors felt that experienced marijuana smokers could readily distinguish the placebo from the 'real thing', and consequently a true placebo control was not possible. Subjects took either the drug or placebo by a standard and uniform inhalation method designed to minimize practice effects and individual differences in smoking technique. Subsequently, they were tested on a battery of standard psychological and psychomotor tasks, and certain physiological measurements were taken in a neutral laboratory setting.

195. The physiological findings were quite straightforward: heart rate was increased moderately, no significant change in respiration rate occurred, blood sugar level was unchanged (although the timing of the samples may not have been optimal), no change in pupil size was seen and a slight swelling of the conjunctival blood vessels (producing a reddening of the membranes around the eye) occurred. The researchers suggest that the near absence of significant physiological effects '. . . makes it unlikely that marijuana has any seriously detrimental physical effects in either a short-term or long-term usage.'

196. The capacity for sustained attention (Continuous Performance Test) was unaffected by cannabis in both the naïve

and chronic user groups, even when a flickering strobe light was presented to provide distraction. Muscular coordination and attention performance (Pursuit Rotor Test) declined as dose was increased in naïve subjects, but improved slightly after marijuana use in the chronic users. (This improvement was considered a result of practice rather than a drug effect but can not be properly evaluated due to the lack of a placebo measurement in the experienced users.) Performance on the Digit Symbol Substitution Test, (a simple test of cognitive function often used in I.Q. tests) was impaired in the naïve groups, while the experienced smokers started off at a reasonable base line and actually improved slightly when they were 'high' – a trend which can not be accounted for solely by practice. A tendency to overestimate time was also noted in these subjects. The researchers caution that the differences between users and non-users in this study must only be considered a trend since the testing situations were not strictly comparable for the two groups.

197. Subjects were given five minutes to talk on 'an interesting or dramatic experience' and the content of the verbal report was analysed. Marijuana did not impair the understandability of the material as measured by the Cloze method, although judges could consistently distinguish the transcripts of pre- and post-drug samples in both the naïve and experienced groups. A 'strange' quality in the post-drug samples was noted but not easily quantified. The investigators suggested that marijuana may temporarily interfere with short-term memory – i.e., the ability to retrieve or remember events occurring in the past few seconds. They feel that this may explain why many marijuana smokers, when very 'high', may have trouble remembering, from moment to moment, the logical thread of what is being said. Controlled investigation of this hypothesis is currently under way.

198. The experienced subjects were asked to rate themselves on a scale from one to ten, with ten representing the 'highest' they had ever been. Ratings given were between seven and ten, with most subjects at eight or nine. This would suggest that the sample was of reasonable potency and the smoking technique

effective. On the other hand, with the same dose and smoking technique, only one of the naïve subjects had a definite marijuana 'high'. (Interestingly, he was the one subject who had earlier expressed an eagerness to 'turn on'.) The researchers point out that the introspective report of an individual is the only way to determine if he is 'high' on marijuana or not. There are, as of yet, no known objective signs which allow one to identify this state.

199. There was no change in mood in the neutral laboratory setting in either naïve or chronic user subjects, as measured by self-rating scales and a content analysis of the verbal sample. There were no adverse marijuana reactions of any kind in any of the subjects, although tobacco cigarettes smoked during a practice session, using the standard technique produced acute nicotine reactions in five subjects which 'were far more spectacular than any effects produced by marijuana'. The authors conclude:

> In a neutral setting persons who are naïve to marijuana do not have strong subjective experiences after smoking low or high doses of the drug, and the effects they do report are not the same as those described by regular users of marijuana who take the drug in the same neutral setting. Marijuana-naïve persons do demonstrate impaired performance on simple intellectual and psychomotor tests after smoking marijuana; the impairment is dose-related in some cases. Regular users of marijuana do get high after smoking marijuana in a neutral setting but do not show the same degree of impairment of performance on the test as do naïve subjects. In some cases, their performance even appears to improve slightly after smoking marijuana.

200. *The New Republic*, in an editorial responding to this report, wrote: 'While pot heads may legitimately ask, "So what else is new?" the study may have a pacifying influence on parents and officials who fear the drug on the basis of unsubstantiated horror stories.'[251] While numerous scientists have expressed similar views, the study does provide a long overdue empirically adequate beginning to the scientific study

of marijuana effects on humans. While this study has implications extending beyond the laboratory, there has been a tendency in the popular press to overgeneralize from the results. It would be imprudent to extrapolate the findings into social and legal areas for which the study was not designed and is not appropriate.

201. IV. Jones and Stone[116] in 1969 reported that smoked marijuana (equivalent to Weil's low dose) compared to a placebo in ten 'heavy users' resulted in: moderately increased heart rate, altered electroencephalogram (EEG), over-estimation of time (but no change in time interval production), no effect on the ability to attend to relevant internal cues to the exclusion of irrelevant external cues (Rod and Frame test), and no effect on the Digit Symbol Substitution Test (the same measure of cognitive functioning employed in the Weil study). A double dose of marijuana (comparable to Weil's high dose) produced a deficit in visual information processing – the only test studied with this quantity of drug.

202. The subjects were asked to rate the low dose and placebo on a scale from 0–100 as to marijuana quality. The mean rating were 66 for the low dose and 57 for the placebo, which was not a significant difference. While this suggests that the dose of marijuana used was probably too low to be very effective and may reduce the significance of the report, it is interesting that the supposedly inactive 'placebo' (with 'only a "trace" of THC') was given a rating suggesting moderate potency by ten heavy marijuana users in San Francisco. However, it appears that the subjective effects of the placebo and low dose marijuana, as measured by a self-rating subjective symptom check-list, may have been different, although no statistics are presented, and the figure containing this information does not clearly identify the placebo. At any rate, these findings suggest that at low doses a simple 'highness' dimension may not be easy to quantify reliably. Unfortunately, Weil did not get ratings on his low dose or placebo, and Jones did not assess the high dose, so a reconciliation is not possible with the present data.

203. The researchers also studied a larger dose of marijuana

extract (equivalent to 20 cigarettes) given orally, compared with a placebo and one dose of alcohol (producing blood alcohol levels of 0.06 to 0.12%). Several tasks were used with the same subjects. Certain comparisons among the conditions and drugs are possible, although the use of a single dose and slight variations in procedure limits the applicability of the findings.

204. The marijuana smoked in low doses produced an 'unimpressive' high with a maximum effect at about 15 minutes and lasting about three hours, while the oral administration had a latency of almost two hours, a peak at three to four hours and mild subjective effects lasting eight to ten hours. The oral dose of marijuana occasionally produced nausea and in one case vomiting, and differed from the smoked material on several subjective dimensions. The results of the comparisons between the oral marijuana and the placebo were essentially the same as those discussed earlier for the smoked material. As a point of reference, the single alcohol dose did not affect performance on the Rod and Frame Test, produced an underestimation of time intervals, decreased rate of information processing, did not affect heart rate, and produced a slight slowing of the E E G. Little meaningful comparison can be made between alcohol and the other treatments at a single dosage level, however.

205. The report is ambiguous and many important details of methodology and results are excluded in what appears to be a preliminary investigation. It should be noted that this study has only single-blind controls and the investigators knew which drugs were administered at the time of the experiment.

206. V. A third recent experimental study of marijuana effects on humans was published by Clark and Nakashima[46] in 1968 and is mentioned here since it is now frequently quoted and, also, to demonstrate some of the problems of interpreting inadequately controlled experiments. Several different doses of marijuana extract (of unknown THC content) were given to 12 marijuana naïve subjects, and the effects recorded on eight psychological tests in 'one control and two or three subsequent sessions'.

207. The study is uninterpretable for a variety of reasons,

some of which follow: since the control session and the various drug doses were given only once, and on separate days, drug and dose effects are indistinguishably confounded with various factors of treatment order (including practice and other learning effects), and natural variations in performance occurring from one day to the next; the researchers describe no basis, statistical or otherwise, for distinguishing the 'effects' from random variation; they report only trends in the data in one or two subjects selected on an unspecified basis, and give no indication of overall group effects; the numerical basis for the figures presented is unspecified; apparently no placebos were given on the 'control' day which was invariably the first session, yet the drug is frequently compared with the 'control' in individual subjects; apparently no 'blind' controls were provided in either the experiment or later data analysis; and the report is presented with a strong negative bias in the introduction and remainder of the article, which is not supported empirically. The authors infer marijuana-induced impairment only on the reaction time and 'digit code memory' tasks, although they provide no reliable evidence for the presence or absence of positive or negative marijuana effects on these or the other tests studied.

Clark concludes that great individual variation exists among individuals in response to the drug. While this would seem a reasonable observation, effects have not been identified, much less the variance of their distribution assessed. The great variability in the data cannot be attributed solely to the drug for reasons outlined above. In summary, this study, conducted, financially supported and published by highly accredited individuals and institutions, adds nothing but confusion to the existing knowledge and should encourage scepticism regarding even modern 'scientific' information on marijuana.

208. VI. Last year Crancer and associates,[61] from the Washington State Department of Motor Vehicles, published the first experimental study of marijuana effects on automobile driving skills. A laboratory driving simulator was employed which had been shown previously to validly predict road accidents and traffic violations on the basis of speedometer, steer-

ing, braking, accelerator and signal errors measured during a programmed series of 'emergency' situations. This study has provoked considerable controversy, some of which may be dissipated if the different sections of the study are examined separately.

209. Using a sophisticated methodological and statistical design, the effects of the single dose of marijuana (2 cigarettes) were assessed in 36 experienced marijuana smokers who used cannabis at least twice a month. In terms of total $\Delta^9 - THC$ administered, the dose was about 22% greater than Weil's high dose and almost $2\frac{1}{2}$ times the standard dose used by Jones. Crancer reports the effects as a 'normal social marijuana high', although this is not quantified in any way and it is not certain how this relates to the overall pattern of marijuana use in the population. Simulator scores were obtained at three intervals over a $4\frac{1}{2}$-hour period. Control (no treatment) sessions were run, although no placebo substance was used since the investigators felt that a placebo would not be effective with experienced marijuana users.

210. Overall performance under the single dose of marijuana was not different from the control. The main study was followed by two 'cursory' investigations. Four subjects were retested with three times the original drug dose and none showed a significant change in performance. Furthermore, four marijuana naïve subjects were tested after smoking enough marijuana to become 'high' (all consumed at least the amount used in the main experiment and demonstrated an increase in heart rate in addition to subjective effects). No significant change in scores occurred with the drug in these subjects either.

The investigators caution that the study does not necessarily indicate that marijuana will not impair driving.

However, we feel that, because the simulator task is a less complex but related task, deterioration in simulator performance implies deterioration in actual driving performance. We are less willing to assume that non-deterioration in simulator performance implies non-deterioration in actual driving.

211. One weakness of this part of the study is that apparently no standard and uniform smoking technique was employed and it is not certain how much of the active principle was actually absorbed. Although a biochemical method for detecting THC in the body has recently been developed, quantitative measurements have not been employed in any experimental marijuana studies. Although higher doses were tested in some subjects, this was not done with the same thoroughness as the main experiment and little can be asserted regarding a dose-response effect of marijuana on driving. It seems likely that if the dose were pushed high enough some impairment would occur, although this has not been empirically demonstrated.

212. In order to obtain some standard reference point for this study, the subjects were also tested under a single dose of alcohol, designed to produce a blood alcohol level corresponding to the legal standard of presumed driving impairment in Washington (i.e., 0.10% blood alcohol level). The average number of errors under alcohol (97.4) was significantly greater than that acquired under either the normal or marijuana condition (each averaging 84.5 errors). While it is clear that a meaningful comparison of the two drugs cannot be based on a single dose of each, the alcohol data were obtained merely to provide a 'recognized standard' of impairment.

Kalant[118] has pointed out that the blood alcohol level of these subjects may have been considerably higher than the desired 0.10%, and that comparisons between the drugs must be made with caution due to the single doses used. He also suggests that although it would not have been easy for the subjects to 'fake' good driving performance under marijuana, an anti-alcohol bias, as often seen in marijuana users, could have resulted in poorer performance in the alcohol condition.

If the limitations of the alcohol-marijuana comparison and the weakness of the marijuana dose-effect generalizations are realized, the over-all study provides interesting tentative information on the effects of a moderate quantity of marijuana on driving skills.

213. VII. In general, studies of the long-term history of marijuana users have been based either on medical or criminal

samples or on subjects selected because of current use. Each of these sources of subjects has considerable intrinsic sampling bias – which greatly complicates the interpretation of results. Recently, however, Robins and associates,[187] reported the first study of the long-term outcome of marijuana use in a group not selected for deviant behaviour. The subjects were 235 Negro men who had gone to public elementary school in the black district of St Louis, Missouri, in the early 1940s. While the characteristics of such a population may have questionable applicability to present marijuana use in Canada, this generally thorough study should be carefully considered. The data are largely based on recent retrospective personal interviews and official records. Subjects were classified according to adolescent drug use.

214. Persons in this sample who had used marijuana (and no other drug except alcohol) differed significantly from non-marijuana users, in that the users had more often: drunk heavily enough to create social or medical problems, failed to graduate from high school, reported their own infidelity or fathering of illegitimate children, received financial aid, had adult police records for non-drug offences, and reported violent behaviour. While these findings indicate an association between marijuana use and these other behavioural characteristics in this population, causal variables have not been identified.

215. The heavy use of alcohol in these subjects complicates the interpretation considerably. Every marijuana user also used alcohol, and drinking usually preceded marijuana use. Among the subjects who used only marijuana and alcohol, 47% had medical or social problems attributable to drinking ('the "shakes", liver trouble, family complaints, arrests, etc.') after the age of 25, and 38% of the users met the criteria for alcoholism. When those subjects who were classified as alcoholics were eliminated from the data (and the remainder of the problem drinkers left in) the only statistically significant difference between the marijuana users and the non-users was with respect to financial aid received in the past five years. Non-significant trends remained, however, which were generally similar to the earlier differences. Subjects who used 'harder' drugs (e.g.,

heroin, amphetamines and barbiturates) in addition to marijuana, were significantly more deviant than the non-users, even after the alcoholics had been eliminated from the sample. Almost one-half of the subjects who had used marijuana also had used other drugs illegally.

The alcoholics, in addition to having a history of early drinking, were also more likely to have used marijuana as adolescents. Unfortunately, no record of intensity of early drinking or marijuana use was obtained. A possible causal relationship between marijuana use and problem drinking, or vice-versa, or a possible third set of factors predisposing certain individuals to both alcoholism and marijuana use cannot be established or denied on the basis of the present data. The relationship between marijuana use and the use of harder drugs is also troublesome.

The authors conclude:

One small study of the effects of drug use in 76 Negro adolescents can hardly serve to determine the laws of the land. But it may at least make us cautious in too readily supporting the view that marijuana is harmless, until some better evidence is available.

216. VIII. The Addiction Research Foundation of Ontario has recently conducted a study of 232 confirmed marijuana users in Toronto.[173] Prisons and court referrals provided about half of the subjects and the remainder were volunteers not contacted through criminal-legal channels. The majority came from middle-class or upper middle-class homes and 16% were students. The average age was 22 (range: 15-42) and males outnumbered females 4 to 1. The average duration of marijuana use was 2.7 years (range: 1-20).

217. Preliminary observations suggest the following characteristics in this sample: the subjects tended to be multiple drug users (tobacco and alcohol were used by almost all of the subjects, more than half had tried LSD and speed, and one-third had tried opiate narcotics); most had 'trafficked' in marijuana, but usually just to friends; cannabis was generally used about twice a week in the company of friends, accompanied by pass-

ive rather than active behaviour; purported reasons for use were increased perception and awareness, other psychedelic effects, improved mood, and conviviality. Almost all subjects found the usual effects favourable although about a third had had at least one unpleasant experience (physiological or psychological) with the drug; about half had driven a car while under the influence of cannabis, and of these subjects, more than half felt that their driving ability was unimpaired by the drug; about half felt that cannabis had improved their lives, while some thought it had worsened things; the subjects 'tended to be underactive physically, engaging in passive pursuits'; about one-third subscribed to the belief in the 'protestant work ethic', while almost as many rejected it; almost one-third had committed non-drug criminal offences; one-half showed a swelling of the fine conjunctival blood vessels around the eye; non-specific deviant EEGs were frequently seen; more than half were thought by a psychiatrist to be psychologically unstable or disturbed; and the group as a whole tended to be more imaginative and creative than what would be expected in the general population.

218. The researchers stress that their findings demonstrate an association, and not necessarily a causal relationship, between the regular use of cannabis and other characteristics in this sample. While some of these results may be attributable to the selection or bias of the sample (e.g., half were contacted through criminal correction channels), much of the information may have general application. On-going analysis of the data should further clarify the results, although the lack of a comparable matched control group will undoubtedly preclude certain generalizations since we have little information regarding the incidence of many of the aforementioned characteristics in non-marijuana using individuals of similar social, economic and educational backgrounds. Furthermore, the frequent use of other drugs by these subjects may limit conclusions specific to cannabis use.

219. IX. In response to questions raised in the British House of Commons, the Government of India, in 1893, appointed a commission to investigate and report on the cannabis ('hemp

drugs') situation in India. The Commission was instructed to inquire into the extent to which the hemp plant was cultivated, the preparation of drugs from it, the trade in those drugs, the extent of their use, and the effects of their consumption upon the social, physical, mental, and moral conditions of the people. The different forms of the drug, especially bhang, ganja, and charas (hashish), were to be studied separately. The Commission '... should ascertain whether, and in what form, the consumption of the drugs is either harmless or even beneficial as has occasionally been maintained'. In addition, they were asked to investigate certain economic aspects of the use of hemp (e.g., tax arrangements and import and export patterns), and also the potential political, social or religious results of prohibition. *The Report of the Indian Hemp Drugs Commission* (1894),[107] including appendices, comprised seven volumes and totalled 3,281 pages.

220. In 1968, Mikuriya,[158] in the first thorough discussion of this report to appear in the Western scientific literature, suggested that this investigation

> ... is by far the most complete and systematic study of marijuana undertaken to date.... It is both surprising and gratifying to note the timeless and lucid quality of the writings of these British colonial bureaucrats. It would be fortunate if studies undertaken by contemporary commissions, task force committees, and study groups could measure up to the standards of thoroughness and general objectivity embodied in this report ... many of the issues concerning marijuana being argued in the United States today were dealt with in the Indian Hemp Drugs Commission Report.

Until recently only about a half dozen copies of this report were available in North America. In the introduction to a new printing of the primary volume in 1969, Kaplan[121] observed:

> That this report, which remains today by far the most complete collection of information on marijuana in existence, should have been so completely forgotten in an era when controversy over the effects of the drug and the wisdom of its

criminalization has increased to such a fervor is almost inexplicable.

221. The Indian Hemp Drugs Commission received testimony from 1,193 witnesses of a total of 80 meetings in 30 cities. Over 300 medical practitioners were consulted and inquiries were made of Commanding Officers of all regiments of the Army. The commissioners investigated the records of every mental hospital in British India and evaluated separately each of the 222 cases admitted during the year 1892, in which some connection between hemp drugs and insanity had been suggested (these made up about 10 per cent of all admissions). Furthermore, all 81 cases of crimes of violence in India purported to have been caused by cannabis over the previous 20 years were investigated and re-examined. In addition, three laboratory experiments were conducted with monkeys to study the effects of cannabis on the nervous system.

222. In the short time during which the full report has been available to us, we have not been able to prepare, at this interim stage, a thorough critical analysis of the document. However, the following quotations, taken from the summary of conclusions regarding the effects of hemp drugs, provide an overview of the findings:

It has been clearly established that the occasional use of hemp in moderate doses may be beneficial. . . . In regard to the physical effects, the Commission have come to the conclusion that the moderate use of hemp drugs is practically attended by no evil results at all. There may be exceptional cases in which, owing to idiosyncrasies of constitution, the drugs in even moderate use may be injurious. . . . The excessive use does cause injury. As in the case of other intoxicants, excessive use tends to weaken the constitution and to render the consumer more susceptible to disease . . . the excessive use of these drugs does not cause asthma . . . it may indirectly cause dysentery . . . (and) it may cause bronchitis.
In respect to the alleged mental effects of the drugs, the Commission have come to the conclusion that the moderate use of hemp drugs produces no injurious effects on the mind. . . . It is otherwise with the excessive use. Excessive use indicates and

intensifies mental instability. . . . It appears that the excessive use of hemp drugs may, especially in cases where there is any weakness or hereditary predisposition, induce insanity. It has been shown that the effect of hemp drugs in this respect has hitherto been greatly exaggerated, but that they do sometimes produce insanity seems beyond question.

In regard to the moral effects of the drugs, the Commission are of opinion that their moderate use produces no moral injury whatever. There is no adequate ground for believing that it injuriously affects the character of the consumer. Excessive consumption, on the other hand, both indicates and intensifies moral weakness or depravity. . . . In respect to his relations with society, however, even the excessive consumer of hemp drugs is ordinarily inoffensive. His excesses may indeed bring him to degraded poverty which may lead him to dishonest practices; and occasionally, but apparently very rarely indeed, excessive indulgence in hemp drugs may lead to violent crime. But for all practical purposes it may be laid down that there is little or no connection between the use of hemp drugs and crime.

Viewing the subject generally, it may be added that the moderate use of these drugs is the rule, and that the excessive use is comparatively exceptional. The moderate use practically produces no ill effects. In all but the most exceptional cases, the injury from habitual moderate use is not appreciable. The excessive use may certainly be accepted as very injurious, though it must be admitted that in many excessive consumers the injury is not clearly marked. The injury done by the excessive use is, however, confined almost exclusively to the consumer himself; the effect on society is rarely appreciable. It has been the most striking feature in this inquiry to find how little the effects of hemp drugs have obtruded themselves on observation.

As noted earlier in this chapter, any generalizations from one culture to another must be made with great caution. In this instance, extrapolation to the present Canadian situation would have to span three-quarters of a century as well. In spite of these clear limitations, the thoroughness of this critical inquiry commands respect and the report deserves careful consideration.

OPIATE NARCOTICS

223. The term *narcotic* has had wide and inconsistent usage in lay, legal and scientific circles. Some use the word to characterize any drug which produces stupor, insensibility or sleep; many apply it only to derivatives of the opium plant ('opiates'); others consider the term equivalent to addiction-producing; and in legal matters, 'narcotics' may refer to almost any allegedly dangerous drugs (for example marijuana and cocaine are often considered with opiate compounds in narcotics regulations in spite of the fact that they have little in common with them). To reduce some of this ambiguity, the specific phrase *opiate narcotic* will be used in this report, and will be restricted to drugs which are derivatives of, or are pharmacologically similar to products of the opium plant *papaver somniferum*.

224. The earliest unambiguous description of opium to which we have access was written in the third century B.C., although some scholars have cited references to opiate-like drugs dated more than 5,000 years ago.[29] Many believe that Homer's 'Nepenthe' was opium. These drugs are obtained from the juice of the unripened seed pod of the opium poppy plant soon after the flower petals begin to fall – no other part of the plant produces psychoactive substances.

Although 'opium eating' has been known in Asia for thousands of years, widespread use of the drug did not occur until the development of the British East India Company's wholesale opium empire in the eighteenth century. The practice of smoking opium developed in China soon after American tobacco was introduced to the Orient. Chinese prohibition of the British opium precipitated the 'opium war' in which the world's greatest naval power forced China to open its door to the British (opium) trade.[223]

225. In 1805, the major active constituent in opium was isolated – an alkaloid given the name morphine, after the Greek God of Dreams, Morpheus. In the next half century, various other alkaloids were discovered, such as codeine and pap-

147

averine, both of which are in general use today. Since then, a variety of semisynthetic (e.g., heroin, in 1874) and synthetic (e.g., methadone, Demerol* and Alvodine*), opiate-like drugs have been developed. These compounds have the potential of producing qualitatively similar actions (at different doses), although there is considerable variability among them in the potency of the different opiate effects. Heroin, more potent on a weight basis than morphine, is usually the choice of the chronic opiate narcotic user. This drug was originally considered 'non-addictive' when put on the market. Those members of the medical and related profession who use these drugs non-medically, as well as others who have become dependent as a result of medical use, tend to use morphine or the synthetics. Because of the similarities among these drugs, they will, with a few exceptions, be dealt with as a group. Heroin (and sometimes other opiate narcotics) is often referred to as 'H', 'horse', 'junk', 'scrag' or 'smack'.

226. Until the nineteenth century, 'raw' opium was either smoked or taken orally. There is a decidedly lower dependence liability with these techniques than with practices which followed, and it was not until the isolation of morphine and the invention of the hypodermic needle that the opiate narcotics became a serious problem in the Western World. Morphine was widely acclaimed among medical practitioners and was used freely to treat pain during the American Civil War, sometimes producing a dependency called 'soldiers' disease'. General use of tincture of opium in many patent medicines (e.g. Paregoric) made the quasi-medical use of opiates a common practice in North America at that time. On the West Coast, the influx of Chinese labourers, some of whom smoked opium, apparently stimulated non-medical use to some degree. The extent of opiate narcotic problems in the nineteenth century is difficult to ascertain; however, it would appear that the use of these drugs was not a major moral issue. In the early part of the twentieth century, some of the problems of morphine and heroin dependence became apparent, and most opiate products were removed from the open market in North America and non-medical possession was prohibited.

227. Because characteristics fluctuate with social change, a description of drug users is necessarily tied to a given population at a given point in time and may have little general application. There is little information on opiate narcotic users in North America prior to this century, but many researchers contend that far more women than men made use of these drugs at that time. Since the general opiate prohibition in the early part of this century, men have become the predominant users. While Chinese opium smokers were not uncommon a half century ago, there appear to be very few Orientals in North America using opiate narcotics today. In recent decades, the use of these drugs in Canada has tended to centre on a few urban areas. Medical and related professions represent a frequently noted high-risk group with respect to the development of drug dependency. For various reasons, statistics on the incidence of dependency in this group are quite inadequate. Many researchers contend that health profession dependents constitute a significant proportion of the total chronic opiate narcotic using population.[28] For many years, the known opiate narcotic users have made up about 0.02 per cent of the overall Canadian population.

228. Although many observers do not feel that the non-medical use of opiate narcotics is currently a major public health problem in Canada, there are numerous reasons for directing attention to this group of drugs. Historically, the popular conception of the 'narcotics addict dope fiend' has established an image of the non-medical drug user which persists and intrudes into almost every examination or investigation of drug use today. Furthermore, the opiate narcotics have played an important role as a model in much of the past and present drug legislation, and in the general crimino-legal approach to the control of socially censured drug use. Although many important questions about the opiate narcotics are still unanswered, it is clear that much of what has commonly passed for fact, is fiction, and often bears little resemblance to scientific information.

229. Most of the current medical uses for the opiate narcotics were fairly well understood and established in Europe by the middle of the sixteenth century, and were probably well-known in certain areas long before that time. These drugs are primarily used in the relief of suffering from pain, in the treatment of diarrhoea and dysentery, and to reduce cough. Hundreds of related compounds have been synthesized in attempts to retain the clinical benefits but reduce the dependence liabilities of the opiate narcotics. These efforts have not been very successful, and thus morphine and related drugs are still considered by physicians to be among the most valuable drugs available to the practitioner today. Heroin is no longer used medically in North America.

Administration, Absorption, Distribution and Physiological Fate

230. Opiate narcotics are produced in a variety of tablets and capsules, elixirs, cough syrups (with codeine), injections, rectal suppositories and, on the illegal market, are also available in a gummy solid or powdered form. Codeine is often mixed with other non-opiate analgesics (e.g. A P C & C*; 222's*). While the opiate narcotics are well absorbed from the gastro-intestinal tract, this route is often erratic and unpredictable compared to injections. Among non-medical users, subcutaneous ('skin popping') and intravenous ('mainlining') injections are commonly used with heroin and morphine. Raw opium is usually eaten or smoked and the powder is sometimes sniffed ('snorted'). Only a minute fraction of the drug absorbed actually enters the central nervous system. The duration and intensity of the effects vary considerably with the different drugs in this class (and as a function of dose), although the major action might typically last from three to six hours. These drugs are usually inactivated in the liver and excreted in the urine, often along with small quantities of free morphine.

231. Pure opiate narcotics produce few significant non-psychological effects in therapeutic doses. The immediate or short-term physiological response usually includes a general reduction in respiratory and cardiovascular activity, a depression of the cough reflex, a constriction of the pupil of the eye, and minor reduction in visual acuity, slight itching, dilation of cutaneous blood vessels, warming of the skin, a decrease in intestinal activity (often causing constipation), and, in some individuals, nausea and vomiting. In higher doses, however, insensibility and unconsciousness result. The primary toxic overdose symptoms are coma, shock and, ultimately, respiratory arrest and death.

232. There appears to be little direct permanent physiological damage from chronic use of pure opiate narcotics. Numerous complications are observed, however, if the overall drug use pattern involves adulterated street samples, unsterile administrations, unhygienic living standards, poor eating habits and inadequate general medical care – all of which are commonly part of the criminal-addict behaviour syndrome. Commonly reported disorders in street users are hepatitis, tetanus, heart and lung abnormalities, scarred veins ('track marks'), local skin infections and abscesses, and obstetrical problems in pregnant females. At one time, malaria was also commonly seen in this population.

233. The general mortality rate among heroin dependents is considerably higher than normally expected for their age group. Sudden collapse and death following intravenous injection has been reported in a number of these individuals. Such fatalities have often been attributed to overdose resulting from erratic and unexpected variations in the purity of drugs obtained from the black market. However, there is considerable evidence that many of these deaths are not merely due to overdose but are a consequence of partly soluble contaminant substances in the sample and, perhaps, some drug hypersensitivity phenomenon.[43]

234. The subjective effects of opiate narcotics may vary considerably among different individuals and situations. Most persons reportedly do not enjoy the experience and may actively avoid its repetition in a controlled or experimental situation, while others describe feelings of warmth, well-being, peacefulness and contentment. Euphoria or dysphoria, nausea, drowsiness, dizziness, inability to concentrate, apathy and lethargy are commonly noted. Certain individuals, especially when fatigued, may be stimulated into feelings of energy and strength. Higher doses produce a turning inward and sleep. Often a pleasant dreamlike state occurs. Some regular users describe their drug experiences in near ecstatic, and often sexual terms (especially the 'rush' of intravenous injection).

The potential of the opiate narcotics to relieve suffering from pain depends upon several mechanisms. The major effect is not on the sensation directly, but on the psychological reaction to it. Often individuals can still feel the pain sensation, and rate its intensity reliably, in spite of the fact that much or all of the negative or unpleasant aspects are absent. In other words, they may still feel the pain, but it does not bother them to the same extent. Morphine has little effect on the other senses, and unlike non-narcotic analgesics and sedatives, it can often control pain at doses which do not necessarily produce marked sedation, gross intoxication or major impairment of motor coordination, intellectual functions, emotional control or judgement.[110] In addition to reducing the anxiety of pain and therefore the motivation to avoid it, the opiate narcotics also tend to decrease other primary motivation associated with sex, food, and aggression.

235. The psychological effects of chronic opiate narcotic use are often rather straightforward extensions of the short-term response. In regular users, much of the variability and unpredictability of the immediate response is lessened, partly because individuals who find the experience unpleasant tend to avoid additional exposure, and also because many who were initially upset by the unusual physiological and psychological sensations caused by the drugs learn to tolerate and even seek them and

may no longer be distressed in the situation. While some individuals who become dependent on the opiate narcotics withdraw from regular social activities, and live what might appear to be an immoral, criminal and slovenly existence, others are able to lead an otherwise normal life with little change in work habits or responsibilities. Possible factors underlying these differences will be discussed later.

Tolerance and Dependence

236. Tolerance to the different actions of opiate narcotics varies with the magnitude and frequency of administration, and the response being measured. In chronic use, a considerable degree of tolerance occurs to the sedative, analgesic, euphoric and respiratory depressant (and, therefore, potentially lethal) effects; less tolerance develops to the constipating and pupil-constricting activity. Consequently, persons who are motivated by the chronic avoidance of pain or other unpleasant subjective conditions, or perhaps simply by the positive euphoric effects of the drug, are likely to increase dose and may eventually tolerate several times the quantity which would be lethal to a normal individual. Occasional use does not produce tolerance, however.

237. The degree of physical dependence acquired to these drugs is closely related to the tolerance developed. With low dose or infrequent use, little dependency occurs and withdrawal symptoms may be nonexistent, or merely resemble the symptoms of a mild flu. Withdrawal of the drug after chronic high-dose use results in a severe and painful pattern of responses which are similar to those associated with alcohol and barbiturate dependence (although it is not as physically dangerous). Usually less than half a day after the last administration, the dependent begins to feel irritable, anxious and weak; he sweats and shivers and his eyes and nose become watery. A few hours of uneasy sleep may intervene before he begins the 'cold turkey' phase. The skin becomes clammy, the pupils dilate, chills, nausea, vomiting, and severe abdominal cramps occur with uncontrollable defecation; tremors and, rarely, convulsions may

develop. While death has been reported, fatalities are much rarer than with sedative withdrawal. The major symptoms of the abstinence syndrome generally last several days, and gross recovery usually occurs within about a week, although complete recuperation may take up to six months.[145] Tolerance is eliminated or greatly reduced with withdrawal. Babies born of dependent mothers are also physically dependent on the drug, and may die if withdrawal symptoms are not recognized and treated soon after birth. It should be noted that the different opiate narcotic drugs have varying dependence-producing potentials, and physical dependence is rarely seen in opium smokers or users of codeine (although strong psychological dependence may occur).

238. Considerable cross-tolerance and cross-dependence exists among the opiate narcotics. An intravenous injection of any of these drugs, in sufficient dose, can completely eliminate the withdrawal syndrome in a matter of minutes. Methadone can prevent withdrawal symptoms at doses which provide little psychological effect, and is frequently used in chronic 'maintenance' programmes designed to rehabilitate dependents. Although the sedatives and opiate narcotics do not usually show significant cross-tolerance and dependence, barbiturates can ease the pain of opiate withdrawal. Nalorphine (Nalline*) antagonizes the effects of the other opiate narcotics and precipitates the withdrawal syndrome in dependent individuals. This drug has been used to 'test' for dependence in suspected users.

239. The role of physical dependence in the overall picture of chronic opiate narcotic use has been the subject of much controversy and many observers feel that the psychological components are the most important. Some investigators argue that the fear of withdrawal is often the primary motivating factor behind continued use, while others emphasize the profound craving seen in some individuals, or the drug's positive reinforcing or reward potential. Many dependent persons return to the drug at some time after withdrawal, and some have occasionally been known to voluntarily undergo withdrawal in order to lose tolerance (for economic reasons), and

immediately initiate chronic use again, at a less expensive level. This practice suggests that, with some individuals, psychological factors other than mere avoidance of the abstinence syndrome can be dominant in the drug dependence. Whether this motivation is related to the desire to escape or avoid a life that is unpleasant, or emotionally painful or depressing, or perhaps a more directly hedonistic demand for pleasure or 'kicks', or even a disguised attempt at self-destruction is not clear – no simple answer could be expected to have much generality or validity. It has frequently been observed that some individuals become dependent on the hypodermic syringe (or 'point') in a way which is, in some respects, independent of the pharmacological properties of the drug. Persons showing such conditioning are often called 'needle freaks'.

240. It is interesting to note that there are only a few middle-aged persons who are dependent on opiate narcotics. Most individuals spontaneously lose interest in the drugs before they turn 45 years of age (barbiturate and alcohol dependents show no such decline in use). Whether this is due to psychological or physiological factors is uncertain.

Opiate Narcotics and Crime

241. A consensus exists among medical, law enforcement and research authorities, as well as drug users themselves, that few crimes of violence are directly produced by the use of the opiate narcotics. On the other hand, there is a considerable relationship between crime and opiate narcotic dependence in North America and many drug dependent persons have non-drug criminal records. This apparent paradox can be explained by two important factors. To begin with, both in Canada and in the United States, many individuals who become dependent on opiate narcotics have a prior history of behavioural problems and delinquency and have continued these practices. The second factor is economical, and is associated with the high cost of heroin on the black market and the demands made by extended tolerance.

Because of the illegal nature of the drug, the cost of a heavy heroin habit may run anywhere from $15.00 to $50.00 a day and higher, in spite of the fact that the medical cost of the drugs involved would just be a few cents. There are very few legitimate ways in which most individuals can afford to meet that kind of an expense. Consequently, when tolerance pushes the cost of drug use above what the user can afford legitimately, he is forced into a decision – either quit the drug and go through withdrawal, or turn to easier, criminal, methods of acquiring the necessary money. While many users refuse to become involved in such activities and stop using the drug, at least temporarily, many turn to petty crime, small robberies, shoplifting and prostitution. These are the individuals who regularly come to the attention of the law enforcement officials. More affluent persons may be able to support the habit and continue indefinitely without running afoul of the law. Medical profession dependents, for example, apparently have less tendency to commit non-drug offences – perhaps (in addition to predisposing psychological and sociological factors) because they can often steal with little risk or purchase the necessary drugs at low cost.

As Jaffe has stated:[111]

> The popular notions that the morphine addict is *necessarily* a cunning, cringing, malicious and degenerate criminal who is shabbily dressed, physically ill and devoid of the social amenities could not be farther from the truth. The addict who is able to obtain an adequate supply of drugs through legitimate channels and has adequate funds, usually dresses properly, maintains his nutrition and is able to discharge his social and occupational obligations with reasonable efficiency. He usually remains in good health, suffers little inconvenience and is, in general, difficult to distinguish from other persons. ... Good health and productive work are thus not incompatible with addiction to *opiates. However, ... such continued productivity is the exception rather than the rule.*

The Development of Dependence

242. There have been a number of popular misconceptions about the pattern of development of opiate narcotic de-

pendence. Rumours have frequently been heard that marijuana and hashish have been 'spiked' with heroin to produce opiate addiction in the unsuspecting user. Similar rumours have been heard about 'spiked' LSD. In fact, there are no known documented cases in Canada of opiate narcotic adulteration of other drugs alleged to be pure. The high price of illicit heroin renders such a hypothesis extremely improbable. Furthermore, it would be highly unlikely, if not impossible, for tolerance and dependence to develop without the user knowing it. The majority of users, both here and in the United States, were apparently first 'turned-on' by their friends and peers. Blum (in the United States Task Force Report) points out:[28]

> There is no evidence from any study, of initiation as a consequence of aggressive peddling to innocents who are 'hooked' against their will or knowledge. . . . The popular image of the fiendish pedlar seducing the innocent child is wholly false.

243. The once popular notion that the opiate narcotic experience is intrinsically so pleasurable, or that physiological dependence develops so rapidly, that most who are subjected to it are promptly addicted is without support. In one experiment, injections of morphine were given to 150 healthy male volunteers. Only three were willing to allow repeated administration and none indicated that he would have actively sought more. The investigators[42] conclude:

> . . . opiates are not inherently attractive, euphoric or stimulant. The danger of addiction to opiates resides in the person and not the drug.

Lasagna et al[126] also report that the majority of normal pain-free individuals found effects of opiates quite unpleasant. Beecher[22] reports that only ten per cent of a normal population liked the morphine experience. Furthermore, many individuals who developed tolerance and physical dependence in a medical situation show little interest in the drug experience itself and tend not to resume use after withdrawal. Even in non-medical cases, there is evidence that only a small proportion of drug users who have experimented with opiate narcotics in the streets become physically dependent on them.[42]

244. Many observers contend that certain social and personality factors predispose some individuals to drug dependence and that otherwise normal individuals rarely, if ever, become chronically dependent. There is considerable evidence that both the ready availability of the drug and a social milieu tolerating or encouraging drug use (either medical or non-medical) are also important factors. Although there are numerous individuals who have gradually worked up from occasional 'skin popping' to chronic 'mainline' dependence, there is, at present, little evidence that a large proportion of the Canadian population is running this particular risk. However, there is cause for apprehension because of the rapidly growing incidence of heroin use among the young in the United States. Although there are no known methods of predicting the likelihood of dependence for any individual at this time, the use of opiate narcotics involves a risk of considerable proportions for anyone.

Opiate Narcotics and Other Drugs

245. In the United States, the opiate narcotic offender coming to the attention of the law enforcement officials was often reported to have previously and concurrently been a heavy user of alcohol, barbiturates, tobacco, and marijuana. In Canada, the pattern appears to be much more variable and heterogeneous. Alcohol and barbiturates (and probably tobacco) have apparently been the drugs most often associated with opiate narcotic use here[246, 215], although recent indications suggest that many new heroin users may have experience with marijuana and other psychedelic drugs as well.[170a] There are reports that LSD is generally not popular with regular heroin users, however.[41] Some opiate narcotic users also make use of stimulants such as amphetamine and cocaine.

246. Much attention has been and is now being given to the 'stepping-stone' or 'progression' theory of opiate narcotic dependence. Although there is no pharmacological basis for the hypothesis that one drug creates a 'need' for, or necessarily leads to another, there are numerous social factors which might

link together the use of various drugs. It may well be that the questions of 'progression' or predisposing experiences can never be definitively answered. Like other characteristics associated with deviant behaviour, they must be continually evaluated anew as the social context changes. Some observations on the possible relationship between marijuana and opiate narcotic use were presented in the previous section on cannabis.

VOLATILE SOLVENTS

247. Although the inhalation of volatile substances and gases for non-medical purposes has been known for well over a century, it has only been within the last decade that such practices have come to the regular attention of public health officials. While the recent practice of adolescent 'glue sniffing' has received the most publicity, a wide variety of other substances and practices have been involved. These drugs have frequently been labelled *deliriants* although delirium is only one of many potential effects and is clearly not restricted to these substances. Some of these drugs have much in common with the sedatives and might be considered in a sub-class of that category. In addition, certain solvents and gases apparently have some psychedelic properties.

248. Many of the chemicals used may be described as volatile hydrocarbon solvents and are highly soluble in lipids (fats) – a major component of living tissue. Most of the substances are either gases at room temperature or rapidly evaporate from a liquid phase to a gaseous state when exposed to the air. This property makes them highly desirable, industrially, in the production of materials in which fast drying is essential. The solvents are also usually highly inflammable.

249. There are literally hundreds of easily accessible sources of these materials, which may run from hardware store and cosmetic sundries to clinical drugs and anaesthetics. Some common products which may contain large quantities of these chemicals are: fast drying glue and cements; many paints and lacquers and their corresponding thinners and removers; gasoline, kerosene and various other petroleum products; lighter

159

fluid, dry cleaning fluid, finger nail polish remover and various aerosol products. Active chemicals in these materials include toluene, acetone, naphtha, benzene, hexane, cyclohexane, trichlorophane, trichloroethylene, perchlorethylene, carbon tetrachloride, chloroform, ethyl ether and various alcohols, ketones and acetates. Closely related chemically to the solvents are the freon gases which are commonly used as aerosol and refrigerant gases. Nitrous oxide, the original inhalant anaesthetic, and related nitrites are also highly volatile substances with long histories of non-medical use. It was recently observed that thirty-eight different products containing such substances were available from the shelves of a service station-hardware store in Ottawa.

It is clear that we have in this drug category a large aggregate of chemically diverse substances from a wide variety of sources. While this heterogeneity precludes any broad and all-encompassing generalizations, many of the substances have common properties which warrant general consideration. Most of these drugs have not been investigated individually in much detail, since only a few have had extended medical use. In most instances, human studies, if any, have been limited to gross investigations of toxicity in industrial situations and may have uncertain application here.

250. Nitrous oxide, ethyl ether and chloroform, three of the best known inhalant anaesthetics, had considerable non-medical recreational use which preceded their general medical acceptance. Over a century ago, the following advertisment was circulated in Hartford, Connecticut:[52]

A Grand Exhibition of the effects produced by inhaling Nitrous Oxide, Exhilarating or Laughing Gas, will be given at Union Hall this (Tuesday) Evening, December 10, 1844.
Forty gallons of Gas will be prepared and administered to all in the audience who desire to inhale.
Twelve Young Men have volunteered to inhale the Gas to commence the entertainment.
Eight Strong Men are engaged to occupy the front seats to protect those under the influence of the Gas from injuring themselves or others. This course is adopted that no appre-

hension or danger may be entertained. Probably no one will attempt to fight.

The effect of the Gas is to make those who inhale it either Laugh, Sing, Dance, Speak or Fight and so forth, according to the leading trait of their character. They seem to retain consciousness enough not to say or do that which they would have occasion to regret.

N.B. – The Gas will be administered only to gentlemen of the first respectability. The object is to make the entertainment in every respect, a genteel affair.

Although occurring several decades before systematic investigation and general medical acceptance of nitrous oxide as an analgesic and anaesthetic, the promoters of this entertainment showed considerable appreciation for the variety of potential effects of the drug and the importance of the individual personalities of those taking it.

251. During the century prior to its introduction into medical practice, ether was widely used as an industrial solvent and often as an intoxicant. It frequently served as a replacement beverage for alcohol during times of liquor scarcity in numerous areas in Europe, Great Britain and North America in the nineteenth century. During World War II, ether consumption increased in Germany when alcohol became unavailable.[168] Inhalation of small amounts of ether and chloroform on special occasions is reported to have been accepted practice in certain sophisticated social circles in North America before the turn of the century.

Ether inhalation parties were not uncommon at that time, especially among students and associates of the healing professions. In fact, it was the observation of one of these ether 'jags' which directly led to the first medical use of ether as a clinical anaesthetic by C. W. Long. Soon after, Oliver Wendell Holmes suggested the word *anesthesia* to describe the state of 'insensibility' which accompanies the unconsciousness or sleep induced by large doses of these substances.[52]

252. Although current non-medical use of volatile solvents has been reported across age groups and spanning social class,

recent surveys concur with law enforcement and public health impressions that chronic use is predominantly a phenomenon of youth, reaching a peak in early teens and dropping off soon after. There are no specific statutes dealing with the use of most of the substances discussed, although chronic users may be apprehended, for example, as juvenile delinquents.

253. The almost unlimited number of potential substances makes specific legislation of questionable value as a deterrent. An alternative approach to control which has frequently been suggested is to add to the products most commonly used, a substance which renders the original material offensive to the user. An irritant chemical or obnoxious odour might serve this purpose, although it might also be unpalatable to the manufacturing staff and the legitimate user of these chemicals as well. The pervasive use of highly volatile, potentially psychoactive substances for largely non-drug purposes in our society makes this approach seem impractical as a general solution. Restricting certain substances would have little overall effect since many materials such as gasoline are easily obtained by any age group. Effective restriction of access to most such substances could not be achieved except at considerable inconvenience to a large segment of the population. This is an area which clearly calls into question the potential of the crimino-legal system in controlling drug use.

Medical Use

254. Most of the substances included in this category have had no regular medical use, although in many instances the general effects produced are similar to those of the clinical inhalant anaesthetics. Ether, nitrous oxide, trichloroethylene (Trilene*) and chloroform have been widely used to reduce pain and produce unconsciousness prior to and during surgical and dental work, and at one time were used as sedatives, and in the treatment of sleeplessness. Other nitrogenous compounds (e.g., amyl nitrite) are used in the therapy and relief of heat pain and, occasionally, asthma.

255. Although in many instances the active agents in the substances used would be absorbed if taken orally, inhalation provides a more rapid and effective means of administration, and a sharpening of effects. Techniques used in inhalation are generally designed to maximize the gas concentration in the air. Frequently the substance is emptied into a plastic or paper bag which is held tightly over the nose and mouth and the fumes inhaled. Alternatively, a cloth may be dipped in a liquid, or the active substance applied to the cloth, which is then rolled up and held against the nose and/or mouth and the gases breathed in. In other instances, the drug may be sniffed directly from an open container or inhaled through a tube. Amyl nitrite is also available in ampules or 'pearls' which are broken to release the fumes.

As noted earlier, drinking of certain relatively pure substances, such as ether, has also been noted. The effects of oral administration are reported to be in many ways similar to ordinary alcohol. The somewhat different initial results of inhalation are probably due to the more rapid rate of absorption from the lung as compared to the gastro-intestinal tract. These observations would again underline the importance of route and rate of administration in determining drug effects.

256. In certain cases some metabolism occurs in body tissue, although many of these drugs are eliminated chemically unchanged by the lungs in gaseous form. Consequently the odour of the substance may be noticeable on the breath of the user for several hours after administration.

Effects

257. The psychological and physiological effects of the volatile solvents are in many respects similar to the sedatives, alcohol and barbiturates. Low doses can produce considerable behavioural and psychological arousal while higher amounts usually result in sedation and a general reduction in activity. Little is known as to the specific mechanism by which these

drugs exert their action. As with most drugs, the effects of the volatile solvents can be expected to vary considerably with the individual, his mental set and the setting in which the substance is used.

258. Little controlled research has been conducted on the psychological effects of the solvents. Frequently reported are: a lessening of inhibitions, a feeling of sociability and well being, and a general elevation of mood. Higher doses may produce laughing and silliness, feelings of floating and being 'out of contact', dizziness, perceptual distortions of time and space, and illusions. Certain of these substances are said to have subjective effects which are in some respects similar to those produced by the psychedelic drugs. Confusion, drunkenness, slurred speech, blurred vision, a feeling of numbness, nasal secretion, watering of the eyes, headache, incoordination and, not infrequently, nausea and vomiting may also occur. As the dose is further increased, the general sedating – anaesthetic effects dominate and drowsiness, stupor, respiratory depression and, finally, unconsciousness result. Additional quantities may inhibit breathing and produce death.[125]

259. During the acute phase of intoxication, judgement may be impaired and considerable confusion and lack of behavioural control may occur. Some individuals become irritated, tense, or frightened, and acute psychoses have been reported. There is no evidence of long-term psychotic reactions, however. Possible results of these conditions include accidents, self-destructive behaviour and impulsive, aggressive, and other anti-social acts.

260. The effects of acute intoxication may be as short as five to ten minutes or last up to an hour depending on the substance used, the dose administered, and a variety of other factors. Recreational users frequently retain their supply and repeat the administration over several hours; attempting to maintain a balance of intoxication often close to but below that producing unconsciousness. The state achieved is somewhat analogous to light (Stage 1) clinical anaesthesia, where mixed stimulation and depression of various psychological and physiological systems

occur. Because of the sensitivity of the nervous system to subtle changes in dose, maintaining this level of intoxication is frequently not an easy task and undesired 'conk-outs' occur.

Medical anaesthetists, in trying to achieve deep anaesthesia in a patient with high doses, generally attempt to pass through this early deliriant stage quickly and may use a variety of techniques and other drugs to minimize the erratic stimulating effects of light anaesthesia. Many individuals may be able to recall the dreamlike experiences and unusual feelings and thoughts which are characteristic of 'going under' with inhalant anaesthetics. Such experiences are not unlike the intoxication effects sought by some individuals in the non-medical use of these substances.

261. The majority of recent reports on volatile solvent inhalation have been concerned with juveniles who had come to the attention of the authorities because of some anti-social or delinquent behaviour, which may or may not have been associated with drug use. Most of these individuals had emotional or behavioural difficulties prior to the use of the drug and no careful investigation has been done with non-delinquent solvent users, even though there are indications that these latter individuals make up the majority of users. Almost no information is available on the long-term psychological outcome of solvent inhalation, although several observers have expressed concern over possible effects of regular drug use by young people coping with the already trying and often troublesome stages of early adolescence.

262. Transient changes or abnormalities resulting from acute intoxication have been reported in kidney and liver function, bone marrow activity, and a variety of psychological and neurophysiological tests. Gastro-enteritis, hepatitis, jaundice and blood abnormalities are among the complications reported to be associated with the use of some of these products.[186] In addition, a number of chronic users have slow-healing ulcers around the mouth and nose. The frequent loss of appetite and resulting poor eating habits of chronic users complicate the situation further, and various nutritional disorders may also occur. It appears, however, that after discontinuing drug use, complete

165

recovery normally occurs from these disorders and with few exceptions, there is little evidence of permanent brain damage or other non-reversible psychological or physiological abnormalities due to the deliberate inhalation of these chemicals. Many solvents have not yet been carefully investigated, however, and generalizations about potential dangers from existing data can not be extended to the vast number of unstudied volatile substances.

263. While the commonly held belief that permanent brain damage is a regular result of glue sniffing can not be supported by scientific data, numerous industrial studies involving related chemicals, as well as certain laboratory animal experiments, suggest that irreversible physiological changes can occur with prolonged exposure to some solvents. In addition, some preliminary results suggest possible chromosome changes in the white blood cells of chronic users of some of these substances, although this effect has not been firmly established.

264. Recently, a number of deaths have been attributed to volatile solvent use. These fatalities have usually occurred when the user was inhaling alone, and often appear to be a subsequent result of the unconsciousness produced by overdose. Such unconsciousness, if of short duration, might normally be quite harmless since fresh air usually produces complete and rapid recovery. However, if the user's mouth and nose is covered by a plastic bag, as is often used for inhalation, suffocation may occur. Also, if the user's face remains close to the source after he loses consciousness, he may continue to breathe fumes and produce further overdose and respiratory arrest due to depression of the brain-stem breathing centres. Other fatalities have been attributed to vomitus suffocation, direct cardiac arrest and, perhaps, damage to lung tissue.

Tolerance and Dependence

265. Although no tolerance occurs with occasional use, the chronic user may find that after several months he may require two or three times as much of the active substance to achieve the desired state of intoxication as was necessary in the be-

ginning. The possibility of physical dependence with withdrawal symptoms has not been adequately investigated to date, although existing clinical reports suggest that this does not occur. This is somewhat surprising given the pharmacological similarities between the volatile solvents and the sedatives, which *do* produce both tolerance and physical dependence. Furthermore, cross-tolerance has been suggested by the frequently reported insensitivity of chronic alcohol and barbiturate users to ether anaesthesia. It is possible, however, that such factors as the rapid excretion rates of most volatile solvents and/or the usual intermittent patterns of solvent use make the development of physical dependence unlikely.

Symptoms of psychological dependence and compulsive use have been recorded, although chronic use is not frequent. Certain regular users reportedly become restless, irritable and depressed if they cannot have access to the drugs.

Solvents and Other Drugs

266. As noted above, cross-tolerance seems to occur between some solvents and the sedative drugs. Although some observers entertain the hypothesis that chronic use of solvents in early youth may predispose one to misuse of other drugs in later life, there is, as yet, no empirical evidence linking solvent use with other forms of drug dependence. It has been noted that solvents are taken in conjunction with alcohol by certain individuals. The use of other drugs currently available on the black market, such as marijuana and amphetamines, has also been reported in some youthful solvent users. Adult users of solvents often have a history of heavy alcohol consumption and may switch from one drug to the other.

REFERENCES AND SELECTED BIBLIOGRAPHY

1. Adams, R. Marihuana. *Harvey Lect.*, 1942, *37*, 168–97.

2. Addiction Research Foundation of Ontario. *Marihuana and its effects: An assessment of current knowledge.* Toronto: ARF, 1968.

3. Addiction Research Foundation of Ontario. *Facts about solvents.* Toronto: ARF, 1969.

4. Addiction Research Foundation of Ontario. Preliminary brief submitted to the Commission of Inquiry Into the Non-Medical Use of Drugs, December, 1969.

5. Advisory Committee on Drug Dependence. *Cannabis.* London: Her Majesty's Stationery Office, 1968 ('The Wootton Report').

6. Allen, J. R., and West, L. J. Flight from violence: Hippies and the green rebellion. *Amer. J. Psychiat.*, 1968, *125*, 364–70

7. Allentuck, S., and Bowman, K. M. The psychiatric aspects of marihuana intoxication. *Amer. J. Psychiat.*, 1968, *99*, 248–51.

8. American Medical Association Committee on Alcoholism and Addiction. Dependence on barbiturates and other sedative drugs. *J.A.M.A.*, 1965, *193*, 673–7.

9. American Medical Association. Dependence on cannabis (marihuana). *J.A.M.A.*, 1967, *201*, 368–71.

10. American Medical Association. Marihuana thing. *J.A.M.A.*, 1968, *204*, 1187–8.

11. Ames, F. A clinical and metabolic study of acute intoxication with cannabis sativa and its role in the model psychoses. *J. Ment. Sci.*, 1958, *104*, 972–99.

12. Andrews, G., and Vinkenoog, S. (Eds.). *The book of grass: An anthology of Indian Hemp.* New York: Grove Press, 1967.

13. Anslinger, H. J., and Cooper, C. R. Marijuana, assassin of youth. *American Magazine*, 1937, *124*, 19–20; 150–53.

14. Arnold, D. O. The meaning of the LaGuardia Report. In J. L. Simmons (Ed.), *Marihuana: Myths and realities.* North Hollywood, California: Brandon House, 1967.

15. *Attack on Narcotic Addiction and Drug Abuse*, 1969, *3* (3), 3–. N.Y. State Narcotic Addict. Control Commission.

16. Ausubel, D. P. *Drug addiction: Physiological, psychological, and sociological aspects.* New York: Random House, 1958.

17. Bakewell, W. E., Jr, and Wikler, A. Non-narcotic addiction:

Incidence in a university hospital psychiatric ward. *J.A.M.A.*, 1966, *196*, 710–13.

18. Banay, R. S. Alcoholism and crime. *Quart. J. Stud. Alcoh.*, 1942, *2*, 686–716.

19. Becker, H. S. Becoming a marihuana user. *Am. J. Sociol.*, 1953, *59*, 235–42.

20. Becker, H. S. Marihuana use and social control. *Soc. Prob.*, 1955, *3*, 35–44.

21. Becker, H. S. History, culture and subjective experience: An exploration of the social bases of drug-induced experiences. *J. Health Soc. Behav.*, 1967, *8*, 163–76.

22. Beecher, H. K. *Quantitative effects of drugs: Measurement of subjective responses.* New York: Oxford University Press, 1959.

23. Bell, D. S. Addiction to stimulants. *Med. J. Austral.*, 1967, Jan. 14, 41–5.

24. Benabud, A. Psycho-Pathological aspects of the cannabis situation in Morocco: Statistical data for 1946. *Bull. Narc.*, 1957, *9*, 1–16.

25. Bloomquist, E. R. *Marijuana.* Beverley Hills: Glencoe Press, 1968.

26. Blum, R. H., and Associates. *Utopiates: Use and users of LSD.* New York: Atherton Press, 1964.

27. Blum, R. H. Mind altering drugs and dangerous behavior: Dangerous drugs. Appendix A-1. Task Force Report: *Narcotics and drug abuse.* Washington, D.C.: U.S. Government Printing Office, 1967 (a).

28. Blum, R. H. Mind altering drugs and dangerous behavior: Narcotics. Appendix A-2. Task Force Report: *Narcotics and drug abuse.* Washington, D.C.: U.S. Government Printing Office, 1967 (b).

29. Blum, R. H., and Associates. *Society and drugs.* Vol. 1. San Francisco: Jossey-Bass Inc., 1969.

30. Bouquet, J. Cannabis. *Bull. Narc.*, 1951, *3*, 22–45.

31. Boyce, S. S. *Hemp (Cannabis sativa). A practical treatise on the culture of hemp for seed and fiber with a sketch of the history and nature of the plant.* New York: Orange Judd, 1912. Quoted by O. J. Kalant (1968).

32. Bracken, J. (Chm.). *Report of the Manitoba Liquor Enquiry Commission.* Winnipeg, 1955.

33. Brill, H. The case against marijuana. *J. Sch. Health*, 1968, *38*, 522–3.

34. Brill, H., and Hirose, T. The rise and fall of a methamphetamine epidemic: Japan 1945–55. *Seminars in Psychiatry*, 1969, *1*, 179–94.

35. Bromberg, W. Marihuana intoxication: A clinical study of cannabis sativa intoxication. *Amer. J. Psychiat.*, 1934, *91*, 303–30.

36. Caldwell, D. F., Myers, S. A., and Domino, E. F. Effects of marihuana smoking on sensory thresholds in man. In D. H. Efron (Ed.), *Psychotomimetic drugs.* New York: Raven Press, 1969.

37. Campbell, E. O'F. Alcohol involvement in fatal motor vehicle accidents. *Mod. Med.*, 1969, *24*, 35–42.

38. Carey, J. T. *The college drug scene.* Englewood Cliffs, N.J.: Prentice-Hall, 1968.

39. Carpenter, J. A. Effects of alcohol on some psychological processes. *Quart. J. Stud. Alcoh.*, 1962, *23*, 274–314.

40. Chapple, P. A. L. Cannabis – a toxic and dangerous substance – a study of eighty takers. *Brit. J. Addict.*, 1966, *61*, 269–82.

41. Cheek, F. E., Newell, S., and Sarett, M. The down-head behind an up-head – the heroin addict takes LSD. *Int. J. Addict.*, 1969, *4*, 101–19.

42. Chein, I., Gerard, D. L., Lee, R. S., Rosenfeld, E., and Wilner, D. M. *The road to H.* New York: Basic Books, 1964.

43. Cherubin, C. E. A review of the medical complications of narcotic addiction. *Int. J. Addict.*, 1968, *3*, 163–75.

44. Chopra, G. S. Man and marijuana. *Int. J. Addict.*, 1969, *4*, 215–47.

45. Chopra, R. N., and Chopra, G. S. The present position of hemp drug addiction in India. *Indian Medical Research Memoirs,* 1939, No. 31, 1,–119.

46. Clark, D. C., and Nakashima, E. N. Experimental studies of marihuana. *Amer. J. Psychiat.*, 1968, *125*, 379–84.

47. Clement, W. R., Solursh, L. P., and Van Ast, W. Abuse of amphetamine and amphetamine-like drugs. In press, 1970.

48. Cohen, M., Marinello, M., and Bach, N. Chromosomal damage in human leukocytes by lysergic acid diethylamide, *Science,* 1967, *155*, 1417–19.

49. Cohen, S. Lysergic acid diethylamide: Side effects and complications. *J. Nerv. Ment. Dis.*, 1960, *130*, 30–40.

50. Cohen, S., and Ditman, K. S. Complications associated with lysergic acid diethylamide (LSD–25). *J.A.M.A.*, 1962, *189,* 181–2.

51. Cohen, S., and Ditman, K. S. Prolonged adverse reactions to lysergic acid diethylamide. *Arch. Gen. Psychiat.*, 1963, *8*, 475–80.

52. Cohen, P. J., and Dripps, R. D. History and theories of general anesthesia. In L. S. Goodman and A. Gilman, *The pharmacological basis for therapeutics.* (3rd ed.) New York: MacMillan, 1965.

53. Cole, J. O., Peeking through the double blind. In D. H. Efron

(Ed.), *Psychopharmacology: A review of progress 1957–1967*. Washington, D.C.: U.S. Government Printing Office, 1968.

54. Commonwealth of Massachusetts. Supreme Judicial Court for the Commonwealth, Suffolk County. December Sitting, 1968, No. 14, 113. Commonwealth v. Joseph D. Leis. Commonwealth v. Ivan Weiss.

55. Connell, K. H. Ether drinking in Ulster. *Quart. J. Stud. Alcoh.*, 1965, *26*, 629–53.

56. Connell, P. H. *Amphetamine psychosis*. London: Chapman and Hall, 1958.

57. Conger, J. J. Reinforcement theory and the dynamics of alcoholism. *Quart. J. Stud. Alcoh.*, 1956, *17*, 296–305.

58. Corey, M. J., Andrews, J. C., McLeod, M. J., MacLean, J. R., and Wilby, W. E. Chromosome studies on patients (in vivo) and cells (in vitro) treated with lysergic acid diethylamide. Paper presented at a meeting of the Commission of Inquiry into the Non-Medical Use of Drugs, Halifax, Jan. 1970. (Also in press, 1970).

59. Council on Mental Health. Marihuana and society. *J.A.M.A.*, 1968, *204*, 91–2.

60. Cox, C., and Smart, R. G. The nature and extent of speed use in North America. Addiction Research Foundation of Ontario, Substudy 1–32 and 7–69, 1969.

61. Crancer, A., Jr, Dille, J. M,. Delay, J. C., Wallace, J. E., and Haykin, M. D. Comparison of the effects of marijuana and alcohol on simulated driving performance. *Science*, 1969, *164*, 851–4.

62. Cumberlidge, M. C. The abuse of barbiturates by heroin addicts. *Canad. Med. Ass. J.*, 1968, *98*, 1045–9.

63. Davidson, R. H., and Barclay, J. F. A rational analysis of the legal status of marihuana with jurisprudential considerations. Brief submitted to the Commission of Inquiry into the Non-Medical Use of Drugs, February, 1970.

64. Davis, M. A. Antidepressants, stimulants, hallucinogens. In *Annual Reports in Medicinal Chemistry*, 1967.

65. Denson, R. Complications of therapy with lysergide. *Canad. Med. Ass. J.*, 1969, *101*, 53–7.

66. De Ropp, R. S. *Drugs and the mind*. New York: Grove Press, 1957.

67. DiPalma, J. R., (Ed.), *Drill's pharmacology in medicine*. (3rd ed.) New York: McGraw-Hill, 1965.

68. Domino, E. F. Psychosedative drugs II: Meprobamate, chlordiazepoxide and miscellaneous agents. In J. R. DiPalma (Ed.), *Drill's pharmacology in medicine*. (3rd ed.) New York: McGraw-Hill, 1965.

69. Eddy, N. B., Halbach, H., Isbell, H., & Seevers, M. H. Drug dependence: Its significance and characteristics. *Bulletin, World Health Organization*, 1965, *32*, 721–33.

70. Efron, D. H. (Ed.) *Psychopharmacology: A review of progress, 1957–67.* Washington, D.C.: U.S. Government Printing Office, 1968.

71. Ellinwood, E. H. Amphetamine psychosis: 1. Description of the individuals and process. *J. Ner. Ment. Dis.*, 1967, *133*, 273–83.

72. Essig, C. F. Addiction to barbiturate and nonbarbiturate sedative drugs. In A. Wikler (Ed.), *The addictive states*. Proceedings of the Association for Research in Nervous and Mental Disease, Vol. XLVI. Baltimore: Williams & Wilkins, 1968.

73. Evans-Wentz, W. Y. (Ed.) *The Tibetan book of the dead.* New York: Oxford University Press, 1960.

74. Farmilo, C. G., Davis, T. W. M., Vandenheuvel, F. A., & Lane, R. Studies on the chemical analysis of marihuana. *Proc. Canad. Soc. Forensic Sci.*, 1962, *1*, 1–50.

75. Farnsworth, D. L., & Oliver, H. K., The drug problem among young people. *Rhode Island Med. J.*, 1968, *51*, 179–82.

76. Fattah, E. A. Pour de nouvelles mesures legislatives sur les drogues et la toxicomanie. *Toxicomanies*, 1969, *2*, 85–108.

77. Finlator, J. Drug abuse control. *F.B.I. Law Enfor. Bull.*, 1967, *6*, 1–5.

78. Finlator, J. The Playboy Panel: The drug revolution. *Playboy*, 1970, *17* (2), 53–.

79. Food and Drug Directorate, Department of National Health and Welfare, 1969. (Personal communication).

80. Forney, R. B., & Harger, R. N. The alcohols. In J. R. DiPalma (Ed.) *Drill's pharmacology in medicine.* (3rd ed.) New York: McGraw-Hill, 1965.

81. Fort, J. The AMA lies about pot. *Ramparts*, 1968, *7*, (August), 12–13.

82. Fort, J. Pot: A rational approach. *Playboy*, 1969, *16* (10), 131–.

83. Franks, C. M. Alcohol, alcoholism and conditioning: A review of the literature and some theoretical considerations. *J. Ment. Sci.*, 1958, *104*, 14–33.

84. Gamage, J. R., & Zerkin, E. L. *A comprehensive guide to the English-language literature on cannabis (marihuana).* Wisconsin: Stash Press, 1969.

85. Geber, W. F., & Schramm, L. C. Effect of marihuana extract on fetal hamsters and rabbits. *Toxic. Appl. Pharmacol.*, 1969, *14*, 276–82.

86. Gellman, V. Glue-sniffing among Winnipeg school children. *Canad. Med. Ass. J.*, 1968, *98*, 411–13.

87. Ginsberg, A. The great marihuana hoax: First manifesto to end the bring-down. *Atlantic Monthly*, 1966, *28* (November), 107–13.

88. Glaser, D., Inciardi, J. T., & Babst, D. Later heroin use by marijuana-using, heroin-using and non-drug-using adolescent offenders in New York City. *Int. J. Addict.*, 1969, *4*, 145–55.

89. Glatt, M. M. The abuse of barbiturates in the United Kingdom. *Bull. Narc.*, 1962, *14*, 19–38.

90. Goode, E. Marijuana and the politics of reality. *J. Health Soc. Behav.*, 1969, *10*, 83–94.

91. Goode, E. Multiple drug use among marijuana smokers. *Soc. Prob.*, 1969, *17*, 48–64.

92. Goode, E. The marijuana market. *Columbia Forum*, 1969, *12* (Winter), 4–8.

93. Goode, E. The marijuana smokers. In press, 1970.

94. Goodman, L. S., & Gilman, A. *The pharmacological basis of therapeutics.* (3rd ed.) New York: MacMillan, 1965.

95. Grinspoon, L. Marihuana. *Sci. Amer.*, 1969, *221* (6), 17–25.

96. Grossman, W. Adverse reactions associated with cannabis products in India. *Ann. Intern. Med.*, 1969, *70*, 529–33.

97. Haas, H., Fink, H., & Klin, B. M. The placebo problem. *Psychopharmacology Service Center Bulletin*, 1963, *2*, (8), 1–65 (Translation).

98. Halliday, R. Barbiturate abuse: An iatrogenic disorder? *B. C. Med. J.*, 1967, *9*, 374–8.

99. Hecht, F., Beals, R. K., Lees, M. H., Jolly, H., & Roberts, P. Lysergic-acid-diethylamide and cannabis as possible teratogens in man. *The Lancet*, 1968, November, 1087–.

100. Hekimian, L. J., & Gershon, S. Characteristics of drug abusers admitted to a psychiatric hospital. *J.A.H.A.*, 1968, *205*, 124–30.

101. Hoffer, A. LSD: A review of its present status. *Clin. Pharm. R Ther.*, 1965, *6*, 183–225.

102. Hofmann, A. Psychotomimetic drugs: Chemical and pharmacological aspects. *Acta Physiologica et Pharmacologica Neerlandica*, 1959, *8*, 240–58.

103. Hofmann, A. The active principles of the seeds of rivea corymbosa and impomoea violacea. *Bot. Mus. Leaflets*, 1963, *20* (6), 194–212.

104. Hollister, L. E., & Gillespie, H. K. Similarities and differences between the effects of lysergic acid diethylamide and tetrahydrocannabinol in man. Paper presented at the Rutgers Sym-

posium on Drug Abuse, Rutgers – New Brunswick, New Jersey, June, 3–5, 1968.

105. Houston, B. K. Brief communications – review of the evidence and qualifications regarding the effects of hallucinogenic drugs on chromosomes and embryos. *Amer. J. Psychiat.*, 1969, *126*, 251–3.

106. Huxley, A. *The doors of perception and heaven and hell.* Harmondsworth: Penguin, 1959.

107. *Indian Hemp Drugs Commission Report.* Simla, India: Government Central Printing Office, 1894. 7 vols.

108. Isbell, H., Fraser, H. F., Wikler, A., Belleville, R. E., & Eisenman, A. J. An experimental study of the etiology of 'rum fits' and delirium tremens. *Quart. J. Stud. Alcoh.*, 1955, *16*, 1–.

109. Isbell, H., Gorodetzsky, C. W., Jasinski, D., Claussen, U., Spulak, F. V., & Korte, K. Effects (–)-delta-9- of trans-tetrahydrocannabinol in Man. *Psychopharmacologia*, 1967, *11*, 184–8.

110. Jaffe, J. H. Narcotic analgesics. In L. S. Goodman & A. Gilman, *The pharmacological basis of therapeutics.* (3rd ed.) New York: MacMillan, 1965. (a)

111. Jaffe, J. H. Drug addiction and drug abuse. In L. S. Goodman and A. Gilman, *The pharmacological basis of therapeutics.* (3rd ed.) New York: MacMillan, 1965. (b)

112. Jellinek, E. M. *The disease concept of alcoholism.* New Haven: Hillhouse Press, 1960.

113. Jellinek, E. M. The symbolism of drinking: A culture-historical approach. Toronto: Addiction Research Foundation of Ontario, Substudy 3-2 & Y-65.

114. Jellinek, E. M., & McFarland, R. A. Analysis of psychological experiments on the effects of alcohol. *Quart. J. Stud. Alcoh.*, 1940, *1*, 272–371.

115. Johnson, R. D. Medico-social aspects of marijuana. *Rhode Island Med. J.*, 1968, *51*, 171–8.

116. Jones, R. T. & Stone, G. C. Psychological studies of marijuana and alcohol in man. Paper presented at the 125th annual meeting of the American Psychiatric Association, Bal Harbour, Florida, May 1969.

117. Joyce, C. R. B. (Ed.) *Psychopharmacology:* Dimensions and perspective. London: Tavistock Publications, 1968.

118. Kalant, H. Marihuana and simulated driving. *Science*, 1969, *166*, 640.

119. Kalant, O. J. *The amphetamines: Toxicity and addiction:* Brookside Monograph No. 5. Toronto: University of Toronto Press, 1966.

120. Kalant, O. J. *An interim guide to the cannabis (marihuana) literature.* Addiction Research Foundation Bibl. Series No. 2, 1968.

121. Kaplan, J. (Ed.) *Marijuana. Report of the Indian Hemp Drugs Commission 1893–1894.* Silver Spring, Maryland: Jefferson, 1969.

122. Kato, T., & Jarvik, L. F. LSD and genetic damage. *Dis. Nerv. Syst.*, 1969, *30*, 43–6.

123. Keeler, M. H. Adverse reactions to marihuana. *Amer. J. Psychiat.*, 1967, *124*, 128–31.

124. Kramer, J. C., Fischman, V. S., & Littlefield, D. C. Amphetamine abuse: Pattern and effects of high doses taken intravenously. *J.A.M.A.*, 1967, *201*, 89–93.

125. Kupperstein, L. R., & Susman, R. M. Bibliography on the inhalation of glue fumes and other toxic vapours – a substance abuse practice among adolescents. *Int. J. Addict.*, 1968, *3*, 177–97.

126. Lasagna, L., von Felsinger, J. M., & Beecher, H. K. Drug-induced mood changes in man. I: Observations on healthy subjects, chronically ill patients, and 'postaddicts'. *J.A.M.A.*, 1955, *157*, 1006–1020.

127. Laurie, P. *Drugs: Medical, psychological and social facts.* Harmondsworth: Penguin, 1967.

128. Leary, T., Metzner, R., & Alpert, R. *The psychedelic experience.* New Hyde Park, N.Y.: University Books, 1964.

129. Leary, T., Metzner, R., Presnell, M., Weil, G., Schwitzgebel, R., Kinne, S. A change program for adult offenders using psilocybin. *Psychotherapy*, 1965, *2*. See also Leary, T., & Clark, W. H. Religious implications of consciousness-expanding drugs. *Relig. Ed.*, 1963, *1*, 251–6.

130. Lehmann, H. E. Phenomenology and pathology of addiction. *Compreh. Psychiat.*, 1963, *4*, 168–80.

131. Lehmann, H. E., & Ban, T. A. Pharmacotherapy of tension and anxiety. In press, 1970.

132. Levine, J. & Ludwig, A. The LSD controversy. *Compreh. Psychiat.*, 1964, *5*, 314–21.

133. Levy, B., & Ahlquist, R. P. Adrenergic drugs. In J. R. DiPalma (Ed.), *Drill's pharmacology in medicine.* (3rd ed.) New York: McGraw-Hill, 1965.

134. Lewis, A. Cannabis. Appendix 1. In Advisory Committee on Drug Dependence, *Cannabis.* London: Her Majesty's Stationery Office, 1968.

135. Lindesmith, A. R. *The addict and the law.* New York: Random House, 1965.

136. Litt, I. F., & Cohen, M. I. Danger ... vapor harmful: Spot-remover sniffing. *New Eng. J. Med.*, 1969, *281*, 543–4.

137. Louria, D. B. *The drug scene*. New York: McGraw-Hill, 1958.

138. Ludwig, A. M., & Levine, J. The clinical effects of psychedelic agents. *Clin. Med.*, 1966, *73*, 22–.

139. Lynch, V. D. Marihuana Research – a perspective. Paper presented at the Tenth Annual Conference, International Narcotic Enforcement Officers' Association, Philadelphia, Sept. 18, 1969.

140. Malcolm, A. I. *On solvent sniffing*. Toronto: Addiction Research Foundation of Ontario, 1969.

141. Manheimer, D. I., & Mellinger, G. D. Marijuana use among urban adults. *Science*, 1969, *166*, 1544–5.

142. Margolis, J. S., & Clorfene, R. *A child's garden of grass*. North Hollywood: Contact Books, 1969.

143. Marshman, J. A further note on the composition of illicit drugs. 1970. Unpublished paper.

144. Marshman, J. A., & Gibbins, R. J. The credibility gap in the illicit drug market. *Addictions*, 1969, *16* (1), 22–5.

145. Martin, W. R., & Jasinski, D. R. Physiological parameters of morphine dependence in man: Tolerance, early abstinence, protracted abstinence. *J. Psychiat. Res.*, 1969, 7, 9–17.

146. Masserman, J. H., and Yum, K. S. An analysis of the influence of alcohol on experimental neurosis in cats. *Psychosom. Med.*, 1946, *8*, 36–52.

147. Masters, R. E. L., & Houston, J. *The varieties of psychedelic experience*. New York: Dell, 1966.

148. Maynert, E. W. Sedatives and hypnotics II. Barbiturates. In J. R. DiPalma (Ed.), *Drill's pharmacology in medicine*. (3rd ed.) New York: McGraw-Hill, 1965.

149. Mayor's Committee on Marihuana. *The marihuana problem in the City of New York: Sociological, medical, psychological and pharmacological studies*. Lancaster, Penn.: Jacques Cattell Press, 1944. ('The La Guardia Report').

150. McGlothlin, W. H. Toward a rational view of marihuana. In J. L. Simmons (Ed.), *Marihuana: Myths and realities*. North Hollywood: Brandon House, 1967.

151. McGlothlin, W. H., Cohen, S., & McGlothlin, M. S. Long lasting effects of LSD on normals. *Arch. Gen. Psychiat.*, 1967, *17*, 521–32.

152. McGlothlin, W. H., Arnold, D. O., & Freedman, D. X. Organacity measures following repeated LSD ingestion. *Arch. Gen. Psychiat.*, 1969, *21*, 704–9.

153. McGlothlin, W. H., Arnold, D. O., & Rowan, P. K. Marijuana use among adults. Psychiatry, 1970, in press.

154. McGlothlin, W. H., & West, L. J. The marihuana problem: An overview. *Amer. J. Psychiat.*, 1968, *125*, 370–78.

155. Mechoulam, R., & Gaoni, Y. Recent advances in the chemistry of hashish. *Fortschr. Chem. Organ. Naturst.*, 1967, *25*, 175–213.

156. Mendelson, J. H. Experimentally induced chronic intoxication and withdrawal in alcoholics. *Quart J. Stud. Alcoh.*, 1964, *25*, suppl. No. 2.

157. Meyer, R. E. *Adverse reactions to hallucinogenic drugs with background papers.* Washington: U.S. Public Health Services Publication No. 1810, 1969.

158. Mikuriya, T. H. Physical, mental, and moral effects of marijuana: The Indian Hemp Drugs Commission Report. *Int. J. Addict.*, 1968, *3*, 253–70.

159. Mikuriya, T. H. Marijuana in medicine: Past, present and future. *Calif. Med.*, *1969*, *110*, 34–40.

160. Miller, D. E. Narcotic drug and marihuana controls. Paper presented at National Association of Student Personnel Administrators Drug Education Conference, Washington, D.C., Nov 7-8, 1966.

161. Miller, R. D. Some principles of psychopharmacology: Implications for the social control of drug abuse. Paper presented at the Sir George Williams Symposium on Drug Abuse, Montreal, February, 1969.

162. Milman, D. H. The role of marihuana in patterns of drug abuse by adolescents. *J. Pediat.*, 1969, *74*, 283–90.

163. Miras, C. J. Experience with chronic hashish smokers. In J. R. Wittenborg (Ed.) *Drugs and youth.* Springfield, Ill.: Charles C. Thomas, 1969.

164. Modell, W. Mass drug catastrophes and the roles of science and technology. *Science*, 1967, *156*, 346–51.

165. Moore, L. A., Jr. *Marijuana (Cannabis) bibliography, 1960–1968.* Los Angeles, Cal.: Bruin Humanist Forum, 1969.

166. Murphy, H. B. M. The cannabis habit: A review of recent psychiatric literature. *Bull. Narc.*, 1963, *15*, 15–23.

167. Murray, N. Covert effects of chlordiazepoxide therapy. *J. Neuropsychiat.*, 1962, *3*, 168–70.

168. Nagle, D. R. Anesthetic addiction and drunkenness: A contemporary and historical survey. *Int. J. Addict.*, 1968, *3*, 25–39.

169. Narcotic Addiction Foundation of B.C. *Glue sniffing.* Vancouver: N.A.F. of B.C., 1968.

170a. Narcotic Addiction Foundation of B.C. Brief submitted to the Commission of Inquiry into the Non-Medical Use of Drugs, 1969.

170b. *New York Times*. January 13, p. 13 and January 19, p. 22, 1968.

171. Nowlis, H. H. Communicating about drugs. Paper presented at National Association of Student Personnel Administrators Drug Education Conference, Washington, D.C. Nov. 7–8, 1966.

172. Nowlis, H. H. *Drugs on the college campus*. Garden City, N.Y.: Doubleday, 1969.

173. Oki, G. Personal communication. 1970.

174. Osmond, H. A review of the clinical effects of psychotomimetic agents. *Ann. N.Y. Acad. Sci.*, 1957, March 14. Reprinted in D. Solomon (ed.) *op. cit.*, 1964.

175. Pahnke, W. N. Drugs and mysticism: An analysis of the relationship between psychedelic drugs and the mystical consciousness (Doctoral dissertation, Harvard University) Cambridge, Massachusetts, 1963. Also discussed in W. Pahnke, & W. Richards, *op. cit.* 1966.

176. Pahnke. W. N. The mystical and/or religious element in the psychedelic experience. Paper presented to the third annual conference of the R. M. Bucke Memorial Society for the Study of Religious Experience, Oct. 13–15, 1967.

177. Pahnke, W. N., & Richards, W. A. Implications of LSD and experimental mysticism. *J. Relig. Health*, 1966, *5*, 175–208.

178. Parry, H. J. Use of psychotropic drugs by U.S. adults. *Pub. Health Rep.*, 1968, *83*, 799–810.

179. Perna, D. Psychotogenic effect of marihuana. *J.A.M.A.*, 1969, *209*, 1085–86.

180. Peterson, E. Psychopharmacology. In J. A. Vernon (ed.), *Introduction to psychology: A self-selection textbook*. Iowa: Brown Co., 1966.

181. Playboy Panel: The drug revolution. *Playboy*, 1970, *17* (2), 53–.

182. Popham, R. E. (Ed.) *Alcohol and alcoholism*. Toronto: University of Toronto Press, 1970.

183. Popham, R. E. & Schmidt, W. The prevention of alcohol problems: Ecological studies of the effects of government control measures. Addiction Research Foundation of Ontario, Toronto. Mimeo, n.d.

184. Rawlin, J. Street level abuse of amphetamines. In J. Russo (Ed.), *Amphetamine abuse*. Springfield, Illinois: Charles C. Thomas, 1968.

185. Richards, L. G., Joffe, M. H., Smith, J. P., & Spratto, G. R. *LSD–25: A factual account.* Washington, D.C.: U.S. Department of Justice, Bureau of Narcotics and Dangerous Drugs, 1969.

186. Ritchie, J. M., The aliphatic alcohols. In L. S. Goodman & A. Gilman, *The pharmacological basis of therapeutics.* (3rd ed.) New York: MacMillan, 1965.

187. Robins, L. N., Darvish, H. S., & Murphy, G. E. The long-term outcome for adolescent drug users. A follow-up study of 76 users and 146 non-users. Paper presented at the American Psycho-pathological Association's Symposium, 'Psychopathology of Adolescence', New York City, February, 1969.

188. Roffman, R. A., & Sapol, E. Marijuana in Vietnam: A survey of use among army enlisted men in the two southern corps. *Technical Report for the Surgeon-General. Department of the Army,* 1969.

189. Rosenthal, S. H. Persistent hallucinosis following repeated administration of hallucogenic drugs. *Amer. J. Psychiat.,* 1964, *121,* 238–44.

190. Rosser, W. W. A survey of barbiturate tranquillizer and amphetamine usage. *Canad. Fam. Physic.,* 1969, *15* (7), 39–41.

191. Rowell, E. A., & Rowell, R. *On the trail of marihuana, the weed of madness.* Mountain View, California: Pacific Press, 1939. Quoted in A. R. Lindesmith *op. cit.*

192. Rutman, L. (Ed.), *Drugs: Use and abuse.* Winnipeg: University of Winnipeg Press, 1969.

193. Savage, C., & Stolaroff, M. J. Clarifying the confusion regarding LSD-25. *J. Nerv. Ment. Dis.,* 1965, *140,* 218–21.

194. Schwarz, C. J. LSD, marihuana and the law. *B. C. Med J.,* 1967, *9,* 274–85.

195. Schwarz, C. J. The complications of LSD: A review of the literature. Paper read at the annual meeting of the North Pacific Society of Psychiatry and Neurology, Vancouver, B.C., April 6–8, 1967.

196. Schwarz, C. J. Towards a medical understanding of marihuana. Paper read at the Western Regional Meeting of the Canadian Psychiatric Association, Vancouver, B.C., January 23, 1969.

197. Seneca. Epistle LXXXIII, On drunkenness. *Quart. J. Stud. Alcoh.,* 1942, *3,* 320–27.

198. Sharpless, S. K. Hypnotics and sedatives. In L. S. Goodman & A. Gilman, *The pharmacological basis of therapeutics.* (3rd ed.) New York: MacMillan, 1965.

199. Shulgin, O. T. Recent developments in cannabis chemistry. *J. Psychedel. Drugs,* 1968, *2,* 15–29.

200. Siegler, M., & Osmond, H. Models of drug addiction. *Int. J. Addict.*, 1968, *3*, 3–24.

201. Siler, J. F., Sheep, W. L., Bates, L. B., Clark, G. F., Cook, G. W., & Smith W. A. Marijuana smoking in Panama. *Mil. Surg.*, 1933, *73*, 269–80.

202. Simmons, J. L. (Ed.) *Marihuana: Myths and realities.* North Hollywood, Cal.: Brandon House, 1967.

203. Smart, R. G. LSD: Problems and promise. *Can. Ment. Health*, 1968, *16*, Suppl. No. 57.

204. Smart, R. G., and Bateman, K. Unfavorable reactions to LSD. *Canad. Med. Ass. J.*, 1967, *97*, 1214–.

205. Smart, R. G., Storm, T., Baker, E. F. W., & Solursh, L. *Lysergic acid diethylamide (LSD) in the treatment of alcoholism.* Toronto: University of Toronto Press, 1967.

206. Smith, D. E. Acute and chronic toxicity of marijuana. *J. Psychedelic Drugs*, 1968, *2*, 37–47.

207. Smith, D. E. Physical vs. psychological dependence and tolerance in high-dose methamphetamine abuse. *Clin. Toxicol.*, 1969, *2*, 99–103.

208. Smith, H. Do drugs have religious import? *J. Phil.*, 1964, *61* (18). Reprinted in D. Soloman (Ed.), *op. cit.*, 1964.

209. Smith, Kline & French Laboratories. *Drug abuse: Escape to nowhere.* Philadelphia: 1967.

210. Solomon, D. (Ed.) *LSD: The consciousness-expanding drug.* New York: G. P. Putman, 1964.

211. Solomon, D. (Ed.) *The marihuana papers.* New York: New American Library, 1966.

212. Solursh, L. P., & Solursh, M. J. *Illusinogenic drugs: Their effects on criminal responsibility.* Toronto: Canadian Mental Health Association, 1969.

213. Solursh, L. P. Some medical observations on the use and abuse of illusinogenic drugs. In L. Rutman (Ed.), *Proceedings of University of Winnipeg Conference.* Winnipeg: University of Winnipeg, 1969.

214. Stafford, P. G., & Golightly, B. H. *LSD: The problem-solving psychedelic.* New York: Universal Publishing, 1967.

215. Stevenson, G. H. *Drug addiction in British Columbia.* Vancouver: University of British Columbia, 1956.

216. Stewart, C.P., & Stolman A. (Eds.) *Toxicology: Mechanisms and analytical methods.* Vol. 1. *The Toxocologist and his work.* New York: Academic Press, 1960.

217. Suchman, E. A. The 'Hang-Loose' ethic and the spirit of drug use. *J. Health Soc. Behav.*, 1968, *9*, 146–55.

218. Talbott, J. A., & Teague, J. W. Marihuana psychosis. *J.A.M.A.*, 1969, *210*, 299–302.

219. Tart, C. T. Marijuana intoxication: Common experimental effects. Paper presented at a meeting of the Faculty of the Langley-Porter Neuropsychiatric Institute, San Francisco, California, January, 1970.

220. Task Force report: *Narcotics and drug abuse. Annotations and consultants, papers.* The President's Commission on Law Enforcement and Administration of Justice. Washington, D.C.: U.S. Government Printing Office, 1967.

221. Task Force report: *Narcotics, marijuana and dangerous drugs. Findings and recommendations.* Special Presidential task force. Washington, D.C.: U.S. Government Printing Office, 1969.

222. Taylor, G. C. An analysis of the problems presented in the use of LSD. *Bull. Narc.*, 1967, *19*, 7–13.

223. Taylor, N. *Narcotics: Nature's dangerous gifts.* (Rev. Ed.) New York: Dell, 1966.

224. Thompson, T., & Schuster, C. R. *Behavioral pharmacology.* Englewood Cliffs, N.J.: Prentice-Hall, 1968.

225. Tijo, J. H., Pahnke, W. N., & Kirland, A. A. LSD and chromosomes. *J.A.M.A.*, 1969, *210*, 849–56.

226. UCLA Interdepartmental Conference. Drug dependency: Investigations of stimulants and depressants. Moderator: Anthony Kales. *Ann. Intern. Med.*, 1969, *70*, 591–614.

227. Uhr, L. (Ed.) *Drugs and behaviour.* New York: Wiley, 1960.

228. Unger, S. M. Mescaline, LSD, Psilocybin, and personality change. *Psychiatry: Journal for the study of Interpersonal Processes*, 1963, *26* (2). Also reprinted in D. Solomon, *op. cit.*, 1964.

229. Ungerleider, J. T., Fisher, D., & Fuller, M. The dangers of LSD: Analysis of seven months' experience in a university hospital's psychiatric service. *J.A.M.A.*, 1966, *197*, 389–92.

230. Ungerleider, J. T., Fisher, D. D., Goldsmith, S. R., Fuller M., & Forgy, E. A statistical survey of adverse reactions to LSD in Los Angeles county. *Amer. J. Psychiat.*, 1968, *125*, 352–7.

231. Unsigned. Cannabis – yet another teratogen. *Brit. Med. J.*, 1969, *I*, 797–.

232. Unwin, J. R. Illicit drug use among Canadian youth. *Canad. Med. Ass. J.*, 1968, *98*, 402–407, 449–54.

233. Unwin, J. R. Non-medical use of drugs with particular reference to youth. *Canad. Med. Ass. J.*, 1969, *101*, 72–88.

234. Victor, M., & Adams, R. D. The effect of alcohol on the nervous system. *Res. Publ. Ass. Nerv. Ment. Dis.*, 1953, *32*, 526–73.

235. Waller, C. W. *The national marihuana program. First annual report.* Bethesda, Maryland: U.S. National Institute of Mental Health, 1969.

236. Walton, R. P. *Marihuana: America's new drug problem.* Philadelphia: Lippincott, 1938.

237. Wasson, R. G. Fly Agaric and man. In D. H. Efron (Ed.), *Ethnopharmacologic search for psychoactive drugs – 1967.* Washington, D.C.: U.S. Government Printing Office, 1967.

238. Weil, A. T. Cannabis, *Science J.*, 1969, *5A*, 36–42.

239. Weil, A. T., & Zinberg, N. E. Acute effects of marihuana on speech. *Nature*, 1969, *222* (3 May), 434–7.

240. Weil, A. T., Zinberg, N. E. & Nelsen, J. M. Clinical and psychological effects of marihuana in man. *Science*, 1968, *162*, 1234–42.

241. Whitaker, R. *Drugs and the law.* Toronto: Methuen, 1969.

242. White House Conference on Narcotic and Drug Abuse. *Proceedings.* Washington, D.C. Sept. 27–28, 1962, 270–90.

243. Wikler, A. Relationship between clinical effects of barbiturates and their neurophysiological mechanisms of action. *Fed. Proc.*, 1952, *11*, 647–52.

244. Wikler, A. *The relation of psychiatry to pharmacology.* Baltimore: Williams & Wilkins, 1957.

245. Williams, E. G., Himmelsbach, C. K., Wikler, A., Ruble, D. C., & Lloyd, B. J. Studies on marihuana and pyrahexyl compound. *Pub. Health Rep.*, 1946, *61*, 1059–85.

246. Williams, H. R. Treatment of the narcotic addict with some observations on other drug dependencies. *B.C. Med. J.*, 1969, *11*, 11–13.

247. Wolfe, T. *The electric kool-aid acid test.* New York: Farrar, Straus & Giroux, 1968.

248. Wolff, P. O. *Marihuana in Latin America: The threat that it constitutes.* Washington, D.C.: Linacre Press, 1949.

249. Wolstenholme, G. E. W., & Knight, J. (Eds.) *Hashish: Its chemistry and pharmacology.* Boston: Little, Brown & Co., 1965.

250. Yolles, S. F. Statement for the National Institute of Mental Health, before the Subcommittee on Public Health and Welfare of the Interstate and Foreign Commerce Committee on House Rule 11701 & House Rule 13743. February, 1970.

251. Zinberg, N. E. , & Weil, A. T. The effects of marijuana on human beings. *The New York Times Magazine*, May 11, 1969.

252. Zunin, L. M. Marijuana: The drug and the problem. *Milit. Med.*, 1969, *134*, 104–110.

CHAPTER THREE

THE EXTENT AND PATTERNS OF
NON-MEDICAL DRUG USE IN CANADA

INTRODUCTION

267. From the outset of its inquiry, the Commission has been concerned with the *extent* of non-medical drug use, and with the channels through which the drugs are distributed. While there has been much speculation and perhaps myth-making about both these matters, it is unfortunate that there is relatively little reliable information about either. The problems of gathering accurate information are formidable. However, the Commission hopes to be able to report in greater detail in its final submission.

There does not seem to have been any consistent pattern to the general statements made to the Commission so far on the extent of drug use. We have heard estimates that would appear either grossly to over-estimate or to under-estimate such use. In general, it seems that drug users tend to exaggerate their own numbers (and there is some research evidence supporting this observation). Some low estimates by adults perhaps reflect an unwillingness to face up to a very real situation – a hope that if a problem is minimized it will go away.

The phenomenon of non-medical drug use is certainly not new in Canada. However, during the past decade, there appears to have been a rather sudden change in the drugs in use, particularly by younger people, but this trend is by no means confined to those under 25.

We have a good deal of information about certain aspects of non-medical drug use. Much excellent research has been carried out into the use of alcohol and tobacco. A reasonable amount of knowledge is available about the extent and patterns of the illicit use of heroin and other opiate narcotics. But we know relatively little about the use of such drugs as LSD and cannabis, especially their use by adults, although there are indications that the extent of their use has increased during the past two or three years, perhaps sharply. We have little precise information about the non-medical use of prescription drugs such as the tranquillizers and amphetamines.

268. At this point we should review the sources of epidemiological information available to the Commission.

Prescription records kept by the Food and Drug Directorate of the Department of National Health and Welfare are of relatively little value in estimating the extent of *non-medical* use of prescribed drugs. Dispensing records kept by physicians, pharmacists and hospitals do not tell us the extent to which drugs may be used for non-medical purposes.

Some inferences can be drawn from other government records, such as statistics showing the volume of manufacture, importation and distribution of certain drugs. These reports would indicate that the available supplies of drugs such as the amphetamines and barbiturates far exceed the most liberal estimates of our proper medical needs. These drugs and the minor tranquillizers are legitimately available only on prescription and there is reason to believe large amounts of them pass from legitimate manufacture to illicit distribution. However, the amount manufactured and imported is so great as to suggest questionable prescribing judgement by some physicians. The Canadian Medical Association recognized this possibility in their brief to the Commission.

269. Government records show that in 1968 Canadians bought almost three billion aspirin tablets.[1] Some 55,600,000 standard doses of amphetamines, and some 556 million standard doses of barbiturates[2] were also produced or imported for consumption in Canada. A study by the Addiction Research Foundation in 1966[3] found evidence indicating that on an average day 7 per cent of the Toronto population over 15 years of age would be using, on prescription, a mood-modifying drug. This study estimates that 24 per cent of all prescriptions written in Toronto were for drugs of this type; 44 per cent of these were for sedative and hypnotic drugs; 40 per cent were anti-depressants and major and minor tranquillizers. It is also reported that '... more than 35 per cent of all mood-modifying

184

prescriptions were dispensed in quantities calculated to last more than four weeks'.

270. Police files provide a record of the number of arrests made in connection with drug offences but they are of limited value for purposes of establishing the true extent of illegal drug use or for estimating trends in such use. Changes in the number of arrests over a period of time may reflect changes in the extent of illegal use. However, they may also reflect changes in enforcement policy, changes in police efficiency, changes in the resources available to the police such as the number of officers assigned to drug squads, or changes in the visibility of drug use. Police statistics provide virtually no information about the extent to which drugs available for medical purposes are also used non-medically. Thus they tell us little about the use of barbiturates, amphetamines or tranquillizers.

At the request of the Commission, the R.C.M. Police presented estimates of the numbers of users of cannabis and LSD. The Force provided us with arrest statistics, figures on the number of known users, whether or not arrests had been made, and estimates of the probable total number of users. The first two of these statistics are no doubt accurate, but as pointed out above, they are of limited value in estimating total use.

The third statistic, the estimate of total number of users, seems to the Commission to be highly conservative and should be interpreted in the context of estimates available from other sources. This statement should not be interpreted as criticism of the R.C.M. Police. Any police force would be handicapped in making accurate estimates of this type and the Commission and the Force were aware of this fact when the estimates were requested.

271. However, the Commission believes that police records may be valuable at this time in estimating the number of persons dependent on heroin, since these users are limited in number, concentrated in certain areas, generally rather visible and are kept under police surveillance for extended periods of time. But if certain emerging patterns of heroin use in the United States appear in Canada, police surveillance will become

far more difficult and consequently their estimates less accurate.

272. Scientific survey data on drug use will be needed before accurate estimates can be made. While a number of surveys have been carried out in Canada in recent years, they have focused on particular populations – usually students and other young people. This particular attention to youth no doubt reflects the general concern for youth in our present society. It was probably also due to the fact that the young are usually more willing to discuss or report their drug experiences than their elders.

There are further limitations on the value of existing survey data. The studies that the Commission have examined have varied widely in quality of research design, adequacy of the samples and in the sophistication and the rigour with which the data have been analysed. In the time available since it was appointed, the Commission has not been able to carry out the survey research which it believes necessary. Consequently, in preparing this chapter we are reporting on information based on a study of surveys carried out during the past two years.

273. However, the Commission has initiated an extensive programme of survey research aimed at determining, as accurately as possible, the extent and patterns of drug use in Canada in 1970.* Studies will be directed at the Canadian people at large, students in Canadian universities and colleges, and Canadian high school students. The result of these studies will be made available at a later date.

274. Properly constructed surveys are the most accurate method of making estimates of drug use. A survey is particularly appropriate to describe social facts which include both overt behaviour and attitudes. While much human behaviour is subject to various forms of investigation, only self-reporting by a representative sample of a population will yield information to describe sets of attitudes and experiences that combine to

* This project is supervised by Dr C. M. Lanphier and Dr Sondra B. Phillips of the Institute for Behavioural Research, Survey Research Centre, York University, Toronto.

determine differences in behaviour within that population. A survey is basically a descriptive tool which will provide a profile on a given question representative of a population from which the sample is drawn. Whatever estimates are drawn from such a survey will carry with them a statement of the probable error of the estimate. The research being carried out by the Commission will be based on highly rigorous sampling methods.

Data upon which to make estimates of drug use have been available to the Commission from sources other than those noted above. Both in public and private hearings we have had the benefit of the estimates of highly trained and sensitive observers of the drug scene such as psychiatrists, psychologists, sociologists and social workers. Some valuable information has also been provided by persons involved in the manufacture and distribution of illicit drugs and by users of these drugs. The Commission is grateful to the many Canadians as well as the institutions such as the Addiction Research Foundation of Ontario who have made their epidemiological data available.

275. With reference to the matter of illicit drug distribution, one of the most confusing areas involves the *market value* of certain drugs. Particularly with respect to psychedelic substances such as cannabis and LSD, the mass media, basing their reports mainly on police and Crown prosecution estimates, tend to present highly exaggerated evaluations of drug seizures – a practice that serves to glamorize an illegal enterprise for some youths, and further reduces, among experienced drug purchasers, the already strained credibility of those who make such gross overestimates.

Basic to any understanding of the illicit drug market is the realization that there are many levels of distribution and that there are price mark-ups and additional expenses at every level. The exact value of any illegal drug, then, depends on the level of distribution with which one is concerned. In fact, a drug's market value at any distribution level is simply its replacement cost to the individual possessing that drug.

Just as in the world of legal commerce, illicit drugs have a varying value depending on whether one is speaking of their production, wholesale, middleman or retail cost. One pound of marijuana, for example, is worth $10 in Mexico, and about $50 in parts of California, and $100 by the time it reaches distributors in Canada. If this same pound of marijuana is divided into ounces, these ounces (or 'lids') are likely worth $10 in California, $15 apiece in New York, and $20 to $25 to their owner in Canada. Further subdivisions into 'nickel' ($5) or 'dime' ($10) lots (generally called 'bags') are worth exactly that – and no more. It has been customary for the police to evaluate large marijuana seizures in terms of the number of nickel or dime bags (or even single marijuana cigarettes – or 'joints') that can be drawn from them. But this inflationary practice contradicts the reality of a market in which there are many distribution levels and in which dealers almost always sell to the next level down (e.g., someone possessing large quantities of marijuana is likely to sell it by the 'brick' – a kilo weighing approximately 2.2 pounds – or by the pound; not by the ounce or smaller quantities). The most accurate means of determining the value of a certain quantity of drugs is to find its purchase price (for the individual acquiring the drugs), not its selling or, worse still, estimated eventual selling price. The value of any drug depends on its location in the distribution network that extends from producer to consumer.

ALCOHOL

276. Although alcohol use dates back to the earliest recorded history of the human race, it has lost little of its appeal as a drug of choice for non-medical purposes. It is estimated that 80 per cent of Canadians over the age of 15 use alcohol. There are no indications that the popularity of alcohol is slipping. In 1967, the per capita consumption of alcohol in the Canadian population 15 years of age and older was 1.83 imperial gallons.[4] That is an increase of almost 25 per cent over the per capita consumption in the same population in 1951 – this, despite an average price increase of 55 per cent.[5]

Along with tobacco, alcohol remains the most popular and widely-used of the legitimately manufactured drugs. While it is probably most often taken to alter mood, it is also used, unlike the tranquillizers and amphetamines, for other reasons. Its use

Chart 1

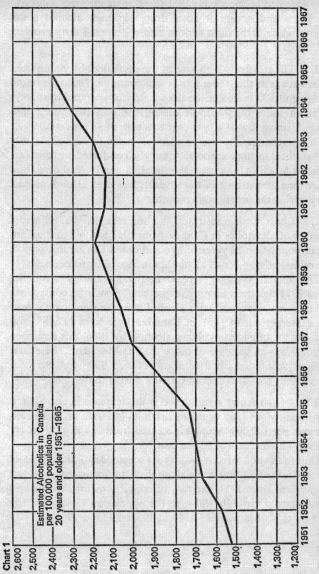

Estimated Alcoholics in Canada
per 100,000 population
20 years and older 1951–1965

Data supplied by Addiction Research Foundation Toronto.

is so accepted in our society that few Canadians seem willing to recognize and accept it as a drug, although alcohol abuse clearly presents the most serious and widespread drug problem in Canada.

277. The relatively high rate of use of alcohol by young Canadians suggests that these trends will continue. The table found in Appendix D indicates the use of alcohol as found in surveys taken in some high schools during the past two years. Use ranged from a low of 40 per cent to a high of 88 per cent.

In universities, the use of alcohol seems to be significantly higher than in high schools. A survey conducted in four faculties at McGill University, Montreal, late in 1969, showed that more than 80 per cent of the students had used alcohol at least once during the previous six months.

278. Chart I demonstrates the increase in the estimated number of alcoholics in Canada from 1951 to 1965 in the Canadian population 20 years of age and older. During this period, the estimated number of alcoholics increased by 63 per cent.

The annual average increase in the number of alcoholics since 1951 has been about five per cent. Similarly, convictions for offences associated with alcohol use rose significantly over the same period. In 1951 in Canada, there were 117,685 convictions for offences involving alcohol; by 1966, this had risen to 302,278 – an increase of more than 150 per cent. These convictions accounted for a total of between 6.3% and 8.5% of convictions for all crimes in Canada during those years.[6]

279. Of particular significance is the increase in convictions for impaired and/or drunken driving. The rate of these convictions per 100,000 vehicles increased from 234 in 1951 to 448 in 1966 – an increase of 92 per cent.[7]

One indication of our society's acceptance of the abuse of alcohol is the fact that while alcoholism has increased by almost 60 per cent since 1951, the rate of convictions for drunkenness has remained virtually stable in the population 15 years of age and older in that period (1,149 in 1951; 1,155 in 1966).[8]

280. The barbiturates and tranquillizers have been in relatively heavy use in Canada since the early fifties. As with the stimulants, development of therapeutic uses for some sedatives was a by-product of wartime research, although in the case of the barbiturates, there are records of use dating back to the early years of this century. Tranquillizers, however, have been in use only in the past 20 years. At the same time, pharmaceutical manufacturers have lost little time in entering the growing market for these drugs. In North America since 1950, more than 12,000 patents have been issued for tranquillizer-barbiturate-stimulant preparations.

According to R.C.M. Police testimony before the Commission, there was no evidence of the illicit manufacture or importation of barbiturates. Likewise, no such evidence exists with respect to tranquillizers. However, because the pattern of use of each of these drugs differs considerably, they will be considered separately.

The Barbiturates

281. There is more accurate and complete information on the volume of barbiturates available in Canada than there is on the tranquillizers. The following table[9] shows the number of standard unit doses of various classes of barbiturates imported in each year from 1964 to 1968:

Year	Barbiturates* Short-acting	Barbiturates Medium-acting	Barbiturates Long-acting
1964............	68,440,000	125,683,333	342,666,666
1965............	122,050,000	160,750,000	432,766,666
1966............	87,590,000	147,350,000	346,733,333
1967............	95,720,000	166,950,000	338,366,666
1968............	88,790,000	145,400,000	322,433,333

* Short-Acting Barbiturates – 100 mg. (Standard Unit Dose.)
Medium-Acting Barbiturates – 60 mg. (Standard Unit Dose.)
Long-Acting Barbiturates – 30 mg. (Standard Unit Dose.)

282. These statistics deal with the importation and production of barbiturates and tell us little about the prevalence of use or abuse. The submission of the R.C.M. Police to the Commission described the abuse of barbiturates generally this way:

Barbiturates are susceptible to two types of abuse. The first is entirely of a medical nature and involves mainly exceeding the dosage prescribed. Not infrequently this results in a dependency which compels the patient to obtain additional supplies in a criminal manner by forgery, theft, or by obtaining prescriptions through more than one physician at the same time . . .

The second type of abuse relates directly to the non-medical use and is most prevalent among alcoholics, old-time criminals and addicts who can no longer support a steady opiate habit. Prior to 1961, it was not uncommon for heroin addicts to be in possession of barbiturates.

These drugs were then readily available from legitimate outlets through the medical profession. Since the enactment of Part III of the Food and Drugs Act, particularly the regulations controlling legal outlets, this problem has been very greatly alleviated. Controlled drugs are still encountered by police in the hands of what would be unauthorized persons if legislation existed. Generally speaking, cases of barbiturates being found in the possession of known drug abusers are not reported, except when such possession can be related to a charge of trafficking or possession for the purpose of trafficking. For this reason, statistical evidence is not readily available.

283. Some statistical evidence does exist of the serious difficulties, both social and medical, brought about by the abuse of barbiturates. In British Columbia, 109 persons died from overdoses of barbiturates in 1967; and 158 in 1968. Metropolitan Toronto Police records show that in 1968, 57 apparent suicides and 322 attempted suicides were attributed to barbiturates. Metro Toronto Police also estimate that 30 per cent of the 2,052 drunken female prisoners encountered in 1968 used barbiturates in conjunction with alcohol.[10]

Incomplete though they may be, statistics from poison control centres across Canada also give some indication of the volume of the non-medical use of barbiturates. The following table shows the number of cases of barbiturate poisoning for the years 1961 to 1967:[11]

1961 – 197 cases	1965 – 422 cases
1962 – 325 cases	1966 – 474 cases
1963 – 463 cases	1967 – 478 cases
1964 – 437 cases	

284. Chart II indicates the trend in reported poisonings resulting from overdoses of both barbiturates and tranquillizers. It is interesting to note the apparent levelling in cases of barbituric poisoning, while tranquillizer poisonings continued to increase sharply.

High school surveys during the past two years show a use of barbiturates ranging from 1.5 per cent to 3.3 per cent (see Appendix D).

The Minor Tranquillizers

285. The minor tranquillizers are among the most widely used mood modifiers. In potency, most of these drugs rank between alcohol and the barbiturates as daytime sedatives, and Canadians and Americans spend well over $500 million annually for them. Since regulations do not require either the manufacturer or the retail pharmacist to keep records of the volume of minor tranquillizers handled, it is not possible to report on the volume of Canadian production or importation. We also lack information on the general distribution of these drugs.

But, again, it is known that the non-medical market for these minor tranquillizers is supplied, indirectly, by drug companies which manufacture or import far more barbiturates and minor tranquillizers than are required for medical puposes. How these excess amounts are then diverted to, and distributed within, the illicit market has not been adequately researched, but it appears certain that the pharmaceutical industry is well aware of their overproduction. There is no evidence that these drugs are produced illegally. It seems probable, rather, that

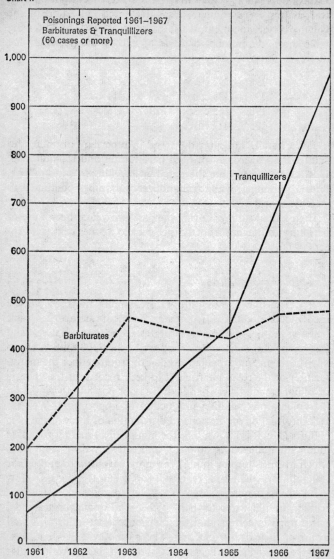

Chart II

Poisonings Reported 1961–1967
Barbiturates & Tranquillizers
(60 cases or more)

Tranquillizers

Barbiturates

many individuals procure large amounts improperly through legitimate prescription channels. They are known to be the toxic agent in a large number of poisoning cases. Poison control centres report the numbers of cases of poisoning from tranquillizers in the years 1961 to 1967 as follows:[12]

1961 – 63 cases	1965 – 445 cases
1962 – 136 cases	1966 – 709 cases
1963 – 233 cases	1967 – 973 cases
1964 – 361 cases	

286. A few surveys have been conducted in high schools in some Canadian centres, indicating a degree of use of tranquillizers among students ranging from six per cent to 27.3 per cent. It will be seen that in all high schools surveyed, use of tranquillizers by females is higher than that by males (See Appendix D).

THE AMPHETAMINES

287. The amphetamines are most commonly prescribed for appetite suppression and weight control, fatigue and the relief of mild depression and certain other special therapeutic applications. Their non-medical use has risen sharply in recent years, and witnesses appearing before the Commission expressed particular concern about the increased use of amphetamines in high dosages by the young.

Canada is not a pioneer in amphetamine use and abuse. A number of reviews have summarized the extensive use of these drugs since World War II in such countries as the United Kingdom, Germany, Japan, Ireland, Switzerland, Sweden, Australia, the United States and Yugoslavia. Indeed, the Swedish government recently responded to the abuse of amphetamines by prohibiting their possession for any purpose – medical or non-medical.

288. In Canada, the oral ingestion of amphetamines has been rising since the mid-forties. By 1964, approximately 60 million standard doses were produced for the Canadian market. This increased to more than 100 million doses in 1966 and dropped to 56 million in 1968, the last year for which statistics are pre-

sently available.[13] But these statistics refer only to the legal manufacture and importation of the drug. They tell us little about the degree of non-medical use of amphetamines and nothing about the volume produced and distributed illicitly in Canada. It has been put to the Commission, however, that the volume of legally manufactured and imported amphetamines greatly exceeds medical needs. As in the case of other drugs used widely for both medical and non-medical purposes – e.g., the barbiturates – it is believed that a significant proportion of the original supply of amphetamines probably finds its way to the user through unlawful channels. The relative frequency of illegal sales and thefts along the route between the manufacturer and the consumer is uncertain, and illegitimate distribution has been widely reported at all social levels of our society.

289. There is also evidence that some individuals make use of legitimate channels by obtaining numerous prescriptions from several physicians at the same time, or by using false identification or forged prescriptions. There has also been some carelessness in the extent to which they have been prescribed by physicians. While the tranquillizers do not appear to be manufactured illegally, there is evidence that amphetamines reach the streets from both legitimate and illegitimate manufacturing sources.

290. It is difficult to determine precisely when non-medical use of amphetamines began in Canada. In his appearance before the Commission, R.C.M. Police Assistant Commissioner Carrière testified:

Prior to 1961, the extent of the abuse of amphetamines and methamphetamines was not known. Following the enactment of Part III of the Food and Drug Act, it was found that an extensive traffic in these drugs existed among long distance truck drivers. By 1963, through the cooperation of several trucking firms, publicity and investigation, the use among drivers was virtually non-existent. With the emergence of marijuana and LSD abuse, the amphetamine drugs, particularly methamphetamine, gained considerable popularity to

196

the point where today a very active illicit traffic is in existence.

Low-dose oral amphetamine use and dependence are not uncommon in every age group. High school students swallow them for kicks, as a cheap, readily available and easily-taken drug; housewives can become habituated to the mood-elevating and energizing effect of amphetamine-type diet pills; tired professionals and executives use them; and even members of men's clubs meet to take these stimulants and strong coffee while their friends enjoy the more traditional pleasures of the afternoon cocktail.

The prevalence of stimulant use can not be determined with any degree of accuracy. Recent surveys, published in Appendix D, show that among high school students in the areas surveyed, use ranged from 3.6 per cent to 9.7 per cent. These surveys do not indicate the circumstances under which the stimulant was taken, nor the dosage.

The 'Speed' Phenomenon

291. In the last year or so there has been increasing reference to the use of 'speed' – prolonged, high-dosage use of amphetamines, usually methamphetamine, and usually by intravenous injection. It should be pointed out, however, that the use of 10 to 15 milligrams, the normal prescribed daily dosage, is not considered an aspect of the 'speed' phenomenon. Rather, this phenomenon is characterized by high levels of dosage rising to 150 to 250 milligrams daily and, in some cases, as much as a gram or more a day.

'Speed' use appears to be on the increase in Canada, particularly in some of the larger urban centres. Distributors have given private testimony with respect to the quantities of amphetamines being used in certain areas.

The young people who have appeared before the Commission have stated that most 'speed freaks' are in their teens or very early twenties. This parallels the findings of studies in Japan which reveal that the 'speed' user is almost invariably young.[14]

292. It is known that in addition to the regular commercial

197

supplies, there exists a considerable amount of 'home-made' amphetamine on the illicit market, produced by clandestine 'speed factories'. Since these drugs are rather easy to synthesize, after even limited formal training in chemistry, and because the chemical ingredients are inexpensive, bootleg production and distribution by amateurs is therefore quite feasible.

Despite the relative ease with which some amphetamines can be produced, analyses of street samples in recent months indicate that alleged 'amphetamines' are by no means invariably free of impurities. Of 38 samples analysed by Dr J. Marshman in Toronto, 45 per cent contained traces of other drugs.[15]

The serious dangers of heavy amphetamine use have been well known to the 'hip' sub-culture for several years, as reflected in the 'Speed Kills' buttons sold at 'head shops'. Many experienced drug users have expressed their anxieties to the Commission in public and private hearings about this drug and its apparent growing use.

At many points the Commission was told that the use of amphetamines is feared by most young people and the 'speed freak' is looked down on by many of his peers.

In the ensuing year, the Commission intends to investigate further the prevalence and characteristics of this phenomenon.

LSD AND THE OTHER STRONG HALLUCINOGENS

293. LSD is by far the most frequently used of the stronger hallucinogenic drugs. It is the only one in this group which appears to be used to any significant extent in some communities. The rapid spread of its use occurred some years after the onset of the cannabis phenomenon.

The R.C.M. Police made the following comments concerning the use of LSD in their brief at the Toronto hearings:

All marijuana users are capable of using LSD; however, it is not suggested that this has yet happened. The consensus of opinion among our investigators is that the large majority of cannabis users also use, or will use, amphetamines, methamphetamines, and LSD. .... It is much more prevalent than previously conceived.

The Force reported that it first became aware of the use of LSD during 1963. At that time only the sale of LSD was prohibited, and police powers for search and seizure of this drug did not exist. The spread of LSD use was influenced to some degree by factors similar to those which contributed to the growth of cannabis use.

294. We have been told repeatedly that LSD use increased rapidly during periods when cannabis was in short supply. Drug users and non-users alike have suggested that the effectiveness of Operation Intercept in the United States in reducing the supply of marijuana available in Canada was a major cause of the increase in the demand for 'acid'. This statement has been repeated by several dealers. A number of other forces have been active in encouraging experimentation with this drug. Individuals such as Dr Timothy Leary, who regard LSD as a sacrament in a new religion, have had an impact. The popular music industry has provided a repertoire of songs that quite directly endorse its use. The psychedelic quality of much modern advertising helps to create an aura in which LSD use becomes more plausible. But as with cannabis, the personal testimony of one friend to another, along with a desire to experiment and find new drug experiences, has played a major role in increasing the use of LSD.

295. During 1968 and 1969, some surveys of the extent of LSD use were carried out in high schools and universities. For example, the Loyola College study in 1969 found that 1.6 per cent of the freshmen had taken the drug. The McGill study of the same year found a 6.0 per cent level. Research at Bishop's University showed a level of 0.7 per cent in the fall of 1968 but this level was later discovered to have jumped more than four times to 3.1 per cent by April 1, 1969, and to have increased very sharply again during that month. Surveys of high school populations during 1968 and 1969 found the level of use ranging from 0.5 per cent to 3 per cent. The findings of certain of these studies are summarized in Appendix D.

The Commission has the impression that in recent months the use of LSD has risen beyond the levels reflected in the high school surveys. The Narcotic Addiction Foundation of British Columbia reports that a survey of students in six school districts of British Columbia during 1969 indicated that 6.6 per cent had used LSD at least once in the previous six months.[16] Representatives of the Department of Justice and other federal officials have testified that they believe the prevalence of LSD use to be rising. The study of Professor Low, McAmmond and Skirrow of the University of Calgary found levels of use of LSD that may reflect more accurately the picture that could emerge in 1970:[17]

> The high incidence of LSD use (49.8 per cent) is surprising only if the wishful thinking of other investigators who have been out of touch with the youth is taken seriously. In our experience most young people do not buy the scare stories about LSD. However, their use of the drug tends to be restrained and carefully structured. It is not the sort of thing they would want to do every week-end.

We have also heard testimony to the effect that in some high schools most of the students who have used drugs at all have used LSD, although this is not supported by survey data.

296. It must again be pointed out that surveys can only determine the proportion of a population who think or believe they have taken a particular drug. The proportion who have in fact taken pure or even relatively pure LSD is very much smaller. In an analysis of samples of street drugs gathered principally in the Toronto region during 1969, it was found that less than half of those purported to be LSD did in fact contain the drug in a relatively pure form. The actual composition of 116 alleged LSD samples was found to be:[18]

Relatively pure LSD	48 per cent
Impure LSD	14 ,, ,,
Mixtures apparently resulting from unsuccessful synthesis of LSD	29 ,, ,,
No drug	7 ,, ,,
Other drug	1 ,, ,,
Not identified	1 ,, ,,
	100 per cent

297. In the early 1960s it was thought that the LSD being used non-medically came primarily, if not exclusively, from legal manufacturing sources in Europe. More recently it has come mainly from clandestine factories in the United States, but there may be a certain limited production in Canada. LSD can be very easily smuggled. In pure liquid form, enough could be brought into the country on a blotter to provide doses for some tens of thousands of individuals. A single average dose in pure crystalline form would be all but invisible to the naked eye. When in liquid form, LSD is tasteless, odourless and colourless. However, most of the LSD brought into Canada comes in the form of tablets of capsules. It has been suggested that as many as 45,000 single doses a week have been reaching the Toronto market. The structure of distribution at the local level seems to parallel that for marijuana, in that most dealers carry several drugs.

Since the production of LSD requires special chemicals, apparatus, and highly trained personnel, improperly synthesized or contaminated substances are often sold as LSD. The illegality of LSD has also led to the clandestine laboratory production of non-prescribed hallucinogens like MDA, STP (DOM) and PCP, the psychological and physiological effects of which are even less well established than those of LSD.

298. STP (the initials stand for Serenity, Tranquillity and Peace or Super-Tested Performance) appeared on the illicit market late in 1967. The drug has in fact only rarely been available in Canada.

DMT and DET (dimethyl-, and diethyltryptamine) are milder hallucinogens producing what has sometimes been called the 'businessman's trip' marked by relatively short-lived effects. These drugs are usually sniffed or smoked with some combustible material such as tobacco. Like STP, they have infrequently been reported in Canada.

There have been a few reports of the availability of psilocybin. However, none of the street samples analysed actually contained this drug.

The Commission is aware of numerous reports of mescaline availability and use. Many experienced drug users have spoken of it as their drug of preference. It is reputed to provide a very smooth 'trip'. However, pure mescaline has seldom been found in this country. Marshman in Toronto analysed 33 street samples purported to be mescaline and found that 12 per cent were impure LSD, 18 per cent were incompletely synthesized LSD, and 40 per cent were relatively pure LSD. None were mescaline.[19] The Commission was informed by the staff of the Haight-Ashbury Clinic in San Francisco that despite frequent reports of its use, they had not found mescaline present in the street samples analysed there.

MDA (methylenedioxyamphetamine) has been found fairly often in Canada since last summer. Some of it is manufactured in this country. A dealer informed the Commission that Canadian-made MDA is thought by many to be the highest quality available in North America.

Among other drugs which may produce similar effects at high dosage and that have received more than passing notice from drug users have been Asthmador (a proprietary medicine for the relief of asthma), nutmeg and Morning Glory seeds (of *Heavenly Blue* and *Pearly Gates* varieties).

When available, all but the drugs mentioned in the last paragraph seem to appear through the same distribution network as LSD and the cannabis products.

CANNABIS

299. Cannabis was included in the schedule of the *Opium and Narcotic Drug Act* in 1923 (see Chapter Five), but there was little evidence of its use in Canada until the early 1960s.

The R.C.M. Police report that in 1969 they had identified some 13,500 users of cannabis and they estimated that there were an additional 45,000 persons who had used the drug. The Commission is of the opinion that this estimate of a total of 58,500 is conservative. If only eight per cent of the students in high schools and only 25 per cent of those in colleges and universities have used the drug, then we should have a total of 215,000. This hypothetical but not unreasonable figure does not include any estimate of the number of users who are neither in high school nor university.

The R.C.M. Police report that cannabis use began to increase after 1962. In that year 20 cases connected with the drug were reported by the police. By 1968 the number had climbed to 2,331 and in 1969 there was a further increase to 4,215. In his presentation of the R.C.M. Police brief to the Commission, Assistant Commissioner Carrière stated:

Prior to 1962, isolated cases of cannabis use were encountered but generally, in connection with entertainers and visitors from the United States. Although marijuana arrests were effected sporadically in the middle 40s, its use on a more frequent basis appeared in Montreal only in 1962, in Toronto in 1963 and in Vancouver in 1965. Abuse arose concurrently with the development of the hippie sub-culture. It began in our universities and spread rapidly to high schools. Today it is most common among the 17 to 25 age group. In addition, it can be found in virtually every suburban centre, regardless of size.

300. It appears to the Commission that there has been a good deal of variation in the development of patterns of marijuana use. Thus, in some centres, the first to experiment with the drug had already used other drugs such as glue, Benzedrex inhalers or cough syrups such as Romilar*. In other places there was no prior history of non-medical drug use except for traditional adolescent drinking. It is unfortunate that there have been almost no carefully executed studies of the spread of marijuana use through particular communities.

301. Several recent surveys (See Appendix D) have reported that a significantly greater number of boys than girls are involved in the use of cannabis and other drugs. (One exception is minor tranquillizers.) Marijuana users, according to a number of studies (London, Toronto, Halifax, Montreal), are twice as likely to be male as female. Non-using males are also said to be twice as willing as non-using females to try cannabis if presented with the opportunity. The authors of one Toronto study suggest the following reasons for this distinction:[20]

Girls tend to be more passive and will usually accept norms of behaviour. Boys, on the other hand, are more aggressive and assume more freedom of behaviour.

302. Several high school studies have found that the proportion of cannabis users to non-users tends to vary according to grade level. However, there is limited agreement on the patterns involved in this variation. Some surveys have revealed that cannabis use peaks in the mid-high school grades and then declines, while others (notably Whitehead's Halifax research[21]) suggest a regular increase from grade seven to 12. Whether this mid-high school peaking process reflects a drop-out syndrome or a period of temporary youthful indiscretion, and whether the Halifax data represent a nationally ascendent or merely local trend, await further research.

While it is generally assumed that youthful cannabis users tend to have middle-class origins, it is impossible to confirm this hypothesis at the present time. The data collected in one large Toronto high school survey suggest that a significant relationship between a student's reported inclination to use drugs and his father's occupation does not exist. On the other hand, the assumption that there is a strong direct relationship between a student's socio-economic status and his use of cannabis is borne out by a recent Maritimes study. The author of this survey reports that:[22]

> There is a steady increase in the rates of marijuana and LSD use as one moves from the lower status occupational category (of a student's father) to the higher occupational categories.

Overall, the most potent factor in the rapid spread of cannabis use is probably the direct influence of one individual or another reporting first-hand the experience as interesting, pleasant and harmless. There is no doubt as well that cannabis experimentation has been encouraged by the amount of public attention paid to the drug controversy and by the increasing volume of literature praising the drug effects and minimizing its hazards. The popular music industry has played a major role in encouraging drug use in general and cannabis use in particular through the lyrics and other aspects of the records it has marketed. (It is reasonable to assert that this industry has, in fact, provided an extensive advertising campaign on behalf of drugs.)

The underground press has also quite openly advocated and encouraged drug use and provided information on the characteristics of specific drugs. The overall message was, of course, reinforced by the presence of a culture that accepts and indeed encourages the use of drugs to influence mood and provide pleasure. In some circles, marijuana seems to have had a particular appropriateness to the general mood of students and young people. In our conversations with them they have frequently contrasted marijuana and alcohol effects to describe the former as a drug of peace, a drug that reduces tendencies to aggression, while suggesting that the latter drug produces hostile, aggressive behaviour. Thus marijuana is seen as particularly appropriate to a generation that emphasizes peace and is, in many ways, anti-competitive.

303. We have been told repeatedly that many young people were initially deterred from experimenting with cannabis by reports of the dangers of drugs. However, from the personal experience of friends, many soon learned that some of these accounts were exaggerated. As a result, the credibility of much of the literature critical of the drug experience was lost, and with it much of the credibility of traditional authority figures such as teachers, parents, physicians and the police.

These are but three of the factors influencing the extent of use. Many other factors have been operative and some of these are dealt with in greater detail in Chapter Four.

304. Some data on the extent of use have been available to the Commission from a number of surveys of cannabis use in certain high schools and universities (see Appendix D).

A 1968 survey of freshmen at Loyola College in Montreal found that 15 per cent of the males and 7 per cent of the females had used the drug at least once.[23] A study at Bishop's University in Lennoxville, Quebec, found that in the fall of the 1968–9 academic year, 19.6 per cent had tried cannabis, but the proportion increased to 27.3 per cent in a second study in the spring of that year.[24] In 1969, surveys were carried out among students at McGill University and the Universities of Toronto, British Columbia and Saskatchewan (Regina Campus). At

McGill it was estimated that 34.6 per cent had used marijuana and 29.3 per cent had used hashish. The surveys at Toronto and British Columbia were limited to the Law faculties and found levels of use to be 35.9 per cent and 45 per cent respectively. At the Regina Campus, use was over 30 per cent. The Commission is presently conducting a survey of the extent of non-medical drug use in a representative sample of university students in Canada.

The results of surveys of a number of Canadian high school populations are outlined in Appendix D. It will be seen that usage estimated on the basis of surveys conducted in 1968 ranged from 5.7 per cent to 19.7 per cent and that the range for similar surveys in 1969 was from 5.9 per cent to 24 per cent. It should be emphasized that these surveys varied in the methods used, the extent to which the samples were adequate and representative, the questionnaire design, the sophistication of the approach, the analysis of the data and the reliability of the findings. Given these limitations, it would be unwise to attempt to generalize from them.

305. There can be no doubt that many of the students who have used cannabis, at both the high school and university levels, have done so only once or, at most, a few times. Others who may have used the drug more frequently may now have terminated their use. For these reasons it becomes important to have data on frequency and patterns of use. Unfortunately, we have even less information on this point than about the prevalence of use, and this makes it more difficult to compare the results of the various studies.

The second Bishop's University[25] study found that about half of those who had used marijuana had used it less than five times. Nearly 20 per cent of those who had used the drug had discontinued their use. A study of 431 marijuana users conducted by faculty members of the University of Calgary[26] revealed that 31 per cent of this group had used the drug once a week or more. Ten per cent had used it only a few times, as an experiment. In the 1968 study of Toronto high schools carried out by the Addiction Research Foundation,[27] 60 per cent of those who had tried marijuana had used it less than four times.

A 1969 survey of some 4,500 Montreal high school students carried out by OPTAT[28] (Office de la Prévention et du Traitement de l'Alcoolisme et des Autres Toxicomanies) revealed that 55 per cent of the students who had used marijuana had used it less than five times, and 67 per cent less than seven times. It is, of course, impossible to apply any generalizations from these few isolated studies to the Canadian student population as a whole.

In its public and private hearings the Commission heard many estimates of the extent and frequency of use. For example, some students have suggested that the proportion who have used cannabis at least once may be as high as 50 per cent in some universities. However, it is difficult to gauge the accuracy of these generally personal and impressionistic reports.

306. The Commission has also been made aware of what appears to be an extensive and growing marijuana use by adults. The evidence of such use has come to us largely from the statements of individuals, many of whom have given private testimony, and from a large volume of correspondence received at the Commission's office. An examination of this mail reveals that, of those who indicated their age, 20 per cent claimed to be over 40, 25 per cent between 30 and 40, and 40 per cent between 20 and 30. Most were married and on the whole claimed to have reached an average or above average level of education. The Commissioners have spoken to physicians, lawyers, bankers, politicians, teachers, scientists, pilots, business executives and journalists, to mention only a few, who have smoked marijuana or hashish. Many of these reported using the drug with colleagues and many expressed the opinion that the use of these drugs would increase among their friends and associates. The purpose of cannabis use in this population seems to be largely for its relaxing and intoxicating properties. A dealer supplying such people said: 'You can achieve the same sort of thing out of a drink or two before dinner.'

307. A further caution must be applied to the reports. Even if we assume the honesty of those who report cannabis use, we cannot assume that the drug in question was in fact cannabis. Analyses of street samples of marijuana have frequently found

that what was claimed or said to be the drug was, in fact, alfalfa, marjoram, dried parsley or marijuana of very low potency. Hashish has almost always proved, on analysis, to be as represented.

308. The supply of both marijuana and hashish has been irregular and has varied widely on a regional basis. Although there is some generally low-grade cannabis grown in Canada, most cannabis products are illegally imported; marijuana from Mexico by way of the United States, and hashish from the Middle and Far East and North Africa. The R.C.M. Police, representatives of the Department of Justice, and a number of witnesses have reported that marijuana, long the staple of the drug-using subculture, is now being replaced by hashish as the widely used illegal drug in some parts of the country. This shift in popularity can probably be attributed to a growing difficulty in obtaining marijuana (American and Mexican authorities lately have been intensifying their efforts to control its cultivation and prevent smuggling activities), the greater ease with which hashish, a concentrated form of cannabis, can be hidden and thus transported, and the greater profits in hashish trafficking. Hashish can be purchased at its source for around $50 a kilo and resold in Canada at $1,400 a kilo, while marijuana costs from $20 a kilo in Mexico to $100 a kilo in southern California, and can be resold in Canada for about $300 a kilo; an ounce of hashish sells for between $75 and $100 in contrast to about $20 for an ounce of marijuana.

The R.C.M. Police have provided the Commission with information about the amounts of cannabis products they have seized. In 1968 they confiscated 857 pounds of marijuana, and 481 pounds in 1969. Hashish seizures increased from 83 pounds in 1968 to 404 pounds in 1969. This shift in popularity of cannabis products can be better understood by indicating that the wholesale value of these seized drugs (based on the above-mentioned Canadian kilo prices) has, in the case of marijuana, declined from approximately $110,000 in 1968 to $66,000 in 1969, while the value of hashish seizures has increased from $53,000 in 1968 to over $250,000 in 1969.

Because of the illegal nature of the operation and the severe legal sanctions against such activities, there are very few reliable studies of the distribution of cannabis. Some preliminary research has been conducted in the United States (for example, E. Goode's *The Marijuana Market* and J. T. Carey's *The College Drug Scene*), but it is primarily limited to the New York and California markets and deals solely with marijuana. The Commissioners have been able to hold discussions with a number of persons involved in the distribution of both hashish and marijuana. However, it is not possible at this time to provide an accurate or comprehensive account of the complex system of cannabis importation and distribution.

The information we do have indicates that a large number of individuals have been involved in the importation of marijuana, often in fairly small amounts (which suggests the desire to provide for personal consumption rather than any mercenary motivation). While it appears true that co-incidental with the spread of cannabis use, an increasingly well-organized importation-distribution network has developed, there is no evidence available to us, beyond unsubstantiated rumours, that organized crime has become involved in the importation of marijuana. Rather, it seems that importation is more likely organized by a number of independent entrepreneurs supplying local markets, parts of local markets, or even a small group of friends and acquaintances. A few dealers across the country are probably involved in the importation of larger amounts of marijuana, up to several hundred pounds in a single or continuing operation. These persons' motivation is primarily commercial and they can be seen as traditional entrepreneurs who choose to trade in a contraband substance, chiefly because of the tremendous profit margin afforded them by the drug's illegality and the steadily rising demand from marijuana consumers. Such dealers are exceptional, though not rare, and it can be safely said that the high degree of centralized importation and distribution that typifies the opiate narcotics traffic is not a characteristic of the marijuana market.

There are several levels of dealers below the importer in the marijuana distribution system, but precise details of its make-up are at the moment impossible to ascertain. This is partly because of the necessarily clandestine nature of such commerce, but also because of rapid changes in personnel, variations in the availability of the drugs, and the difficulty in drawing any clear-cut distinction between sellers and buyers since essentially all dealers use marijuana and nearly every regular marijuana user has at some time sold some of his 'stash' (personal marijuana supply).

If the original marijuana shipment is large enough, it is usually sold in lots of several pounds or kilos to a local dealer who, in turn, sells it to more junior dealers by the pound, or half or quarter pound. These dealers are likely to subdivide their purchases still further, and occasionally will dilute the product with various substances resembling the crushed plant. At each level of distribution the monetary value of the cannabis is increased, but the dealer's total profit concomitantly decreases. There are few, if any, 'rich' dealers below the very upper echelons of the distribution hierarchy, and many persons involved in the selling of marijuana do so only to supplement their regular income. As well, as has been noted earlier, most cannabis dealers are likely to distribute other psychedelic drugs besides marijuana and hashish.

309. It is essential to any understanding of marijuana distribution to realize that, at the level of the user, transactions are so far removed from the impersonality that characterizes conventional purchasing relations that one sociologist has described the marijuana dealing-using sub-culture as 'an island of tribalism in a sea of commercial ethic'.[29] There is no doubt that among users much of it is given away, offered to visiting friends, or used as barter currency. As Erich Goode explains it:[30]

> The closest thing to marijuana in the 'straight' world is food. It is an act of hospitality to feed one's guests, a breach of good manners to allow them to go hungry. Smoking marijuana like eating together, binds people into a primitive sense of fellowship.

At the local level the distribution of hashish seems to be virtually identical to that of marijuana. There may, however, be a more complex system of importation. It seems reasonable that organized crime might be attracted to hashish distribution because of its place of origin and the relative ease with which it can be smuggled, compared with marijuana.

OPIATE NARCOTICS

310. Users of the opiate narcotics are more readily identifiable because of their serious dependency that arises from the use of these drugs. According to the Division of Narcotic Control, Department of National Health and Welfare, there are more than 4,000 known addicts in Canada of whom 62 per cent are in British Columbia and 23 per cent in Ontario.[31]

The extent of use in the sixties revealed by the statistics of the Division of Narcotic Control is as follows:

TABLE

Year	Criminal* Addicts	Medical† Addicts	Professional‡ Addicts	Total
1961	3,048	224	123	3,395
1962	3,136	306	134	3,576
1963	2,963	262	130	3,355
1964	2,947	273	132	3,352
1965	3,180	251	142	3,573
1966	3,182	259	151	3,592
1967	3,335	231	149	3,715
1968	3,459	200	145	3,804
1969	3,733	178	149	4,060

* Criminal addicts include all cases where the Narcotic Control Division has some record of the individual for ten years, not necessarily a criminal record, but perhaps criminal associations.

† Medical, or therapeutic addicts, are those whose addiction has arisen through medical treatment and who have no criminal record. Names are dropped after five years.

‡ Professional addicts are members of the medical profession, nurses and pharmacists. These names, too, are dropped after five years.

311. An analysis of the above table reveals that although the population of Canada increased almost ten per cent between 1961 and 1966, the criminal addict population increased only 4.4 per cent during the same period, and the total addict population

only 5.6 per cent. In effect, the opiate narcotic addict population has declined in proportion to the total population of Canada and is continuing to do so.

Further analysis of the 1969 statistical evidence reveals that 69 per cent of the criminal addicts were males. By occupation, the criminal addict population broke down as follows:

Labourers and unskilled	23·0	per cent
Service Occupations	12·2	,, ,,
Skilled Workers	7·0	,, ,,
Natural Resources Workers	5·5	,, ,,
Prostitutes	4·4	,, ,,
Clerical and sales	4·4	,, ,,
Housewife	3·8	,, ,,
Transportation	4·0	,, ,,
Other Occupations	2·4	,, ,,
Not known	33·3	,, ,,

312. The age groupings of the criminal addict population in Canada provide some indication of the pattern of use. The statistics for the calendar year 1969 are as follows:

Under 20 years	1·5	per cent
20–24	9·8	,, ,,
25–29	17·9	,, ,,
30–34	16·5	,, ,,
35–39	13·8	,, ,,
40–49	17·3	,, ,,
50–59	7·5	,, ,,
60–69	3·5	,, ,,
70–over	·8	,, ,,
Unknown	11·4	,, ,,

There are some indications that the number of young addicts in Canada is increasing, although the overall opiate narcotic dependent population has been dropping on a basis proportionate to the whole population since 1959. The Narcotic Addiction Foundation of British Columbia has reported that 81 new heroin users coming to its attention in 1969 (all of whom had also used other drugs) were in the 16-23 age group. Whether these persons were in fact 'addicts' is unclear. In any case, the latest Division of Narcotic Control statistics for British Columbia report an increase of only 44 criminal addicts (from 252 in 1968 to 296 in 1969) in the under-25 category. The Commission does not have further statistical evidence of this pattern of heroin use by the young in Canada, although this has been reported in some areas of the United States in recent months.

SOLVENTS

313. As mentioned in Chapter Two, solvent inhalation has become more widespread in recent years, confined mostly to the relatively young. Because the substances being inhaled (plastic glue, nail polish and remover, paint thinner, lighter fluid, etc.) can be obtained legally and with no difficulty, and because they have a multitude of both industrial and domestic applications, it is virtually impossible to determine accurately the degree of abuse to which they are put.

For decades there have been accounts of intoxication brought on by the inhalation of toluene and gasoline fumes. Ether has been used in this way for almost a century. In addition, prison workers have long known of the deliberate sniffing of paint thinner and gasoline as a means of intoxication. Only in the early sixties, however, did the prevalence of solvent inhalation among the relatively young come into prominence in the United States and Canada.

314. How widespread is solvent sniffing in Canada today? Surveys in some high schools in Canada in 1968 and 1969 indicate that between 2 and 13 per cent or more of the students surveyed had used the solvents at least once in the previous six months. (See Appendix D.)

Other indications of the prevalence of solvent use among children can be found in poison control reports to the Department of National Health and Welfare.[32] These reports will, of course, contain some cases of accidental ingestion, although many are suspected of being deliberate. Incomplete reports for the years 1968 and 1969 provide additional insights. Nail polish remover and plastic glue are the most popular, although there

213

are a number of cases of poisoning from naphtha, chlorine, paint remover, ether and liniment.

315. Ages of the users in the reported cases ranged from nine years (glue sniffing) to 22 years (nail polish remover sniffing), with an average of 14.5 years. This tends to bear out the suspicion that solvent inhalation is most common among older children and younger adolescents.

REFERENCES

1. Department of National Health and Welfare. December, 1969.

2. Department of National Health and Welfare. *Consumption of barbiturates and amphetamines.* September, 1969.

3. Cooperstock, R., & Sims, M. Mood-modifying drugs prescribed in a Canadian city: Hidden problems. Addiction Research Foundation of Ontario, Substudy 1–31 and 29–69, 1969.

4. *Eighteenth annual report of the Alcoholism and Drug Addiction Research Foundation.* Toronto: Addiction Research Foundation of Ontario, 1969.

5. Ibid.

6. Ibid.

7. Ibid.

8. Ibid.

9. See reference 2.

10. Brief of the R.C.M. Police to the Commission. October, 1969.

11. Department of National Health and Welfare. Poison control programme statistics. 1968.

12. Ibid.

13. See reference 2.

14. Brill, H., & Hirose, T. The rise and fall of a methamphetamine epidemic: Japan 1945–55. *Seminars in Psychiatry,* 1969, *1*, 179–94.

15. Marshman, J. A further note on the composition of illicit drugs. 1970. Mimeo.

16. Russell, J. *Survey of drug use in selected British Columbia school districts.* Vancouver: Narcotic Addiction Foundation of British Columbia, 1970.

17. Low, K., McAmmond, D., & Skirrow, J. The marijuana user. 1969. Mimeo.

18. See reference 15.

19. Ibid.

20. Smart, R. G., & Jackson, D. J. *A preliminary report on the attitudes and behaviour of Toronto students in relation to drugs.* Toronto: Addiction Research Foundation, 1969.

21. Whitehead, P. The incidence of drug use among Halifax adolescents. June, 1969. Mimeo.

22. Ibid.

23. Menard, L. C. In *Loyola conference on student use and abuse of drugs*. Montreal: Canadian Student Affairs Association, 1968.

24. Campbell, I. Marihuana use at Bishop's University. (A preliminary statistical report). January, 1969. Mimeo.

25. Campbell, I. Marihuana use at Bishop's University. (A second preliminary statistical report). May, 1969. Mimeo.

26. See reference 17.

27. See reference 20.

28. Laforest, L. *La consommation de drogues chez les étudiants du secondaire et du collégial de l'île de Montréal.* Quebec: Office de la prévention et du Traitement de l'Alcoolisme et des Autres Toxicomanies, 1969.

29. Goode, E. The marijuana market. *Columbia Forum,* 1969, *12* (Winter), 4–8.

30. Ibid.

31. Department of National Health and Welfare, Division of Narcotic Control. Total addict population in Canada, by class, province and sex, for 1969.

32. See reference 11.

CHAPTER FOUR

SOME CAUSES OF NON-MEDICAL
DRUG USE

316. The recommendations of the Minister of National Health and Welfare which gave rise to the appointment of the Commission, and the Commission's terms of reference, place particular stress on the desire to understand the causes of the non-medical use of drugs. We regard our inquiry into these aspects of the phenomenon to be one of our most important functions. The terms of reference speak of motivation, and they speak of the social, economic, educational and philosophical factors that have led to such use.

317. By cause we understand not merely the immediate, direct motivation for a particular drug experience, but the larger social significance of the phenomenon – how it relates to various aspects of life today – family relations, education, work, institutions, and conditions of life generally. In what way is it a response to the problems of modern living? What are its philosophical or spiritual implications? What does it say about our value structure? How does it reflect the way people think about the future?

At this time it is clearly impossible to provide a full and comprehensive statement of cause in these terms. At best we can hope to convey some of the interpretive themes and to describe some of the characteristics that have struck us as significant – that seem to have the merit of illuminating from one perspective or another this complex phenomenon. We seek to do this for a variety of reasons: to report in general some of our reactions and impressions; to assist in a preliminary way to add to the common understanding of a phenomenon that has aroused great interest, but that has also caused concern and anxiety, and has brought anguish to many parents; to suggest to citizens, especially parents and guardians, avenues of approach that may be helpful to them in understanding with sympathy and perhaps empathy a social fact that is to them strange and bewildering. But we must emphasize the tentative nature of these comments. They are not to be taken as a conceptual framework for an understanding of the changes or responses about which we are concerned. They do not constitute such a framework for the Commission. They are impressions. We intend to test them as rigorously as possible by intensive investigation. We invite critical comment from all quarters. In this way the interim report may serve a useful dialectical function, assisting us in consultation with our fellow citizens, to arrive at a full and sound understanding of this phenomenon.

318. The first problem we face is how to get at the facts of motivation and other related factors. What are we to accept as evidence of these facts? These are very subjective matters. Can we ever be sure that we know the truth? Whether we can or not, it seems to us that we must rely primarily on what drug users themselves say about their personal motivation and other factors predisposing them to use drugs. These statements must be weighed for credibility and carefully considered for proper interpretation but they are the primary and best source of an understanding of motivation. This was the approach followed by William James in his *Varieties of Religious Experience*, a phenomenon which has certain affinities with the subject-matter of our inquiry. The best evidence of the experience, the subjective effects of which may be presumed to be the primary motivation or cause, comes from the words of those who have undergone it. This is not to say that insight cannot be gained from the observations and interpretations of psychologists, social philosophers, sociologists and other informed and qualified students of our society. Thus we shall have recourse, in trying to explain this phenomenon, to both the words of drug users and the interpretations of observers. Finally, we shall offer our own interpretation, although this can only be a tentative one at this time – one that is offered as a basis for further consideration and discussion by the people of Canada.

319. Our inquiry has taken several forms: the public hearing of the traditional kind in which briefs have been submitted but in which there has been a full opportunity for questioning and

discussion by everyone present; private hearings with groups and individuals; numerous discussions with drug users and various experts having not only theoretical insight into the problem but active points of contact with it through some professional involvement; presentation of evidence regarding law enforcement and correction; and we have heard from experts in the areas of education; medical services; family life and social welfare. Although we intend to inquire further into motivation (as well as extent of use, perception of the problem, and general attitudes) in the surveys to be carried out this year, we do not necessarily rely on the answers to survey questionnaires as the most reliable evidence of motivation. Motivation is too subtle, complex, and full of nuance to be adequately elicited through questionnaires. We place as much or more reliance on the impressions derived from hearing individual drug users speak at length in public and private meetings about their experience and what they think to be the causes. In many ways we are closer here to the art of the novelist than that of the social scientist. We can only offer hypotheses – the validity and acceptance of which will depend on their ability to make sense of this phenomenon – to provide a meaning which is satisfactory to Canadians. It is like the ultimate test of any philosophy or religion. But it is important to emphasize once again that what is recorded here is merely our first impression gleaned from initial contacts during the first six months or so of our inquiry.

320. The explanations of motivation and the other related factors vary considerably. They vary between the different drug-using populations and they vary within a particular population. It is idle to seek a single, unifying explanation or theory. This whole area is characterized by bewildering diversity and conflicting impressions, but certain dominant themes do seem to emerge.

321. The motivational patterns underlying drug use also vary to some extent from drug to drug. In the case of cannabis, a major factor appears to be the simple pleasure of the experience. Time after time witnesses have said to us in effect: 'We do it for fun. Do not try to find a complicated explanation for it. We do it for pleasure.' This is the explanation frequently

offered for the use of cannabis, particularly by college students and adults in the working world. A mother of four and a teacher said: 'When I smoke grass I do it in the same social way that I take a glass of wine at dinner or have a drink at a party. I do not feel that it is one of the great and beautiful experiences of my life; I simply feel that it is pleasant and I think it ought to be legalized.'

A person involved in work with drug users expressed it this way: 'I think maybe it is time we stopped all the sociological nonsense about social milieux, and how your daddy fell off a horse, and how your mommy burnt the pablum or whatever it is – or what kind of sociological trip you want to blast off on, and just say in front what you mean which is "I get loaded because I love to do it".'

322. Many of us think of human behaviour in general as a consequence of needs that are either inherited or learned. There is some tendency to think of behaviour such as drug use as a consequence of pathological need patterns. However, we feel it would be a serious error, at least as far as cannabis use is concerned, to think of use as symbolic of or manifesting a pathological, psychological or even sociological state. Simple pleasure, similar to that claimed for the moderate use of alcohol, or food, or sex, is frequently offered as the general explanation for most current drug use. This is particularly true of the growing number of adult users (who share perhaps little else but their taste for cannabis with the members of the 'hip' culture). It is no doubt true that for some the use of drugs is a reflection of personal and social problems. But the desire for certain kinds of psychological gratification or release is not peculiar to the drug user or to our generations. It is an old and universal theme of human history. Man has always sought gratifications of the kind afforded by the psychotropic drugs.

323. They will vary with the particular drug used and, to some extent, with the personality of the user. In the case of *cannabis*, the positive points which are claimed for it include the following: it is a relaxant; it is disinhibiting; it increases self-confidence and the feeling of creativity (whether justified by

objective results or not); it increases sensual awareness and appreciation; it facilitates concentration and gives one a greater sense of control over time; it facilitates self-acceptance and in this way makes it easier to accept others; it serves a sacramental function in promoting a sense of spiritual community among users; it is a shared pleasure; because it is illicit and the object of strong disapproval from those who are, by and large, opposed to social change, it is a symbol of protest and a means of strengthening the sense of identity among those who are strongly critical of certain aspects of our society and value structure today.

324. Those who have used cannabis are not unanimous in its praise, although clearly the vast majority seem to regard it as either a harmless pastime or the source of real advantages and gain. Those who have used the drug and then criticize it tend most often to say: it can dominate a weak personality; it can take too much time; it can become an excuse for procrastination; it lessens the ability to persevere with unpleasant, boring or routine tasks.

325. Often a cannabis user has said, 'We can't explain it to you. Why don't you try it?' It has been implied that there is something ineffable about the experience, although this is more often the case when speaking of the effects of LSD. Sometimes one wonders if what is being conveyed is not a certain sense of exclusiveness, a smugness of the initiated. But we prefer to believe that it is the subtle and multifaceted aspect of its psychological and social significance for the average user that makes words seem inadequate to convey the whole of its meaning. Indeed, many users have insisted that the smokers of cannabis are able to communicate without the use of words; that they recognize and understand one another and share important assumptions and attitudes. Whether this silent communication is more than the knowledge of a common experience is not clear. But users speak of a sense of affinity, a larger consciousness of which they are made to feel a party by the drug experience.

326. Thus there is unquestionably a strong suggestion of community, of cultural solidarity, among cannabis users. And there is a definite tendency to proselytize, to encourage others to

221

take up the practice. It may be that this tendency is partly due to the illicit status of the practice which makes users want to increase the numbers involved and thus the concern of society about its present policy. But there is also a definite impression that the cannabis user seeks to convert others to what he sincerely believes to be a superior outlook and life style. The smoking of cannabis becomes a rite of initiation to a new society and value system. These are aspects of cannabis use, particularly among the younger, more idealistic members of our society, which merit serious consideration in any attempt to measure its potential for growth.

327. We gather from the statements of cannabis users that the drug is predominantly used in groups to enhance, enrich and ease social intercourse. However, the statements of LSD users imply that their experience is much more. L S D is spoken of as a very profound experience, not to be lightly entered into. With some it is never to be repeated; with others, its profound character, the sense of venture into the unknown, the very real risks of adverse effect, make it a practice which seems likely to remain fairly restricted. It is cheaper than psychoanalysis but appears to carry with it some of the same implications: the promise of greater self-knowledge and self-acceptance, but at the same time uncertainty as to the personality that will emerge. Except for a relatively few devotees, LSD is not a regular experience having social or communal significance. It is rather a venture into self-discovery which sometimes takes on turning-point significance for the subject. The self-revelation experienced may or may not become a basis for attitudinal change. It is thus a foundational experience rather than a casual one, as is the case of cannabis.

328. It is with reference to L S D that the most serious claims for spiritual significance are made. Timothy Leary has spoken in terms of a new quest for religious truth and experience. 'It's the same old pursuit. The aims of our religion are those of every religion of the past: we work to find the God within, the divinity which lies within each person's body.'[1] Users frequently speak of the LSD experience in mystical terms. There is repeated testimony to a feeling of oneness with others – of a loss

of the sense of personal identity in a sense of being a part of everything that is around one. There is a strong suggestion of a pantheistic sense of affinity and identification.

329. While pleasure, curiosity, the desire to experiment, and even the sense of adventure, are dominant motivations in drug use, there is no doubt that a search for self-knowledge and self-integration and for spiritual meanings are strong motivations with many. We have been profoundly impressed by the natural and unaffected manner in which drug users have responded to the question of religious significance. They are not embarrassed by the mention of God. Indeed, as Paul Goodman has observed, their reactions are in interesting contrast to those of the 'God is dead' theologian. It may be an exaggeration to say that we are witnessing the manifestations of a genuine religious revival, but there does appear to be a definite revival of interest in the religious or spiritual attitude towards life. As one drug user put it: 'The whole culture is saying, "Where is God?" I don't believe in your institutions, but now I know it's there someplace.' Another witness said, 'I just find that a lot of people are becoming a lot more aware of what's happening and joining in on a universal cause, a cosmic sort of joyousness and people are getting interested in spiritual things as well, because this is what our generation and the previous generations have lacked. . . .'

330. Drug use is by no means indispensable to the new outlook. Some people are fortunate enough to be what users call a natural 'turn on'. It is conceded that you can be 'turned on' without drugs – vital, human, and aware of all your senses, enjoying authentic, non-exploitative human relations, and alive to beauty and the possibilities of the moment. Indeed, there is an active doctrine of transcendence which sees drug use as a catalytic or transitional thing to be abandoned as soon as it has enabled you to glimpse another way of looking at things and of relating to life and people. The doctrine of transcendence carries much hope for the future. One witness said: 'I don't do too many drugs anymore because I have gone beyond them. They have taught me the lesson and there isn't so much need for them any more. I mean it's still fun to get stoned but there's a lot more to it. There is more to it than just fun. After you

have learned the lesson, you have fun in virtually anything.'

331. Many users have stated that the insights gained through drug use have carried over and remained with them, continuing to shape their attitudes and outlook and style of relating when they were not using drugs. In other words the drug has been a means of discovering a new way to be – more relaxed and self-accepting, more accepting and indeed loving, more appreciative of the intensity and value of being human in the moment, less anxious about time and specific goals. In listening to these statements one can not help feeling that this discovery was often made in other ways in the past – through traditional religious experience, for instance.

Modern drug use would definitely seem to be related in some measure to the collapse of religious values – the ability to find a religious meaning of life. The positive values that young people claim to find in the drug experience bear a striking similarity to traditional religious values, including the concern with the soul, or inner self. The spirit of renunciation, the emphasis on openness and the closely knit community, are part of it, but there is definitely the sense of identification with something larger, something to which one belongs as part of the human race.

332. Young drug users are highly critical of many aspects of our modern life. In this they are perhaps not much different than the critical minority that one finds in each generation. But this one has its own unique history and has lived through a formative period unlike any other. What are the distinguishing features of that backgound? In what way is it truly different from the one which shaped the outlook of previous generations of young people? The distinguishing marks would seem to be: a generalized middle-class affluence; a very rapid rate of technological change; the oppressive, almost foreboding character of certain problems or menaces which cast a serious doubt about man's ability to survive – nuclear power, overpopulation, environmental pollution, racial hostility and the widening gap between wealth and poverty. All these and other aspects of the human predicament today impart a distinctive character to the outlook and response of our youth. An example of the criti-

cism of the economic system is the following statement by a university student:

I think it is essential that there should be some manner by which we could break down the economic system. We still need productivity. But you can get away from the economic basis, from the competitive basis on which people, once they have gone into something, have to beat you down. You have this aspect of wanting to share which we should develop. You should be willing to share together. But you can still have productivity without competition.

333. To this point we have been concerned largely with the statements and interpretations of drug users themselves. We turn now to interpretation – our own and that of other commentators. Present-day affluence plays a curious role. Without it there could not be the freedom for speculation and experiment – the luxury of cultivating the inner self. At the same time it repels. It is both taken for granted and repudiated. There is a love-hate relationship. The drug-taking minority of this generation cannot be inspired by the goals of their fathers. They do not feel the same urgency to achieve material success and do not seek self-fulfilment that way. It may be that they see no way of achieving their own sense of personal identity in attempting to repeat, probably with less success, what their fathers have already done. There is reason to believe that young people from less comfortable circumstances are more strongly motivated towards traditional career patterns and material success. But there would seem to be more than merely trying to find a role different from that of one's father. The materially more sophisticated young people, those more familiar with material well-being and less anxious about their ability to maintain it, think they see a future in which it will be impossible to avoid. They envisage a society which will be obliged to assure a sufficient amount of material security to everyone in order to maintain itself politically and economically. They therefore conclude that it is a goal for which it is now unnecessary to plan or to which it is futile to devote a significant amount of one's time and energy.

334. There is also a strong impression that young people are,

as it were, unconsciously adapting or preparing themselves for a time when there will be much less work to go around. The rapid rate of technological change and the pervading threat of work obsolescence makes them very uncertain about their own occupational future. They seem to suspect that a high proportion of them may have to learn to live happily with relatively little work. Those of us who are well-established in work tend to talk glibly of a future in which there will be increasing leisure. Little thought or practical effort has been devoted to the problem of how to fill that leisure in constructive and satisfying ways. The exploration of the inner self, the expansion of consciousness, the development of spiritual potential, may well be purposes to which young people are turning in anticipation of a life in which they will have to find sustaining interest in the absence of external demands and challenges.

335. Young people speak often of a desire to overcome the division of life into work and play, to achieve a way of life that is less divided, less seemingly schizophrenic, and more unified. They seem to be talking about the increasingly rare privilege of work that one can fully enjoy – of work that is like one's play. They claim to be prepared to make considerable renunciations or sacrifice of traditional satisfactions like status and material success for work in which they can take pleasure. Indeed, one of their frequent commentaries on the older generation is that it does not seem to enjoy its work, that it does not seem to be happy. This is said sadly, even sympathetically. It is not said contemptuously. The young say, in effect, 'Why should we repeat this pattern?' The use of drugs for many is part of a largely hedonistic life style in which happiness and pleasure are taken as self-evidently valid goals of human life.

336. Role rejection is an important theme of the cultural reaction that is associated with much of contemporary drug use. One young person suggested that letting one's hair grow was in part at least a rejection of the manhood role. Young people do not deny the historic validity or necessity of these roles for the older generation nor the positive achievements which must be credited to them; they simply say that they are no longer relevant or desirable. The role which many reject is that of the

achievement-oriented male, committed body and soul to the big corporation, and feeling increasingly the need to give proofs of his masculinity. Some have spoken of drugs as dehabituating, desophisticating, and deconceptualizing – as helping the personality to break out of old moulds. They speak of a release or recovery of child-like innocence – the essential perspective of the artist.

337. There can be no doubt that there is a search for authenticity in thought, in stance, in personal relations. The drug becomes a means of dissolving the mask, of escaping from pretence, affectation and stereotyped reaction and attitude, although their place may be taken by other stereotypes – a cultist enthusiasm which expresses itself in knowing smiles and a private language. What happens under LSD is far from clear, but users speak of blowing holes in the conscious mind through which bits of the subconscious emerge, to be always accessible in the future. It is the language of self-discovery – the eternal search for the main-springs of one's personality – the attempt to find liberation from psychological burdens, from 'hang ups', as they are popularly called.

These human desires, these goals, are not new: they may be summed up as the attempt to become a 'real person'. This has been a goal of religious or spiritual concern down through the centuries; the attempt to pull together the dispersed or fragmented pieces of the self. It is often expressed as the search for an identity.

338. There is in man a powerful and long-term tendency to attempt to weave the experience and perceptions of the individual into a logically consistent whole, centred when possible on a single cosmological principle or theme. In such a whole, man seeks for a meaning to life in the broad sense, for goals towards which to direct himself and the means by which he can reasonably hope to attain these goals. Through such a structure man hopes to find the nature of his own relationship to existence in general and to his fellows. When such a synthesis of experience is available, not only to an individual but in a form that can be shared and accepted by some large numbers of people, it can become the ideological basis for social life and, as such, serve as a unifying principle for a society. Such syntheses of

experiences were achieved by minds such as those of Saint Thomas Aquinas, John Calvin and Karl Marx. In the absence of such syntheses, man and society suffer. The responses that are made by man in periods of ideological vacuum often appear strikingly similar. For instance, there seem to be striking parallels between the orientation of the stoics and cynics at the time of the collapse of the Greek world, and the response of the 'Beat Generation' and the 'Hippies'. In both instances the individual seems to withdraw from his society and to seek reality within himself.

339. Are there special elements in the present human situation that impose particular stresses and burdens that would account for the increasing dependence of old and young on drugs? In this context we repeatedly encounter the term 'alienation'. The use of this term has been discussed by Kenneth Keniston in these words:[2]

> Although formal discussions of alienation itself are largely limited to the last 150 years, the theme of alienation – of estrangement, outcastness and loss – is an archetypal theme in human life and history. . . . The ambiguous concept of alienation has in recent years become increasingly fashionable and, partly as result, increasingly devoid of any specific meaning. More and more the term is used to characterize whatever the author considers the dominant maladies of the twentieth century; and since views differ as to what these maladies are, the meaning of alienation fluctuates with each writer. . . . Writers like Fromm, Kahler and Pappenheim use 'alienation' to describe a variety of conditions ranging from separation of man from nature to the loss of pre-capitalist work relationships, from man's defensive use of language to his estrangement from his own creative potential, and from the worker's loss of control over the productive process to the individual's feeling of social or political powerlessness. Of course, the purpose of such writers is to suggest that all of these different phenomena are connected, that all result from some characteristic of modern society.

In the testimony we have heard, the term 'alienation' is most often used to refer to the estrangement of many young people and adults from the institutions, processes and dominant economic, social and political values of our society; to this inability to think of a good and meaningful life being available to them in the society; to their sense of inability to affect or influence the course that society will follow or the great issues of peace and war, poverty, pollution and others.

340. Many of our modern youth are undoubtedly suffering from too great self-expectation. This is partly the result of exaggerated paternal expectation – parents confusing their own affluence (which may be as often the product of an aggressive acquisitiveness as innate intelligence) with the inherited characteristics which they are capable of passing on. It is also partly the result of a sense of wider opportunity reflected in universal education. More is possible; more is expected. There develops a disquieting gap between expectation and ability. Dr Vivian Rakoff said: 'We use drugs to find out how far we can go, rather than as a device for passivity. Drugs can be a spurious way to fill the gap between aspiration and capacity.'

341. Witnesses appearing before the Commission have sometimes referred to the word '*anomie*' to express one of the possible 'causes' of the non-medical use of drugs. Whether these speakers referred to the literal 'Anomie' or to some other state of confusion or estrangement closer to 'alienation' is not easy to determine. But, in fact, and in any case, the Commission was told that a certain anomie in which the Canadian society lives does call for a response, a reaction: self-search, integration, new values, evasion, etc. Literally, *anomie* means 'normlessness'. This state, well described by the French sociologist, Emile Durkheim (especially in relation to suicide), does not often result from the total absence of norms but emerges from the co-existence of conflicting norms, rendering the aiming towards precise goals very difficult; contradicting values are expressing themselves through co-existing norms.

The Commission thinks that the concept of anomie and the existence of anomic situations may be part of the explanation that it will be trying to discern, in the course of its mandate. However, anomie and alienation are used all encompassingly as two of the 'causes' of nearly all social problems; these concepts will have to be treated carefully, and critically. The term 'anomie' is neither specific nor very useful operationally (it cannot account for *a* specific problem. *e.g.,* How is it that all people living under anomic conditions do not resort to drugs?)

342. Contemporary drug use is also associated with a loss of faith in reason and a new emphasis on emotion. As one young high school student put it, 'Young people today want to learn feelings more than facts.' Paul Goodman has described the loss of faith thus:[3]

> There is a lapse of faith in science. Science has not produced the general happiness that people expected, and now it has come under the sway of greed and power; whatever its beneficent past, people fear that its further progress will do more harm than good. And rationality itself is discredited. Probably it is more significant than we like to think that intelligent young people dabble in astrology, witchcraft, psychedelic dreams, and whatever else is despised by science; in some sense they are not kidding. They need to control their fate, but they hate scientific explanations.

Keniston has spoken of a 'cult of experience' and declares:[4]

> Central to this cult is a focus on the present – on today, on the here-and-now. Thus, rather than to defer gratification and enjoyment for a distant future, immediate pleasure and satisfaction are emphasized. Rather than reverence for the traditions of the past, experience in the present is stressed. Psychologically, then, such human qualities as control, planning, waiting, saving, and postponing on the one hand, and revering, recalling, remembering and respecting on the other, are equally de-emphasized. In contrast, activity, adventure, responsiveness, genuineness, spontaneity and sentience are the new experimental values. Since neither the future nor the past can be assumed to hold life's meaning, the meaning of life must be sought within present experience, within the self, within its activity and responsiveness in the here-and-now.

343. This emphasis on feeling and immediate experience reflects itself in an interest in the arts and in nature. Many young people speak of a heightened appreciation of the beauties of nature. This is related to the aesthetic repugnance they feel towards many of the physical aspects of modern urban life. One student said that he did not feel any desire for drugs for two weeks when he was on a canoe trip in the Canadian north. The drugs may often be an attempt to escape from a pervading urban ugliness into a world of interior beauty.

344. We suspect that much contemporary drug use simply serves the purpose of relieving the stress and tension which most people, young and old, experience in modern living. Certainly this is a dominant function of alcohol and nicotine which are still the most prevalent drugs in all age groups (see Chapter Three). It is also true of the large quantities of barbiturates consumed by adults. In the vast majority of cases it is idle to look beyond the relief of tension for an explanation. This is the pleasure or gratification most generally sought by the drug user.[5]

... Chemical comforts are extremely varied in their chemical nature, but what they do have in common is their ability to produce pleasure. In this it can be noted that people only become dependent on substances which they report produce pleasure and the dependency potential of any substance, drug or food, may be predicted by seeing how much pleasure it gives to the patient. The pleasure they produce is reduction of tension, in addition to any other social or physical effects they might have.

345. Some commentators have identified a degree of strain that is peculiar to the impact of communications in our age. Keniston has referred to it as 'stimulus flooding and psychological numbing'. Dr Paul Christie, the superintendent of the Queen Street Mental Health Centre in Toronto has spoken of 'chronic confusion'. As Keniston puts it:[6]

One of the conditions of life in any modern technological society is continual sensory, intellectual, and emotional stimulation which produces or requires a high tendency towards psychological numbing ... the quantity, intensity and variety of inputs to which the average American is subjected in an average day probably has no precedent in any other historical society. ... The problem arises, however, because the shells we erect to protect ourselves from the clamours of the inner and outer world often prove harder and less permeable than we had originally wanted. ... Thus, in at least a minority of Americans, the normal capacity to defend oneself against undue stimulation and inner excitation is exaggerated and automatized, so that it not only protects but walls off the individual from inner and outer experience ... the feeling and fear of psychological numbing leads to a pursuit, even a cult, of experiences for its own sake.

346. Many observers tend to characterize the psychological predisposition to the use of *methamphetamines* ('speed') as one of deep depression. Wilfrid Clement, who has had extensive clinical experience with 'speed freaks', has expressed the opinion that 'we are faced with major generalized social depression as a reaction to our technological society'. Both Mr Herb Tookey and Mr Barry Luger, who have had a great deal of contact with the 'speed' community through their work with *The Trailer* in Toronto (see Chapter Six), have emphasized this depression. Tookey says, 'The methedrine user is usually chronically depressed with a passive-dependent personality.'[7] The depression seems to come from the feeling of powerlessness and inability to cope with various environmental problems and the demands of modern life. Luger puts it this way: 'Most potential speed freaks are depressed because of their past environmental and institutional problems and see no positive experiences in the foreseeable future. They were not able to cope with the problems at home, at school or with their middle-class group.'[8] The depression, Tookey says, is 'often manifested behaviourally by a lack of goal orientated behaviour. The methedrine user has considerable difficulty in constructing and carrying out long range plans (i.e. getting and maintaining a job, going to school, etc.)' The feeling of being able to cope is very important. 'Coupled with chronic depression', says Tookey, 'is episodic angry agitation which appears to result from feelings of im-

232

potency, rejection, inferiority, and lack of control over the environment.'[9]

The 'speed freak' can be seen as a casualty of the increasing complexity of the demands for adaptation and survival in a technological society. Says Tookey, 'The "speed freak" usually has poor interpersonal skills and invariably is unable to make the discriminations necessary to deal with a complex technological society.'[10] Clement sees the problem as one of adaptation in a time of rapid change and contrasts the 'speed freak' with what he calls the 'super-adaptive' youth. Clement expresses the view that the 'speed freak's' depression relates to his perception of his peers and their relative ability to cope with the demands on them – not only the demands of the educational system but also the demands of social adaptation. They experience anxiety about their function and identity in the future. They can see peers able to tolerate the speed and bewildering demands of modern life. The sight of the 'super-adaptive' peer fills the average young person with a sense of inadequacy. The contrast in abilities is shown most clearly in after-school activity – in response to the demands of sociability.

The desire for a supportive, reinforcing community is a strong motivation for the use of speed. 'For the vast majority', says Tookey, 'the speed community provides a very strong, though anonymous identity. Paradoxically, identity is found by losing personal identity to the group. "I'm a speed freak".'[11] The speed freak community has few moral standards but it shows a rough loyalty to its members. John Bradford, President of Rochdale College, said, 'One reason why kids use speed is that they are trying to imitate a life style they're not part of and don't understand.' He was referring to the life style of the 'heads' – the users of psychedelics.

347. Many young people profess to have little belief in the future – to find it difficult to visualize a future for themselves. In one small group we met with during our hearings one of the women said, 'Very few in our generation believe we are going to live to be forty.' There was general agreement in the group with this statement. Paul Goodman in his article, 'The New Reformation', has emphasized this point: 'Again and again stu-

233

dents have told me that they take it for granted they will not survive the next ten years.'[12]

348. There is also a suggestion that this emphasis on experience in the present reflects a reaction against the constraints on the personality produced by the habit-forming, role-imposing, conformity of modern society. It is a reaction against role and rule – an attempt to find spontaneity, variety, and unstructured expression in personality and experience. This reflects again the importance of the dehabituating effect of the drugs – their capacity to break down moulds into which behaviour and personality are threatened with confinement by the various pressures towards conformity. Benjamin DeMott has written very perceptively of this reaction in an article entitled '*The Sixties: A Cultural Revolution*'. He emphasizes that it is common to all age groups. DeMott sums up this new longing and reaching out which cuts across all age groups as:[13]

The will to possess one's experience rather than be possessed by it, the longing to live one's own life rather than be lived by it, the drive for a more various selfhood than men have known before. . . . Young, old, black, white, rich and poor are pursuing the dream of a more vital experience . . . at the root of our yearning stand the twin convictions: that we can be more, as men, than we're permitted to be by the rule of role and profession, and that the life of dailiness and habit, the life that lives us, precedes us, directs us to the point of suppressing moral conscience and imagination, is in truth no life at all.

One witness reflected something of the same emphasis in his explanation of the effects of drugs:

Marijuana makes a person child-like. L S D and mescaline are a ticket to childhood. They are desophisticators, they break down the conceptual structure through which the person interprets or views the world. Categories which were always perfectly acceptable are now of questionable value, things which were never noticed or were always taken for granted now jump out to the person presenting unsolvable metaphysical problems. Every event has deep meaning, every thought is profound.

234

349. This phenomenon can also be viewed from the perspectives of psychiatry and abnormal psychology. There are many in the public who tend to view the non-medical use of drugs as symptomatic of a pathological psychological state. There is no doubt but that some of those who use drugs such as cannabis or LSD are mentally ill; this is also true of some proportion of those who use alcohol and the mental illness is causative to some degree of their use. However, it is the view of the Commission that the majority of drug users do not take drugs as a result of pathological motivation. Nevertheless it is desirable to draw attention to some of the psychological and psychiatric problems that are suggested to be contributing factors underlying non-medical drug use.

350. From the psychological point of view, overstimulation and exposure to an overwhelming stressful and complex environment, which requires the individual to perfom too many and too difficult differentiations and to solve problems which surpass his coping ability, are likely to lead to a disturbance ('a jamming') of his capacity to deal effectively with the excessive in-put to his central nervous system. In animals, such situations produce pathological states of maladaptive behaviour which are often referred to as 'experimental neuroses'. In man, it is likely that similar mechanisms prevail, and pathological states of neurosis or personality disorder, even psychosis, may develop under these conditions.

Looking once more at the experimental animal model, it is interesting that animals whose behaviour has become severely disturbed through environmentally-produced stress can be temporarily 'normalized' by the administration of tranquillizing drugs. Animals under these conditions prefer, in fact, water with added alcohol or tranquillizing drugs to plain water.

This suggests that severely disturbed humans, too, may often resort to drugs which produce relaxation or 'instant rest' as a temporary escape from intolerable tensions in a world which offers less and less natural opportunities to do so. It is noteworthy and apparently paradoxical, that amphetamines – the stimulating 'speed' drugs – are among the most effective medical means of alleviating states of pathological nervous overactivity in children, and that these drugs can often help such children to regain increased self-confidence and greater powers of concentration. Claims for similar effects of 'speed' are often made by the teenager who is plagued by the awareness of his own inadequacy. This may be interpreted as the choice of a different 'chemical defence' against the threat of an overwhelming environment – instead of 'instant rest', the young person chooses 'instant efficiency'. Thus, the non-medical use of psychotropic drugs may frequently be an abortive and poorly directed attempt by an emotionally sick person to treat his own condition. But because he does not know precisely how, when and in what dosage to apply these drugs, he not only usually fails in his attempts but more often than not makes things worse.

351. In the language of ego psychology, a person's ability to cope with external demands depends on his ego structure; that is, that part of the personality which mediates between inner needs and outer reality. Ego strength, in turn, depends on undisturbed processes of growth, development and maturation throughout childhood. Since a child is an extremely vulnerable organism, disruptive early experiences may lead to imbalanced development and result in a poorly adjusted personality structure. Such a maladjusted person would then be inadequately equipped to deal with the complex demands of today's world.

352. The Commission has very often been told by young people that they reject all that is traditional, conventional and stereotyped, because they consider it to be hypocritical, phony, dehumanizing, threatening, and ugly. As a result, they may become alienated and some may be plunged into a frantic search for an identity which may be acceptable to them by their own standards. This search for identity may go in two directions: one leading to a pathological adjustment – the other simply to a non-pathological parting from conformity.

In the pathological outcome, the individual may substitute a spurious identity for an authentic one, for instance, by accepting his belonging to a drug community as his new identity. Also, by displacing his inner needs, projecting his aspirations and denying his limitations, the person might settle for a drug-induced illusion of false power, rather than real achievement, and for chemically induced comfort rather than true resolution of conflicts and tensions.

By contrast, in the non-pathological choice, the drug user may opt exclusively for the inner world of personal experience and genuine emotional awareness instead of the despised external hall-marks of success in the world of our present-day society, as we have often been told by young people. In making this choice, the young individual apparently replaces the prevailing social, technological and scientific values which require consensual verification, with the immanent and immutable values of emotional, interpersonal, spiritual, creative – but not necessarily productive – achievement. It might well be reassuring to him that personal experience, emotional awareness, spirituality and creativeness are forever free from the danger of being usurped by dehumanizing automation (the one power the neo-nonconformist hates and fears perhaps more than anything else, as we have repeatedly been told). However, this choice of deliberate withdrawal and restructuring of his value system is probably only open to a highly differentiated, sensitive and introspective person.

353. Many others who reject today's society probably do so for more personal and less philosophical reasons – for instance, because of unresolved conflicts with their parents and with authority in general. Many also adopt more pathological defences, rather than an orderly withdrawal, as their way of rejecting the 'establishment'. Such defences – when induced and sustained by psychotropic drugs – may consist in the vicarious building of an illusionary world with LSD or in frenzied and aggressive overstimulation with the help of 'speed', or in a passive walling off and isolation of the self from all contacts, with cannabis.

354. Even more pathological responses may occur as disguised self-destructive behaviour. For instance, some 'speed' users who inject almost suicidal doses of methamphetamine into their veins without any regard for their safety and health, may actually be trying to test the truth of the youth slogan 'Speed Kills'. The role of the doomed person who is at once a

martyr sacrificing himself, a hero braving the confrontation with certain destruction and a gambler playing dice with death, is a role which seems to have a strong seductive pull for some young people who are morbidly hungry for compassion, admiration and excitement. For these individuals the slogan 'Speed Kills', may, paradoxically, carry more attractive than deterrent power – and thus may not serve the purpose for which it is being promoted.

355. The sick individual who relies on cannabis, speed or other psychotropic drugs, almost as his only means of escape, who uses them always as a crutch, and structures his whole existence around them as the only providers of pleasure (the 'pothead', the 'speed-freak' and the 'acidhead'), is in need of medical and psychiatric or psychological treatment. Prolonged counselling, psychotherapy and comprehensive social follow-up care are usually required. Medically prescribed and supervised drug treatment may also be indicated in many cases.

On the other hand, the neo-noncomformist who is using drugs but is not sick in the medical or psychiatric sense, may not need treatment. If it seems desirable to bring about a change in his behaviour, only a philosophical and spiritual reorientation, which would have to touch the cultural roots of his values and existential attitudes, could achieve this goal.

REFERENCES

1. Leary, T. Statement prepared for a Canadian audience in 1967.

2. Keniston, K. *The uncommitted: Alienated youth in American society.* New York: Delta, 1965.

3. Goodman, P. The new reformation. *New York Times Magazine,* September 14, 1969.

4. See reference 2.

5. Holmes, S. J. Keeping perspective re: Chemical comforts. Paper delivered to the College of Family Physicians of Canada, October 2, 1969.

6. See reference 2.

7. Tookey, H. The increasing use of methamphetamine ('speed') among young people. 1969. Mimeo.

8. Luger, B. Basic facts on speed. 1969. Mimeo.

9. See reference 7.

10. Ibid.

11. Ibid.

12. See reference 3.

13. De Mott, B. The Sixties: A cultural revolution. *New York Times Magazine,* December 14, 1969.

CHAPTER FIVE

PRESENT CANADIAN POLICY – THE LAW

A. INTRODUCTION

356. Present Canadian policy with respect to the non-medical use of psychotropic drugs is mainly reflected in a heavy emphasis on law and law enforcement. Moreover, it is an emphasis on the use of criminal law. Since this law is affecting or threatening to affect more and more Canadians in all age groups and all walks of life, it is not surprising that there should be such a preoccupation with the appropriateness and limitations of the criminal law as a means of controlling non-medical drug use. In the initial phase of our inquiry, by far the greatest proportion of the testimony we have heard has been concerned directly or indirectly with this problem. It is in the very forefront of Canadian perceptions of the phenomenon of non-medical drug use. Until our conception of the role of law in this field has been re-examined, and certain assumptions agreed upon, it is going to be very difficult to develop a coordinated and effective system of social responses to this phenomenon.

357. Law is, of course, not the only means of social response to the phenomenon of non-medical drug use. As we suggest in Chapter Six, social response runs through a whole gamut, including law and administrative regulation; research, information and education; various social influences, such as those of family, church, peer-group, media and entertainment; medical treatment and other supportive services; and corporate and individual responsibility and self-restraint, reflected in such matters as production, distribution and prescription of drugs. There are no doubt more. It is sufficient to observe here that law is only one of these responses, and it is far from clear what its relative importance is in the long run. It is, nevertheless, the dominant response at present, and it colours our approach to all the others. It inevitably invites special consideration at this time.

358. A full consideration of Canadian policy with respect to the non-medical use of drugs requires a detailed knowledge and understanding of how the various institutions in our society are responding to this phenomenon, particularly those in the fields of law, science, education, medicine, social service, and mass communication and entertainment. We do not have that knowledge at this time although we have glimpses of certain issues and problems on which we shall comment to a limited extent, with some interim recommendations of a very general nature, in Chapter Six. For example, we do not yet have a sufficiently intimate knowledge of the way in which our scientific, educational and medical institutions are responding to this problem to be able either to give a full description of current policy in these fields or to make detailed recommendations, although we believe that certain general observations are both possible and appropriate at this time. We plan to deal more fully with these matters in our final report.

359. Because, however, of the present importance of law in public perceptions of the phenomenon of non-medical drug use, we believe that we should venture some general outline of the content and application of the law in this field. The statement which follows is not by any means intended to be exhaustive or definitive, but simply to serve as a sufficient background for the identification and discussion of some of the issues at this time. It also serves as a frame of reference for the interim recommendations with respect to law which we make in Chapter Six. During the ensuing year we intend to deepen our study of the law, from both a doctrinal and empirical point of view, to examine the policy and practices of other countries in greater depth than has been possible so far, and to consider more fully the policy options that are available to Canada.

360. Some of the Canadian attitudes towards the present law and law enforcement are referred to in Chapter Six to indicate the issues that have been raised during the initial phase of the inquiry, but we do not think it would be appropriate at this time, when we are less than half way through, to attempt a comprehensive description of these attitudes which might appear to assign relative *weight*, in terms of popular opinion, to them.

We do not yet have a sufficient basis to speak with any degree of confidence about the relative weight of Canadian attitudes towards the non-medical use of drugs. In the initial phase of our inquiry, we have gathered a great variety of impressions but we have no way of knowing how representative any of them are of Canadian attitudes generally. We cannot, for example, venture a statement of what we think to be the majority view or consensus, if there is such a thing at the present time. Perhaps we shall not even be in a position by the end of this inquiry to speak with assurance about the weight of public opinion on the various issues involved in the non-medical use of drugs. We hope to be able to throw more light on this subject as a result of a national survey to be carried out in 1970. (See Chapters One and Three.) This will give us some base data concerning attitudes. We hope also that our interim report and our public hearings in 1970 will draw out segments of opinion that we may not have heard from as yet, or that we may not have heard from in a sufficiently representative manner. Hopefully, the interim report may assist us to focus expression of opinion and attitudes more directly upon the precise issues involved in the determination of the proper social response to the non-medical use of drugs.

361. Insofar as the other institutional responses, and attitudes towards them, are concerned – in the fields, for example, of science, education and medicine – we have reserved such descriptive observations as we are able to make at this time to Chapter Six.

B. LAW AND LAW ENFORCEMENT

1. Some Historical Background[1]

362. The history of Canadian legislative policy with respect to the control of drugs may be traced to 1908, when legislation to control the traffic in opium was adopted,[2] following a report on *The Need for the Suppression of the Opium Traffic in Canada* by William Lyon Mackenzie King, then Deputy Minister of Labour. King had come upon the traffic in opium rather by accident while investigating claims for compensation arising

out of the anti-Asiatic riots which took place in Vancouver in 1907.

363. Gradually, over the years, an increasing number of drugs were brought under the control of the *Opium and Narcotic Drug Act*,[3] and the severity of the penalties was increased. There can be no doubt that Canada's drug laws were for a long time primarily associated in the minds of its legislators and the public with general attitudes and policy towards persons of Asiatic origin. For example, in 1922 when the law was amended to provide for mandatory deportation of convicted aliens, two members of the House of Commons expressed the hope that such deportation would help 'to solve the oriental question in this country'.[4]

364. The inclusion of marijuana in the *Opium and Narcotic Drug Act* in 1923[5] is thought to have been influenced in some measure by a book entitled *The Black Candle*,[6] which was written by Mrs Emily S. Murphy, a police magistrate and a judge of the Juvenile Court in Edmonton, Alberta. The book was based on a series of articles on drugs which she wrote for Maclean's Magazine, and it contained a chapter which referred to marijuana as a 'new drug menace'. It also referred to legislation against marijuana in certain American states. It quoted statements to the effect that marijuana causes insanity and loss of 'all sense of moral responsibility' and leads to violence. There is no suggestion that the extent of use or public concern about marijuana were factors which led to its inclusion in the Act in 1923. Nor does there appear to have been any particular attempt to justify this decision on the basis of scientific evidence.

365. In 1955 a Special Committee of the Senate of Canada was appointed to inquire into and report upon the traffic in narcotic drugs in Canada. The Committee was chiefly concerned with the opiate narcotics, particularly heroin. Its report, published in 1955, contains the following observations with respect to marijuana:[7]

Marijuana is not a drug commonly used for addiction in

Canada, but it is used in the United States and also in the United Kingdom by addicts.

No problem exists in Canada at present in regard to this particular drug. A few isolated seizures have been made, but these have been from visitors to this country or in one or two instances from Canadians who have developed addiction while being in other countries.

The Committee recommended more severe penalties for trafficking in the drugs covered by the *Opium and Narcotic Drug Act*, including 'heavy compulsory minimum sentences', and a 'penalty of the utmost severity' for importation.[8] It opposed any distinction between the addict trafficker and the non-addict trafficker and declared that the trafficking provisions should be directed to making distribution by street peddlers and addicts so hazardous that the 'higher up' would have difficulty finding outlets. 'The elimination of trafficking in drugs,' said the Committee, 'is the goal of enforcement and the attainment of this goal is not assisted by artificial distinctions between motives for trafficking.' In justifying severe penalties the Committee referred, in part, to testimony by Mr Harry J. Anslinger, U.S. Commissioner of Narcotics, before a Special Committee of the United States Senate.

The recommendations of the Special Committee on the Traffic in Narcotic Drugs in Canada were implemented in some measure by the *Narcotic Control Act*,[9] which replaced the *Opium and Narcotic Drug Act* in 1961. It increased the severity of the penalties for trafficking and possession for the purpose of trafficking, and imposed a minimum penalty of seven years imprisonment for importation. The Act did not, however, adopt the Committee's recommendation of a severe *minimum* penalty for trafficking. It also made provision for preventive detention and compulsory treatment,[10] although these provisions of the Act have not been put into force by proclamation.

II. *International Framework*

366. Canadian legislative policy on the non-medical use of drugs must be viewed against the background of Canada's

international agreements and obligations on this subject. The *Single Convention on Narcotic Drugs, 1961*,[11] to which Canada is a party, provides that the drugs specified by it, including heroin and cannabis, shall be subject to a system of strict controls. More particularly, the parties to the Convention agree 'to limit exclusively to medical and scientific purposes the production, manufacture, export, import, distribution of, trade in, use and possession' of the drugs covered by it (Article 4), and to make certain acts contrary to the provisions of the Convention penal offences. Article 36, paragraph 1, reads as follows:

> 1. Subject to its constitutional limitations, each Party shall adopt such measures as will ensure that cultivation, production, manufacture, extraction, preparation, possession, offering, offering for sale, distribution, purchase, sale, delivery on any terms whatsoever, brokerage, dispatch, dispatch in transit, transport, importation and exportation of drugs contrary to the provisions of this Convention, and any other action which in the opinion of such Party may be contrary to the provisions of this Convention, shall be punishable offences when committed intentionally, and that serious offences shall be liable to adequate punishment particularly by imprisonment or other penalties of deprivation of liberty.

Canada fulfils its obligations under this Convention by the system of controls which it has established under the *Narcotic Control Act* and the *Food and Drugs Act*.[12] As long as a state remains a party to the Convention it is bound by its terms. If it wishes to be released from a particular provision it must either obtain an amendment to the Convention, which may involve an international conference (Article 47) or else withdraw from the Convention by giving the notice called 'denunciation' in accordance with (Article 46), which reads as follows:

> 1. After the expiry of two years from the date of the coming into force of this Convention (Article 41, paragraph 1) any Party may, on its own behalf or on behalf of a territory for which it has international responsibility, and which has with-

drawn its consent given in accordance with Article 42, denounce this convention by an instrument in writing deposited with the Secretary-General.

2. The denunciation, if received by the Secretary-General on or before the first day of July in any year, shall take effect on the first day of January in the succeeding year, and, if received after the first day of July, shall take effect as if it had been received on or before the first day of July in the succeeding year.

3. This Convention shall be terminated if, as a result of denunciations made in accordance with paragraph 1, the conditions for its coming into force as laid down in Article 41, paragraph 1, cease to exist.

367. Policy decisions with respect to the international control of drugs are developed by the Commission on Narcotic Drugs of the United Nations Economic and Social Council. The principal functions of the Commission are to assist the Council in the supervision of international agreements respecting drug control and to make policy recommendations to the Council and to governments. The Commission reports to the Council, submits draft resolutions for adoption by the Council, and makes decision for its own action or guidance, or as suggestions for action by governments.

The membership of the Commission includes representatives of countries which are important in the field of manufacture of narcotic drugs and the countries in which drug dependency or the illicit traffic in narcotic drugs constitutes and important problem.

The Commission has power to amend the schedules of the *Single Convention on Narcotic Drugs, 1961*, by adding or deleting drugs. A party to the Convention may require review of any such decision by the Economic and Social Council.

The World Health Organization plays an important role in the development of international drug control policy. The Convention contemplates that the WHO will make recommendations to the Commission concerning the effects and proper classification for purposes of international control of the various drugs. The technical findings and recommendations of the WHO in this field are developed by its Expert Committee on

Drug Dependence. The Commission may accept or reject the recommendations of the WHO as to the control measures to be applied to a certain drug under the *Single Convention on Narcotic Drugs, 1961,* but it may not modify them.

The Commission on Narcotic Drugs has now developed a draft Protocol on the control of psychotropic drugs outside the scope of the *Single Convention on Narcotic Drugs, 1961,* which will be considered for adoption at an international conference in 1971. The draft Protocol contemplates the international control of drugs which presently fall in the 'controlled' and 'restricted' categories of the *Food and Drugs Act,* including the amphetamines, the barbiturates, and the hallucinogens, such as LSD, DET and STP (DOM). It also contemplates control of tranquillizers. It is assumed that Canada will not incur international obligations with respect to the control of these drugs before it has had an opportunity to consider the final report of our Commission.

III. Constitutional Framework

368. A proper appreciation of Canadian legislative policy on the non-medical use of drugs also requires some awareness of the constitutional framework. Because of the limited scope of the federal power to regulate trade and commerce – one which has been confined essentially to international and inter-provincial trade and commerce – federal drug legislation has rested on the criminal law power.[13] What this means is that federal legislation, if it is to reach transactions taking place wholly within a province, probably has to have a criminal law character, whether or not an alternative type of regulation might be more desirable. The prohibitions in both the *Narcotic Control Act* and the *Food and Drugs Act* form part of the criminal law of Canada, and violations of these prohibitions constitute criminal offences. A misapprehension was evident during the course of our hearings that offences under the *Food and Drugs Act* had in some sense a different legal status or character than those under the *Narcotic Control Act.* They do not, although there are significant differences in the severity of the penalties under the two statutes, and a wider opportunity to proceed by

way of summary conviction instead of by way of indictment under the *Food and Drugs Act.*

369. It is doubtful if the Federal Government has any constitutional basis other than the criminal law power for a comprehensive regulation of non-medical drug use. The chief possibilities would be the general power (or 'Peace, Order and Good Government' clause) based on the importance such use has assumed for the country as a whole, and a broader application of the trade and commerce power, based on the international and interprovincial character of the drug traffic as a whole. It is doubtful, however, if either of these possible bases of jurisdiction could be successfully invoked to support a federal regulation of any particular drug, similar to the provincial regulation of alcohol, which involves a government monopoly of distribution as well as a licensing system.

370. On the other hand, the provinces can not create penal offences unless they are properly ancillary to otherwise valid provincial legislation. There would seem to be no doubt about provincial jurisdiction to develop a system of administrative regulation of a particular drug similar to that which applies to alcohol, if the Federal Government were to withdraw its criminal law proscription of the drug, or at least permit 'local option'. But the possible scope for provincial penal legislation to control the distribution and use of drugs, even in the absence of federal criminal law, is not so clear. There is some judicial support for the view that such penal provisions might be validly grafted on to provincial health legislation, but it is doubtful.[14] The judicial authority supporting provincial liquor prohibition legislation as the suppression of a 'local evil' would appear to be a constitutional anomaly which could not be relied on as a basis for further prohibitions of this sort.[15]

371. In sum, the Federal Government controls the criminal law approach to non-medical drug use and the provinces would appear to control the approach of 'legalization', involving government monopoly of distribution.

The division of constitutional responsibility with respect to other aspects of the social response to non-medical drug use – in

248

particular, research, education and treatment – also indicates the appropriateness of federal-provincial consultation and co-operation to develop a coordinated national policy. We touch on these areas in our interim recommendations in Chapter Six.

IV. Federal Legislation and its Enforcement

372. *1. The Statutes and Administrative Regulations.* The non-medical use of psychotropic drugs is presently regulated by the *Narcotic Control Act* and the *Food and Drugs Act*. Each statute makes a rigid distinction between legitimate and illegitimate use of the drugs with which it deals. Total criminal prohibition is deemed impossible because of the desirability of the drugs for certain medical or scientific purposes. Hence one major function of the legislation is to devise a system of controls which isolates this type of legitimate use and ensures that no leakage or diversion of the drugs for illegitimate purposes occurs. This system of controls is established by the regulations under each act and is administered by the Food and Drug Directorate of the Department of National Health and Welfare.

The Department estimates the yearly requirements for legitimate use in Canada and issues permits to licensed dealers to manufacture or import certain quantities. Wholesalers can dispose of the drugs only to other licensed dealers, pharmacists, practitioners, or hospitals. The pharmacists can dispense the drugs only under a prescription which they have undertaken, reasonably, to verify. For narcotics, a prescription can be filled only once, and refilling for controlled drugs is limited. Both dealers and pharmacists are required to keep complete records of the persons with whom they have transacted business involving narcotics or controlled drugs, together with the quantities which are involved. Reports are sent to the Directorate and reviewed, and periodic audits or inspections are made to verify their accuracy. Records must be kept by hospitals, although not by practitioners. The latter are required to account, though, for the use made of drugs they purchase for professional treatment.

The rigid system of controls and records is designed to enable

249

the flow of drugs in the legitimate distribution system to be maintained and verified. If excessive amounts appear at any one point, investigation may be made of the reasons for this. The objective of this whole effort is the preservation of the integrity of criminal law controls on all other kinds of use by preventing leakage from the legal to the illegal market.

373. *The Narcotic Control Act* applies to opium and its derivatives, such as heroin and morphine, the synthetic narcotics and cannabis (marijuana and hashish), which is classified as a narcotic for purposes of the Act. Unauthorized possession, trafficking in, and import and export of narcotics and cannabis, as well as the cultivation of the opium poppy or marijuana, are prohibited by the Act with penal consequences as follows:

(*a*) Unauthorized possession is punishable

(i) upon summary conviction for a first offence, by a fine of one thousand dollars or by imprisonment for six months or by both fine and imprisonment and for a subsequent offence, by a fine of two thousand dollars or by imprisonment for one year or both by fine and imprisonment; or (ii) upon conviction on indictment, by imprisonment for seven years (Sec. 3, as amended by 1969 Stat. Can., c. 41, s. 12)

(*b*) Trafficking is punishable upon conviction on indictment by imprisonment for life. (Sec. 4)

(*c*) Being in possession for the purpose of trafficking is punishable in the same way. (Sec. 4)

(*d*) Unauthorized importing or exporting is punishable upon conviction on indictment by imprisonment for life, and in any case by imprisonment for not less than seven years. (Sec. 5)

(*e*) Unauthorized cultivation of opium poppy or marijuana is punishable by imprisonment for seven years. (Sec. 6)

374. Unauthorized conduct with respect to certain other psychotropic drugs which are the subject of this inquiry is prohibited by the *Food and Drugs Act.*

Part III of the Act,[17] dealing with 'controlled drugs' (which include the amphetamines, methamphetamines, and barbiturates) prohibits trafficking in, and possession for the purpose of trafficking in those drugs as follows:

> (a) Trafficking is punishable upon summary conviction by imprisonment for eighteen months, or upon conviction on indictment, by imprisonment for ten years. (Sec. 32)
> (b) Possession for the purpose of trafficking is punishable in the same way. (Sec. 32)

Part IV of the Act,[18] dealing with 'restricted drugs' (which include LSD, DET, DMT, STP (DOM), MDA, MMDA and LBJ) prohibits possession, trafficking in, and possession for the purpose of trafficking in, these drugs as follows:

> (a) Unauthorized possession is punishable
> (i) upon summary conviction for a first offence, by a fine of one thousand dollars or by imprisonment for six months or by both fine and imprisonment, and for a subsequent offence, by a fine of two thousand dollars or by imprisonment for one year, or by both fine and imprisonment; or (ii) upon conviction on indictment, by a fine of five thousand dollars or by imprisonment for three years or by both fine and imprisonment. (Sec. 40)
> (b) Trafficking and possession for the purpose of trafficking are punishable
> (i) upon summary conviction, by imprisonment for eighteen months; or (ii) upon conviction on indictment, by imprisonment for ten years. (Sec. 41)

A person may also be charged with conspiracy to traffic under S. 408 (1) (d) of the Criminal Code, which makes him liable upon indictment to the same punishment as one convicted upon indictment of trafficking under the *Narcotic Control Act* or the *Food and Drugs Act*.

375. 2. *The Role of Possession and the Possessional Offence in the Law.* Both statutes have as their purpose the prevention of non-medical or non-scientific use of drugs. However, neither of them makes use, as such, a criminal offence. Yet, under the *Narcotic Control Act*, simple possession of the drug is a crimi-

nal offence. To the extent that 'use' requires 'possession', the effect of this Act is to make all unauthorized users criminals. The same is true of 'restricted drugs' (e.g., LSD) under part IV of the *Food and Drugs Act*. However, for 'controlled drugs' (e.g., amphetamines) under Part III of the Act there is no such prohibition of simple possession (and thus, 'use'), and the object of criminal law regulations is the distribution system.

376. Under both statutes, and for all three legal categories of drugs – narcotics, controlled drugs and restricted drugs – there are two prohibitions directed against illegal distribution: a prohibition against trafficking and a prohibition against possession for the purpose of trafficking.

Importing or exporting is a separate offence under the *Narcotic Control Act,* carrying a minimum sentence of seven years imprisonment, but it falls within the definition of trafficking for both 'controlled' and 'restricted' drugs under the *Food and Drugs Act*.

For purposes of the *Narcotic Control Act* and the *Food and Drugs Act*, 'possession' has the same meaning that it has under the *Criminal Code*, where it is defined in Section 3 (4) as follows:

(a) 'A person has anything in possession when he has it in his personal possession or knowingly
  (i) has it in the actual possession or custody of another person, or
  (ii) has it in any place, whether or not that place belongs or is occupied by him for the use or benefit of himself or of another person; and
(b) Where one of two or more persons, with the knowledge and consent of the rest, has anything in his custody or possession, it shall be deemed to be in the custody and possession of each and all of them.'

377. It has been held that there is no 'minimal' amount required to establish the offence of simple possession,[19] but an 'infinitesimal' amount found in traces of the accused's clothing has been held insufficient for conviction.[20] The accused must know that he has a prohibited drug in his possession. In other words, he must have the necessary intention or *mens rea* tra-

ditionally required for criminal responsibility.[21] Where the accused is charged with being in constructive possession by virtue of the fact that another person has possession with his knowledge and consent,[22] it is not sufficient to show mere acquiescence; it is necessary to show some kind of control[23] over a common venture regarding the drug.[24]

378. In their submissions to the Commission, officers of the R.C.M. Police contended that a 'possessional offence' was essential to effective law enforcement against trafficking. They claimed that there should be possessional offences for other prohibited drugs, such as the amphetamines. At the present time, we have no basis for comparing the effectiveness of the law enforcement against trafficking, where there is an offence of simple possession, such as in the case of heroin, cannabis, and LSD, with the effectiveness where there is not such an offence, as in the case of the amphetamines, but this is undoubtedly a matter of importance requiring further examination, if possible. The existence of a possessional offence apparently makes it less risky to proceed for trafficking. As the submission on behalf of one division of the R.C.M. Police put it: 'Our main target is the trafficker. At times we are unable to obtain sufficient evidence for a trafficking offence, then we might proceed with a straight possession charge which helps to serve the purpose.' An officer speaking for another division told the Commission that it was difficult to have enforcement without a possessional offence. And another agreed that a possessional offence for 'controlled' drugs would be beneficial for law enforcement.

379. *3. Burden of Proof.* The role of possession in drug offences is also closely related to the question of burden of proof, in which the law reflects a significant departure from the traditional approach of criminal justice. The offence of possession for the purpose of trafficking is important as a means of enforcing trafficking laws in the face of the great difficulties in detecting and proving the prohibited transaction. It enables the prosecution to rely on the simple fact of possession, once proved, as evidence which can justify a finding of possession for trafficking, even for 'controlled' drugs for which there is not an

offence of simple possession. In all three categories – narcotics,[25] controlled drugs[26] and restricted drugs[27] – it is provided that in a prosecution for possession for the purpose of trafficking there is first to be a finding by the Court as to simple possession. If possession in law is found by the Court to be established on the evidence, the accused is to 'be given an opportunity of establishing that he was not in possession of the narcotic (or controlled or restricted drug, as the case may be) for the purpose of trafficking'. If he fails to do so, he is convicted of possession for the purpose of trafficking; if he succeeds, he is convicted of simple possession or acquitted according to the category of drugs involved.

It is obvious that, in the absence of an admission, proof of an ulterior motive such as the intention to traffic must be by way of inference from circumstantial evidence, most often the quantity of the drug discovered in the accused's possession.[28] Hence the reason for putting some onus on the accused for an explanation of unauthorized possession. The serious question is the precise nature of the burden thrown on the accused by this procedure and the extent to which it operates, in practice, as a departure from the traditional presumption of his innocence and other protection of the accused.

The Courts have distinguished the secondary burden of adducing evidence from the primary burden of proving a fact when all the evidence is in.[29] The primary burden is always on the Crown to establish all the elements of a crime, including the purpose of trafficking in this offence. Because this onus always requires proof beyond a reasonable doubt, the presumption of innocence remains unaffected. However, the legislation has deemed that evidence of unauthorized possession may support an inference of the mental element without any further affirmative evidence on this point, unless the accused gives a reasonable probable alternative explanation for his possession, whether from his own evidence, or other witnesses, or from evidence already before the Court.[30] The Court need not draw this inference even when the accused does not adduce any evidence, but he takes the risk it will do so.[31] In all cases, though, if the accused by argument or evidence or cross-examination of the Crown witnesses establishes a reasonable doubt about his alleged purpose of trafficking, he must be acquitted of the offence of possession for the purpose of trafficking.[32]

380. *4. The Definition of Trafficking.* To traffic under the *Narcotic Control Act* means 'to manufacture, sell, give, administer, transport, send, deliver or distribute', 'or 'to offer to do' any of these things without authority.[33] Under the *Food and Drugs Act*, Parts III and IV, applicable to controlled and restricted drugs, it means 'to manufacture, sell, export from or import into Canada, transport or deliver', without authority.[34] Thus under the *Food and Drugs Act* trafficking includes importing or exporting, which is a separate offence calling for a minimum of seven years imprisonment under the *Narcotic Control Act*, but it does not include *offering* to do any of the things mentioned above. It is not clear whether any significance is to be attached to the absence of the words 'give' and 'administer' in the definition of trafficking in the *Food and Drug Act*. It is not necessary to be in possession to be a trafficker, and thus the offences of trafficking and being in possession for the purpose of trafficking are quite distinct, although they may be proved by the same facts.[35] The offence of trafficking by offering to do so does not require actual possession of the drug which is offered.[36]

Some attempts have been made to extend the definition of trafficking by relying on the word 'transport' in the definition, and arguing that any movement of the drug from one place to another is sufficient for trafficking, but the Courts have rejected this argument, stating that the word 'transport', when read in the context of other words in the definition, can not be applied to movement of the drug connected with the accused's own use.[37] The very fact that there are separate offences for possession, possession for trafficking, and trafficking, requires some notion, in the case of trafficking, of a transaction of some kind with another person.

The statutes express no distinction at all between qualitatively different kinds of trafficking and the Courts have not read any such distinction into the legislation. There is obviously a big difference between selling the drug for monetary consideration and giving it to a friend. Selling it at cost to an acquaintance is different from selling it to a variety of people to make a profit. Selling it on a small scale to make a marginal profit – perhaps to support one's own usage – is not the same as organizing and controlling a large entrepreneurial organization. As can be seen, trafficking activities range along a spectrum from a kind of act not far removed in seriousness from simple possession to the extensive activities of the stereotyped exploiter and profiteer whose image led to the kinds of penalties associated with trafficking. The legislature has left it to the Courts to develop sentencing policies reflecting important differences.

For the offence of trafficking, unlike that of simple possession (or possession for the purpose of trafficking), it is not necessary that the substance actually be one of the prohibited drugs; it is sufficient that it be represented or held out to be such by the accused.

381. *5. Methods of Enforcement.* Special enforcement difficulties, calling for special enforcement methods, arise from the fact that drug offences do not involve a victim, such as exists in the case of crimes against person or property. There are important consequences of this distinction. The victim of a crime against person or property usually complains to the police, gives them information, and assists them to commence an investigation. The police react to what they have been told about a specific offence. If, on the other hand, someone has a drug in his possession, and has bought it from someone else, it is rare that anyone will feel affected enough to lay a complaint. Hence, instead of reacting to a specific request, the police must go out themselves and look for offences. Moreover, it is difficult to discover these offences. Because the parties to the offence or transaction are all willing participants, they can agree to carry out the prohibited conduct in a place of privacy where it is not likely to be seen either by witnesses or police officers.

This problem of enforcement has generated legal responses that are relatively peculiar to the drug context. First of all, under the statutes, the powers of search and seizure by police officers have been radically expanded. Under the ordinary law, a person can be searched only after an arrest has been made, and in order to discover any evidence of the crime for which the arrest is made. Where there is not an arrest, there is no power to search premises without a search warrant. Again, such warrants assume specific evidence that the particular premises contain something incriminating. The point of these rules is to prevent indiscriminate interference with privacy in an attempt to turn up evidence of a crime and to prevent such interference by requiring cogent evidence that the person or premises affected are peculiarly worthy of search, before such search is authorized by an independent judicial officer who reviews this evidence.

382. Under the *Narcotic Control Act* and the *Food and Drugs Act*, the powers of search are widened in an extraordinary way.[38] The test to be applied remains theoretically the same – does the officer reasonably believe that there is a narcotic or other proscribed drug on the premises searched? But there is no longer a real requirement that the police obtain external review and confirmation of their judgement concerning this reasonable belief. Any police officer can enter and search any place other than a dwelling house without a warrant, if he has this reasonable belief. If it is a dwelling house, the demands of privacy require a warrant or a Writ of Assistance.

A warrant is obtained from a magistrate who is satisfied by information under oath that there are reasonable grounds for believing that there is a narcotic or other proscribed drug by means of or in respect of which an offence has been committed, in a particular dwelling house. On the other hand, the Writ of Assistance,[39] which was introduced in 1929, is a blanket warrant which must be issued by a judge of the Exchequer Court of Canada to an enforcement officer upon application by the Minister. It remains valid so long as the officer retains his authority and it empowers him to enter any dwelling in Canada at any time, with such assistance as he may require, and search for narcotics and other proscribed drugs. As in the case of a warrant, he must reasonably believe that the dwelling contains the narcotic or other proscribed drug by means of or in respect of which an offence has been committed, but his reasons for such belief are not reviewable before the authority is conferred.

A peace officer having authority under the *Narcotic Control*

Act or the *Food and Drugs Act* to enter a place and search without warrant, or to do so with a warrant or a Writ of Assistance may 'with such assistance as he deems necessary, break open any door, window, lock, fastener, floor, wall, ceiling, compartment, plumbing, box, container or any other thing'; may search any person found in such place; and may seize and take away any narcotic or other proscribed drug in such place, as well as anything that may be evidence of the commission of an offence under the Act.

Judicial reaction to these extraordinary powers thought to be necessary for the enforcement of the drug laws, is reflected in the words of the Ontario Court of Appeal in *Regina v. Brezack*,[40] where it was held that a constable who reasonably believes that an arrested person has a narcotic in his mouth may force his own fingers into the mouth to obtain the drug. The Court said:

> ... it is well known that, in making arrests in these narcotic cases, it would often be impossible to find evidence of the offence upon the person arrested if he had the slightest suspicion that he might be searched. Constables have a task of great difficulty in their efforts to check the illegal traffic in opium and other prohibited drugs. Those who carry on the traffic are cunning, crafty and unscrupulous almost beyond belief. While, therefore, it is important that constables should be instructed that there are limits upon their right of search, including search of the person, they are not to be encumbered by technicalities in handling the situations with which they often have to deal in narcotic cases, which permit them little time for deliberation and require the stern exercise of such rights of search as they possess.

The difficulties of enforcement in this field have led to another unusual practice – what is known in other jurisdictions as 'entrapment' but which may be described as 'police encouragement'. A person is encouraged by a police agent to commit an offence. It is impossible to say how extensive this practice is, but it is reflected in a number of cases.

It is unclear whether there is any lawful authority for police officers or their agents to engage, for purposes of law enforcement, in conduct which would otherwise be an offence. The decision in *Regina v. Ormerod*[41] throws considerable doubt on the legality of this practice. Should police involvement in the transaction have any bearing on the guilt of the accused? The American courts have developed the defence of 'entrapment' in order to deter overly aggressive police encouragement of offences.[42] The Ouimet Committee on Corrections has recommended the legislative adoption of a similar defence in Canada in favour of a person who does not have 'a pre-existing intention to commit the offence'.[43] In the case of *Regina v. Shipley*[44] the doctrine was applied for the first time to stay prosecution. The court found that the undercover R.C.M. Police officer befriended the rather 'naïve' young defendant, asked the latter to obtain drugs for him, and refused to repay a loan until it was done. The judge held that the Court had an inherent power to prevent abuse of its processes. The Courts have also considered the involvement of police agents in drug offences as relevant to mitigation of sentence.[45]

383. 6. *Sentencing Policy*. The approach to sentencing has varied considerably across Canada in the four or five years since offences involving drugs other than heroin have assumed importance. Table I shows the distribution and range of sentences by province for marijuana and hashish offences from January 1 to October 31, 1969,[46] from the brief of the Solicitor General's Department.

The upsurge in drug use, especially among the young in recent years, has generated a substantial difference of opinion in the Courts as to appropriateness of sentences within the statutory limitations. Basically, this has involved the question of the appropriateness of prison for young first offenders, whether for possession or marginal trafficking. There have been more written, reported, appellate opinions, and more discussion of the appropriate principles of sentencing policy in these drug cases than for all other offences put together. This is probably the best evidence there can be of the uneasiness the Courts feel about the difficult problem which has been left to them.

The picture of sentencing policy or attitudes which emerges

TABLE FIVE

NUMBER OF CONVICTIONS FOR MARIJUANA AND HASHISH OFFENCES BY TYPES OF SENTENCES AND PROVINCE RECORDED BETWEEN 1ST JANUARY AND 21 OCTOBER, 1969

(Division of Narcotic Control, Department of National Health and Welfare)*

Province	Fine Only	Probation S/S	Indefinite period	Under 6 mos.	6 mos. to less than 1 yr.	1 yr. to less than 2 yrs.	2 yrs. to less than 3 yrs.	3 yrs. to less than 4 yrs.	4 yrs. to less than 5 yrs.	5 yrs. to less than 6 yrs.	6 yrs. to less than 7 yrs.	7 yrs. to less than 8 yrs.	8 yrs. to less than 9 yrs.	9 yrs. to less than 10 yrs.	10 yrs. and over	Total
Newfoundland	—	1	—	—	—	—	—	1	—	—	—	—	—	—	—	2
Prince Edward Island	7	3	—	1	—	—	—	—	—	—	—	—	—	—	—	11
New Brunswick	—	9	1	6	—	3	—	—	1	1	—	—	—	—	1	22
Quebec	20	129	1	117	22	10	19	1	2	1	—	2	—	—	—	324
Nova Scotia	4	23	—	4	—	—	—	—	—	—	—	—	—	—	—	31
Ontario	30	483	7	108	61	17	4	1	—	—	—	—	—	—	—	711
Manitoba	9	33	1	27	5	6	2	—	—	—	—	—	—	—	—	83
Alberta	2	99	—	27	26	16	7	1	—	—	—	—	—	—	—	178
Saskatchewan	—	19	—	15	2	—	—	—	—	—	—	—	—	—	—	36
British Columbia	37	201	12	230	62	35	8	3	3	2	—	1	—	—	—	594
Yukon	—	—	—	1	—	—	—	—	—	—	—	—	—	—	—	1
Total	109	1,000	21	536	178	87	40	8	6	4	—	3	—	—	1	1,993

* From the Brief of the Department of the Solicitor General

from an examination of sentences over the last four or five years, prior to cases of simple possession arising under the new legislation in August 1969,[47] is that the provincial courts of appeal have steeled themselves against the costs to the offender and have laid down the principle that the 'public interest' in general deterrence calls for a substantial prison sentence for the drug offender. Trial judges and magistrates, in actual contact with the offender, have been much more ambivalent about this policy, and in several cases prison sentences have been imposed or increased on appeal.[48] Probably the most influential Court in the determination of sentencing policy has been the British Columbia Court of Appeal. Beginning with the case of *Regina v. Budd* in 1965,[49] where the Court dismissed an appeal by a twenty-one year old female student from a six-month jail sentence for possession of marijuana, the Court has emphasized deterrence. In *Regina v. Hartley and McCallum (No. 2)* in 1968,[50] they upheld six months terms for eighteen and twenty-one year old first offenders and spoke as follows about the significance of the offence of simple possession:

The predominant factor in this case is the deterrent effect upon others. This Court two years ago in the Budd case . . . said that the possession of marijuana is a serious offence and it must be punished severely. The purpose of course was to deter the use of marijuana, among other reasons, because users must obtain supplies, and the supply of the drug involves trafficking, and that, as the market increases, that traffic becomes organized, and the organized traffic tends to increase the use of the drug. It was our hope then, although I was not party to that decision, that substantial gaol sentences imposed upon people convicted of having possession of marijuana for their own use would reduce the number of users, and consequently the trafficking necessary to supply the market. We also feared that if we did not treat this offence seriously that the traffic would continue to develop and users would increase. Our fears have been borne out by the experience over the past few years. Our hopes have been disappointed because with deference some of the members of the magisterial bench have failed to fully appreciate our purpose in the Budd case. Too many of these convictions for possession of marijuana have been treated too leniently . . .

In this case the deterrent aspect, as I said, is the important one. The rehabilitation of the offenders is secondary. If the use of this drug is not stopped, it is going to be followed by an organized marketing system. That must be prevented if possible. We think that is the principal consideration which should move us.

The general approach of the British Columbia Court of Appeal seems to have influenced the courts in other provinces in which prison sentences have been imposed in recent years for the offence of simple possession. Since the amendment to the law in August, 1969, providing the option of proceeding by way of summary conviction, instead of indictment in cases of simple possession of marijuana and hashish, sentencing policy with respect to this offence has shown a marked change that is revealed by statistics for the balance of the year 1969. The pattern they reveal is that imprisonment is now being rarely, if at all, resorted to in cases of simple possession of marijuana and hashish and, it would appear, LSD, and that such cases are now generally disposed of by suspended sentence, probation or fine. It would appear that the policy now is, as a general rule, not to impose prison sentences for typical first offenders. The amendment of August, 1969, applied equally to simple possession of heroin, but the information received by the Commission suggests that prison sentences are still being imposed for this offence.

As indicated above, the statute law does not make any distinction between differently motivated kinds of trafficking for purposes of penalty. On the whole, the sentencing policy for trafficking has been one of severity, with sentences in some cases of as much as 20 years.[51] The courts have attempted to distinguish to some extent between different kinds of trafficking for purposes of sentence,[52] but an attempt to single out a certain category of trafficker for special treatment has been abandoned. In *Regina v. Hudson*,[53] the Ontario Court of Appeal ruled that suspended sentence and probation were more appropriate for the typical trafficker in the youthful, alienated sub-culture of Yorkville. The Court said:

Those, of whom the accused is one, who have accepted the use of psychedelic drugs as socially desirable as well as a personally desirable course of conduct are not as likely to be discouraged by the type of punishment ordinarily meted out to other traffickers. Such treatment will likely serve to confirm them in their belief in the drug cult . . .

The same court reconsidered this attitude in *Regina v. Simpson*,[54] where sentences of nine months definite and six months indefinite were upheld because of the alleged failure of the earlier policy. The Court said:

Some six months or more have elapsed since the decision in *R. v. Hudson* and in the case at bar statistical information was introduced demonstrating that the evil of trafficking in marijuana in the city of Toronto is markedly on the increase, that such trafficking is reaching into the secondary schools and that cases of such trafficking among juveniles now are a matter of frequent occurrence in the Juvenile Courts of the city . . . the protection of the public must include consideration of the interests, health and well-being of the vast majority of young people comprising individuals presently uncommitted to the use of this drug. As I have said, the sentence was appropriate; it is by no means a severe one, bearing in mind the gravity with which the offence must be regarded by reason of the maximum penalty of life imprisonment provided by the statute.

Following this case, there were several cases in other provinces where prison sentences were imposed, and in some instances increased on appeal in cases of marginal trafficking.

384. 7. *Empirical Study of Law Enforcement and Correctional System.* The Commission has so far been able only to make a preliminary pilot study in one major locality of actual enforcement of the drug laws, but it intends in the ensuing year to carry out a more comprehensive and thorough empirical study of such enforcement, with particular reference to such matters as: the relative cost of the enforcement of the drug laws, the extent and patterns of enforcement, including percenttage of offences dealt with and kinds of offender affected, the

manner in which discretions are exercised, the attitudes of police to their role, and sentencing policies and practices.

The pilot study suggests the urgent need for improvement in the present methods of collecting and recording statistical data with respect to the administration of criminal justice in this field. The kind of analysis for which reliable statistics are required is shown by the model of a flow chart in Figure I. Some of the difficulties with respect to statistics arise from the fact that there are three agencies primarily responsible for the collection of data, namely: the Food and Drug Directorate of the Department of National Health & Welfare, the R.C.M. Police and the Dominion Bureau of Statistics. The pilot study found a certain amount of duplication, but also inadequacies and inconsistencies in the reliability and validity of information compiled. Moreover, the delay between the conviction of drug offenders and the publication of statistical reports ranged between two months and three years. Due to rapid changes in the nature and extent of drug use and the way in which society responds to it through its official agencies, it is essential that this delay be reduced as much as possible. A rational policy depends on adequate, up-to-date information and steps should be taken to ensure that this is available on a continuing basis.

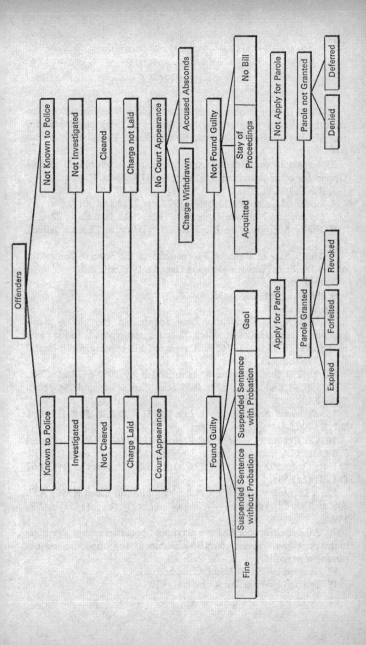

REFERENCES

1. Based in part upon a paper on the 'Social Background of Narcotic Legislation' prepared by Mrs Shirley J. Cook and others for the Alcoholism and Drug Addiction Research Foundation of Ontario.

2. An Act to prohibit the importation, manufacture and sale of Opium for other than medicinal purposes, 1908 Stat. Can., c.50.

3. R.S.C. 1952, c.201.

4. House of Commons Debates, 1922, pp. 2824 and 3017.

5. Opium and Narcotic Drug Act, 1923, 1923 Stat. Can., 22.

6. Emily Murphy, *The Black Candle* (Toronto, Thomas Allen), 1922.

7. The Senate of Canada: Proceedings of the Special Committee on the Traffic in Narcotic Drugs in Canada, 1955, xii.

8. Ibid, xx-xxi.

9. 1960–61, Stat. Can., c.35.

10. Secs. 15–19.

11. The Single Convention was adopted in 1961 by a plenipotentiary conferences in which 73 states participated, and it came into force on Dec. 13, 1964. It replaced all existing multi-lateral treaties in the field.

12. 1952–3 Stat. Can., c.38, as amended by 1960–61 Stat. Can., c.37; 1962–3 Stat. Can., c.15; 1969 Stat. Can., c.41; and 1969 Stat. Can., c.49.

13. *Standard Sausage Co. v Lee* [1933] 4 D.L.R. 501, [1934] 1 D.L.R. 706.

14. Cf. *Regina v. Synder and Fletcher* (1967) 61 W.W.R. 112 and 576 (Alta C.A.); and *Regina v. Simpson, Mack and Lewis* [1969] 1 D.L.R. (3rd.) 597, (1969) 3 C.C.C. 101 (B.C.C.A.), rev'g. [1968] 67 D.L.R. (2d) 585.

15. A.G. Ont. v. A.G. Can. (Local Prohibition Case) [1896] A.C. 348 at 370; Cf. *Switzman v. Elbling and A.G. Que.,* [1957] S.C.R. 299.

16. All penalties specified are maximum penalties except the minimum penalty of seven years imprisonment for importing or exporting a narcotic.

17. Enacted by 1960–61 Stat. Can., c.37. s.1.

18. Enacted by 1969 Stat. Can., c.41, s.10.

19. *R. v. McLeod*, (1955), 21 CR. 137 (B.C.C.A.).

20. *R. v. Ling*, (1954), 19 C.R. 173 (Alta.) 109 C.C.C. 306 (Alta.); but compare *Regina v. Quigley*, (1955), 20 C.R. 152; 111 C.C.C. 81, where it was held that the only reasonable conclusion was that the amount found was the residue of a larger amount.

21. *R. v. Beaver*, (1957), S.C.R. 531; 118 C.C.C. 129.

22. See paragraph (b) of section 3 (4) of the Criminal Code quoted above.

23. *R. v. Colvin and Gladue*, (1943), 1 D.L.R. 20, 78 C.C.C. 282 (B.C.C.A.); *R. v. Larier*, 129 C.C.C. 297 (Sask. C.A.); *R. v. Harvey*, 7 C.R.N.S. 183 (N.B.C.A.); *R. v. Marshall* (1969), 3 C.C.C. 149 (Alta. C.A.)

24. What is required is control over the drug but this may presumably be inferred from control over the person or persons in actual possession of it.

25. *Narcotic Control Act*, s.8.

26. *Food and Drugs Act*, s.33 (as amended by 1969 Stat. Can., c.41, s.8).

27. *Food and Drugs Act*, s.42 (as enacted by 1969 Stat. Can., c.41, s.10).

28. See *R. v. Wilson*, (1954), 11 W.W.R. 282, but compare with *R. v. MacDonald*; *R. v. Harrington*, (1963), 43 W.W.R. 337 (C.A.). Other circumstantial evidence most commonly relied on are exhibits suggesting sale or distribution, such as containers, scales and measuring spoons, lists of names and telephone numbers, large amounts of cash in small denominations, and the like; and evidence of the accused's movements suggestive of contact for purposes other than his regular employment.

29. See *R. v. Sharpe*, (1961), O.W.N. 261, 131 C.C.C. 75 (Ont. C.A.), a case under the *Opium and Narcotic Drug Act*, and predecessor of the *Narcotic Control Act*.

30. *R. v. Capello*, 122 C.C.C. 342 (B.C.C.A.).

31. *R. v. Huper, Forsyth and Patterson*, 122 C.C.C. 346 (B.C.C.A.).

32. *R. v. Hartley and McCallum* (No. 1), (1968) 2 C.C.C. 183 (B.C.C.A.); See also *R. v. Hupe*, et al, *supra*; *R. v. Capello, supra*. In *R. v. Sharpe, supra*, the Ontario Court of Appeal held that the secondary burden on the accused of adducing evidence could be discharged by a balance of probabilities, that the primary burden of proving guilt beyond a reasonable doubt rests on the Crown throughout, and that for this reason the burden on the accused was not an infringement of the right under the *Canadian Bill of Rights* 'to be presumed innocent until proved guilty according to law'.

33. Sec. 2 (i).

34. Secs. 31 (c) and 39 (d).

35. *R. v. MacDonald*; *R. v. Vickers*, (1963), 43 W.W.R. 238 (B.C.C.A.). See also *R. v. Wells*, [1963,] 2 C.C.C. 279, in which the accused was convicted of trafficking for her aid to a distributor who actually passed the drugs to the buyers. She drew up a list of potential buyers, received their money, and checked their names off the list as they received their purchase.

36. *R. v. Brown*, (1953), 17 C.R. 257.

37. *R. v. Macdonald; R. v. Harrington*, (1963), 41 C.R. 75, 43 W.W.R. 337; [1964] 1 C.C.C. 189 (B.C.C.A.). *R. v. Cushman*, 5 C.R. N.S 359.

38. See *Narcotic Control Act*, s.10; *Food and Drugs Act*, ss. 36 and 44.

39. See Traswick, E. W., 'Search Warrants and Writs of Assistance', (1962) 5 Criminal Law Quarterly 362.

40. [1950], 2 D.L.R. 265 at 270 (Ont. C.A.).

41. (1969), 6 C.R.N.S. 37 (Ont. C.A)

42. *Sorrells v. United States*, 287 U.S. 435 (1932).

43. Report of the Canadian Committee on Corrections, pp. 75–80.

44. Judgement of County Court of Ottawa, October 22, 1969, not yet reported.

45. *R. v. Ormerod, supra*; *R. v. Mills,* judgement of the British Columbia Court of Appeal, May 28, 1969 not yet reported. Cf. however, *R. v. Granbois*, (1969), 6 C.R.N.S. 313 in which no reference was made to the fact that the sale was made to an undercover agent.

46. From the brief of the Department of the Solicitor General to the Commission.

47. 1969 Stat. Can., c.41.

48. E.g. *R. v. McNicol,* (1968), 5 C.R.N.S. 242, 66 W.W.R. 612, 1 D.L.R. (3rd) 328, (Man CA); *R. v. Racine*, judgement of the British Columbia Court of Appeal, April 2, 1969, not yet reported; *R. v. Robichaud*, judgement of the New Brunswick Court of Appeal, November 25, 1969, not yet reported; *R. v. Lehrmann*, 61 W.W.R. 625, [1968] 2 C.C.C. 198 (Alta. C.A.); *R. v. Adelman*, [1968] 3 C.C.C. 311 (B.C.C.A.).

49. Judgement of the British Columbia Court of Appeal, January 15, 1965, unreported, but synopsized at 5 C.R.N.S. 248–9.

50. [1968] 2 C.C.C. 187 at 188–189.

51. *R. v. Babcock* [1967] 2 C.C.C. 235 (B.C.C.A.); *R. v. Cipolla*

[1965] 2 O.R. 673, (Ont. C.A.), aff'd. by S.C.C., June 14, 1965. Both of these were serious trafficking cases.

52. E.g. *R. v. Kazmer*, 105 C.C.C. 153 (B.C.C.A.); *R. v. Campbell*, (1969), 67 W.W.R 678 (B.C.C.A.), dealing with hard narcotic cases.

53. [1967] 2 O.R. 501, 2 C.R.N.S. 189, [1968] 2 C.C.C. 43 (Ont. C.A.).

54. [1968] 2 O.R. 270; 3 C.R.N.S. 353, [1969] 1 C.C.C. 93 (Ont. C.A.).

CHAPTER SIX

THE ISSUES – SOME INTERIM RECOMMENDATIONS

A. INTRODUCTION

385. *Terms of Reference.* As set out more fully in Chapter One, the Commission is required by its terms of reference to inquire into and report on the effects, the extent and the causes of the non-medical use of psychotropic drugs and substances in Canada and to make recommendation to the Federal Government as to what it can do, alone or with other levels of government, to reduce 'the dimensions of the problems involved in such use'. The Commission has interpreted its terms of reference as applying to all drugs and substances which alter sensation, mood, consciousness or other psychological or behavioural functions in the living organism and to such use of these drugs and substances as is not indicated (or justified) for generally accepted medical reasons. As explained in Chapter Two, the Commission has classified these psychotropic drugs and substances into eight major categories: sedatives and hypnotics; stimulants; psychedelics and hallucinogens; opiate narcotics; volatile solvents; non-narcotic analgesics; clinical anti-depressants and major tranquillizers. The Commission is devoting particular attention at this time to the barbiturates, alcohol, the minor tranquillizers, the amphetamines, LSD, cannabis (marijuana and hashish), the opiate narcotics such as heroin, and the volatile solvents and gases.

386. *The requirement of an interim report.* The Commission is required to make a final report within two years from the date of its appointment, but it is also required to make an interim report 'at the expiration of six months' from the date of the appointment of the Commission. It is left to the discretion of the Commission to determine the appropriate scope of the interim report. The Commission has interpreted this requirement to mean that there should be an initial period of inquiry of at least six months to serve as the basis for an interim report, and that the Com-

mission should prepare its interim report upon the expiration of this period. The manner in which the issues have developed during the initial phase of the inquiry, as well as public and governmental expectations concerning the scope of the interim report, have suggested to the Commission that the interim report would have to be more comprehensive than was originally contemplated in order to meet the felt needs for perspective and information at this time. Accordingly, its preparation has taken longer than was originally planned, but the additional time has made it possible to take into consideration the submissions which the Commission has received in public and private hearings since the beginning of 1970. The interim report thus has a broader basis than would have been the case had it been confined to information obtained through public hearings and other means of inquiry up to the end of November 1969.

387. *Function of the interim report*. As explained more fully in Chapter One, the Commission conceives of the interim report as helping to put the phenomenon of non-medical drug use in some perspective, identifying the issues, and disclosing tentative findings or assumptions concerning the effects, extent and causes of such use. We also feel that it is appropriate, in the interim report, to make such recommendations as seem urgent and for which there is a sufficient basis at this time. But generally speaking, the interim report is primarily concerned with the statement of the issues and applicable principles, and the final report is to be concerned with the detailed application of these principles to the development of a satisfactory system of social response to the phenomenon of non-medical drug use. It is also hoped that the interim report will serve as a basis for further discussion and analysis, and by attracting opinion to our preliminary definition of the issues, assist us in arriving at a fuller and more informed understanding of this phenomenon.

We must emphasize two characteristics of the interim report:
(A) The preliminary nature of our findings at this time; and
(B) The selective treatment of the subject.

388. *The problems involved in non-medical drug use*. The Commission is required by its terms of reference to identify the 'problems involved in' the non-medical use of psychotropic drugs

and substances. These problems emerge from a study of the effects, the extent and the causes of non-medical drug use, as well as the social response to it. In the initial phase of our inquiry our attention has been drawn to many matters which are alleged to be problems involved in non-medical drug use. At the very outset, a fundamental question (which we attempt to deal with below) is formulated: to what extent is non-medical drug use in itself to be considered a problem? Beyond this general question our inquiry so far suggests that the following matters are among the most important to be considered as problems within the meaning of our terms of reference:

(a) the harm (whether personal or social) produced by certain non-medical drug use;

(b) the extent and patterns of such use, and in particular its increase among certain age groups in the population;

(c) the aspects of our personal relations and social conditions today which encourage such use;

(d) the proliferation and adulteration of drugs;

(e) the lack of sufficient scientifically valid and accepted information concerning the phenomenon of non-medical drug use;

(f) the lack of a coordinated and otherwise effective approach to the timely collection and dissemination of such information as does exist, including appropriate drug education programmes;

(g) our present approach to treatment and the other supportive services required to assist people suffering from the adverse effects of non-medical drug use; and

(h) the content and application of the criminal law in the field of non-medical drug use.

389. *The concept of social response.* We see non-medical drug use generally as presenting a complex social challenge for which we must find a wise and effective range of social responses. We believe that we must explore the full range of possible responses, including research, information and education; legislation and administrative regulation; treatment and supportive services; personal and corporate responsibility and self-restraint; and, generally individual and social efforts to correct the deficiencies

272

in our personal relations and social conditions which encourage the non-medical use of drugs. We attach importance to the general emphasis in this range of social responses. We believe that this emphasis must shift, as we develop and strengthen the non-coercive aspects of our social response, from a reliance on suppression to a reliance on the wise exercise of freedom of choice.

The problems involved in the non-medical use of psychotropic drugs and substances are one thing; the proper social responses are another. In other words, the identification of the problem does not necessarily indicate what the wise social response should be. However, some of the problems 'involved' in non-medical drug use today arise out of our present social responses. The responses are themselves problems in some cases. The role which the Federal Government will be able to play, alone or with other levels of government, in relation to the various aspects of the social responses required will vary considerably. In some cases it will be very direct; in others it will be indirect or remote; and in still others, there will be no apparent role for government to play. At the same time, we feel that our duty to report on the effects, extent and causes of non-medical drug use (including the related social factors), and by implication on the social responses to this phenomenon, requires us to *suggest* the action which may be taken by other institutions or agencies in our society.

390. *The general attitude towards non-medical drug use.* It is necessary to decide how far the mere existence of non-medical drug use is to be considered a problem. What is to be our general attitude towards non-medical drug use? Is such use to be regarded as wholly bad, or are there distinctions to be made? The concept of drug abuse as developed by the World Health Organization does not appear to be a helpful criterion of distinction among various kinds of non-medical use since it defines abuse with reference to 'acceptable medical practice'. One thing is clear: our society is very heavily involved in non-medical drug use of all kinds. It would therefore be unrealistic to condemn it all in principle. We drink coffee and tea, smoke cigarettes, drink alcohol, take tranquillizers and 'pep pills'. As adults, we are constantly setting an example of non-medical drug use to our

273

children. From infancy we are conditioned to think that there is a pharmaceutical cure for every ailment. The full resources of modern advertising are used to reinforce the reliance on drugs of all kinds. The achievements of chemistry are constantly dramatized. We live in a chemical age, the drugs are a part of our life.

The medical use of drugs is one of the boons of this chemical age. Drugs of all kinds have enormously increased our capacity to cure illness and to relieve pain. One has only to think of penicillin and the other antibiotics to recall how much we owe to the medical use of drugs. Moreover, the line between the medical use and the non-medical use of drugs is often a difficult one to draw. Is not the relief of disease-producing tension a legitimate therapeutic purpose? Certainly, more and more adults think so. The widespread use of tranquillizers and sedatives is common knowledge. Is the moderate use of tranquillizers such a bad thing, particularly for those whose tension might otherwise lead to heart trouble or other organic damage? Have we, as a society, taken a moral position against the tranquillizers? Obviously, we have not. At least, if we have, it is a very faint and hardly audible one.

Alcohol is a sedative which is widely used for the relief of tension. Have we taken a strong moral position against its use? Some have done so and still do, but they are obviously in a minority, and the vast majority of the society pays little attention to them. As for the stimulants, we take in enormous quantities of caffeine and nicotine. We stimulate our systems and modify our mood by cup after cup of coffee through the day. The nicotine in tobacco is clearly a psychotropic drug used to modify one's mood. Have we adopted a moral position against the use of caffeine and nicotine? Hardly. We are beginning to react against tobacco because of its clear danger to health, but the effect on sales is so far unimpressive.

We know that there is increasing use of the amphetamines by adults in all walks of life to overcome fatigue and to maintain energy and drive. Many can not face the challenge of daily life without their daily ration of 'pep pills'. Then there is also the use of the barbiturates – the 'downers' – to permit the over-stimulated system to relax sufficiently for sleep. One could go on. The point is that there must be very few people who do not use some psychotropic drug for non-medical reasons. The general climate, therefore, is not one of moral condemnation of the use of drugs for mood-modifying purposes, but rather one of acceptance of such use.

At the same time, while the use of certain mood-modifying drugs has become an accepted part of our way of life, the prevailing opinion in society still reserves varying degrees of disapproval or condemnation for the non-medical use of other drugs. Nor is society overly embarrassed or deterred from this attitude by being told that it does not practise what it preaches; that there is a hypocritical gap between its moral condemnations and its actual behaviour. The general response to this charge assumes a variety of forms which boil down to the general proposition that the fact we are in trouble with certain drug use is no reason why we should increase the trouble merely to be consistent. Those who take this view do not attempt to justify the present excessive use of alcohol, for instance; indeed, they generally deplore it. They merely say that it is too deeply ingrained in our society to be suppressed. Similarly, it is conceded that if we are considering tobacco for the first time, in light of what we have reason to believe about its possible effects, we might adopt a much stricter attitude towards it than it is feasible to adopt now. Such discrepancies or inconsistencies in our social policy, often the result of historical factors, may give rise to a sense of injustice, but they can not be the determinants of future policy. There is more than the claim of consistency involved in considering social responsibility.

Society is not obliged to repeat its errors. On the other hand, such inconsistencies do place a particular burden on society to justify its current policies. It is generally assumed that the burden of proof is on those who seek any change in public policy, but it may be that apparent inconsistencies in current policy impose a special burden to demonstrate the merits of such policy, apart from the question of consistency.

What then should be the criteria of current social policy in respect of non-medical drug use? **Our own view is that while we can not say that any and all non-medical use of psychotropic drugs is to be condemned in principle, the potential for harm of non-medical drug use as a whole is such that it must be regarded, on** balance, as a phenomenon to be controlled. The extent to which any particular drug use is to be deemed to be undesirable will depend upon its relative potential for harm, both personal and social.

By personal harm, we mean the adverse physiological or psychological effect of the drug upon the user; by social harm we mean the general adverse effects of non-medical drug use upon society. Reference to some of the concerns that have been expressed may serve to illuminate the concept of social harm. Many have expressed the concern that non-medical drug use, if allowed to increase and spread unchecked, will result in a general impairment of individual economic and social utility – an undermining of the will and capacity for moral choice and decisive action – that will weaken and undermine our society. More particularly, the concern has been expressed that such use will impair the capacity of the society to sustain its political, social and economic viability. In addition to this more general effect, there is concern for the immediate burdens which the adverse effects of non-medical drug use may place on individuals depending in some measure on the user and upon social agencies having some responsibility for his and their welfare.

In considering the relative potential for harm of any drug and the social response to its use which such harm would seem to justify, it is important to keep in mind the values which we seek to protect from harm. We must also remember that such values may be threatened by our social response to drug use, as well as by the use itself. We believe that most of these values can be related to two general conditions. They are *vitality* – that is, the condition of a person who is in command of his full capacity to act – and the *opportunity for the full development* of one's potential as a human being.

B. THE EFFECTS OF THE DRUGS

1. General

391. The Commission is required by its terms of reference 'to report on the current state of medical knowledge' respecting the effects of psychotropic drugs and substances. The task of the Commission, therefore, is to undertake a critical review of the literature rather than to engage in original experimental or

clinical research. In the six months or so of active inquiry which the Commission has had as a basis for the Interim Report there has been little enough time for the review of a voluminous literature, but the Commission has been exceptionally fortunate in the experience, ability and effort which its research staff have been able to bring to bear on this subject, and in view of these special circumstances and the urgent call on every side for 'more information', it has felt justified in issuing the preliminary statement on the drugs and their effects which is contained in Chapter Two. We recognize that this statement may have to be modified in some respects in the Final Report, because of new knowledge which comes to our attention. It is essential, however, if there is to be an Interim Report at all, that we disclose our assumptions at this stage concerning the effects of the drugs. We invite others to give us the benefit of their views during the ensuing year.

392. *The drugs to be considered at this time.* It is not our purpose in this chapter to attempt to summarize the main conclusions of Chapter Two, but merely to identify certain issues concerning the effects of the drugs which seem to be particularly relevant for purposes of public policy and social response at this stage. Our treatment is therefore necessarily selective and tends to focus on matters which have assumed a certain urgency. This selectivity should not be mistaken for an over-all perspective or sense of priorities concerning non-medical drug use as a whole. These we hope to be in a better position to convey in the Final Report after we have had the opportunity of further study and reflection. The matters of effect which we select for comment here are those which indicate the need for certain action now. In terms of short-term public policy decisions, the drugs which call for special comment at this time are cannabis, and the other hallucinogens (particularly LSD), and the amphetamines. This is not to detract in any way from the relative importance of the other drugs described in Chapter Two, in particular, alcohol, the barbiturates, and the opiate narcotics, but there seems to be less urgency concerning public policy decision with respect to them. They are of immediate concern, though, in their possible relationship to the hallucinogens and the amphetamines, and in the place

277

which they assume in the whole phenomenon of multiple-drug use.

2. *Cannabis*

393. *The kinds of effects to be considered.* It is customary to distinguish between short-term or 'acute' effects and the effects of long-term or 'chronic' drug use, and between physiological effects and psychological effects. There is also the distinction between the effects on the individual and the effects on third persons and society as a whole. The Indian Hemp Drugs Commission adopted the simple, three-fold classification of physical, mental and moral effects. We shall refer to physiological, psychological and social effects. Social effects will often be sufficiently considered in an estimation of the behavioural manifestations of physiological and psychological effects.

394. *The problem of knowing what is being referred to.* Rational discussion of the drug generally referred to as 'marijuana' is frequently impeded by looseness of terminology and failure to identify the substance we are referring to. It is often difficult to compare studies and to generalize from them because of differences in substance, potency, and administration. When one adds to these variables, differences in the psychological and physiological make-up of the subjects, their socio-economic background, their expectation of the drug experience (the 'set') and the circumstances or environment in which the drug is taken (the 'setting'), all of which have an important bearing on the drug's effect, it is no wonder that there is such confusion and conflict of opinion in the field. Most of the time, we simply do not know what we are comparing.

The term *cannabis* (although it is the name of the plant) is to be preferred to marijuana, to indicate this general class of drug, because it is more comprehensive and covers a number of substances and derivatives, of which marijuana is but one. Cannabis is the term used in the *Single Convention on Narcotic Drugs*, 1961. The *Narcotic Control Act* is less precise, using cannabis and marijuana somewhat interchangeably. We use cannabis here to refer chiefly to marijuana, hashish, cannabis extracts, and the active principles of these materials, such as tetrahydrocannabinol

(THC). Marijuana is made up of the crushed leaves, flowers and other parts of the plant. It is generally smoked in the form of cigarettes, or in a pipe, but may be taken orally in foods and beverages. Hashish consists of the relatively pure resin and is several times more potent than marijuana. It is smoked usually on the tip of a cigarette or in a pipe, or it is ingested, and in the latter form, it is sometimes mixed with food. Tetrahydrocannabinol is an active element isolated from cannabis and recently synthesized. It could be incorporated into a tobacco but is usually administered orally. It is considerably more potent than either marijuana or hashish. The essential point of emphasis here is that the potency of the various cannabis products and derivatives may vary considerably. The potency of the cannabis plant, which depends in part on soil and climatic conditions, as well as certain genetic factors, varies considerably from one country to another. Thus it may be quite difficult to compare cannabis products from one country with those from another. In India there have been traditionally three kinds of preparations of varying strength: *bhang*, a comparatively mild marijuana preparation; *ganja*, a slightly stronger kind of marijuana-type preparation and *charas*, which is the Indian form of hashish. In evaluating studies of cannabis use it is essential to distinguish between the milder and stronger forms of preparation. Moderate use of the milder forms is one thing; excessive use of the stronger forms may be quite another. While *bhang* and *ganja* have been tolerated as relatively innocuous when used moderately, *charas* has been more generally condemned. The marijuana used in North America comes mainly from Mexico or the southern United States and is usually considered to be less potent than the products of certain varieties of cannabis plant grown elsewhere in the world. This is only one of the difficulties in applying the results of studies abroad to the North American context.

In their brief to the Commission, the R.C.M. Police emphasized the importance of keeping the distinction between marijuana and hashish in mind in considering the effects of cannabis. There is evidence of an increasing use of hashish. This may be attributable in part to shortage, from time to time, in the supply of marijuana, but also to the greater potency of hashish. It has been pointed out that there is a distinction between potency and power; that potency simply means the relative strength or concentration of the active principle by weight or volume of the carrier; and that a difference in potency does not necessarily mean a difference in power – that is, in the effects which the psychoactive substance is capable of producing when administered in sufficient strength or quantity. At the same time, the degree of intoxication will undoubtedly depend upon the total strength administered at a particular time, which in turn will be influenced by availability, form and route of administration, and general practices or fashions in use. The fact that the average preparation of hashish may be five or six times as potent as the average preparation of North American marijuana does not mean that a person is necessarily going to smoke sufficient marijuana to produce the effect that would be produced by ingestion of a given amount of hashish. While the 'power' potential of these substances may be similar, given the required quantities of each, the effects actually experienced in practice may be different if the difference in potency is not adjusted by difference in the quantities actually consumed. It appears that most *experienced* cannabis users in North America compensate for variations in potency in different samples by altering dose to achieve a certain level or intensity of effect. Heavy, chronic users seem to prefer the stronger forms, however.

In considering the few studies which have been made of the effects of cannabis on humans, one is struck by the possible significance of the distinction between inhaling and ingestion as routes of administration. This distinction is important, for example, in comparing the results of such studies as those of the Mayor's Committee on Marijuana (La Guardia Report) with the results of other reports. The mayor's committee's investigators, on the one hand, relied on the oral administration of a 'red-oil' concentrate from cannabis, in most instances (and employed smoked materials in only a few experiments) while Isbell and co-workers, on the other hand, administered various strengths of purified THC, both by smoking and ingestion, to ex-opiate addicts in Lexington, Kentucky. One may well question the basis for comparing the effects of an orally administered concentrate or synthetic derivative with the effects of marijuana which is absorbed through inhalation. All this emphasizes the importance of dose and route of administration in evaluating the effects of a particular cannabis substance or derivative. Meaningful research can not be done on cannabis effects until we agree on a standardized substance and dose ranges which bear some reasonable resemblance to real and potential patterns of consumption under various conditions of availability in the North American social context. Such patterns may have little relationship to those which would develop if cannabis were more freely available. At the present time we do not know what should be regarded as a normal frequency of use. There are two problems: one is to be able to compare the results of different studies; the other, is to have studies that produce results which have some relevance to the conditions which are likely to be encountered in actual life. Standard cannabis research samples are being developed although it will not be possible to determine how useful or relevant they will be until we know more about the doses, route of administration, and frequency of use in the general population. What is important to remember now is that when we talk about marijuana we are talking about smoking the mildest form of cannabis preparation; when we talk about hashish we are talking about a more potent form of cannabis preparation that is also generally smoked but may increasingly (as people shy away from smoking for reasons already associated with tobacco) be ingested in the form of food-stuffs; and that when we talk about THC or other synthetics we are talking about a cannabis preparation that is apparently not yet used outside of a research setting. Thus, in discussing effects we shall attempt to bear these distinctions in mind.

395. *The proper classification of cannabis.* There is universal agreement that cannabis is not a narcotic and should not be classified legally with the opiate narcotics. Such classification is misleading and undermines respect for the rationality of law. There is not such scientific agreement as to what its proper classification should be, but there seems to be a general consensus that if it is to be classed with any other group it may be regarded as a mild hallucinogen, although some point out that its character is rather that of an intoxicant than a hallucinogen. On the question of legal classification we agree with the Canadian

Medical Association's suggestion that it has greatest affinity with the restricted drugs in Schedule J of Part IV of the Food and Drugs Act. We shall have more to say on this point in our interim recommendations for changes in the law.

396. *Short-term physical effects.* After centuries of use in a great number of countries, and extensive opportunities for clinical observation, the short-term physical effects of cannabis which have been brought to the attention of trained observers and mankind in general are relatively insignificant. There is no record of fatality directly attributable to cannabis, nor of irreparable injury to organs or tissue. The short-term physical effects which have been reported or observed form a relatively short and innocuous list, including an increase in pulse rate (but not, in the opinion of most observers, in blood pressure), conjunctivitis or a reddening of the membranes around the eyes (but not as often stated, a widening of the pupils), and dryness of the throat. Effects on psychomotor abilities, insofar as these may be considered to have a physiological aspect, will be discussed below.

397. *Short-term psychological effects.* The psychological effects of cannabis are so subjective and depend so much on a number of variables, including the dose level, the particular personality of the subject, the set, and the setting, that generalizations are difficult and of questionable value. It seems unnecessary here to dwell upon the allegedly positive or beneficial effects of cannabis. It is probably sufficient to observe that an increasing number of people in all age groups appear to find the experience a pleasurable one. Cannabis is an intoxicant and a euphoriant, and it generally acts as a relaxant. In this it resembles alcohol. Like alcohol, it is felt to reduce inhibitions and to facilitate social relations. It would appear to produce a more introspective, self-absorbed mood than alcohol. The social aspect of its use may be the enjoyment of its effects in the company of others, each sensing a common bond in the knowledge that the others are undergoing a similar experience. There may be less interaction than is stimulated by social drinking, although it often stimulates laughter and hilarity. Cannabis is reported to intensify sensory perceptions of various kinds, particularly the appreciation of

282

colour and music. It also stimulates the appetite. It is not believed, as is sometimes contended, to be an aphrodisiac, although it is claimed to heighten the pleasure of sexual experience. It has been suggested that cannabis, like alcohol, brings out the fundamental traits of the personality. It heightens or emphasizes what is already there rather than adding something different, or producing a fundamental change in character. Thus the psychological predispositions and prevailing mood of the subject are likely to be reflected in the cannabis experience. 'Bad trips' (that is, panic or more serious psychological reactions) from cannabis are infrequently reported, and upon examination have generally been found to be unusual cases, involving a special set of predisposing factors, such as strong anxiety or feelings of guilt. Instances of 'cannabis psychosis' as a short-term effect would also appear to be very rare, and a reflection of very special personality difficulties in the subjects involved or exceptional dose levels. This observation would seem to apply particularly to the cases of psychosis reported by the La Guardia Report and by the Lexington study of ex-opiate addicts by Isbell and others. Several recent clinical reports suggest, however, that psychotic reactions may occur in some individuals without clear prior psychopathology.

398. *Effect on cognitive functions and psychomotor abilities.* The most important issue concerning the short-term effects of cannabis would appear to be its effect on cognitive functions and psychomotor abilities – those capacities which affect learning, performance in an occupation, the operation of machinery and similar activity having significant social consequences. Whether or not a person is more excited or more relaxed under the influence of cannabis, whether his coordination is impaired, his perception and judgement of distance, speed and other relationships in space and time are affected, or his reaction time prolonged, are only a few of the factors of crucial importance for driving a car, controlling machinery, or performing many other functions in daily life. Unimpaired vigilance, that is, a high level of sustained attention, is even more important for such functions as controlling traffic on city streets, in rail yards and at airports. This issue is of particular importance with respect to cannabis

at this time because (*a*) it is generally agreed that one can not tell if another person is 'high' on cannabis unless he tells you, and (*b*) as yet, no simple means has been devised for detecting the presence and dose level of cannabis in the blood although there is optimism that scientists will develop such techniques shortly. At present, cannabis intoxication is unrecognizable and undetectable. **Existing scientific knowledge and opinion concerning the effects of cannabis on cognitive functions and psychomotor abilities is not of such an order as can be relied on at this time for purposes of public policy decision-making.** Some of the existing opinion is quite impressive and at least raises a serious presumption as to the nature of such effects but more research is required to command the acceptance of the scientific community.

The report by the New York Mayor's Committee on Marijuana (the 'La Guardia Report'), notes that simple psychomotor functions were only affected slightly by large doses of marijuana, and negligibly or not at all by small doses. More complex functions, hand steadiness, static equilibrium, and complex reaction time were impaired by both doses. Generally, non-users were more affected by the marijuana than those with previous experience. Strength of grip, speed of tapping, and estimations of short time intervals and linear distances were unchanged. Although no statistical analyses were done in this section, it appears that marijuana produced impairment in some intellectual functions, little or no change in others and, in a few instances, may even have resulted in an improvement in performance.

Although the La Guardia study as a whole was well planned and its different sections assigned to competent authorities, the experimental designs are not up to modern standards: no double-blind or placebo controls were used in the clinical and psychological investigations; statistical evidence was usually not presented; the reporting of results (for example, in the section on Intellectual Functioning) was not entirely unbiased; the subject samples may have been too small in some of the studies (for example, on the occurrence of addiction) to draw valid conclusions; and the type of subjects (prison inmates) chosen for some of the investigations severely limits the extent to which we may generalize from the results. These reservations apply to both the positive and negative conclusions of the report – to the alleged existence, as well as non-existence, of harmful effects.

The experiment by Weil, Zinberg and Nelsen, in which two different doses of cannabis were administered to non-experienced subjects in a double-blind situation (and a single dose given to chronic users), is, so far as it goes, an adequately controlled study to modern scientific standards. With respect to effects on intellectual functioning and psychomotor abilities the investigators found:

Marijuana-naïve persons do demonstrate impaired performance on simple intellectual and psychomotor tests after smoking marijuana; the impairment is dose-related in some cases.

Regular users of marijuana do get high after smoking marijuana in a neutral setting but do not show the same degree of impairment of performance on the tests as do naïve subjects. In some cases, their performance even appears to improve slightly after smoking marijuana.

The researchers caution that the apparent differences in the effects on experienced and non-experienced users must only be considered as trends since the testing situations were not strictly comparable for the two groups. Furthermore, they suggest that the commonly observed tendency for many marijuana users to lose their train of thought when very 'high' might be considered a temporary reduction in 'short-term' memory.

Clearly, the Weil study can not be considered an adequate basis for generalizations regarding effects on driving ability. On this point the authors observe:

Although the motor skills measured by the pursuit rotor are represented in driving ability, they are only components of that ability. The influence of marijuana on driving skill remains an open question of high medical-legal priority.

Crancer and associates of the Department of Motor Vehicles, State of Washington, studied the effects of cannabis and alcohol (at a single dose of each) on driving ability in a laboratory simulated driving test. When subjects experienced 'a social marijuana high', overall performance was not different from the control. Furthermore, no significant change was observed when four subjects were retested at three times the original marijuana dose. However, on this limited data little can be asserted regarding a dose-response effect of marijuana on driving. It seems likely that if the dose were pushed high enough some impairment would occur, although this has not been empirically demonstrated. The investigators caution that the study does not necessarily indicate that marijuana will not impair driving.

However, we feel that, because the simulator task is a less complex but related task, deterioration in simulator performance implies deterioration in actual driving performance. We are less willing to assume that non-deterioration in simulator performance implies non-deterioration in actual driving.

The subjects were also tested after a relatively large dose of alcohol (probably more than required for an ordinary 'social alcohol high') which did produce significant impairment in driving ability. However, it is clear that a general comparison between alcohol and marijuana can not be based on a single quantity of each, and a more complete dose-response relationship for both drugs would be necessary for a meaningful assessment of either individual or relative effects on driving skills.

399. *Long-term effects.* There is hardly any reliable information applicable to North American conditions concerning the long-term effects of cannabis. Because of the likelihood of significant differences in the many variables determining drug effects (physiological and psychological condition of subjects; conditions of nutrition, sanitation, climate and the like; potency, dose levels and frequency of use, as well as other drug use) the results of studies in other countries are of highly questionable applicability to North American conditions. Much further investigation is required to determine the extent to which the experience in other countries with cannabis might be utilized by properly controlled retrospective studies to yield results that would have relevance for North America.

The existing opinion as to the long-term effects of cannabis use presents an unclear picture. The conclusions of the Indian Hemp

Drugs Commission (1894) include the following statements regarding the effects of cannabis in India:

... Speaking generally, the Commission are of the opinion that the moderate use of hemp drugs appears to cause no appreciable physical injury of any kind. The excessive use does cause injury.

In respect to the alleged mental effects of the drugs, the Commission have come to the conclusion that the moderate use of hemp drugs produces no injurious effects on the mind. ... It is otherwise with the excessive use. Excessive use indicates and intensifies mental instability. ... It has been shown that the effect of hemp drugs in this respect has hitherto been greatly exaggerated, but that they do sometimes produce insanity seems beyond question.

In regard to the moral effects of the drugs, the Commission are of the opinion that their moderate use produces no moral injury whatever. ... Excessive consumption, on the other hand, both indicates and intensifies moral weakness or depravity ... apparently very rarely indeed, excessive indulgence in hemp drugs may lead to violent crime. But for all practical purposes it may be laid down that there is little or no connection between the use of hemp drugs and crime.

In their report of an eight year study of 1,238 cannabis users in India, as well as 600 cases of mental illness attributed to the use of cannabis, R. N. Chopra and G. S. Chopra came to similar general conclusions – that moderate use of cannabis, particularly of the milder form like *bhang*, was not harmful, but that excessive use, particularly of the stronger forms like *ganja* and *charas*, was harmful. The evidence of possible connection between cannabis use and various psychiatric disorders, as well as criminal behaviour, is far from clear. It would appear that excessive cannabis use may emphasize or aggravate a predisposition to psychiatric disorders or criminal behaviour, rather than being the direct cause of them. In her excellent critical review of the Chopras' study, O. J. Kalant observes that its chief weakness and source of possible error is the absence of data from a control sample of non-users, as well as differences in routes of administration and the psychological and social characteristics of the two groups of users (moderate and heavy) which were compared. She sums up the conclusions of the study as follows:

> Despite the foregoing reservations it can be concluded that, in general, the moderate users of bhang were reasonably healthy, well-adjusted individuals whose use of the drug resulted in a pleasant and mild degree of intoxication which did not interfere with their routine activities. On the other hand, the smoking of ganja and charas, particularly in excess, was unquestionably correlated with a higher incidence of ill effects, the most conspicuous of which were diseases of the respiratory and digestive systems, a lower than normal number of offspring in their families, and emotional and social maladjustment. In addition, the degree of intoxication sought and achieved by ganja and charas users was much more intense than in the case of bhang users. It was not conclusively demonstrated that all characteristics of the former group were attributable to the specific pharmacological action of cannabis. Thus, the respiratory illnesses might have been caused by other components of the smoke, or by the smoke of tobacco origin, and the emotional and social maladjustment might have been, at least in part, the cause rather than the result of habitual intoxication.

With respect to long-term effects, the Mayor's Committee on Marijuana (the La Guardia Report) concluded:

> ... marijuana users accustomed to daily smoking for a period of from two and a half to sixteen years showed no abnormal system functioning which would differentiate them from the non-users.
> There is definite evidence in this study that the marijuana users were not inferior in intelligence to the general population and that they had suffered no mental or physical deterioration as a result of their use of the drug.

The report on *Cannabis* in 1968 of the Advisory Committee on Drug Dependence of the United Kingdom (the Wootton Report) concluded:

> Having reviewed all the material available to us we find our-

selves in agreement with the conclusion reached by the Indian Hemp Drugs Commission appointed by the Government of India (1893–4) and the New York Mayor's Committee on Marijuana (1944), that the long-term consumption of cannabis in moderate doses has no harmful effects.

Recently, Robins and associates reported a retrospective study of the long-term outcome of marijuana use in a group of 235 Negro men in St Louis, Missouri. The characteristics of such a population may have limited applicability to present marijuana use in Canada. Persons in this sample who had used marijuana (and no other drug except alcohol) as adolescents differed significantly from non-marijuana users, in that the users had more often: drunk heavily enough to create social or medical problems, failed to graduate from high school, reported their own infidelity or fathering of illegitimate children, received financial aid, had adult police records for non-drug offences, and reported violent behaviour.

The heavy use of alcohol by those who used marijuana complicates the interpretation considerably: 47 per cent had 'medical or social problems attributable to drinking' and 38 per cent of the users were alcoholics. When those subjects who were classified as alcoholics were eliminated from the data the only statistically significant difference between the marijuana users and the non-users was with respect to financial aid received in the past five years. Non-significant trends remained which were generally similar to the earlier differences, however. Subjects who used 'harder' drugs (e.g. heroin, amphetamines and barbiturates) in addition to marijuana were significantly more deviant than the non-users, even after the alcoholics had been eliminated from the sample.

A possible causal relationship between marijuana use and problem drinking, or vice-versa, or a possible third set of factors predisposing certain individuals to alcoholism, marijuana use and other deviant behaviours can not be established or denied on the basis of the present data. The authors point out that in this study, '. . . *marijuana could not be demonstrated to be harmless*'.

On the whole, then, the existing evidence, such as it is, affords no clear guidance for predicting what would be the long-term effects of cannabis use at various levels of dose and frequency. It is probably fair to say, however, that such evidence as there is affords the basis for a cautious rather than an optimistic approach. There is no way of telling how the 'moderate use' referred to in the Indian Hemp Commission and Wootton Reports would compare with the levels of use that might be established in North America under conditions of free availability and social acceptance. We would not hazard a guess as to what might be the average daily intake of hashish by inhalation or ingestion.

As has been found elsewhere, the difficulty with research into long-term effects, whether retrospective or prospective, is to find a suitably matched control group of non-users. As Weil has observed, this may become increasingly difficult as marijuana use spreads through the society.

The priorities of research into long-term effects would appear to include the possibility, at levels of dose and frequency of use likely to be attained under conditions of free availability and social acceptance, of (*a*) personality change, particularly in adolescent users; (*b*) impairment of mental capacity; (*c*) psychosis and other psychiatric disorders; (*d*) lung cancer or other serious effects on the bronchial and respiratory system; and (*e*) psychological and physiological dependence.

3. LSD

400. *The problem of knowing what is being referred to.* LSD, which stands for d-lysergic acid diethylamide-25 and, in the idiom of the user, is usually referred to as 'acid', has been studied widely by pharmacologists, psychiatrists and psychologists since the startling psychotropic properties of this synthetic drug were accidentally discovered by the Swiss pharmacologist, Hofmann, in 1943. Several thousand scientific papers have been published on LSD during the last 27 years. Although the drug had been put to occasional non-medical and non-scientific use during the 1950s, its general adoption by the non-medical drug users, as the principal representative of the psychedelic-hallucinogenic class of drugs, took place only during the last decade.

Since 1963 the Canadian Government has controlled the distribution of LSD, making it available only for scientific and medical purposes, and in 1969 possession of LSD without authorization was made a criminal offence. Thus, any supply of the drug for non-medical drug users has to come through illicit channels and is, almost without exception, either imported illegally or produced in clandestine laboratories by private entrepreneurs. The drug is not as easily produced as the amphetamines, but can be made by a person with some chemical knowledge who has the equipment and the basic material available. Because of the constantly growing demand by the drug community for illicit LSD, the supply is often relatively limited, and much of the drug that is sold on the illegal market is not pure. Chemically, LSD is an ergot derivative, and street samples frequently contain other chemical compounds also related to ergot, but possessing pharmacological properties which differ from those of LSD. Although most street samples in Canada which were analysed contained some LSD, many were also mixed with these chemical impurities resulting from poorly controlled procedures of production. On rare occasions street samples have proven to contain powerful chemicals with atropine-like effects. Furthermore, amphetamines ('speed') have been alleged to be added to some illicit LSD samples, which combination may potentiate or considerably change the effect of LSD. Such contaminated samples may often be responsible for 'bad trips' but they are by no means their only cause. Furthermore, the admixture of chemicals with atropine-like properties to LSD changes the response to the usual antidotes to LSD which may, under these circumstances, instead of lessening the effects of a 'bad trip', actually increase the toxic reaction. Thus, for the proper medical treatment of LSD reactions which have gone out of control, it is very important, though often not feasible, to know the real composition of the alleged 'LSD' sample which has been consumed.

401. *The proper classification of LSD*. LSD belongs clearly in the category of *psychedelic-hallucinogen* drugs. It may, in fact, be considered the most characteristic representative of this *psychotropic* drug class. Because of its almost incredible potency, extremely small quantities of the drug will produce powerful

effects which are typical of drugs of this classification. In the same category is mescaline which is found in peyote, the flowering heads of a cactus (lophophora williamsii), whose habitat is the desert areas of southern U.S.A., Mexico and other parts of Central and South America. DMT (dimethyltryptamine), DET (diethyltryptamine) and other synthetically produced compounds are also in this category.

402. *Short-term physical effects.* The most important effects of LSD manifest themselves in the psychological sphere. Physical effects of the drug are less pronounced and occur mainly in the early phases of an LSD reaction, when the drug produces a stimulating effect on many autonomic nervous functions. It increases heart-rate and blood pressure, enlarges the pupils, may increase body temperature and blood sugar level and, not uncommonly, also induces nausea, vomiting and headache in the early stages of the drug reaction. It increases the electrical activity of the brain (as indicated by the EEG), blocks sleep and rarely, in high doses, produces convulsions. Surprisingly, in spite of its great potency, pure LSD is of low physical toxicity, and no human fatalities due to overdosage have been reported to date. (The human organism may be particularly resistant to the physical effects of LSD, since an elephant was killed by a dose which was calculated on the basis of the human dose multiplied by the different weight factor.)

A few years ago, a possible adverse effect of LSD on human chromosomes was described. Studies to test this finding have yielded conflicting results. In some studies, the finding has been confirmed, but in several others it has not. Several recent, well controlled prospective studies with clinically pure LSD administered to humans under laboratory conditions produced little or no evidence of significant chromosomal change. However, due to the seriousness of the possible consequences if such damage should occur, research in this area must continue until the following issues are unequivocally settled:

1. Does LSD damage human chromosomes in users?
2. Does such damage, if it does occur, predispose the affected person to cancer or other serious diseases, or otherwise produce any adverse effects?

3. Does chromosome damage, if it does occur, produce malformation in the children born of parents affected in this manner?

Furthermore, there is evidence that large doses of LSD, injected during pregnancy, can produce deformities in the offspring in certain strains of rodent but not in others. Although such effects have not been clearly demonstrated in humans, the possibility must be given careful consideration.

403. *Short-term psychological effects*. LSD, like all drugs classified in the psychedelic-hallucinogenic category, disorganizes normal mental activity. One of its earliest effects is a distortion of space perception and a profound disturbance of the normal time sense. Profound alterations in the detail and quality of sensory impressions occur. Colours are greatly intensified, sounds and visual perceptions may fuse, so that the sounds are 'seen' and colours are 'heard' (synesthesia), feelings of insight and lucid thoughts occur, and illusions and, more rarely, hallucinations may be experienced by a person under the effects of LSD. Since such profound disturbances of perceptual processes are hardly ever observed, except in naturally occurring mental disease (psychosis), the LSD reaction is sometimes referred to as a 'model psychosis'. On the other hand, this change in normal mental function is called an 'expansion of the mind' by many of those who advocate this experience.

Some clinical observers who have worked with hallucinogenic drugs suggest that these substances may induce a regression to more basic types of psychological functioning, weaken normally prevailing defence mechanisms, facilitate the emergence of ordinarily forgotten or repressed memories and render the individual under the influence of these drugs more dependent on the persons and circumstances in his immediate environment.

Some LSD users, but by no means all, may have 'true' psychedelic experiences, that is, transcendental 'peak' experiences which have been compared to mystical states and to religious ecstasy. As with all true mystical states, these experiences can not be clearly communicated to others by means of verbal description, but remain at an intensely private, introspective level.

293

Others may have a 'bad trip' and suffer the agonizing anxiety of doubting that they are alive or that they will ever become normal again. To some extent it is possible to control the type of reaction a person will have under the influence of LSD, but in most cases it is impossible, even for an expert, to predict whether or not a person under the effects of LSD will experience a 'bad trip'. Even the fact that a person may already have had several gratifying experiences with LSD is no guarantee that he will not suffer a horrifying experience the next time.

Many persons under the influence of LSD refuse to be tested by the usual psychological procedures and lack the motivation to cooperate with a standard clinical, systematic assessment of their psychological functions, because they feel that these tests are meaningless. However, most persons who have been tested while under the effects of LSD have revealed a definite impairment of coordination and of many other psychomotor functions.

Their cognitive functioning is even more affected. Their verbal fluency may be reduced and they may show marked impairment of their critical faculties, but particularly of the ability to analyse perceptions and concepts. They are also often severely handicapped in their capacity to synthesize appropriate behavioural patterns. Because of this impairment of cognitive functions, persons under the effects of LSD not infrequently lose their contact with 'reality', become irrational and may develop delusions of persecution or other strange beliefs, such as not being subject to the force of gravity or of being invulnerable. Thus, it is evident that the judgement of a person under the effect of LSD may be greatly impaired, along with his ability to protect himself against common dangers.

404. *Long-term effects.* One of the most important issues concerning the non-medical use of drugs is their long-term effect. What happens in the long run after a person has taken a drug once or twice, or perhaps many times? LSD is capable of producing lasting effects on the personality structure and, for this reason, has been used by psychiatrists for the medical treatment of such personality disorders as alcoholism and chronic neuroses. Notwithstanding some early enthusiastic reports on the therapeutic value of LSD in these conditions, it is still doubtful to

what extent and in what conditions – if at all – LSD may be of value in the treatment of psychiatric illness. But there is no doubt that LSD frequently has produced profound changes of personality. Especially if somebody has had a true psychedelic experience, he might experience a change in his whole attitude towards life, which may at times be as momentous as that associated with a religious conversion. However, the drug-induced psychedelic state is still only poorly understood and remains to a considerable extent uncontrollable. Once such an experience has occurred, there is often little anyone can do to direct its future influence on the person. This influence could, indeed, range from a rapid, profound and lasting beneficial change to a fleeting, insignificant impact – or to a shattering mental breakdown. While it is true that many who have used LSD claim that they have gained new and better insights into the essential issues of life and have acquired greater sensitivity and a more genuine way of interacting with other people, it is also true that many have suffered such critical adverse effects as suicidal or accidental death, severe panic, prolonged depressive and psychotic episodes, for which they had to be treated in mental hospitals, and disturbing recurrences of the LSD experience without a new exposure to the drug ('echo effect'; 'flash-backs').

Statistical evidence for the incidence of lasting effects of self-administered LSD on the personality structure is still very sketchy, but there is perhaps more clinical support for the unfavourable than for the favourable changes. It appears, however, that under expert psychological or psychiatric supervision the risk of an unpleasant LSD experience can be reduced, since a limited measure of control is possible under these conditions.

No physical dependence occurs with LSD, although there are reports of individuals who have become psychologically dependent on the drug. An acute tolerance to the effects of LSD develops which is dissipated after a few days. There is usually no tendency for users to increase dose.

On balance, it may be concluded that the significant incidence of very serious unfavourable effects, coupled with the impossibility of predicting or effectively controlling the effects of self-administered LSD, constitute, at present, serious potential dangers. One must also consider the risk that even a single administration of LSD might be highly traumatic to emotionally unstable persons, and especially to adolescents whose personality structure is still in a critical stage of development.

4. Amphetamines

405. *The problem of knowing what is being referred to.* The quality and potency of the drugs sold as amphetamines ('speed') on the illicit market, are apparently less variable than are those of cannabis or LSD. Amphetamines have been in wide medical use for more than 30 years and are legally produced in large quantities by the pharmaceutical industries. Thus, the problems of illegal production and quality control which beset cannabis and LSD are much less in evidence with the amphetamines. It appears that a large proportion of the amphetamines available on the illicit market has simply been diverted from authorized industrial production into illegal channels of importation and distribution.

Many of the orally administered tablets and capsules of prescription drugs such as dextroamphetamine (Dexedrine*), and the great variety of amphetamines contained in 'diet pills' (e.g., phenmetrazine or Preludin*) which are prescribed for weight control are legally produced. This also applies to methylphenidate (Ritalin*), or pipradol (Meratran*) which are pharmacologically closely related to the amphetamines.

But there is some evidence that much of the amphetamine which is most frequently used by the 'speed freaks' for intravenous injection (e.g., methamphetamine or Methedrine*) is produced in small clandestine laboratories which may sometimes be run by amateur chemists. In these cases, there is little adequate quality control and the user can not be sure of the chemical nature of the drug alleged to be methamphetamine, or of its dose.

It is important to keep these different forms of amphetamines or 'speed' in mind:

1. Pure prescription amphetamines (e.g., Dexedrine*) or closely related drugs (e.g., Ritalin*).
2. Prescription amphetamines in combination drugs (e.g., 'diet pills').

3. Illegally produced and distributed amphetamines (e.g., methamphetamine) in tablet or powdered form.

While there is a dependence problem with the prescription amphetamines and the 'diet pills', this is usually not the same as the newer 'speed' problem. 'Speed freaks' are almost without exception young, under 25 years of age, and 'shoot' (inject) amphetamines intravenously in very large doses (e.g. from several hundred to several thousand milligrams). Amphetamine-dependent persons who use prescription drugs tend to be older, between 30 and 50 years of age, take the drug orally and use much smaller doses (e.g., from 10 to 100 milligrams).

406. *The proper classification of amphetamines.* Amphetamines and drugs with amphetamine-like effects are generally classified in the pharmacological category of *stimulants*, although one might find them occasionally included in the category of anti-depressants. It was assumed originally, when these drugs were introduced into clinical medicine in the 1930s, that amphetamines would be useful in the treatment of morbid depression, because they frequently induced euphoria in normal subjects. But it was soon observed that in severely depressed persons these drugs would often not elevate the mood and thus did not serve as true anti-depressants, but simply increase tension, restlessness and insomnia. Today, amphetamines and amphetamine-like drugs are used only occasionally in the treatment of severe depression; drugs more frequently used for this therapeutic purpose are those generally classified as anti-depressants (see classification table in Chapter Two) and are used almost exclusively on a medical basis. Many stimulants, on the other hand, enjoy wide non-medical use. Amphetamines are controlled drugs under Schedule G of Part III of the *Food and Drugs Act*.

407. *Short-term physical effects.* More than 30 years of medical use have allowed for thorough investigation of the short-term physical effects of the amphetamines. Moderate doses produce EEG signs of electro-physiological arousal of the central nervous system and peripheral effects indicative of activation of the sympathetic (adrenalin-like) part of the autonomic nervous system, which manifest themselves as increased pulse rate, in-

creased blood pressure, dilatation of the pupil and some relaxation of smooth muscle (e.g., in the gastro-intestinal tract). Another regular, immediate effect is suppression of appetite (anorexogenic effect), produced through some action on the appetite-regulating centres in the brain.

408. *Short-term psychological effects.* Typical short-term psychological effects are a feeling of increased energy, drive and initiative, often leading to an awareness of greater vitality and heightened self-confidence, and thus often resulting in a mood change in the direction of euphoria. Fatigue and boredom are diminished, pre-existing drowsiness is overcome and prolonged wakefulness is induced. In general, persons under the influence of amphetamines find it easier to tackle cognitive and emotional problems, work faster and often more efficiently – although they may be somewhat more easily distracted – and experience a facilitation of their interaction with other people.

It should be noted, however, that these effects occur by no means regularly in everyone exposed to the drug. Individuals who are chronically anxious or temporarily under stress, and therefore irritable and tense, frequently react to amphetamines with a further increase of anxiety, tension or irritability. Under these circumstances, they experience, of course, no euphoria, and their general functioning tends to be impaired rather than improved.

Test performance on simple mental tasks is frequently improved under the effects of amphetamines, particularly when rapidity of response, staying power and speed of sustained activity are being tested, and when the subject is fatigued or bored. General intelligence, however, is not improved by amphetamines when measured by the usual tests except perhaps very occasionally, and in a secondary way, through a temporary increase of motivation. A person's judgement is, as a rule, not affected by moderate doses of amphetamines, but when high doses are administered, as by the 'speed' user, judgement may be greatly impaired. Also, with higher doses, it becomes increasingly difficult for the subject to concentrate, and thus a marked deterioration of cognitive functioning might result.

Psychomotor abilities may be temporarily facilitated, and athletic performance might improve under the influence of moderate doses of amphetamines. This fact has recently made it necessary to enforce strict regulations against 'doping' with these drugs in those taking part in athletic competitions.

With extremely high doses of amphetamines, which the 'speed' user might employ (up to 1000 times the therapeutic dose) all mental activity loses its focus, concentration becomes impaired, all critical faculties are seriously reduced and the person's judgement becomes blurred. Psychomotor coordination suffers, as well, once this state has been reached, and emotional control is often lost. Nevertheless, the person under the influence of these extremely high doses of amphetamines, far from being aware of his mental limitations, experiences a 'rush' of pleasant feelings and becomes convinced that he is more capable and more powerful than ever. This sequence of drug-induced psychological events, creating unrealistically inflated feelings of self-confidence, self-righteousness and power, might lead to delinquent behaviour, as the result of 'acting out' of latent aggression and hostility.

409. *Long-term effects.* If moderate doses of amphetamines, such as are prescribed for medical purposes, are taken over long periods of time, three different categories of outcome may be observed:

1. No adverse effects may occur, and the person for whom the drug was prescribed or who took it without medical authorization, but in moderate doses, may go on for months or even years, taking the same dose regularly and suffering no ill effects from it. Many mildly depressed or chronically fatigued people ('tired housewife syndrome') who obtain their amphetamines on prescription, fall into this category. Also in this category are a sizable number of persons who feel the need for mild stimulation of the amphetamine type at regular intervals because of the special kind of stress their work is placing on them, e.g., journalists, commercial artists, public speakers or performers who are required to work to deadlines, or 'produce' original ideas on demand. There is considerable evidence – though little systematic documentation – of the existence of a large group of such people who regularly use amphetamines, often without a prescription.

2. More frequently, however, a person who has started taking an amphetamine, with or without medical prescription, becomes dependent, not only on the therapeutic effects for which the drug has been taken originally (e.g., a reduction of appetite, to facilitate weight loss), but even more so, on its 'fringe benefits', such as the feelings of euphoria and increased energy produced by the drug. Tolerance to these particular effects of the amphetamines develops rapidly in most people, with the result that they are inclined to increase their doses. Although this might enable them to extend the period of time during which they can experience the particular drug effects on which they have become dependent, they now also induce a number of highly undesirable effects which are the result of the prolonged ingestion of doses of amphetamines which are considerably higher than those with which they started.

These new undesirable effects consist primarily of insomnia, loss of appetite and general nervousness, which often make it necessary for the person thus affected to take gradually increasing doses of sedatives, setting up in this way, a vicious cycle of forced stimulation and sedation – of ups and downs – which greatly disrupts his normal rhythm of functioning. If continued for several months, this pattern often results in general debilitation and exhaustion and might finally lead to a psychotic breakdown. At this stage, the chronic amphetamine user has become irresponsible, expresses delusions of persecution and requires treatment and hospitalization for mental illness.

There is, unfortunately, no reliable way of predicting which persons will fall into the first category and be able to take amphetamines regularly without increasing their dose (and thus with relative impunity) and which persons will become dependent on the drug, develop tolerance, increase dose and then invariably suffer effects destructive to their physical and mental health. Since the risk that this might occur is high, amphetamines should not be taken without close medical supervision, nor should they ever be prescribed by physicians who are not thoroughly informed about the dependency potential of amphetamines.

3. The third category of amphetamine users is constituted of

'speed freaks', usually young persons who most often inject intravenously extremely large quantities of the drug. Users in categories 1 and 2 may start taking amphetamines for medical reasons and could continue obtaining amphetamines on prescription, which then might later be used for non-medical purposes; but the 'speed freaks' rarely start the drug under medical supervision and rarely, if ever, begin use through legitimate prescription channels.

To this date there is little evidence that the slogan 'speed kills' has concrete applicability. The disastrous effects of massive doses of 'speed' on the user's physical and mental health, appearance and behaviour either cause him to quit using the drug on his own initiative, or to be hospitalized for physical or mental breakdown, or to be arrested for delinquent behaviour, long before his drug habit has killed him. This interruption of his exposure to the toxic effects of 'speed' may save his life, and may help him to give up amphetamines, while his body can still repair the damage he has inflicted on it. There seems to be little doubt, however, that nobody could survive a long, uninterrupted exposure to the devastating effects of high 'speed' doses of amphetamines on his cardiovascular system, his resistance to infection and his central nervous system.

5. Multiple Drug Use

410. In Chapter Two we have touched on possible relationships between the various drugs under study – in particular the phenomenon of cross-tolerance and cross-dependence and the extent to which the use of certain drugs may predispose one towards the use of others. (See paragraphs 57–8, 74–5, 86, 104, 140, 172–6, 245–6, 266).

In the R.C.M.P. brief to the Commission, one of the contentions of the law enforcement authorities put forward in defence of their position to maintain the present legal status for cannabis is that it leads to the use of stronger drugs, eventually leading the user to 'hard' drugs, such as heroin. This contention, often referred to as the 'stepping-stone' theory, assumes the character of a contagion theory. The R.C.M.P. drug law enforcement experts envisage this contagion operating in a multiple drug use context, and not merely as a simple, direct progression from cannabis to heroin.

The multiple-drug-use-contagion theory is a general one of multiple drug use to which the use of cannabis is said to be a predisposing factor. What the contention amounts to is – that the use of one of these psychotropic drugs increases the probability of the use of others. The R.C.M.P. do not contend that drug progression occurs as a result of a kind of pharmacological action, but rather it is the result of exposure to, and involvement in, a drug sub-culture which encourages experimentation with drugs and a search for new and increasingly potent drug experiences. The R.C.M.P. base the theory on a 'two-year study of this problem' from which they conclude:

> ... documented evidence proves indisputably that in many cases a transition to heroin does take place, but not necessarily directly and certainly not in every case. The transition is generally from marijuana to hashish to methamphetamine and LSD and then to the opiates.

We are not able to find either the documented evidence for this conclusion nor the study to which the Force alludes.

In its Annual Summary for 1969, the Narcotic Addiction Foundation of British Columbia noted a 'marked increase in the number of young people (125) who had become involved in multiple drug use, including heroin'. The Foundation reported that this group, of which 81 were in the age range of 16 to 23, were users of 'a wide variety of drugs from marijuana, LSD, amphetamines and barbiturates, prior to heroin use'. This report does not specify what proportion of these young people who sought the help of the Foundation were addicted to heroin and what proportion were occasional users. Data published by the Narcotic Control Division of the Department of National Health and Welfare for the year 1969, report only 44 additional addicts under the age of 25 in British Columbia.

However, there may be significance in the fact that from 1959–69, 99 younger aged people reported a history of multiple drug use prior to heroin use, to the Narcotic Addiction Foundation, while in 1969 alone, the number reporting such use reached 81.

411. Several hypotheses might be advanced to support the

contention that the use of one drug leads or predisposes an individual to experiment with others. In the general view and among drug users, drugs are ranked in a hierarchy of increasing psychotropic potency and of potential danger, running from cannabis, the least potent and dangerous, through the amphetamines to the opiate narcotics which are believed to be the most potent and dangerous. It is reasonable to believe that the notion of hierarchy attracts some individuals to work towards drugs higher on the scale. A number of motives might be suggested: the search for greater 'kicks' or more intense pleasures; the thrill of taking new and greater risks; a desire for attention from other drug users or a high reputation among them; a wish to show increasing disdain or contempt for the values of our society. Some people may be attracted to the drugs which have a dangerous reputation either because they have personality problems and tendencies to self destruction, or because they lack foresight and compulsively seek new experiences and thrills.

We also find it reasonable to think that the users of one drug might be led to the use of other drugs simply by their presence and use among their friends and their availability from the dealers they patronize. It must be recognized that an increasing number of persons have multiple drug experiences in society. They can influence others to similar drug use patterns by their mere presence and by reporting their pleasures in other drug use, and by attributing value to their use, or by the fact that any untoward effects of their multiple drug use may not be clearly visible.

It is reasonable to be concerned that many younger drug users may experiment with a number of drugs because they lack knowledge of their dangers and may not be concerned with harmful but distant consequences. The tendency of some youth to stress feeling and emotion rather than reason emphasizes their desire for immediate gratification.

Frequently and plausibly it has been suggested to us that the belief that young people are being 'lied to' about the dangers of cannabis has led them to shrug off or deny the warnings about other drugs given to them by traditional authority figures.

It may be that the first drug experience is a greater step and a more difficult one to take than to move on and experiment with other drugs. Once having taken this first step, there may be a strong attraction for many to try more potent and exotic substances.

We think too, that the presence of a drug fad in society encourages multiple drug use and we recognize that in many groups there is probably a pressure on those who seek acceptance by the group to take part in drug experimentation.

We have also been told that the shortage of one drug, such as cannabis, 'forced' those who would use drugs to accept other drugs from the dealers. **We feel we must take seriously the fact of multiple drug use and further investigate the contention of drug contagion or drug progression.** At the present time there is evidence of multiple drug use, but not of a type to establish a causal link or specific pattern between the use of one drug and the use of others.

6. Drugs and Crime

412. Various relationships between the use of drugs and criminal behaviour have been suggested to us, particularly by the R.C.M. Police and the Solicitor General's Department. It has been put to us by the R.C.M. Police that the use of drugs such as cannabis is or will be related to subsequent criminal activity. The Solicitor General's Department has drawn our attention to the fact that a large number of convicted heroin addicts had records of non-drug criminal activity prior to their drug convictions. It has also been asserted that some crimes are committed by individuals while under the influence of drugs.

The R.C.M. Police stated: 'We are inclined to believe that most users will eventually be convicted for an offence not related to drugs.' With reference to cannabis, they report that users of this drug are found in possession of firearms more frequently than are those who use heroin. The Solicitor General's Department note that this is also true of users of and traffickers in heroin. Apart from this, the R.C.M. Police say that while they 'lack evidence of crimes committed in Canada by cannabis users' such evidence is available from other societies. They cite studies in India (the Chopras'),[1] Greece (Gardikas)[2] and in the United States (Eddy,[3] Blumquist[4] and Miller[5]).

The R.C.M. Police, and others, referred to a number of criminal acts alleged to have been committed by individuals under the influence of drugs. They report a number of cases of nudity and other nuisance by those under the influence of LSD. Those who have taken this drug are also reported by the R.C.M.P. to have committed 'vicious assault', and to have endangered or lost their lives by believing they could fly or that they were impervious to injury. They also drew attention to a large number of suicides and attempted suicides by users of barbiturates. They report that there have been a number of arrests of individuals who had used alcohol and barbiturates concurrently.

The amphetamines have a widely accepted reputation for producing aggressive and violent behaviour. Cocaine has been said to be used by criminals to produce false courage. Alcohol has long been recognized to be highly criminogenic.

Our attention was drawn, by the Solicitor General's Department, and the R.C.M.P., to the number of criminal addicts who have records of earlier criminal behaviour. It was reported that 85 per cent (3,450 of a sample of 3,804) of persons convicted of drug offences, who were addicted to hard drugs, had 'criminal antecedents'. It was also reported that 567 of 583 addicts in penitentiaries had committed at least one crime prior to conviction for a drug offence.

We were also told that individuals dependent on heroin are often moved to crimes such as theft and prostitution to meet the high cost of buying drugs.

We feel that at present there is a lack of adequate evidence to support the contention that the use of drugs under discussion leads significantly or generally to other forms of criminal activity with the exception of the heroin user's criminal behaviour to 'support his habit'. We feel it would be dangerous to draw general conclusions from the records of prison inmates insofar as they can not be considered to be a representative sample of the present population of drug users.

The Commission intends to investigate further the allegations of relationship between drug use and other criminal activity.

C. EXTENT AND PATTERNS OF NON-MEDICAL
DRUG USE

413. At this time only general statements can be made about the extent of non-medical drug use in Canada. There can be no doubt that it is widespread. Clearly there has been growing interest in and use of the psychoactive drugs by the young and indeed by all ages.

The Commission has gathered epidemiological information from a number of sources: governmental records, police statistics and estimates, various surveys of drug use among students and the informed and sensitive opinions of experts, drug users and distributors. While this information, taken together, gives the Commission some sense of the extent of the phenomenon, it does not provide the basis for any detailed or specific epidemiological statements. **A major research project is being carried out on behalf of the Commission. It is expected that the results of this study will provide a basis for more accurate estimates of the extent of drug use in Canada.**

Alcohol has been and remains the most popular psychoactive drug among Canadians of all ages and classes. Its use continues as our most serious drug problem. However, during the early 1960s, the acceptance and use of other psychoactive drugs such as cannabis and LSD began to be noteworthy. Marijuana had been used previously but its use had been confined to a small number of musicians and entertainers. The spread of the use of the drug appears to have begun among university students and among the mobile, alienated, out-of-school young people of the cities. It did not take long for it to appear in the high schools and its use probably spread more rapidly there than in the universities. While the phenomenon began in the larger cities, it also appeared relatively quickly in smaller urban centres and in rural communities.

It seems reasonable to think that probably more than 8 or 10 per cent of high school students have used cannabis. Some studies have found much higher proportions. For instance, a recently published British Columbia study estimates the level of cannabis use in the schools which were studied at 20 per cent. In the hearings we have heard extreme estimates. Many parents and teachers provide low estimates and strongly contend that the extent of use has been grossly exaggerated. Students, notably those who use drugs, suggest that as many as 60 or 70 per cent of their fellows have smoked cannabis. At the university level, the data we have seen suggest that more than 25 per cent of students have at least experimented with it. There is not as great a tendency to deny widespread use among college students as there is to deny it at the secondary school level.

The use of LSD seems to have emanated from the 'hip' subculture of the cities. Its spread began somewhat later than that of cannabis, but today its use has probably reached virtually the same population, although involving fewer individuals. Initially, the acceptance of LSD use was inhibited by the statements of a probable medical and genetic risk. The persuasive force of these statements seems to have been greatly attenuated during the past year or 18 months. An increasing repertoire of other new hallucinogenic drugs has appeared, and has been accepted for use by the drug communities. It is more difficult than in the case of cannabis to estimate the extent of use of these drugs. In large part this is due to the fact that their use is much more recent and there have been virtually no current attempts at measurement by surveys. However, we have heard estimates that in some high schools as many students have now used LSD as have smoked cannabis and there seems to be an awareness in the public of an increased use of hallucinogenic drugs, notably LSD, by both high school and university students.

The non-medical use of stimulants, particularly the high dosage administration of the amphetamines, is a matter of serious concern. There are conflicting reports of the extent of the so-called 'speed' phenomenon but there can be little doubt of a rapid increase in the use of these dangerous drugs in recent years. This increase seems to have taken place after the spread of cannabis and LSD. The intravenous use of amphetamines does not appear to have a wide following among university students, but these drugs seem to have achieved their greatest popularity for oral use among high school students and for intravenous use among out-of-school young people. The use of this drug has been deplored in virtually all quarters, including the cannabis and LSD communities. We have heard estimates that several thousand young people were making dangerously regular high dose use of amphetamines in Toronto. Such estimates have been accompanied by forecasts of anticipated high death and disease rates among the users.

It has come to the Commission's attention that an increasing number of young drug users are probably using or experimenting with a wide variety of drugs or drug combinations. Unfortunately, there is little survey data to indicate the extent or the pattern. We have considered the causes of multiple-drug use above.

It is quite clear that many students at the high school and college levels have had drug experiences, notably with cannabis and LSD. There is no evidence that the number involved is diminishing, or that the frequency of use is lessening. Among high school and school drop-out users, there seems also to have been an increase in multiple-drug use.

The system of distribution of cannabis and LSD appears to differ significantly from that of heroin. There does not appear to be an organized crime involvement at this time, although hashish distribution might be attractive to organized crime in the future. In many cities there are large importers of marijuana, hashish, and LSD who supply a multi-levelled network of distributors. Most of the distributors at the street level can not properly be thought of as pushers in the sense of the traditional heroin pushers. There is also a large number of smaller importers. Much of the distribution of these drugs seems to be informal and even casual. They often seem to move among friends in a fashion similar to alcohol or tobacco in 'straight' society. It is probable that the most important factor in the rapid development of this phenomenon has been the influence of one individual upon another – the reporting of one's own drug experiences to friends and acquaintances.

The use of heroin and the other opiate narcotics has been a problem in Canada for a number of years. However, the last available government statistics indicate that the proportion of addicts in the total population has declined.[6] The Commission is concerned, however, by reports in Canada and the United States of the increasing use of heroin, particularly by young people.

It is important to realize that the non-medical use of psycho-tropic drugs has been increasing among adults as well as among the young. We have cited statistics to show the increase in the use of alcohol and such drugs as the barbiturates, stimulants and minor tranquillizers. We have also heard much about the purported increased use of cannabis by adults for recreational purposes.

D. CAUSES OF NON-MEDICAL DRUG USE

414. The Commission feels that one of its most important responsibilities is to provide some reasonable explanations of non-medical drug use and to give the Canadian people assistance in understanding at least some of the major causes and causal patterns. There are causal forces involved at the individual, the group and the society-wide levels. Our primary concern is with those pressures to drug use that have a wide applicability, although we do not ignore the idiosyncratic.

We feel that it is important to stress that there is no single or simple explanation available – nor is one likely to be found. Motives vary widely between users and groups of users. The motivation of the individual user may vary through time. Motivation is also a function of the real and expected effects of the various drugs.

There has been some tendency to think of the motives for drug use as pathological or as reflecting a pathological psychological condition. This is shown by the tendency to turn to the physician, and particularly to psychiatrists, for help in understanding the drug phenomenon. There is no doubt that some drug users are to some degree mentally ill. However we are convinced that the vast majority fall within the normal range of psychological functioning.

Probably the most important single factor that has encouraged an increase in the use of cannabis has been the description by one individual to another of the drug's effects as being pleasant, fun, interesting or exciting. The search for fun, pleasure and excite-ment is also probably the most important factor favouring the continued use of this drug. While newspapers, magazines and the popular music industry have played a role in creating an interest in drug use and experimentation and have provided information about the effects of the drugs, it seems likely that their influence has been far less than that of individuals upon each other. There is also now a fad of drug-taking and experimentation.

The smoking of marijuana and hashish is primarily a group practice, although there are solitary smokers. While it is often said that smoking cannabis aids communication, lessens inhibitions, and causes laughter and gaiety, there is also much emphasis on its capacity to alter perception and enhance the enjoyment of music. LSD is much more an individual experience and there is a stress on new insights into the self and existence that are said to follow its use. We are told that both drugs provide the user with new perspectives of reality and new contexts in which to absorb experience. LSD is often spoken of almost as a sacrament. Its effects are said to be essentially indescribable and hence capable of being understood or fully appreciated only by those who have experienced the drug.

The introspection, the search for meaning within the self, the desire to explore what are said to be new frontiers of the mind seem to be related to a collapse of many traditional explanations of existence including religious expressions and syntheses of experience. In the past, when ideologies or religions lost their appropriateness, man has similarly turned inwards to find meaning and satisfaction within the self.

There also seems to be a relationship between drug use and the concern of the young for the future. Many appear to have lost faith not only in a traditional God but in the power and capacity of human reason. They fear that reason can not cope with the problems of nuclear arms, pollution, over-population, poverty and racial hostility. Their doubt of man's capacity to survive and their loss of faith in reason seem to have encouraged an emphasis on feeling and emotion and on life and pleasure in the here-and-now.

The general affluence of our society has also been a factor. This affluence has paradoxically become a source of boredom from which drugs provide an escape. It also permits the luxury of time for introspection to a large number. There is also a rejection of the life style characteristics of the affluent society with its emphasis on striving for material gain and competitive success and its perceived willingness to place material gain above the psychological and spiritual needs of the individual. Drugs are said to have the capacity to help liberate the user from these moulds and structures.

Many have used the term alienation in trying to explain the sources of drug use to us. This is not an easy word to define. But as used in our hearings it has tended to refer to what some feel to be an estrangement from the institutions, processes and dominant values of the society, a sense of powerlessness to affect the future of the society or of themselves within it, and a lack of belief that a full and meaningful life is available for them in the society.

Some of the young seem fearful that they can not live up to the expectations that have been set for them or feel that to do so would demand too much sacrifice of their personalities.

The increased use of 'speed' has been interpreted as symptomatic of a widespread depression and sense of powerlessness.

We make no full attempt at this stage to present a statement of the causes of the spread of non-medical drug use. In Chapter Four, we point to some explanatory themes that we feel might help to illuminate the phenomenon.

E. SOCIAL RESPONSE

1. Research, Information and Education

415. *The relative lack of adequate information concerning the non-medical use of drugs.* There is general agreement that we lack sufficient reliable information to make sound social policy decisions and wise personal choices in relation to non-medical drug use. The Commission has heard repeatedly of the desire for more information. Not only citizens, but administrative officials, legislators, physicians and scientists have confessed to feeling that they have an inadequate basis for judgement on this subject.

416. *The state of research.* Until recently, research on certain of the psychotropic drugs, such as cannabis, has been impeded or discouraged by several factors: the lack of clearly established medical uses for the drug, the lack of previous wide-spread non-

medical use in the Western World, the illegal character of the drugs and the reluctance of government agencies to authorize such research. Although it has been possible for governments, under the terms of the United Nations Single Convention on Narcotic Drugs, to authorize the possession of cannabis for medical or scientific purposes, there is reason to believe that such steps as have been taken nationally, and internationally, have not substantially encouraged such research. Public policy on this point would appear to have been heavily influenced by the attitude of law enforcement authorities rather than by scientific advisers. With the increasing concern over the spread of cannabis use, the relative ineffectiveness of the criminal law as a deterrent, and the mounting demand for the 'legalization' of cannabis, there has been some change in the attitudes of government towards research with this drug. Both the Canadian and American governments have indicated their willingness to support such research. The Canadian government, through the Department of National Health and Welfare, has invited applications for research authorization. The American government has initiated a programme of research through the National Institute of Mental Health. We hope that the necessary care which governments must exercise in the approval of projects for research into the effects of cannabis and other psychotropic drugs upon humans will not place unnecessary difficulties in the path of such research and discourage those who are willing and able to undertake it.

There is a fundamental question concerning the responsibility of the scientist to provide information to society regarding the benefits and risks of the use of different drugs. Many scientists interested in such research have expressed feelings of dissatisfaction and frustration with governmental research policy. They have stated to the Commission that they have been unable to carry out such work under their own authority as scientists in the present atmosphere of restraint. They say that they have been frustrated by the administration of the formal and unwritten governmental policies which surround the right to undertake research in this field. An important public policy question to be answered is: 'To whom should the scientific researcher be primarily accountable?' What are his responsibilities to government authorities, his peers in the scientific community and to society in general?

In the initial phase of our inquiry, reference has been made on several occasions to the impossibility of obtaining authorization for research in cannabis and other psychotropic drugs in Canada, and a certain scepticism has been expressed as to whether recently announced policy changes (for example, the Food and Drug Directorate's 'Policy Statement On Use of Cannabis Preparations for Research Purposes') will really facilitate such research. **The Commission invites scientists interested in research on psychotropic substances to comment on such protocols and regulations which may affect their research, their planning of new projects and the public communication of results.**

417. *The need for research*. The need for research referred to above in the section on effects is very urgent. The public, including interested scientists, are justly dissatisfied and impatient with the present state of research. The public does not know whom to blame, but it will not lightly tolerate an indefinite reliance on inadequate knowledge to justify a social policy which is coming under increasingly severe criticism. Moreover, it is essential that we provide accurate information to the Canadian people on which to base their own exercise of personal choice. **In our opinion, research into the effects, the extent, the causes, and the prevention and treatment of dangerous aspects of non-medical drug use should be pursued with all possible vigour in an environment of flexibility and freedom.**

418. *Some current research on cannabis*. In Canada a number of surveys, including those of the Commission, are being conducted into the extent and patterns of use of cannabis and other psychotropic drugs. In addition, the Addiction Research Foundation is conducting a behavioural and physiological study of regular cannabis users and is planning an experimental study on the effects of cannabis on humans.

The United States National Institute of Mental Health (N.I.M.H.) has informed the Commission of various plans for research into the chemical, physiological, psychological and legal aspects of cannabis. The present emphasis in the United States is on the qualitative and quantitative chemical composition of cannabis and on effects in animals. There is little ongoing human research, although much is planned. Several projects are concerned with cannabis effects on some perceptual and cognitive functions and on driving skills.

Some additional information on current research projects is presented in Appendix E. **The Commission intends to maintain close contact with, and critically evaluate, research in these areas and to report thereon.**

419. *Expectations of current and proposed cannabis research during the following year.* As a result of ongoing research in North America and abroad, it appears that by the spring of 1971 we may have a good deal more information on the chemistry, basic pharmacology and toxicology of cannabis in animals. A few human studies may be conducted which might provide new data on the short term effects of cannabis on driving skills, and on some elementary cognitive, perceptual and psychomotor functions. Furthermore, it is feasible that more definite information could be available by that time on the potential of cannabis to produce tolerance and/or dependence with extremely heavy chronic use, although no such investigations are under way.

On the other hand, it may well be a decade or more before we have adequate information on a number of possibly important issues: long-term physiological effects of cannabis on respiratory function and on the central nervous system; the possibility of effects on chromosomes and developing offspring; long-term psychological effects of social and psychiatric importance; the frequency and characteristics of potential patterns of moderate and extreme cannabis use in North America.

420. *The role of the Federal Government in relation to research.* **We recommend that the Federal Government actively encourage research into the phenomenon of non-medical drug use, and in particular, research into the effects of psychotropic drugs and substances on humans. The Government should not only give its approval to such research, upon reasonable conditions, but should encourage, solicit and assist it with financial support in the form of research grants.** We reserve our opinion, for the present, as to the extent to which the Federal Government should itself carry out such research. This raises the question, which we consider

below, as to whether there should be a new federal agency for the collection and evaluation of data in the field of non-medical drug use. We also comment below on the field for cooperation and coordination in respect of research between the federal and the provincial governments.

It is recommended that the Federal Government make available to researchers, as soon as possible, standard preparations of cannabis and pure cannabinols. While cooperation with scientists and government authorities of other countries would clearly be advisable, it is recommended that Canada take the initiative to develop a separate and independent research programme at this time. Under the present circumstances this calls for government-controlled cultivation, production and standardization of cannabis and cannabinols in Canada.

It is further recommended that experimental investigation into the effects of cannabis on humans, as well as animal and basic chemical research, be encouraged and financially supported by the Federal Government immediately. Although a certain amount of this work might be conducted by governmental personnel, it is recommended that independent scientists (in university laboratories, for example) be significantly involved in the overall research effort. Applications to the Federal Government for research authorization should be evaluated by independent scientists as well as civil servants, and the basis for governmental decisions made public.

421. *The problem of collecting and exchanging data.* There is at present no national system for the collection and exchange of data on non-medical drug use. There is no coordinated approach to the problem of documentation. There is urgently needed some coordinating mechanism at the national level to collect data from all over the country. There is also a need for cooperation in the development of a uniform system of classification and indexing of information.

422. *The need for an evaluation and authenticating process.* There is a need for a national system whereby information on non-medical drug use can be evaluated for scientific validity. There must be some source of disinterested and authoritative opinion to which those seeking information can turn for guidance

to determine what can be relied upon for public policy and drug education. This system must be one which commands widespread confidence because of its independence from political pressures, its competence, and its reputation for objective evaluation. People are confused by the babble of voices on non-medical drug use and by the conflict of opinion among respectable authorities. Someone must be given the responsibility to sift out and clarify.

423. *The need for timely information.* The proliferation of drugs and the rapid change in patterns of drug use make it difficult to provide timely information. Witnesses have impressed upon us the problems created by the new drug technology. The possible combinations of new drugs are infinite, and the speed with which they can be manufactured and brought to distribution is astonishing. We are told that the illicit facilities for drug manufacture dispose of technical skill equal to, and in some cases, exceeding that of legitimate manufacturers. Physicians can not be sure of what they are required to deal with in drug cases unless they have access to timely information on the kinds of drugs that are available and being consumed locally. We further believe that if we are serious about seeking to control and reduce the harm caused by non-medical drug use, such information should be made available to drug users and potential drug users. This is particularly important with respect to drug adulteration, about which many witnesses have testified. This raises a question about the desirability of local or regional drug analysis laboratories.

424. *The need for decentralized analysis of drug samples.* It is clear that the facilities of the Food and Drug Directorate in Ottawa can not meet the requirements of the country for the analysis of drugs in non-medical use. It is hardly possible for the Directorate to meet the requirements of the R.C.M.P. for forensic chemical analysis. There has been some decentralization of Food and Drug Directorate and R.C.M.P. laboratory facilities, but the overall capacity remains inadequate, and it is not a timely or an appropriate source of information for those involved with treatment. Several witnesses before the Commission have proposed that the Federal Government support the establishment of local or regional drug analysis facilities for the

316

purpose of providing timely information to all who may seek it.

It is feared by some that such facilities and information may encourage the use of drugs by advertising their availability and reducing dangers. It has been further suggested that distributors will take advantage of these facilities to have their products tested and, as it were, approved. Whatever force there may be in these arguments, they are outweighed, it would seem, by the necessity of a thorough and effective commitment to know as much as possible about what is happening in non-medical drug use and to make such knowledge available for the benefit of those who may be prudent enough to be guided by it. We have more to fear from wilful ignorance than we do from knowledge in this field. In this risk-taking generation, young people are going to continue to experiment with drugs, regardless of what we do. It is better that they should see the whole sordid picture of fraud, adulteration and crass commercial exploitation. In its own pretensions to idealism, the drug culture tends to conceal from itself the extent to which it has become infected with many of the evils which it deplores in the established society. Sample analysis and wide dissemination of the results can only serve in the long run to deglamorize drugs and drug-taking.

We recommend that the Federal Government actively investigate the establishment of regional drug analytical laboratories at strategic points across the country. There is reason to believe, however, that the problems of staffing and financing, to assure an adequate service for quantitative as well as qualitative analysis, might have been underestimated by persons who have urged the establishment of such services. Such laboratories should not be connected with government or law enforcement, and should be free from day-to-day interference by public authorities. It is sufficient for the government to retain ultimate control through the necessity of its approval which may be withdrawn for cause. The Commission will also study the matter. The location, financing and staffing of such a psychotropic drug assay service could well be a matter of federal-provincial cooperation. **In the meantime, we would recommend that, pending our final report, arrangements be made where possible through universities and other agencies for the provision of laboratory facilities to render such service.**

425. *Problems in the dissemination of drug information.* Not only is there a problem of timeliness of information in a rapidly changing scene, but there is also a problem of the credibility of the sources of information. Many witnesses have testified to this problem. We have no doubt that it may sometimes be exaggerated to justify the claim of a particular group or individual to some special role in drug information or education, but we believe that it is a real problem. There is evidence that young people lack confidence in certain sources of information. This is partly because they feel they have been misinformed and misled by certain kinds of approach to drug information and education. It is our impression that the development and evaluation of reliable data may be one thing and its effective dissemination another, and that these two functions may best be carried out by different agencies or individuals. There may be grounds for supporting the dissemination of drug information by local groups or individuals – for example, those involved in Innovative Services – who have high credibility with young people. There have to be strong, well-informed points of local contact with the drug scene if there is to be effective data collection and dissemination.

426. *The role of the media.* In the initial phase of its inquiry the Commission has heard conflicting opinion on the role and performance of the media in relation to the phenomenon of non-medical drug use. Some have criticized the media for sensationalism and even for drawing undue attention to the subject. Others have commended the media for arousing public concern and helping to fill the information gap. There is no doubt that the media have an important role to play in reporting the news in as objective and balanced a manner as possible, and in providing a forum for the exchange of information and opinion. **We recommend that the Federal Government keep the media as fully informed as possible of its own information about non-medical drug use.**

427. *Drug education.* The capacity of this society to learn to live wisely in a world in which chemicals and chemical change will increasingly be significant will depend, in very large measure, on the understanding our citizens have of both themselves and the effects, dangerous and beneficial, of an ever-growing list of

chemical compounds. In this context, the necessity for effective drug education is paramount.

In the Commission's view, the notion of drug education implies more than a mere random conveying of information: it implies selection, system, purpose and perspective. And in this definitional setting, we have discussed with many witnesses the general approach to drug education. From this dialogue, a number of requisites have emerged. For one thing, there has been a general insistence that any drug education programme must provide a full disclosure of all facts concerning the drugs, whether these be positive or unfavourable. There has also been a general agreement by those to whom we have spoken that the *whole truth* be told as far as is humanly possible. We have been advised, particularly by the young, that education about drugs will be ineffectual unless moralizing and patronizing attitudes are changed. The facts, we have been told, must be presented with a proper sense of proportion and perspective so that the overall impression conveyed is truthful and realistic. Witnesses have complained that the overall impression is sometimes a distorted or misleading one in which alleged dangers are either overdrawn or understated. We ourselves can testify to the difficulty of achieving the necessary balance. The attempt to state the facts will often reflect some reaction (and sometimes over-reaction) to what are felt to have been excesses or deficiencies in previous statements. It is probably impossible to exclude some bias, conscious or unconscious, from one's purpose in conveying drug information. Clearly, the universal conviction that we need drug education implies some assumption as to purpose and effect. We believe that the purpose must be to provide the basis for informed and wise personal choice. The ultimate effect that we would hope for is reasonable control and even overall reduction in the non-medical use of drugs. But in our opinion that effect is unlikely to be achieved by exhortation or propaganda, but rather by helping people to see where their real personal interest lies – in the long run. Drug education that is not based on a realistic view of human motivation is doomed to failure. We can no longer rely on the appeal to a sense of morality. In the long run the issue is: Does non-medical drug use enhance or impair one's capacity for effective and satisfying life? What counts with the individual is

319

its effect on vitality, self-development and self-realization. The individual will remain the judge of this on the basis of his own experience and the information which is brought to his attention. Drug education should be merely an aspect of general education and should be directed to the same general objective: the kind of understanding that will permit an individual to live wisely, in harmony with himself and his environment.

Many of the young people who have appeared before us have been critical of the drug education to which they have been exposed. In particular, they have said that the attempts to use 'scare tactics' have 'backfired' and destroyed the credibility of sound information. On the other hand, there is reason to believe that many young people have been deterred from the use of LSD and the amphetamines by the presumptive evidence of their potential for harm. In other words, despite their spirit of risk-taking, they are responsive to serious evidence of the probability of harm. One of the most heartening aspects of the present drug situation is that despite the depression and lack of belief in the future that is reflected in some drug users, young people are concerned to preserve their own capacity to have healthy children and not to visit the consequences of their own risk-taking upon another generation. The conclusion we draw from the testimony we have heard is that it is a grave error to indulge in deliberate distortion or exaggeration concerning the alleged dangers of a particular drug, or to base a programme of drug education upon a strategy of fear. It is no use playing 'chicken' with young people; in nine cases out of ten they will accept the challenge. What we have to ask is whether drug use is the way to life; the way to the greater vitality, consciousness and sense of self-worth which they seek.

Opinion differs as to whether drug education should be a separate course taught by specialists or whether it should be taught more pervasively as part of the general health and physical education programme. There appear to be two considerations to reconcile here: the need for some special training to give the regular teacher a sufficient background and competence; and the desirability of having the subject taught as an aspect of general education. On balance, we believe that there will have to be some degree of specialization if drug education is to command the respect

320

of young people. They themselves are already very knowledgeable, and the teacher must show at least a comparable degree of sophistication if he or she is to hold their interest.

It has been suggested that young people may themselves make effective teachers on the subject of non-medical drug use. It is felt that they are likely to have more credibility with their peers, particularly where they have had experience of drug use. **We believe that serious consideration should be given to training young people for participation in drug education.**

428. *The need for a nationally coordinated system of information and education.* All of the above needs – research, evaluation, local data collection and dissemination and drug education – would appear to call for a coordinated system on a national scale. On the basis of the preliminary information the Commission has received regarding a number of existing drug education programmes, it is evident that no national or regional coordination exists, although provincial and municipal governments, as well as a number of non-governmental institutions, have devised programmes to provide drug education. We are not yet able to perceive the precise outlines, much less the detail of the system which should be established, but we **strongly recommend that the development of an appropriate system be given high priority as a matter of Federal-Provincial cooperation.** We venture at this interim stage to suggest some of the considerations to which further study and discussion may be directed.

The Canadian Medical Association has recommended the formation of regional multi-disciplinary groups or 'teams' to develop an adequate understanding of and community response to the phenomenon of non-medical drug use. These would be non-governmental groups composed of representatives of the various disciplines and services having a special contribution to make in this field. It is contemplated that the community could turn to such a group for reliable information, policy guidance and service of various kinds. There is much that is attractive in this recommendation – particularly the non-governmental, regional and multi-disciplinary character of the proposed groups – but it is not yet clear where the initiative will come from to establish them and how their representative character is to be assured. The danger is that such a group, having to be representative of all specialities and interests connected with drug use, may tend to be filled up by established professional figures and 'leading citizens' and to have an inadequate representation of young people. In this way, it can quickly take on an 'establishment' colour that can undermine its effectiveness. In the course of our public hearings we noted that one provincial 'task force', although a commendable initiative along the lines suggested by the Canadian Medical Association, was composed in this way with little or no independent representation of youth. This may well be the inevitable result of attempting to develop a sufficiently representative provincial or regional body. It will turn out to be representative of the various professions and institutions having some involvement in non-medical drug use, instead of a 'grass-roots' activity in which the people most directly affected can have a true sense of participation. **We therefore approve the Canadian Medical Association recommendation with some reservation or caution, and we hope to have an opportunity in the ensuing year to observe how effective it can be.** There is some ambiguity as to the precise role of these multidisciplinary teams. It is doubtful if regional groups can be as effective as a national body in the development of reliable data. Their effectiveness as a local source of information will depend upon the kind of credibility which they can establish with those most concerned. This credibility will also be affected by the role which they assume in the development of regional policy on non-medical drug use. Finally, it is unlikely that such a group can play any direct role in treatment or rehabilitation, although they may be able to perform a referral service if they command sufficient confidence with drug users.

The Canadian Medical Association brief contemplates a kind of federation of such regional bodies with federal coordination. The function of the regional bodies would be 'to marshal information from all concerned disciplines and subsequently apply or direct the application of this information towards the problems of non-medical drug use'. The federal body would 'centralize information disbursal' and 'act as a catalyst in the interaction between the provincial bodies.'

The issue here is whether the Federal Government should

assume some clear initiative and establish a national agency for data collection and dissemination or whether coordination at the federal level should be left to non-governmental initiative. **In our opinion, the system contemplated by the Canadian Medical Association does not exclude an important role for Federal Government initiative. We believe that the need for an acceptable system of evaluation and authentication on which the entire country can rely calls for the establishment of a national agency to stimulate and coordinate research, and to collect, evaluate and disseminate the resulting data.**

We have not yet come to precise conclusions as to the form this agency should take, nor what its relationship should be to the federal and provincial governments. We presently contemplate, however, that it would be established as a result of federal-provincial consultation, and that both levels of government would participate in the constitution of its membership, but that once established it would be independent of government and free from political interference. It would have to be a body of pre-eminent scientific authority.

We believe that the stimulation and coordination of research and the evaluation of data are best carried out by an independent agency that has no connections with the responsibility for law enforcement. It is our impression that the intimate association of the law enforcement and scientific functions in the past has prejudiced research and the credibility of scientific performance. The government preoccupation with policy, heavily influenced by law enforcement considerations, makes it desirable that the scientific function be given an independent status.

The federal role with respect to drug education presents more complex issues. It is assumed that the information collected and evaluated at the national level would constitute the material to be put into suitable educational form. The development of these educational materials would require close federal-provincial consultation and cooperation because of the provincial responsibility for education. **It is probable that in addition to the national scientific agency there should be a Federal-Provincial institution for the development of drug education materials.** The collection and evaluation of information is really a separate process from its utilization in an educational process, and the two are not necessarily compatible or capable of being carried out by the same agencies. There might be some overlapping of scientific personnel in these two bodies, but the development of effective educational devices and techniques calls for a variety of other professional skills that would not be involved in scientific research and evaluation. Education today is a major specialization calling for utilization of a variety of techniques of communication. The drug education agency would also be the forum for serious considerations of educational policy which are better separated from the process of scientific evaluation. For example, it has been suggested that we may require at least four kinds of drug education: education for children, education for users, education for non-users, and education for parents. Be that as it may, there are probably important distinctions to be drawn between education for pre-adolescents and education for others. Many existing agencies, among them the National Film Board, have indicated an interest in developing effective drug education materials. There is no doubt that a federal-provincial drug education institution would be able to draw on a variety of technical resources in the country.

There is obviously a provincial role with respect to research, and this is presently reflected in the work of addiction research foundations. It is contemplated that a national scientific agency might carry out some research directly, but (in addition to its function of data collection and evaluation) would be chiefly concerned with the development of a coordinated national programme of research and the evaluation of research proposals for federal government financial support.

2. The Law

429. *The Commission's Terms of Reference.* As indicated above, although the Commission's terms of reference do not refer expressly to law, they clearly invited a consideration of its role in relation to the phenomenon of non-medical drug use. The nature and application of the law in this field is one of the social factors presently related to drug use, and it is also an essential factor to be considered in determining what the Federal Government may do to reduce the problems involved in such use. It would be idle to seek recommendations for governmental action if a consideration of law were to be excluded.

430. *International framework*. As indicated in Chapter Five, federal law in relation to non-medical drug use fulfils international obligations arising under the *Single Convention on Narcotic Drugs, 1961*. Canada is required by this Convention to make the manufacture, distribution, and possession of certain drugs for non-medical (or non-scientific) purposes a penal offence, although considerable discretion is left as to the choice of appropriate penalties. The Convention can only be amended by agreement; if a country can not secure amendment it must abide by the Convention as it is or withdraw from it altogether by denouncing it.

431. *Constitutional framework – The criminal law basis of Canadian legislation*. Canadian legislation in this field, consisting principally of the *Narcotic Control Act* and the *Food and Drugs Act* (more fully described in Chapter Five), rests constitutionally on federal legislative jurisdiction with respect to the criminal law. The prohibitions in these statutes are as much a part of the criminal law as the Criminal Code of Canada. The offences created under both statutes are criminal offences. There is no way in which a federal legislative prohibition, violation of which is punishable by fine or imprisonment, can be considered as other than criminal law.

432. Canadian legislative policy is to make certain drugs available for medical or scientific use, under strict controls, but to prohibit the distribution, and in some cases the possession, of some drugs for other purposes. A violation of any of the legislative prohibitions, whether applicable to drugs for medical or non-medical purposes, is a criminal offence. The regulatory aspects of quality control, licensing, inspection, information returns, and the like, merely establish the conditions on which certain conduct is permitted. Conduct which does not comply with these conditions is prohibited as a matter of criminal law. This, at any rate, is a rationale for treating Canadian food and drug legislation as resting on criminal law power rather than on jurisdiction over trade and commerce, which, being limited to

interprovincial and international trade, is too restrictive for the control of transactions taking place wholly within a province.

433. Within the present international and constitutional framework, the legislative options – that is, the choice of general approaches to legal regulation of non-medical drug use – are not very wide. Unless it is possible, because of the national dimensions of the problem of non-medical drug use, to find a new constitutional basis for such regulation in the general power (or 'Peace, Order and Good Government' clause) it would appear that federal regulation must continue to rest on the criminal law power, as directed to the prevention of harm from dangerous substances.

434. *The appropriateness of the criminal law in relation to non-medical drug use.* In the initial phase of this inquiry, serious questions have been raised concerning the appropriate role, if any, of the criminal law in relation to conduct in the field of non-medical drug use. Some witnesses have asserted that the criminal law should not concern itself at all with the manufacture, distribution, possession or use of drugs for non-medical purposes, although witnesses taking this extreme position suggest that the state has a responsibility for seeing that its citizens are properly informed of the dangers of drugs produced and distributed under these conditions. Other witnesses take an intermediate position that the state has a responsibility to restrict the availability of harmful drugs and substances (and that at the federal level this necessarily involves criminal sanctions) but that the criminal law should not be applied to prevent an individual from doing alleged harm to himself. In other words, this view would concede the role of the criminal law in prohibiting the distribution of harmful drugs, but would deny it any application to simple possession for use. A third view that has been put before us is that the criminal law may be properly applied against possession for use but only on a clear showing of serious potential for harm to the individual concerned. In fact, this view is indistinguishable in principle from that which holds that the effective restriction of availability (justified on the ground of potential for harm) requires the prohibition of possession for use.

435. These contentions, and others to be referred to below concerning the present administration of the law, require us to consider the nature of the criminal law and its general appropriateness and effectiveness in relation to the phenomenon of non-medical drug use. A radical challenge has been laid down to the philosophic basis of the law in this area.

436. *The John Stuart Mill thesis*. Those who contend that the criminal law has no application to the conduct involved in the manufacture, distribution and possession of drugs for non-medical use rest their case, for the most part, on the notion that the prohibited conduct is an example of crime without a victim. They contend that the criminal law should be reserved for conduct which clearly causes serious harm to third persons or to society generally and that it should not be used to prevent the individual from causing harm to himself. They often invoke John Stuart Mill's celebrated essay *On Liberty* as philosophical authority for their position. In it, Mill states as his central proposition:

> The object of this Essay is to assert one very simple principle, as entitled to govern absolutely the dealings of society with the individual in the way of compulsion and control, whether the means used be physical force in the form of legal penalties, or the moral coercion of public opinion. That principle is, that the sole end for which mankind are warranted, individually or collectively, in interfering with the liberty of action of any of their number, is self-protection. That the only purpose for which power can be rightfully exercised over any member of a civilized community, against his will, is to prevent harm to others. His own good, either physical or moral, is not a sufficient warrant. He can not rightfully be compelled to do or forbear because it will be better for him to do so, because it will make him happier, because, in the opinions of others, to do so would be wise, or even right. These are good reasons for remonstrating with him, or reasoning with him, or persuading him, or entreating him, but not for compelling him, or visiting him with any evil in case he do otherwise. To justify that, the conduct from which it is desired to deter him, must be calculated to produce evil to some one else. The only part of

the conduct of any one, for which he is amenable to society, is that which concerns others. In the part which merely concerns himself, his independence is, of right, absolute. Over himself, over his own body and mind, the individual is sovereign.

Mill goes on, in a passage which is not as often quoted, to make an exception to this doctrine where persons below the age of maturity are concerned:

It is, perhaps, hardly necessary to say that this doctrine is meant to apply only to human beings in the maturity of their faculties. We are not speaking of children, or of young persons below the age which the law may fix as that of manhood or womanhood. Those who are still in a state to require being taken care of by others, must be protected against their own actions as well as against external injury.

What he would justify in the way of coercion to prevent the young from causing injury to themselves is not clear. But it is clear that his doctrine necessarily assumes the capacity for truly free and responsible choice. This is an important qualification insofar as the problems presented by non-medical drug use are concerned.

437. Mill argues against restrictions on the availability of allegedly dangerous substances as an interference with the liberty of the individual who may seek to use them, but once again he makes an exception in favour of protection of the young. Pertinent passages on this point include the following:

... On the other hand, there are questions relating to interference with trade, which are essentially questions on liberty; such as the Maine Law, already touched upon; the prohibition of the importation of opium into China; the restriction of the sale of poisons; all cases, in short, where the object of the interference is to make it impossible or difficult to obtain a particular commodity. These interferences are objectionable, not as infringements on the liberty of the producer or seller, but on that of the buyer ... when there is not a certainty, but only a danger of mischief, no one but the person himself can judge of the sufficiency of the motive which may prompt him to incur the risk: in this case, therefore (unless he is a child, or delirious, or in some state of excitement or absorption incompatible with the full use of the reflecting faculty) he ought, I conceive, to be only warned of the danger; not forcibly prevented from exposing himself to it.

438. Mill meets head on the argument that there is no such thing as harm to oneself that does not cause some harm to third persons or society in general.

The distinction here pointed out between the part of a person's life which concerns only himself, and that which concerns others, many persons will refuse to admit. How (it may be asked) can any part of the conduct of a member of society be a matter of indifference to the other members? No person is an entirely isolated being; it is impossible for a person to do anything seriously or permanently hurtful to himself, without mischief reaching at least to his near connections, and often far beyond them . . .
I fully admit that the mischief which a person does to himself may seriously affect, both through their sympathies and their interests, those nearly connected with him, and in a minor degree, society at large. When, by conduct of this sort, a person is led to violate a distinct and assignable obligation to any other person or persons, the case is taken out of the self-regarding class and becomes amenable to moral disapprobation in the proper sense of the term. . . . Whoever fails in the consideration generally due to the interests and feelings of others, not being compelled by some more imperative duty, or justified by allowable self-preference, is a subject of moral disapprobation for that failure, but not for the cause of it, nor for the errors, merely personal to himself, which may have remotely led to it. In like manner, when a person disables himself, by conduct purely self-regarding, from the performance of some definite duty incumbent on him to the public, he is guilty of a social offence. No person ought to be punished simply for being drunk; but a soldier or a policeman should be punished for being drunk on duty. Whenever, in short, there is a definite damage, or a definite risk of damage, either to an individual or to the public, the case is taken out of the province of liberty and placed in that of morality or law.

But with regard to the merely contingent, or, as it may be called, constructive injury which a person causes to society, by conduct which neither violates any specific duty to the public, nor occasions perceptible hurt to any assignable individual except himself; the inconvenience is one which society can afford to bear, for the sake of the greater good of human freedom. If grown persons are to be punished for not taking proper care of themselves, I would rather it were for their own sake, than under pretence of preventing them from impairing their capacity of rendering to society benefits which society does not pretend it has a right to exact. But I can not consent to argue the point as if society had no means of bringing its weaker members up to its ordinary standard of rational conduct, except waiting till they do something irrational and then punishing them, legally or morally, for it. Society has had absolute power over them during all the early portion of their existence; it has had the whole period of childhood and nonage in which to try whether it could make them capable of rational conduct in life.

439. *The Hart-Devlin controversy.* The principles affirmed by Mill have been a point of reference for divergent legal philosophies concerning the conduct which is appropriate for criminal law sanction. The issue is often referred to as one of 'law and morals'. The two leading exponents of the contending points of view in modern times have been the English legal philosopher, H. L. A. Hart, and the English judge, Lord Devlin. Hart has expressed various ways in which the issue has been put as follows:

Is the fact that certain conduct is by common standards immoral, sufficient to justify making that conduct punishable by law? Is it morally permissible to enforce morality as such? Ought immorality as such to be a crime?

Hart's answer is no, as is Mill's, but he adds that 'I do not propose to defend all that Mill said; for I myself think there may be grounds justifying the legal coercion of the individual other than the prevention of harm to others.' (*Law, Liberty and Morality.*[8])

Devlin's answer is yes, on the general ground that 'Society is

330

entitled by means of its laws to protect itself from dangers, whether from within or without.' (*The Enforcement of Morals.*⁹)

440. As Hart himself points out, however, the expression of the issue as one of law and morals is not strictly appropriate to the drug crimes, in which the concern is the protection of the individual from physical and psychological harm, albeit harm to which he may voluntarily expose himself. It is not the suppression of conduct simply on the ground that it fails to conform to an established code of morality, although moral judgement on the deviant character of the conduct is no doubt involved to some extent. Hart refers to this protection of the individual against himself as 'paternalism'. He says:

> But paternalism – the protection of people against themselves – is a perfectly coherent policy. Indeed, it seems very strange in mid-twentieth century to insist upon this, for the wane of laissez faire since Mill's day is one of the commonplaces of social history, and instances of paternalism now abound in our law – criminal and civil. The supply of drugs or narcotics, even to adults, except under medical prescription is punishable by the criminal law, and it would seem very dogmatic to say of the law creating this offence that 'there is only one explanation', namely, 'that the law was concerned not with the protection of the would-be purchasers against themselves, but only with the punishment of the seller for his immorality'. If, as seems obvious, paternalism is a possible explanation of such laws, it is also possible in the case of the rule excluding the consent of the victim as a defence to a charge of assault.

441. Hart finds Mill's argument against restriction of the availability of harmful substances extreme, and inapplicable now in the light of the far-reaching paternalism of the modern state. On this point he says:

> Certainly a modification in Mill's principles is required, if they are to accommodate the rule of criminal law under discussion or other instances of paternalism. But the modified principles would not abandon the objection to the use of the criminal law merely to enforce positive morality. They would only have to provide that harming others is something we may still seek

to prevent by use of the criminal law, even when the victims consent to or assist in the acts which are harmful to them.

442. *The right of the state to restrict the availability of harmful substances*. Thus it is important to keep in mind, and particularly in view of the exception which Mill makes to his own doctrine in favour of protection of the young, the distinction which Hart makes between paternalism and 'legal moralism'. In our opinion, the state has a responsibility to restrict the *availability* of harmful substances – and in particular to prevent the exposure of the young to them – and that such restriction is a proper object of the criminal law. We cannot agree with Mill's thesis that the extent of the state's responsibility and permissible interference is to attempt to assure that people are warned of the dangers. At least, this is our present position, particularly in the light of such recent experience as the thalidomide tragedies. Obviously the state must be selective. It can not attempt to restrict the availability of any and all substances which may have a potential for harm. In many cases it must be satisfied with assuring adequate information. We simply say that, in principle, the state can not be denied the right to use the criminal law to restrict availability where, in its opinion, the potential for harm appears to call for such a policy.

443. *The right of society to protect itself from certain kinds of harm*. Without entering into the distinction between law and morality, we also subscribe to the general proposition that society has a right to use the criminal law to protect itself from harm which truly threatens its existence as a politically, socially and economically viable order for sustaining a creative and democratic process of human development and self-realization.

444. *The criminal law should not be used for the enforcement of morality without regard to potential for harm*. In this sense we subscribe to what Hart refers to as the 'moderate thesis' of Lord Devlin. We do not subscribe to the 'extreme thesis' that it is appropriate to use the criminal law to enforce morality, regardless of the potential for harm to the individual or society.

If we admit the right of society to use the criminal law to restrict the availability of harmful substances in order to protect individuals (particularly young people) and society from resultant harm, it does not necessarily follow that the criminal law should be applied against the user as well as the distributor of such substances. There is no principle of consistency that requires the criminal law to be used as fully as possible, or not at all, in a field in which it may have some degree of appropriateness. We do not exclude in principle the application of the criminal law against the user since it is a measure which can have an effect upon availability and the exposure of others to the opportunity for use, but the appropriateness or utility of such an application must be evaluated in the light of the relative costs and benefits.

445. As indicated in Chapter Five, the law enforcement authorities and the courts have tended to see the offence of simple possession as related to the effective suppression of trafficking. The officers of the R.C.M.P. have testified that law enforcement against trafficking is more difficult without a prohibition against simple possession.

The judicial approach is reflected in the reasoning of the British Columbia Court of Appeal in the *Budd* and the *Hartley and McCallum* cases, in which the Court saw the suppression of use as the most effective means of suppressing trafficking. 'If the use of this drug is not stopped,' the Court said, 'it is going to be followed by an organized marketing system.'

446. During the initial phase of the inquiry we have received recommendations for changes in the law respecting the offence of simple possession. Some have proposed the repeal of the present prohibition against the simple possession of marijuana. Others have suggested that the simple possession of the amphetamines without a prescription should be made a criminal offence. These proposals and the experience so far with law enforcement in the field of non-medical drug use oblige us at this time to consider the merits of the offence of simple possession.

447. The present state of our empirical studies of law enforcement in the field of non-medical drug use does not permit us to express a considered opinion of the operational relationship between the offence of simple possession and the offence of trafficking. We are unable to estimate the relative effect on

enforcement against trafficking of the absence of an offence of simple possession. We are unable, for example, to draw comparisons, in this respect, between the enforcement against trafficking in narcotics, cannabis, and restricted drugs, and enforcement against trafficking in controlled drugs, for which there is not an offence of simple possession. We do not know if meaningful comparisons of this kind can ever be drawn, in view of the many other factors in each case which may influence the patterns of trafficking and their detection. **At the present time we are not convinced of the necessary relationship between the offence of simple possession and trafficking, or of the necessity of such an offence for effective law enforcement against trafficking. We do feel, however, that further study and consideration must be given to the contention of the law enforcement authorities on this point, and for this reason we are not prepared AT THIS TIME to recommend the total elimination of the offence of simple possession in respect of non-medical drug use.**

448. At the same time we have very serious reservations concerning the offence of simple possession for use which prompt us, as an interim measure, to recommend a change in the law respecting it. Our reservations apply to the offence of simple possession generally in the field of non-medical drug use and not to any one or more of the psychotropic drugs, in particular. **In effect, while we feel the offence of simple possession should be retained on the statute book, pending further investigation and analysis, which we hope to carry out in the ensuing year, its impact on the individual should be reduced as much as possible.**

449. Our basic reservation at this time concerning the prohibition against simple possession for use is that its enforcement would appear to cost far too much, in individual and social terms, for any utility which it may be shown to have. **We feel that the probability of this is such that there is justification at this time to reduce the impact of the offence of simple possession as much as possible, pending further study and consideration as to whether it should be retained at all.** The present cost of its enforcement, and the individual and social harm caused by it, are in our opinion, one of the major problems involved in the non-medical use of drugs.

450. Insofar as cannabis, and possibly the stronger hallucin-ogens like LSD, are concerned, the present law against simple possession would appear to be unenforceable, except in a very selective and discriminatory kind of way. This results necessarily from the extent of use and the kinds of individual involved. It is obvious that the police can not make a serious attempt at full enforcement of the law against simple possession. **We intend during the ensuing year to attempt to determine the relative cost in actual dollars and allocation of time of the enforcement of the drug laws, but it is our initial impression from our observations so far that it is out of all proportion to the relative effectiveness of the law.** Although accurate statistics are not available to us at this time of either the extent of cannabis use or the number of cases of simple possession of cannabis cleared by the law enforce-ment authorities during the past year, conservative estimates of both suggest that the total number of cannabis users brought to court may be under one per cent.

The law which appears to stand on the statute book as a mere convenience to be applied from time to time, on a very selective and discriminatory basis, to 'make an example' of someone, is bound to create a strong sense of injustice and a corresponding disrespect for law and law enforcement. It is also bound to have an adverse effect upon the morale of law enforcement authorities.

451. Moreover, it is doubtful if its deterrent effect justifies the injury inflicted upon the individuals who have the misfortune to be prosecuted under it. It is, of course, impossible to determine the extent to which the law against simple possession has deter-rent effect, but certainly the increase in use, as well as the state-ments of users, would suggest that it has relatively little. The relative risk of detection and prosecution may be presumed to have a bearing upon deterrent effect.

452. The harm caused by a conviction for simple possession appears to be out of all proportion to any good it is likely to achieve in relation to the phenomenon of non-medical drug use. Because of the nature of the phenomenon involved, it is bound to impinge more heavily on the young than on other segments of the population. Moreover, it is bound to blight the life of some of the most promising of the country's youth. Once again there

335

is the accumulating social cost of a profound sense of injustice, not only at being the unlucky one whom the authorities have decided to prosecute, but at having to pay such an enormous price for conduct which does not seem to concern anyone but oneself. This sense of injustice is aggravated by the disparity in sentences made possible by the large discretion presently left to the courts.

453. Finally, the extreme methods which appear to be necessary in the enforcement of a prohibition against simple possession – informers, entrapment, Writs of Assistance, and occasionally force to recover the prohibited substance – add considerably to the burden of justifying the necessity or even the utility of such a provision.

454. **Despite these reservations, the Commission is not prepared to recommend the total repeal of the prohibition against simple possession without an opportunity to give further study and consideration to:**

   (a) **The possible effect of permitted use on the nature and development of trafficking; and**
   (b) **The possible effect of the lack of an offence of simple possession on the effectiveness of law enforcement against trafficking.**

455. **At the same time the Commission is of the opinion that no one should be liable to imprisonment for simple possession of a psychotropic drug for non-medical purposes.** Moreover, it believes that the discretion as to whether to proceed by way of indictment or summary conviction should be removed. **Accordingly, the Commission recommends as an interim measure, pending its final report, that the Narcotic Control Act and the Food and Drugs Act be amended to make the offence of simple possession under these acts punishable upon summary conviction by a fine not exceeding a reasonable amount. The Commission suggests a maximum fine of $100.** Such a change would in fact reflect, and bring the law into closer conformity with recent sentencing practices, at least for first offenders, in cases of simple possession of cannabis or LSD.

Furthermore, this change would be within the scope of Article

36 of the *Single Convention on Narcotic Drugs, 1961*, which only requires 'imprisonment or other penalties of deprivation of liberty' (see Chapter Five, Paragraph 366) for 'serious offences'.

The Commission also recommends that the power conferred by section 694(2) of the Criminal Code to impose imprisonment in default of payment of a fine should not be exercisable in respect of offences of simple possession of psychotropic drugs. In such cases, the Crown should rely on civil proceedings to recover payment.

456. The Commission would further recommend that the police, prosecutors and courts exercise the discretion entrusted to them at various stages of the criminal law process so as to minimize the impact of the criminal law upon the simple possessor of psychotropic drugs, pending decision as to the whole future of possessional offences in this field.

457. During the initial phase of its inquiry the Commission has received representations from several witnesses, including some who have differed strongly on the proper legal treatment of cannabis, that the simple possession of the 'controlled' drugs in Schedule G of the *Food and Drugs Act* – particularly, the amphetamines and methamphetamines – be made a criminal offence. **The Commission is not disposed to make this recommendation at the present time.** Apart from its general reservations concerning the offence of simple possession, it sees particular problems with respect to such an offence in the case of the controlled drugs.

Unless we are prepared to prohibit some or all of the controlled drugs altogether, whether under prescription or not, as some countries have done, we see serious difficulties (perhaps even greater than those which have arisen with cannabis) in attempting to enforce a criminal law prohibition against simple possession for non-medical use. In the first place, it would not be practicable to impose or attempt to enforce such a prohibition for possession of drugs obtained under prescription, even though the use might no longer be justified on generally accepted medical grounds. The same would apply to members of the same family or to friends to whom such drugs might be given for non-medical use. In other words, the extent to which these drugs can presently be obtained and used under prescription by the adult world – and indeed are used, if we are to draw the logical inferences from production figures – is such that the enforcement of a prohibition against simple possession for the non-medical use of such drugs would inevitably involve even greater discrimination and sense of injustice than that which is bringing the law with respect to cannabis into disrepute. Since such a prohibition might be expected to be directed and enforced mainly against what the police considered to be *excessive* use by young people it would be a further cause of youthful alienation and resentment of the older generation. This would only be reinforced by increasing use of amphetamines and barbiturates by adults.

Further, in view of the paranoia associated with the excessive use of amphetamines and methamphetamines (the level of use which characterizes the 'speed freak'), we do not think it would be socially helpful or desirable to attempt to apply the criminal law and the enforcement methods which seem to be necessary to the simple possession of these drugs for non-medical use. We believe that such a course could lead to a substantial increase in violence and other undesirable social effects. We place much more hope and confidence in education and cultural controls as a means of reducing the use of 'speed'. There is reason to believe that such controls may be beginning to operate effectively through the influence of peer group opinion and the judgement of leading opinion formers in the drug culture.

458. We fully share the general concern which has been expressed to us concerning the extent and effects of amphetamine and methamphetamine use, but we do not feel that we have a sufficient understanding of the phenomenon at this time to make long-term recommendations with respect to it. In the first place, we do not have a reliable impression of its extent, although there are reasonable grounds for believing that it has in recent years been steadily increasing. But is it still increasing, or is it levelling off, or is it declining? We do not know. Is 'speed' likely to be a temporary phenomenon which will burn itself out in a relatively few years, as a result of the problems which it creates and the general contempt in which it is held by large sections of the youthful drug culture? Who can say? We do not at this time have any real sense of conviction about the probable future pattern and extent of amphetamine use in Canada. Other countries, such as post-war

Japan, have experienced amphetamine epidemics. Because of very extensive use, and particularly use by adults, Sweden has seen fit to proscribe their use altogether. We have not yet been able to judge how successful they have been and what the social effects of such repression are, although we understand from preliminary impressions that there is now an extensive illicit traffic in such drugs from neighbouring countries such as Germany and the Netherlands, and that the unlawful possession of amphetamines has become a middle-class status symbol with conspiratorial overtones, which history has shown to be the inevitable consequence of the prohibition of a substance which a large proportion of the population desires.

It would not appear that the excessive use of amphetamines by young people has assumed the same relative importance in Scandinavia as it has here. The emphasis is rather on excessive adult use. Are we moving in Canada into a similar pattern of excessive adult use? It has been suggested to us that this may be the case, but we do not feel confident about expressing an opinion on this possibility at the present time. We would want to give further consideration to the conditions which have produced this phenomenon in other countries during the post-war period, and to compare them with present conditions in this country. It is our impression at this time that the government would not be warranted in following the example of other countries in a total prohibition of amphetamines or barbiturates without clear evidence that such a step is warranted by the extent and levels of use. We doubt very much if such a step would ever be justified in Canada. **At the present time, we advocate closer controls on the availability of these drugs, including controls on production, importation and prescription.**

459. Strong representations have been made to the Commission during the initial phase of its inquiry for radical change in the law respecting cannabis. In particular, many witnesses have urged the 'legalization' of marijuana – that is, that this drug be made legally available through government-licensed or operated channels of production and distribution. Several witnesses have urged that if the Commission is not prepared to recommend such legalization at the present time, it should at least recommend a 'moratorium'

or suspension of all marijuana prosecutions pending publication of its final report. The Commission has also frequently heard the proposal that cannabis should be removed from the *Narcotic Control Act* and placed under the *Food and Drugs Act*.

460. Several arguments are advanced for the legalization of marijuana. They may be summarized as follows:

1. The use of marijuana is increasing in popularity among all age groups of the population, and particularly among the young;
2. This increase indicates that the attempt to suppress, or even to control its use, is failing and will continue to fail – that people are not deterred by the criminal law prohibition against its use;
3. The present legislative policy has not been justified by clear and unequivocal evidence of short term or long term harm caused by cannabis;
4. The individual and social harm (including the destruction of young lives and growing disrespect for law) caused by the present use of the criminal law to attempt to suppress cannabis far outweighs any potential for harm which cannabis could conceivably possess, having regard to the long history of its use and the present lack of evidence;
5. The illicit status of cannabis invites exploitation by criminal elements, and other abuses such as adulteration; it also brings cannabis users into contact with such criminal elements and with other drugs, such as heroin, which they might not otherwise be induced to consider.

For all these reasons, it is said, cannabis should be made available under government-controlled conditions of quality and availability.

461. It should be observed that many of the witnesses who have advocated the legalization of cannabis have also advocated an age limit under which it should not be available, similar to the prohibition against the sale of alcohol to minors. Eighteen and over has been an age limit frequently suggested. Thus, even among those who advocate the legalization of cannabis, there are those who have reservations about its use among young

340

people, and the implications of criminal law proscription of it, insofar as they are concerned, are among the chief problems involved in such use today. A 'legalization' of cannabis which continued to prohibit its sale to persons under 18 years of age would be one which favoured adults rather than young people, and although it would undoubtedly have the indirect effect of making cannabis more easily available to young people, it would leave the issue of the use of cannabis by the young essentially unresolved. We think it is significant that a number of those who advocate the legalization of cannabis are sufficiently concerned about its potential for harm to young people to advocate an age limit for its availability. This obviously deepens as one seeks to ascertain what is considered to be the appropriate age limit – is it 18, 17, 16, 15, 14, 13, 12, 11, 10, 9, 8, 7? We do not mean to suggest that such concern necessarily justifies the maintenence of the present legal status of cannabis, but merely that it throws additional perspective on the debate concerning its potential for harm.

462. This is, of course, the essential question with respect to cannabis at this time. It is idle to pretend that cannabis was brought under its present criminal law proscription on the basis of clear and unequivocal scientific evidence of its potential for harm. Although the precise historical reasons for the decision to suppress its use are somewhat obscure, there is no evidence that scientific judgement played a leading role. There did, however, develop an international climate of official opinion, strongly opposed to its use. This opinion was based in part on the experience of certain countries, but it was also strongly influenced by American insistence. Thus it is fair to say that Canadian policy found increasing support in the opinion of the international community. The spread of the use of cannabis, particularly among the young, and the effects of the criminal law attempt to suppress it now call for a fresh look at the justification of the law, and in particular, at the alleged personal and social harm caused by such use.

463. The issue now is whether Canadian policy is to turn on potential for harm, or whether it is to turn on the extent of use and the apparent incapacity of the law to prevent the spread of

341

such use. It is a difficult judgement to make. The law has had to throw up its hands in the past, as in the case of the failure to enforce the prohibition against alcohol. It is not clear, however, that we are yet at this point with cannabis. The debate and the perception of the issues have turned on a difference of opinion as to the potential for harm. At this point, it is not possible to give assurance concerning potential for harm. We refer to the section on cannabis in Chapter Two and to the section on effects in this chapter as indicating the lack of essential knowledge on pertinent issues.

The question is: How long can society wait for the necessary information? It is very serious that the scientific information concerning cannabis lags so far behind the rapidly developing social problem caused by its illegal status. It is useless to apportion blame. We have referred above to the necessity of research and a fundamental change in the attitude of government towards research. Given a sufficiently comprehensive and aggressive programme of research, when are we likely to know enough, one way or the other, to justify a decision on legalization on the basis of potential for harm? It may be that we shall not be able to learn enough in time, at least with respect to potential for long-term harm, before we are obliged to take a decision on another basis – that is, on the basis of calculated risk, or the lesser of evils.

At this time, we do not feel that Canadian perceptions of this problem or our knowledge warrant a recommendation by us on the basis of calculated risk or the lesser of evils.

464. For the following reasons we are not prepared at this time to recommend the legalization of cannabis:

1. First, it is our impression that there has not yet been enough informed public debate. Certainly there has been much debate, but too often it has been based on hearsay, myth and ill-informed opinion about the effects of the drug. We hope that this report will assist in providing a basis for informed debate not only as to the effects, but as to other issues, including the extent to which science is capable of providing a basis for public policy decision on this question.

2. There is a body of further scientific information, important for

legislation, that can be gathered by short-term research – for example, the effects of the drug at various dose levels on psychomotor skills, such as those used in driving.

3. Further consideration should be given to what may be necessarily implied by legalization. Would a decision by the government to assume responsibility for the quality control and distribution of cannabis imply, or be taken to imply, approval of its use and an assurance as to the absence of significant potential for harm?

4. A decision on the merits of legalization can not be taken without further consideration of jurisdictional and technical questions involved in the control of quality and availability.

465. The proposal for legalization raises important issues of international and constitutional law, although these have not determined our judgement on the merits of legalization at this time.

If Canada were to decide to legalize cannabis or any of its derivatives, it could not do so without violating its international obligations under the *Single Convention on Narcotic Drugs, 1961*, unless it obtained international agreement to an amendment to the Convention or withdrew from the Convention by giving the notice described as 'denunciation'. It will be recalled from Chapter Five that the Convention presently requires the parties to prohibit, with penal consequences, the production, distribution and possession of cannabis for other than medical and scientific purposes. Denunciation by the required notice of six clear months, to take effect on any January 1st, would not, of course, be in violation of international obligations since it is a right expressly provided for in the Convention. It would however, take Canada out of the framework of international agreement with respect to narcotic drugs. We do not speculate on the effect which the legalization of cannabis might have on Canada's international relations through its effect on the enforcement policies of other countries, such as the United States.

Insofar as constitutional law is concerned, the proposal to legalize cannabis raises a question as to the kind of control of availability and quality which would be constitutionally possible for the Federal Government. The proposals for legalization have generally contemplated a government monopoly of production

343

and distribution. We have not considered the necessity or merits of this degree of government intervention because of our judgement on the general issue of legalization at this time, but justifiable public concern about commercial exploitation of psychotropic drugs could well make such a degree of control necessary if a decision were taken to make any particular cannabis preparation or preparations legally available. Such an intervention would appear to involve a regulation of trade and commerce in the provinces that would have difficulty finding constitutional support within the present range of federal power, as judicially interpreted, particularly if legalization were decided on the basis of a judgement as to relative absence of potential for harm. Although we do not exclude the possibility of finding a constitutional basis for an effective control of availability and quality in the general power ('Peace, Order and Good Government' clause) of the federal parliament, in view of the national importance which a controlled use of cannabis would be deemed to have assumed if legalization were considered necessary, the difficulties at first impression are such that we would presume any such decision would be preceded by federal-provincial consultation. There would appear to be good political reasons for this procedure as well. In effect, legalization would appear to involve the abandonment of the present criminal law basis of federal regulation and the necessity of finding another constitutional basis for it. It is doubtful if there is a sufficient basis at this time for a federal system of regulation similar to the provincial regulation of alcohol. We would, therefore, assume that any such scheme would require provincial action.

466. The proposal that there be a 'moratorium' or suspension on prosecutions in respect of cannabis offences pending publication of the final report is indistinguishable, as a practical matter, from a decision to legalize. It would amount to *de facto* legalization without government assumption of responsibility for control of availability and quality. It would be virtually impossible to reverse should it be decided later to be ill-advised in any particular. At best it would create an intolerable uncertainty as to the ultimate application of the criminal law. We do not believe that a 'moratorium' is a practical measure. At the same time, we

have recommended (see paragraph 456) that discretion be exercised by police, prosecutors and judges in such manner as to minimize the impact of the criminal law in respect of the offence of simple possession of cannabis.

467. Since cannabis is clearly not a narcotic (see paragraph 147) we recommend that the control of cannabis be removed from the Narcotic Control Act and placed under the Food and Drugs Act. Since it is generally considered to be a mild hallucinogenic or intoxicant, it would not be inappropriate to classify it with the restricted drugs in Schedule J of Part IV of the *Food and Drugs Act*, although it could be given a separate classification of its own. This change can be made by the Government without the necessity of legislation in virtue of Section 14 of the *Narcotic Control Act* which provides that 'The Governor-in-Council may, from time to time, amend the Schedule by adding thereto or deleting therefrom any substance, the inclusion or exclusion of which, as the case may be, is deemed necessary by him in the public interest' and the provision to the same effect which is applicable to Part IV of the *Food and Drugs Act*. Changes in the penalties governing drug offences will of course require legislation.

468. Considerable concern has been expressed during the initial phase of our inquiry over the severity of the penalty and some of the sentences for trafficking in cannabis, particularly for the marginal trafficking of a relatively petty nature which takes place between users. We share this concern. Under the *Narcotic Control Act* trafficking is defined very broadly not only to include giving but also offering to give, and a person convicted of trafficking or possession for the purpose of trafficking in cannabis is liable to life imprisonment. A person convicted of importing or exporting cannabis is liable to imprisonment for a minimum of seven years and for as much as life. These penalties are obviously grossly excessive, in view of what we now know of the likelihood of harm and the patterns of use and distribution of cannabis. They would no longer apply if cannabis was brought under the control of Part IV of the *Food and Drugs Act*. Certainly, there is no reason why the penalties for trafficking in cannabis should exceed those for trafficking in LSD. The question is whether they should be as severe. Part IV of the Act provides

that trafficking or possession for the purposes of trafficking in a restricted drug is punishable upon summary conviction by imprisonment for eighteen months or upon conviction on indictment, by imprisonment for ten years. We wonder if the penalty for trafficking in the restricted drugs should not be confined to that which is provided upon summary conviction. **In any event, we would recommend that this be the case with trafficking or possession for the purpose of trafficking in cannabis. We further recommend that the definition of trafficking be amended so as to exclude the giving, without exchange of value, by one user to another of a quantity of cannabis which could reasonably be consumed on a single occasion. Such an act should be subject at most to the penalty for simple possession.**

469. Many of the criticisms of the criminal law in respect of the offence of simple possession for use (see paragraph 453 above) may appear to apply equally to the other drug offences – in particular, trafficking and possession for the purpose of trafficking. We refer to methods of enforcement which are considered necessary as a result of the fact that there is seldom, if ever, a third party complainant. During the initial phase of our inquiry, we have heard bitter complaints and criticisms of the use of entrapment and physical violence to obtain evidence. We have not verified the particular circumstances of these complaints and criticisms, so that we make no charge of any kind at this time but we deplore the use of such methods to the extent they may be resorted to on occasion. We believe that such methods are not only a serious violation of respect for the human person, but they are counter-productive in that they create contempt for law and law enforcement. The price that is paid for them is far too great for any good that they may do.

We recommend that instructions be given to police officers to abstain from such methods of enforcement, and that the R.C.M.P. use its influence with other police forces involved in the enforcement of the drug laws to try to assure that there is a uniform policy in this regard. Because of its primary identification with enforcement of these laws, the Force may sometimes be unfairly associated with such methods when it has not, in fact, been guilty of them.

470. We have also heard criticisms of the Writ of Assistance under which the police are empowered at any time to enter and search a dwelling (using force to effect such entry) and of the employment of undercover agents and informants. Since these methods are apparently necessary because of the extreme difficulty of detecting and securing evidence of drug violations, we make no comment on them at this time other than to observe that they reflect a part of the special price which society must pay for enforcement of the drug laws. As we have indicated, the price may be altogether too high in the case of the offence of simple possession. We reluctantly concede its continuing necessity so long as there must be a serious effort to control trafficking.

471. The same observations apply to another aspect of the drug laws which has attracted critical comment during the initial phase of our inquiry – namely the extent to which the traditional burden of proof is shifted to the accused. The primary burden to prove the fact of possession in a charge of simple possession is on the Crown, but the burden is on the accused to prove any exception, exemption, excuse or qualification by law which operates in his favour – for example, that such possession is authorized by the Act or regulations.

In the case of the offence of possession for the purpose of trafficking, once the Court has found, in what amounts to the first trial, that the accused was in possession within the meaning of the Act, the burden is on the accused to show that such possession was not for the purpose of trafficking. The Crown may establish the inference of intent to traffic from such circumstantial evidence as the quantity of drugs found in the possession of the accused, implements or devices suggesting distribution, and contacts of the accused with others, and the burden on the accused is a difficult one to discharge.

In fact, however, proof of possession does not by itself establish intent to traffic, so that there must be some evidence of intent to justify a conviction. What the burden on the accused does, in most cases, is to compel him to testify, which is contrary to the general principles of criminal justice. **Is this departure from our general standards of protection of the accused really justified by the evil to which the law is directed and the special difficulties** of enforcement? The parliament of Canada has said that it is. We find it difficult to believe that this is so.

472. Great concern has been expressed during the initial phase of our inquiry concerning the serious effects of a criminal conviction and record upon the lives of drug users, particularly the young. These effects are cited, in the case of cannabis, as indicating that the harm caused by the law exceeds the harm which it is supposed to prevent. A criminal record may mar a young life, forever being an impediment to professional or other vocational opportunity and interfering with free movement and the full enjoyment of public rights. We believe this reasoning applies to all criminal convictions, and we do not believe that there should be a special rule in favour of drug offenders. **For this reason, we recommend the enactment of general legislation to provide for the destruction of all records of a criminal conviction after a reasonable period of time.**

In addition to legislation which is actually pending, **we would urge the adoption of the recommendation of the Canadian Committee on Corrections with respect to records of summary convictions which is as follows:**[10]

(*a*) That criminal records resulting from summary conviction be annulled automatically after a crime-free period of two years from the end of the sentence;

(*b*) That 'end of a sentence' be taken to mean, in the case of a fine or other punishment not involving probation or prison, from the date of conviction; in the case of probation, from the end of the probation period; in the case of prison, from the end of the prison sentence; in the case of parole, from the end of the parole period;

(*c*) That an annulled record of summary conviction not be activated in the event of any later conviction, which would be dealt with as a first offence.

The above recommendation deals with the removal of a criminal record after some reasonable period of time, but we believe the courts should have discretion to avoid a conviction in certain cases where an offence has been established. **For this reason we recommend the adoption, at least for first offenders in** cases of simple possession of psychotropic drugs, of the recommendation of the committee in favour of absolute discharge, which reads as follows:

> The Committee recommends that where a person, not having previously been given an absolute discharge, is charged, the trial court or the court that hears the appeal, although finding that the charge has been proved, after considering the evidence and having regard to the circumstances including the nature of the charge and the character of the accused may, without conviction, make an order of absolute discharge with or without conditions; that when a person named in an order of absolute discharge with conditions has violated any of the conditions therein, the court may convict the person and, on the basis of evidence heard at the original trial, make whatever disposition it could have made when the matter was originally heard; that either the offender or probation officer be empowered to request and have heard an application to reconsider and/or vary the conditions of the order; that an order of absolute discharge with conditions be in effect for a period of up to one year.

3. Treatment and Supportive Services

The Commission has not yet been able to examine in detail the various complex aspects of the treatment response to non-medical use of drugs. For this interim report, therefore, the Commission wishes merely to draw attention to what it believes are *two urgent and pressing situations that require immediate response*. It also identifies *other areas of concern* that it intends to examine in detail in the ensuing year.

Problems of immediate urgency

473. *Medical response to immediate short-term toxic effects of drug use*. The Commission has been repeatedly informed by members of the medical profession, parents and drug users, that there are insufficient facilities and staff available to persons in need of immediate crisis treatment for drug effects. This problem is said to be compounded by a lack of patience, and sometimes

even by expressed hostility towards the drug user by both physicians and hospital staff. We have been told that all too often medical practitioners may lack the knowledge to treat a particular drug crisis.

The number of persons, both old and young who are in need of short-term treatment for *acute* drug effects threatens to outstrip the available number of hospital spaces in this country if it has not already done so. This, of course, adds to the interpersonal frustrations on all sides.

The Commission suggests that the medical profession, through its regional medical associations and licensing bodies, undertake immediate negotiations with provincial departments of health for the development of special facilities to treat the short-term toxic effects of drug use. These facilities could be developed within existing hospital complexes.

The Commission also suggests that special care be taken in the recruitment and training of the personnel to staff these facilities. The qualities of empathy, understanding and tolerance generally required of hospital staff, are especially important in dealing with patients suffering from adverse drug effects.

474. *Innovative services**. The Commission has been very favourably impressed by the response of young people in developing innovative services to deal with the many problems faced by youth all over Canada. Although these innovative services are not solely concerned with the phenomenon of drug use, they are very much involved in the treatment of adverse drug effects. **At this time the Commission makes the following recommendations with respect to these services based on the analysis in appendix F:**

1. That the Federal Government recognize the necessary and important role to be played by innovative services in communities across the country. Where possible, federal facilities should be made available to assist them in informing the public of their existence and of the services they are providing. They should enjoy the whole-hearted moral support and official recognition of the Federal Government.

* For definition and fuller description of these services, see Appendix F.

2. That the Federal Government examine, with the provinces, the possibility of providing more direct financial assistance to innovative services to meet the problems of funding discussed in Appendix F.

3. That the Federal Government, with the provinces, encourage the early establishment of joint coordinating committees to serve as intermediaries for the receipt and distribution of financial support for innovative services in the large communities. These committees should be comprised of a representative membership drawn from the community agencies and individuals having a particular interest in the work of innovative services. Such committees could be given a discretionary 'reserve fund' to help with the financing activities of its member innovative services. The criteria governing the eligibility for such assistance would have to be the subject of discussions between the various services themselves and the appropriate levels of government.

4. That the Federal Government consult with the provinces and, through them, with the municipalities on matters of municipal zoning, public health regulations and police practices as they affect innovative services. It is further suggested that the municipalities in which innovative services are located examine their programmes in detail and, once satisfied that they are providing a necessary service, do whatever is in their power to facilitate the operations of such services.

5. Noting the risks involved to the innovative services in sheltering runaway youngsters who are afraid to present themselves to other more formal institutions, the Federal Government should urge upon the provinces the need to examine the problems arising from the rigid interpretation and enforcement of existing child protection statutes.

6. As pointed out earlier, young people in need of medical or psychiatric treatment as a result of drug use are frequently afraid to avail themselves of existing facilities in their communities. Therefore, it is recommended that representatives of the medical profession (including psychiatrists, and hospital emergency staffs), psychologists and other members of the counselling professions, establish some system of continuing consultation and assistance with the innovative services in their areas.

475. *Street clinics.* A medically focused innovative service which has grown out of new concepts of community medicine has involved the setting up of street clinics ('store-front clinics', walk-in clinics').

Such facilities make it possible for anyone in a stressful situation and in need of immediate help to be seen without delay, and if indicated, to receive emergency medical treatment. If the treatment required surpasses the capacity of the street clinic, all necessary arrangements for immediate transfer to a more fully equipped hospital facility can then be expedited with a minimum of strain and confusion.

Such street clinics also function as centres for continuing therapeutic relationships, either through treatment at the clinic or through appropriate referral to other sources.

The Commission recommends that the Federal Government examine with the provinces, the possibility of providing more direct financial assistance to such street clinics.

Other areas of concern

476. *Physical dependence.* Treatment and cure are available from the medical profession for physical addiction resulting from the use of opiates, barbiturates, tranquillizers and alcohol. Although withdrawal from some of these drugs can sometimes carry with it serious dangers, it is in most cases possible to effect a satisfactory physical withdrawal from any of these drugs within two to six weeks.

The major problems in this area appear to be:

(*a*) Many individuals who are physically dependent on one of the drugs mentioned above do not seek help for this problem.
(*b*) Of those who do seek assistance for physical addiction, many are not sufficiently motivated to abstain from further excessive use. Thus, in a few weeks or months, they may again be physically dependent.

At this time the Commission has no specific recommendations on this problem other than to draw attention to the urgent need of sufficient, short-term facilities for those who wish to avail themselves of established treatment procedure.

Psychological dependence. We refer to what has already been said (Chapter Two, Para. 40) concerning the elusive character of this concept, which is underscored by the following observation of the Addiction Research Foundation of Ontario:

> Psychological dependence is merely a descriptive label for a pattern of behaviour which can vary from a trivial and inconsequential reliance on some generally harmless substance or practice, such as one's morning paper or coffee, to an intensive need for a drug which dominates virtually the whole pattern of an individual's life.

Those seeking to deal with 'psychological dependence' resulting from chronic drug use range from prison staff in wilderness forest camps to private psychoanalysts and group therapists. They also include the ex-users of drugs who utilize encounter techniques in 24-hour a day self-help halfway houses that are often modelled after the Synanon Program in California.

There are also psychiatric treatment facilities in Canada and abroad which utilize high and low dosage methadone treatment. This is a treatment using the long-term administration of an opiate substitute which prevents the person from experiencing the euphoric effect of heroin, or suffering the discomfort of any withdrawal symptom. A large scale trial of this treatment appears to be yielding positive results.

In the coming year the Commission intends to examine in detail both the concept of psychological dependence and the treatment programmes that have evolved, both in Canada and abroad.

477. *Compulsory treatment.* There have been suggestions from groups, including the Canadian Medical Association, that consideration be given to legislation that would provide for the compulsory treatment of chronic heavy drug users. The Commission is aware of the highly complex and controversial nature of these proposals. We have been told that many users are baffled as to their supposed need for 'treatment'. Some have stated to the Commission that they wonder if it is any more feasible to treat drug dependency in a compulsory fashion than it is to treat neurotic behaviour in this manner. Concern has also been expressed that involuntary commitment programmes could be

...ed as a means of removing 'undesirable people' from society. ...ot the least of the difficulties is the question as to whether or not there is in fact any method of treatment that can be imposed on a drug user that will offer any real hope of treating a phenomenon as imprecisely defined as 'psychological dependence', unless the drug-dependent user is very strongly motivated in this direction.

The Commission recognizes that one of its major tasks in the preparation of its final report will be a thorough examination of the proposals for legislation that would result in compulsory treatment of heavy chronic drug users.

478. *The proper relationship of treatment to other community services.* The Commission has received a number of briefs which have concerned themselves with the question of how drug treatment programmes can best be located in particular communities. Some have urged the development of highly specialized drug treatment centres where ongoing research and treatment experimentation could take place. This might compound the difficulties of drug users who often feel themselves to be outside the larger community. Moreover, some experts in the public health and social welfare fields have strongly urged that any treatment facilities developed for drug users should be part of multi-purpose social service centres in order to make the most efficient use of resources.

The Commission intends to study this question and to make specific recommendations in its final report with regard to the form and organization of treatment facilities for drug users.

4. Prescribing Practices and Controls

479. Medical associations and many individuals appearing before the Commission deplored the 'loose' prescription writing habits of many physicians in Canada. At the present time, all prescriptions for controlled drugs are recorded by federal authorities (a branch of the Food and Drug Directorate, Department of National Health and Welfare), but there is at present no effective system of record analysis. Also, the Directorate does not receive reports of all prescriptions issued in Canada, but

only those involving certain opiate narcotics or controlled drugs. The present system does not include reports of tranquillizer prescriptions, although these psychotropic drugs are among the most widely used of all drugs, both medically and non-medically.

480. There appear to be three areas of concern in this respect, involving the patient, the pharmacist and the physician.

If someone wants to take a certain drug for non-medical reasons, he may build up a supply by obtaining prescriptions from several different physicians. Or he may persuade someone else (a friend, perhaps, or a member of his family) to obtain a prescription on his behalf.

To cope with this problem, a number of measures would appear to be in order. Every physician could be required to record his medical license number, as well as the patient's Social Insurance Number on all prescriptions he writes, thus rendering forgery more difficult and allowing positive identification by the authorities for record analysis. At the same time, everyone presenting a physician's prescription might similarly be required to produce his Social Insurance Card, which would then also be noted on the prescription itself.

It is generally acknowledged by physicians that unless there are cogent reasons to the contrary, it is inadvisable to prescribe stimulants or sedative drugs for periods of more than two or three weeks, since any accumulation of such drugs by the patient is considered potentially dangerous because of the increased risk of accidental or deliberate overdosage. Also, the risk of inducing psychological or physical dependency might be greatly increased.

But it was pointed out during the public hearings that physicians are too often inclined to prescribe the 'easy pill' for insistent and persistent patients to whom they would otherwise have to allocate more time for a personal visit or a therapeutic interview. More specific professional education is needed to make every practising physician aware of these potential hazards in his prescribing patterns. **The Commission recommends that the Federal Government urge all provincial medical licensing bodies to implement such an education programme for all practising physicians.**

In addition, the question of drug prescription by telephone

should be examined. Although some form of control in this area is needed, it should be kept in mind that any outright prohibition of such a practice would impose a certain hardship on many patients. It would mean that each time they needed a prescription, they would have to make a trip to the physician's office. Perhaps telephone prescriptions might be permitted in cases where the prescribing physician is personally known to the pharmacist. Also, the possibility of some electronic identification could be investigated. However, a general policy to require prescription for all therapeutic drugs would not be reasonable because of the inconvenience in time and expense which would be caused to the individual.

Over-the-Counter Drugs

481. The Canadian Medical Association and the College of Pharmacists of the Province of Quebec both asked that measures be taken to restrict the dispensing of certain antihistamines, cough and cold remedies, analgesics, etc., to licensed pharmacists. It was noted that the prolonged excessive use of some analgesics (those contining phenacetin) is known to have resulted in kidney disease in some cases.

The Commission recommends that a systematic study be undertaken of all over-the-counter drugs and that those found to be especially hazardous be dispensed only by prescription.

DISAGREEMENT

March 15, 1970.

I find myself in disagreement with my colleagues on the Commission in respect of the offence of simple possession of cannabis. In my opinion the prohibition against such possession should be removed altogether. I believe that this course is dictated at the present time by the following considerations: the extent of use and the age groups involved; the relative impossibility of enforcing the law; the social consequences of its enforcement; and the uncertainty as to the relative potential for harm of cannabis.

Marie-A. Bertrand

REFERENCES

1. Chopra, I. C., and Chopra, R. N. The use of the Cannabis drugs in India. *Bull. Narc.,* 1957, *9,* 23–.

2. Gardikas, C. G. Hashish and crime. *Engephale,* 1950, August, 5–.

3. Eddy, N. B., Halbach, H., Isbell, H., and Seevers, M. Drug dependence: Its significance and characteristics. *Bull. WHO,* 1965, *37,* 1–12.

4. Blumquist, E. R. *Marihuana.* Beverly Hills: Glencoe, 1968.

5. Miller, D. E. What a policeman should know about marijuana. *Eighth annual conference report.* International Narcotic Enforcement Officers Association, 1967.

6. Department of National Health and Welfare, Division of Narcotic Control. Total addict population in Canada for 1969.

7. Mill, John Stuart. *On liberty.* Indianapolis: Bobbs-Merrill, 1965.

8. Hart, H. L. A. *Law, liberty and morality.* Stanford, Calif.: Stanford University Press, 1963.

9. Devlin, Patrick. *Enforcement of morals: seven essays.* London: Oxford University Press, 1968.

10. Canadian Committee on Corrections. *Report.* Ottawa: Queen's Printer, 1969.

11. Addiction Research Foundation of Ontario. Preliminary brief submitted to the Commission of Inquiry into the Non-Medical Use of Drugs. December, 1969.

SUBMISSIONS BY ORGANIZATIONS

Activators, The,
Vancouver, British
Columbia.

Alcohol Education Service
(Manitoba),
Winnipeg, Manitoba.

Alcoholism and Drug Addiction
Foundation of Newfoundland,
St John's, Newfoundland

Alcoholism and Drug Addiction
Research Foundation of
Ontario,
Toronto, Ontario.

Alcoholism Foundation of
British Columbia,
Vancouver, British
Columbia.

Alcoholism Foundation of
Manitoba,
Winnipeg, Manitoba.

Bible Holiness Mission,
Vancouver, British
Columbia.

Board of School
Commissioners,
Special Services
Department,
Halifax, Nova Scotia.

British Columbia Special
Counsellors' Association,
Vancouver, British
Columbia.

Canadian Civil Liberties
Association,
New Brunswick Chapter,
Fredericton, New
Brunswick.

Canadian Home & School and
Parent-Techer Federation
Inc.,
Laval des Rapides, Quebec.

Canadian Medical
Association,
Ottawa, Ontario.

Canadian Mental Health
Association,
Toronto, Ontario.

Canadian Psychiatric
Association,
Ottawa, Ontario.

Canadian Rehabilitation
Association,
Ottawa, Ontario.

Canadian Student Liberals,
Ottawa, Ontario.

Charlottetown Inter-Faith
Group, and the Priests' Senate
of the Diocese of
Charlottetown,
Charlottetown, Prince
Edward Island.

Centre d'Orientation,
Montreal, Quebec.

Children's Aid Society,
Vancouver, British
Columbia.

Christian Reformed Church,
Ladies Society,
Ottawa, Ontario.

Civil Liberties Association of
British Columbia,
Vancouver, British
Columbia.

College des Pharmaciens de la
Province de Quebec,
Montreal, Quebec.

Committee Representing Youth
Problems of Today,
(CRYPT),
Winnipeg, Manitoba.

Community Services
Organization,
St Paul's Avenue Road United
Church,
Toronto, Ontario.

Council on Drug Abuse,
Toronto, Ontario.

Dawson College,
Westmount, Quebec.

Department of the Attorney
General,
Province of Prince Edward
Island,
Charlottetown, Prince
Edward Island.

Department of Education,
Province of Nova Scotia,
Halifax, Nova Scotia.

Departement de
Pharmacologie,
Université Laval,
Quebec, Quebec.

Department of Public Health,
Province of Nova Scotia,
Halifax, Nova Scotia.

Department of Public
Welfare,
Province of Nova Scotia,
Halifax, Nova Scotia.

Department of the Solicitor-
General of Canada,
Ottawa, Ontario.

Elizabeth Fry Society,
Toronto, Ontario.

Elizabeth Fry Society of British
Columbia,
Social Action Committee,
Vancouver, British
Columbia.

Elizabeth Fry Society,
Kingston, Ontario.

First United Church,
Port Alberni, British
Columbia.

Greater Moncton Committee on
Non-Medical Use of Drugs,
Moncton, New Brunswick.

Greater Vancouver Youth
Communications Centre,
(Cool-Aid),
Vancouver, British
Columbia.

Greater Victoria Alcoholism
Foundation,
Victoria, British Columbia.

Greater Victoria School
Board,
Special Educational
Services,
Victoria, British Columbia.

Humanist Association of
Canada,
Montreal, Quebec.

Humanist Association of
Ottawa,
Ottawa, Ontario.

Interdepartmental Committee
on Drug Abuse of the
Province of New
Brunswick,
Fredericton, New
Brunswick.

Inter-Service Club Council and
Kiwanis Club of Kingston,
Kingston, Ontario.

Jewish Family and Child Service
of Metropolitan Toronto,
Trailer Project,
Toronto, Ontario.

John Howard Society of British
Columbia,
Vancouver, British
Columbia.

John Howard Society of
Ontario,
Toronto, Ontario.

Kingston Rotary Club,
Kingston, Ontario.

Knights of Columbus,
Charlettetown Council No.
824,
Charlottetown, Prince
Edward Island.

Legalize Marihuana
Committee,
London, Ontario.

Manitoba Association for
Children with Learning
Disabilities,
Winnipeg, Manitoba.

Manitoba Medical Association,
Committee on Drug Abuse,
Winnipeg, Manitoba.

Mayor's Committee on
Youth,
Ottawa, Ontario.

Memorial University,
The Students' Union,
Committee on Drugs,
St John's, Newfoundland.

Merri-Go-Round,
Youth Group,
Halifax, Nova Scotia.

Montreal Police Department,
Montreal, Quebec.

Mysterious East,
Fredericton, New
Brunswick.

Narcotic Addiction Foundation
of British Columbia,
Vancouver, British
Columbia.

National Film Board,
Montreal, Quebec.

New Brunswick Teachers'
Association,
Fredericton, New
Brunswick.

Newfoundland Medical
Association,
St John's, Newfoundland.

Newfoundland Pharmaceutical
Association,
St John's, Newfoundland.

Newfoundland Teachers'
Association,
St John's, Newfoundland.

North Shore Unitarian
Church,
Social Action Committee,
North Vancouver, British
Columbia.

Nova Scotia Task Force on the
Non-Medical Use of Drugs,
Halifax, Nova Scotia.

Operation Crime Check,
Montreal, Quebec.

L'Office de la Prévention et du
Traitement de l'Alcoolisme et
des autres Toxicomanies,
(OPTAT),
Ste Foy, Québec.

Ottawa Roman Catholic
Separate School Board,
Ottawa, Ontario.

Penny Farthing Victorian Coffee
House,
Toronto, Ontario.

Pharmaceutical Association of
the Province of British
Columbia,
Vancouver, British
Columbia.

Premier's Task Force,
Charlottetown, Prince
Edward Island.

Prince Edward Island
Federation of Home & School
Associations,
Charlottetown, Prince
Edward Island.

Prince Edward Island
Federation of Labour,
Charlottetown, Prince
Edward Island.

Progressive Conservative
Students' Federation,
Ottawa, Ontario.

Protestant School Board of
Greater Montreal,
Montreal, Quebec.

Radicals for Capitalism,
Toronto, Ontario.

Rochdale College,
Board of Directors,
Toronto, Ontario.

Rochdale Medical Clinic,
Toronto, Ontario.

Royal Canadian Mounted
Police,
Ottawa, Ontario.

St Thomas University Students'
Council,
Fredericton, New
Brunswick.

Social Planning Council of
Metropolitan Toronto,
Toronto, Ontario.

Students' Council of Carleton
University,
Ottawa, Ontario.

Students' Society of McGill
University,
Montreal, Quebec.

Tell-It-As-It-Is,
Board of Directors,
Montreal, Quebec.

Thirteenth Floor Cooperative
Community for Participants
of the Utopian Research
Institute,
Rochdale College,
Toronto, Ontario.

Toronto Board of
Education,
Toronto, Ontario.

United Nations Association,
Montreal, Quebec.

Vancouver City Police
Department,
Vancouver, British
Columbia.

Victoria Youth Council,
Victoria, British Columbia.

Western Half-Yearly Meeting of
Friends,
Argenta, British Columbia.

West Island Social Action
Committee,
Youth Clinic,
Montreal, Quebec.

Women's Christian Temperance
Union,
Vancouver District,
Vancouver, British
Columbia.

Women's Christian Temperance
Union,
Winnipeg, Manitoba.

Women's Institutes of Prince
Edward Island,
Charlottetown, Prince
Edward Island.

X-Kalay Foundation Society,
Vancouver, British
Columbia.
YM-YWCA Drop-In Centre,

Ottawa, Ontario.
Young Women's Christian
Association of Toronto,
Toronto, Ontario.

SUBMISSIONS BY INDIVIDUALS

Aimers, Mr John L.,
Montreal, Quebec.
Aldous, Dr J. G.,
Department of
Pharmacology,
Dalhousie University,
Halifax, Nova Scotia.
Amaron, Mr Robert,
Renfrew, Ontario.
Barclay, Mr J. F.,
Edmonton, Alberta.
Beach, Dr Horace D.,
Psychological Services
Centre,
Dalhousie University,
Halifax, Nova Scotia.
Beaulieu, Professor Claude,
Department des Sciences de
l'Éducation,
Université de Québec à
Montréal,
Montréal, Québec.
Bennett, Mr Wayne,
Regina, Saskatchewan.
Boddie, Dr Charles,
Student Health Services,
Memorial University of
Newfoundland,
St John's, Newfoundland.
Boden, Rev Robert,
Church of the Nazarene,
Fredericton, New
Brunswick.
Brigg, Dr Robert,
Queen's University,
Kingston, Ontario.

Burke, Dr H. C.,
Mount Allison University,
Sackville, New Brunswick.
Buckner, Professor T.,
Department of Sociology,
Sir George Williams
University,
Montreal, Quebec.
Campbell, Mr Brian,
Vancouver, British
Columbia.
Carter, Professor Robert E.,
Department of Philosophy,
Sir George Williams
University,
Montreal, Quebec.
Cathcart, Dr L. M.,
Medical School,
University of British
Columbia,
Vancouver, British
Columbia.
Charlmers, Q.C., Mr N. A.,
Department of Justice of
Canada,
Toronto, Ontario.
Chapman, Mr Bruce,
Mount Allison University,
Sackville, New Brunswick.
Christie, Q.C., Miss Norma,
Department of Justice of
Canada,
Vancouver, British
Columbia.

Clement, Mr Wilfrid C.,
Queen Street Mental Health
Centre,
Toronto, Ontario.

Cloud, Professor Jonathan,
Department of Sociology,
York University,
Toronto, Ontario.

Cody, Dr Howard,
Vancouver, British
Columbia.

Cohen, Dr M.,
Children's Hospital,
Buffalo, New York.

Cook, Mrs Shirley J.,
Department of Sociology,
University of Toronto,
Toronto, Ontario.

Corey, Dr Margaret,
Department of Pediatrics,
Dalhousie University,
Halifax, Nova Scotia.

Cornil, Professor Paul,
Visiting Professor,
Department of
Criminology,
University of Montreal,
Montreal, Quebec.

Gould, Miss Rebecca,
Sackville High School,
Sackville, New Brunswick.

Crawford, Mr Thomas,
Sackville, New Brunswick.

Cundill, Mr G.,
Calgary, Alberta.

Decarie, Professor M. G.,
University of Prince Edward
Island,
Charlottetown, Prince
Edward Island.

Delaney, Dr J. A.,
City Coroner,
Fredericton, New
Brunswick.

Devlin, Mr Terry,
Vancouver, British
Columbia.

Donovan, Mr Greg,
Nova Scotia Youth Agency,
Halifax, Nova Scotia.

Douyon, Professor Emerson,
Department of
Criminology,
University of Montreal,
Montreal, Quebec.

Ellenberger, Dr Henri F.,
Department of
Criminology,
University of Montreal,
Montreal, Quebec.

Fattah Professor M. E.,
Department of
Criminology,
University of Montreal,
Montreal, Quebec.

Fenske, Reverend T.,
Department of National
Defence,
Halifax, Nova Scotia.

Flight, Mr Harvey,
Pharmacist,
St John's, Newfoundland.

Floyd, Mr and Mrs Stan,
Thunderbird Winter Sports
Centre,
University of British
Columbia,
Vancouver, British
Columbia.

Forestell, Mr Francis,
Department of Justice,
Probation Service,
Fredericton, New
Brunswick.

Foulks, Dr James G.,
Department of
Pharmacology,
University of British
Columbia,
Vancouver, British
Columbia.

Fowells, Mr Gavin,
Ottawa, Ontario.

Gagnon, Mr Claude,
Institute of Medieval
Studies,
University of Montreal,
Montreal, Quebec.

Gaussiran, Mr Michel,
Department of
Criminology,
University of Montreal,
Montreal, Quebec.

Ghan, Mr Leonard,
Regina, Saskatchewan.

Gigseghen, M. Hubert,
Centre d'Orientation,
Montréal, Québec.

Green, Mr B.,
Toronto, Ontario.

Grossman, Professor Brian,
Faculty of Law, McGill
University,
Montreal, Quebec.

Hagen, Dr Derek L.,
Fredericton, New
Brunswick.

Hansen, Dr E. S.,
Provost and Dean of Student
Affairs,
Acadia University,
Wolfville, Nova Scotia.

Hatfield, Mr Richard,
Leader of the Opposition,
Fredericton, New
Brunswick.

Hawboldt, Mrs L. S.,
Halifax, Nova Scotia.

Hill, Mr J.,
Vancouver, British
Columbia.

Hill, Mr Terry,
Toronto, Ontario.

Howell, Mrs Sheila,
Kingston, Ontario.

Jamieson, Dr W. R. E.,
Fredericton, New
Brunswick.

Jobson, Mr K. B.,
Faculty of Law,
Dalhousie University,
Halifax, Nova Scotia.

Kitz, Q.C., Mr Leonard,
Halifax, Nova Scotia.

Kuropatwa, Mr Ralph,
Winnipeg, Manitoba.

Lalonde, Dr Pierre,
University of Montreal,
Montreal, Quebec.

Lamrock, Mr Leonard,
Guidance Counsellor,
Mount Allison University,
Sackville, New Brunswick.

Landry, Q.C., Mr L. P.,
Montreal Regional Office,
Department of Justice,
Montreal, Quebec.

LaPointe, Mr John,
Toronto, Ontario.

Laverty, Professor S. G.,
Alcoholism and Addiction
Research Foundation of
Ontario,
Kingston, Ontario.

LeBel, Mr Bernard,
    Department of
    Criminology,
    University of Montreal,
    Montreal, Quebec.
Leon, Dr Wolf,
    Provincial Department of
    Health,
    Charlottetown, Prince
    Edward Island.
Levin, Dr George,
    Sociology Department,
    Mount Allison University,
    Sackville, New Brunswick.
Linde, Mr Cary,
    Law Students' Association,
    University of British
    Columbia,
    Vancouver, British
    Columbia.
Ling, Dr George,
    Department of
    Pharmacology,
    University of Ottawa,
    Ottawa, Ontario.
Lorimer, Dr Roland,
    Vancouver, British
    Columbia.
Love, Mr D.,
    Calgary, Alberta.
Low, Professor Kenneth,
    Calgary, Alberta.
Luka, Mr Leslie B.,
    Guidance Department,
    Don Mills Collegiate
    Institute,
    Don Mills, Ontario.
Mahoney, Mr Michael,
    Kingston, Ontario.
Malloy, Brother Kevin,
    Brother Rice High School,
    St John's, Newfoundland.

Mansfield, Mr N.,
    Vancouver, British
    Columbia.
Mason, Mr Ian,
    University of Toronto,
    Toronto, Ontario.
Moghadam, Dr Hossein K.,
    School of Hygiene,
    University of Toronto,
    Toronto, Ontario.
Morrison, Dr William,
    Sociology Department,
    University of Winnipeg,
    Winnipeg, Manitoba.
Morton, Dr A.,
    Nova Scotia Mental
    Hospital,
    Dartmouth, Nova Scotia.
Mouledoux, Professor Joseph,
    Department of Sociology,
    Sir George Williams
    University,
    Montreal, Quebec.
MacLean, Reverend Ian,
    United Church of Canada,
    Fredericton, New
    Brunswick.
McAmmond, Professor D.,
    University of Calgary,
    Calgary, Alberta.
McLeod, Miss Illette,
    Vancouver, British
    Columbia.
Naidu, Dr S. B.,
    University of Moncton,
    Moncton, New Brunswick.
Nelson, Mrs Sally,
    Montreal, Quebec.
Nickerson, Dr Mark,
    Department of Pharmacology
    & Therapeutics,
    McGill University, Montreal,
    Quebec.

Nixon, Mr Gary,
   Vancouver, British
   Columbia.
Ogden, Mr Frank,
   Montreal, Quebec.
Paterson, Mr J. Craig,
   Faculty of Law,
   University of Western
   Ontario,
   London, Ontario.
Penner, Professor Rolland,
   Faculty of Law,
   University of Manitoba,
   Winnipeg, Manitoba.
Porter, Professor James,
   Department of Sociology,
   York University,
   Toronto, Ontario.
Rakoff, Dr Vivien,
   Clarke Institute of
   Psychiatry,
   Toronto, Ontario.
Reed, Mr Jerry,
   Vancouver, British
   Columbia.
Richmond Dr R. E. G.,
   Corrections Branch,
   Department of Attorney
   General,
   Vancouver, British
   Columbia.
Robertson, Professor A. H.,
   University of New
   Brunswick,
   Fredericton, New
   Brunswick.
Robins, Dr Lee,
   Washington University,
   St Louis, Missouri.
Rush, Professor, G. B.,
   Simon Fraser University,
   Vancouver, British
   Columbia.

Rutman, Professor Len,
   Department of Sociology,
   University of Winnipeg,
   Winnipeg, Manitoba.
Ryan, Professor Stuart,
   Queen's University,
   Kingston, Ontario.
Sabba, Mr Arnold,
   Vancouver, British
   Columbia.
Samuels, Mr Jeffery,
   Osgoode Hall,
   York University,
   Toronto, Ontario.
Saulnier, Mr Maurice,
   Director of Student
   Services,
   Maisonneuve College,
   Montreal, Quebec.
Schwarz, Professor Conrad J.,
   Department of Health
   Services,
   University of British
   Columbia,
   Vancouver, British
   Columbia.
Scott, Dr George,
   Canadian Penitentiary
   Service,
   Kingston, Ontario.
Segal, Dr Mark,
   Department of
   Pharmacology,
   Dalhousie University,
   Halifax, Nova Scotia.
Sharpe, Mr Robin,
   Bistro Coffee House,
   Vancouver, British
   Columbia.

Siegel, Mr Ronald K.,
Department of Pharmacology
and Psychology,
Dalhousie University,
Halifax, Nova Scotia.

Silverman, Dr Saul,
Faculty of Political Science,
Prince Edward Island
University,
Charlottetown, Prince
Edward Island.

Simms, Mr Thomas M.,
Department of Education,
Saint Thomas University,
Fredericton, New
Brunswick.

Simons, Mr Sidney,
Vancouver, British
Columbia.

Skirrow, Professor J.,
University of Calgary,
Calgary, Alberta.

Slauenwhite, Mr Bradley,
Sackville, New Brunswick.

Smith, Mr G. Brian,
Sackville, New Brunswick.

Solomon, Professor David,
Faculty of Arts and Science,
York University,
Toronto, Ontario.

Solursh, Dr L. P.,
Department of Psychiatry,
Toronto Western Hospital,
Toronto, Ontario.

Spector, Dr Malcolm,
Professor of Sociology,
McGill University,
Montreal, Quebec.

Steinhart, Mr James,
Ottawa, Ontario.

Suzuki, Dr D.,
Department of Zoology,
University of British
Columbia,
Vancouver, British
Columbia.

Szabo, Dr Denis,
Department of
Criminology,
University of Montreal,
Montreal, Quebec.

Taylor, Mr G.,
Calgary, Alberta.

Topping, Professor C. W.,
Department of Anthropology
& Sociology,
University of British
Columbia,
Vancouver, British
Columbia.

Trivett, Rev. D. F. L.,
Dalhousie University,
Halifax, Nova Scotia.

Unwin, Dr J. Robertson,
Allen Memorial Institute,
Montreal, Quebec.

Vikander, Professor Nils,
Department of Sociology and
Anthropology,
St Thomas University,
Fredericton, New
Brunswick.

Watt, Mrs. Donna,
Vancouver, British
Columbia.

Watt, Mr F. B.,
Ottawa, Ontario.

Westmiller, Mr W. J.,
Kingston, Ontario.

Whealy, Mr Arthur,
Toronto, Ontario.

Whitehead, Professor Paul C.,
  Department of Sociology and
  Anthropology,
  Dalhousie University,
  Halifax, Nova Scotia.
Wilson, Mr S. L.,
  Sackville, New Brunswick.

Wright, Mrs Jane E.,
  Toronto, Ontario.
Zlotkin, Mr N. K.,
  Toronto, Ontario.

LETTERS FROM PRIVATE CITIZENS

These letters, or excerpts of letters written by private citizens across the country, are in no way intended to represent a consensus of the opinions expressed in the great volume of correspondence the Commission has received during the initial phase of its inquiry.

They have been selected simply to show the *type* of public response so far encountered, as well as the wide divergency of viewpoints held by those who have had some personal involvement with the question of drug use in Canada.

The Commission would like to express its appreciation to all those who have written for the careful thought they have so clearly given to the subject.

Since the Commission guaranteed anonymity when it was requested, every effort has been made to conceal the identity of the authors of these letters, or even their point of origin in Canada.

From a 19-year-old female who says she has been gainfully employed and living on her own for the past year:

'I have smoked marijuana and hashish for the past two years – with no ill effects as far as I can tell. I have yet to experience physical or mental withdrawal symptoms – even after smoking for a week steadily.

I must admit that I don't work well after smoking more than one jay of good weed. I guess that marijuana and derivatives are relaxing drugs rather than stimulants.

I have obtained an increased awareness of the stupidity of many of our laws – (i.e., those relating to drug usage, sex, and crimes without victims as well as many other injustices). I have developed a disdain for most law enforcers, especially undercover narcotic agents. Their consciences must be unbearable.

I have also done some chemicals – namely: acid, mescaline, psilocybin. I don't do these drugs often and never again in the city. They bring an increased awareness of just everything, and an increased awareness of city trips can cause a pretty freaky trip.

The main trouble with weed is that it is usually unavailable or of poor quality – often sending people on to chemical trips. Also, since it is illegal, many innocent people are being subjected to har=

assment from the R.C.M.P., from the underworld, gangster element, and from unwanted additives in their drugs.

Please legalize marijuana and hash. Listen to what people (are) saying.

About the best thing you could do would be to get some good Mexican or Vietnamese weed, go to the country and smoke it. It'll do us all good.'

From a 25-year-old female film technician in a major Canadian city:

'I have on many occasions smoked grass and hash and feel that I can speak with some authority on their effects. Grass, especially if it is known to be pure, is almost universally harmless. Close friends have, however, suffered paranoia trips of a minor yet upsetting nature as a result of smoking hash, especially kif. I usually do very little of either, preferring to take it coolly and wait for the slow reaction. In the cases of paranoia, the users have done quite a lot more than I – say 6 small chips to my 2 or 3. But overall, grass and hash are pretty innocuous and I can see no harm in their moderate use. My experiences have been happy – it stimulates my interest (already well stimulated!) in food and gives the illusion of enhanced sensory perception (I believe this to be an illusion, however pleasant at the time).

Excessive use of grass and hash as I've observed in my friends and acquaintances causes reddening of the eyes and eyelids and a slight slowing down of reflexes and reactions. I consider these adverse effects but they *are* brought about by excess.

I know of no instance of grass or hash being spiked other than one batch of grass which apparently contained a small amount of unpleasant speed. The worst that happens with grass is that you get alfalfa or some other non-intoxicating substitute.

As far as other drugs are concerned I have to speak without personal knowledge as I've never used any myself. I have, however, discussed their use and effects at great length with friends. From these discussions I've concluded that:

(a) I would never touch any chemical bought off the street. They are definitely a risk.

(b) If I were to get a chemist's approval, I'd probably do some mescaline as I've read "Doors of Perception" by Aldous Huxley and have never spoken to anyone who went on a "bum" mescaline trip. All speak highly of its effects in expanding awareness.

(c) Acid is a risky drug. Reports of "bummers" are frequent and disturbing.

(d) Speed is definitely OUT. Far too dangerous.

In conclusion, I think that the treatment of drug users is barbaric. The search and destroy technique used by many R.C.M.P. officers is sickening. I consider it an outrageous invasion of privacy and citizens' rights that an R.C.M.P. officer can charge into a house unannounced, with no warrant and proceed with his search. (This, by the way, has never happened to me.) With laws as they stand it is the obvious duty of the R.C.M.P. to apprehend law breakers, but the fervour with which this is carried out far exceeds the "crime".

Changes in the laws are called for. I think the legalization of grass and hash and the continuance of the present laws against pushers and users of stronger drugs would ease the embarrassing situation wherein a large number of Canadians are officially "criminals".'

From the mother of two teen-age sons living in a surburban town:

'Please, help my sons. With my older boy, my husband and I have failed. We don't know how. We obey the law. We admire the guardians of our freedom, our government and our police. We vote. We work hard and pay taxes, not joyfully perhaps, but honestly.

But the older boy, soon as he reached his teens, laughed at the "pigs", flaunted the law, and, until this commission on narcotics started, regarded any government as useless. Freedom he believes in wholeheartedly – his freedom. His freedom is all important. He must be free to experience drugs. And to practise his freedom, he infringes on mine. He steals from my purse, my husband's wallet, his brother's bank, his widowed grandmother's small savings. His allowance is $1.50, too little to exercise his freedom to buy a nickle bag so he must, because he lives in a democracy, get the difference somehow.

He knows the law inside out. Possession can land him in trouble. So he never carries it with him. He knows he can use it as much as he likes as long as he doesn't have it on him when he's picked up. And he is picked up. Our very efficient, very overworked R.C.M.P. here have hauled him in and each time the young officers have bent over backwards to help him. He's cried. He's vowed repentance. And they let him go. And he laughs out loud later about the stupid narcs he conned.

Right now, he is on an unofficial probation for a year because he exercised his freedom to have something by stealing from a gas station. Charges weren't pressed because my son is a charming boy.

But he knows to the minute when the year will be up. Then, armed with the published opinions of experts – doctors, psychiatrists, ministers, etc. who have favoured the Commission with their expertise, he will get lost in the shadow of drugs because his mom and dad don't know which end is up.

Should we chain him to his bed? Should we follow him whenever he leaves the house? How do we save him?

My younger boy said last night, "Mom, if the government is growing marijuana themselves, well, maybe Dick is right. And if they can get the real LSD, maybe that would be alright too."

No one takes one drink with the express purpose of becoming an alcoholic. No one lights up one cigarette thinking the day will come when it will become almost impossible to quit. No one sniffs glue, smokes marijuana, or tries LSD with the slightest thought of becoming an addict or statistic. Even someone playing Russian Roulette expects to escape unharmed.

Attempted murder is a punishable offence. So is attempted suicide. Drugs are murder weapons. Punish the seller. Punish the user. Don't consider throwing open the door to nightmare.

If my sons must die for freedom, let it be on a battlefield, not on an induced trip. Please, please *help*.'

From a new Canadian living in a western city:

'I am not insane. I am not morally degenerate. I have committed no crimes of violence. And yet for a period of more than six years I used the "killer drug" – marijuana! For about five years I consumed relatively large quantities of marijuana, followed by perhaps a year and a half of use of rather large quantities of hashish. Over this period of time there were probably not more than thirty days on which I did not smoke a quantity of one of these drugs or the other. Over the entire period I was employed by a research laboratory operated by a university in one of the western United States, and my use of cannabis was terminated only by my immigration to this country. After arriving here, knowing no one, and seeing the high degree of infiltration into the so-called drug sub-culture by various police agencies, I decided that the danger to my personal freedom was entirely too great to continue the use of my favourite intoxicants.

My gainful employment did not suffer because of my use of these drugs, which I restricted to evenings and week-ends, although the performance of several of my fellow workers was rather obviously degraded by their use of alcohol.

It was my observation that I used larger quantities of these two drugs than virtually any of my close friends, all but one of whom used marijuana. I believe this may be explained by the fact that about a year before trying marijuana for the first time I had kicked a three-and-a-half-pack-a-day cigarette habit. I never gave up the urge to smoke, although I have not used a tobacco cigarette in eight years.

My experience with other drugs is comparatively meagre. I tried opium once, with no effect. I tried cocaine once, and did not care for it. I tried mescaline once, and found it to be a most rewarding experience. I have never tried LSD, because I felt that I was not prepared for an experience as powerful as that described by my friends.

Nearly all of my friends use LSD repeatedly. In the group of 30 or more people I know who used this drug, no one had been hurt by it, although several had had unpleasant experiences. I did know several people who appeared to me to have made a mess of themselves through use of methedrine.

I have presented testimony in this form because I believe my own history may be of somewhat more value than another set of opinions. It is my belief that neither society nor I have been harmed by my use of marijuana and hashish. It is quite obvious, however, that many people have been harmed by society because of their disregard of the drug prohibition laws. Even disregarding the prosecution and imprisonment of people for using marijuana, I believe that the eroding away of the warmth and trust one wishes to feel towards other people, by the infiltration of undercover police officers, has done a great deal of harm.

I do not care for the effects of alcohol. I smoked marijuana because I enjoyed it. I have not been stoned in a long time now, and would like to get stoned again – legally! I hope you can do something about it.'

From a member of the medical profession, signed: 'One who cares'.

'Insofar as marijuana is concerned, as a member of the medical profession, I am familiar with the known effects of this drug, most of which are not negative, except in the hands of irresponsible and immature adolescents and adults (I might add) for whom the abuse of this substance is an escape from the responsibilities and realities of life to the degree that it interferes with their ability to function and produce effectively. However, it seems apparent that these types of people are basically unstable to begin with and it is not the use of "pot" that interferes with their productivity so much as the accompanying use of amphetamines, LSD, mescaline and the likes. The effects (negative) with which I will not argue. These are the drugs which should be wiped right off the market. These are the drugs which may produce a mad society.

I have worked extensively with addicts, hard-core addicts, neurotics, psychotics and alcoholics in my profession as a Psychiatric Nurse. I am quite familiar with the abuse of dangerous drugs and their consequences. I am also familiar with the underlying causes behind this sort of behaviour. Our efforts should be spent attacking these causes-prevention – so as to eliminate the necessity for treatment after much of the damage has already been done, often irreparable. Present circumstances make it apparent, we are in such a situation that it is now necessary to slap hard controls on the illicit drug market as well as attacking the basic root of the problem.

I can assure you that incarceration of young people for simply the use of marijuana is one of the deadliest mistakes of our time. I know only too well the effect that a prison environment has on a young, impressionable and relatively naïve mind. To expose such a youngster to hard-core addicts, thieves, prostitutes and the lot is a damaging and very disillusioning traumatic experience from which it would take a great deal of personal strength to recover intact. Punitive and primitive measures which provide such an "education" can mark a young one for life.

I will go so far as to say that we have hard-core addicts because our laws and institutions have been such as to produce them – the laws have made it necessary for these people to support their habit; activities and associations being such as to reinforce negative and antisocial behaviour. Thus, ignorance, sickness and abuse multiply themselves and are perpetuated in a vicious-circle-like syndrome.

An addict is, basically, a person with a personality problem – social and emotional – and as such needs treatment, guidance, direction in accepting responsibility and most of all someone who cares enough to help him work out his fears and insecurities. I know how these people think and feel – beyond mere superficialities – beyond the hard wall of self-protection behind which they hide. In my work I was fortunate enough to win their trust and respect and therefore, their confidence, simply because I have cared enough to get involved, take the time and make the effort to understand. The complexities of our present drug problem are too numerous to account but, rest assured, we are only reinforcing the problems by our present laws and methods of "treatment". If more constructive laws

375

and remedies are not soon devised by our government in Ottawa, this generation will become a generation of addicts – sick, hopeless and completely disillusioned with life. The addicts in prison are only a small and extreme indication of the abuse of drugs, although they are bearing the brunt of all of society's malady – they are the focal point – they are the ones who are reaping the punishment for the masses. We use them, as if we were a pack of wolves screaming for blood. But, stop: let us look around us, at ourselves and our acquaintances. We are the respectable and responsible citizens of our society.

My friends and my acquaintances cover a cross-section of our society – businessmen, teachers, social workers, doctors, nurses, white-collar workers, tradesmen – average straight citizens. Pot, liquor and cigarettes are numbered among their indulgences which I can accept as a normal part of life, providing they are used in moderation and do not interfere with their personal well-being and social contributory output. But, I also see, over and above the afore-mentioned, many, many people hooked on tranquillizers, sleeping pills, 'pep' pills and all such legitimately prescribed drugs. As someone once said, "Take all the prescription drugs away and there would be a nationwide nervous breakdown." He hit it right on, as far as my observations are concerned.

In view of this well-known but undermined fact, are we not being just a little harsh and a little hypocritical in our laws and in our indignation? Are we not wise or intelligent enough to recognize the reality that we are perpetuating the illness of our whole society? That unless we take stock of ourselves first and then the laws which create social injustice, our society is doomed to sickness and corruption? Let us not be naïve, and let us not delude ourselves. The responsibility for the current situation and the rectification of the results lie at our feet. Let us hope that we have the stamina, the insight and the courage with which we like to pride ourselves, to change ourselves, and in so doing, effect positive change in our environment. This is the responsibility of each and every one of us. Lip service, obviously, is not enough. Action, and immediate action is imperative.

Respected members of the drug inquiry commission, you have embarked upon a vast and challenging undertaking which envelopes a problem which is so widespread that the future well-being of our country may rest in the outcome of your efforts made on my behalf and on the behalf of all with whom I identify – our people. Do not minimize the dire importance of your task. The action you take may make or break the whole concept of a free society – the effective functioning of a democracy in which basic love, respect, kindness and understanding towards each other as individuals must flourish in order for us to survive in accordance with the principles in which we must believe.'

From the father of a teenager who is using marijuana, peyote, LSD and 'Speed'.

'I must point out to you that during the late summer of 1966 my wife and myself had been "scoffed" at by members of the R.C.M.P. and been given the "brush off" by our local school board and also the Superintendent of Schools in our municipality while we were trying to bring it to their attention that drugs were being used by the students of the high school.

Between that time and the present our son has gone through various stages of deterioration. In June 1967 he married the obvious source of his drug, (a female assistant teacher) who made no secret of the fact that she obtained her supply of LSD and Synthetic Marijuana from the laboratory of the university and that she felt that life was not worth living without drugs.

Recently our son came home during a "hangover" following a trip, he had been refused help at his psychiatrist's office. We took him to a neighbouring town to a physician whom we know and he was admitted to the hospital there. The next morning he demanded to be released and the doctors could do nothing but comply with his demands and release him. The doctor who attended him at this time informed us that our son will be lucky to live two or more years if he does not stop using drugs.

To summarize, we can only blame our educators who use and recommend the use of so-called soft drugs for the increasing numbers of students who fall by the wayside.'

From a female, first-year university student who has smoked mari= juana since she was in grade 10:

'At first I was afraid, but since the boy I liked at the time also smoked it, I decided to also, not wanting to be left out. At first, nothing happened to me, but I got psychologically stoned and I laughed hysterically and walked around with glazed eyes like you were *supposed* to do. For a period of time I could hardly wait for each week-end so that I could go out and get stoned. I was sort of a fanatic. My marks were A – B and they stayed there. After this initial frenzy I began to do it with more of a purpose. I did it because it was relaxing – not particularly for an "escape". It was a social bond, really. Several people would get together and do up together. We would sit around after and talk or listen to records. I guess we felt closer because we had "partaken" together. In this way, I met some of the finest people I have ever had the pleasure to meet, and I got to know people I had only previously superficially known. On the other hand, I met some pretty screwed up people. They had become psychologically dependent on marijuana. I am not a doctor by a long shot, but I figured that they were. Many of them at the time of writing have come out of it, though (me, for one). I also did hash. It makes you "stoned" (I hate that expression) faster, but has the same general effect only perhaps stronger, depending on its quality. Soon enough, both hash and grass became sort of a pleasant treat at a party. I never took it when depressed because it only seemed to deepen my depression. But, if I were in a good mood, it made me feel very contented, warm and glad. Some of my most pleasant experiences have been after I have smoked either of those drugs. (This doesn't mean I have never had pleasant experiences when "down".) I never tried LSD until this summer. I am sure it was relatively good as I obtained it from someone I trusted. After taking it I fell asleep for half an hour or so until my boyfriend came to pick me up to go to a party. On the way I had such a gas. Driving (I was a passenger) over town was more fun than it has ever been in my life. Everything seemed new and fresh – the trees, the road and just EVERYTHING. Then I became very cold although it was a warm summer night. I was very cold, and tiny things made me cry a lot. If the fly I had been watching flew from the room, tears came to my eyes because I took it for a bad omen. (Of what I don't know). I was left alone for a while in which time I came to the conclusion that I had no friends, I was a rotten, horrible, mean person and that deep down inside everyone hated my guts. I have never been so totally miserable. I am sure I lost 5 quarts of water crying. But then, my girlfriend came up to me and told me it was a bunch of crap and that I had tons of friends. All these people that I knew came to me and told me sincerely that they really and truly liked me. I have never felt such happiness. I doubt I will do acid again, but I am glad I did. I learned many things about myself – the hard way. Now I am trying to be a better person. Truthfully, I am sure I would not be the person I am today if it were not for my taking these drugs. I realize that I must go on now by myself. They started it, but I have to go on to find and become myself. I do not smoke dope very often anymore. Maybe once in a while with a few friends, but hardly at all. I am not sure whether legalizing it would be wise unless there were restrictions such as there are for alcohol. (I feel that the effects are the same, having tried both.)'

From a first-year, male university student, age 23, who has used cannabis and mescaline for the past three years:

'My main contact with these drugs has been through my own use of marijuana, hashish and mescaline and association with others who have taken LSD and methedrine as well as the aforementioned.

I first started smoking marijuana three years ago at the age of twenty. At this time the quality was high and the price was inexpensive. I found a major change in my personality which in all probability had been latent up to that point. That is to say that I do not believe that this drug has an effect, such that it can change one's ideas and ideals through some chemical action. The effect I found it to have was that it relaxed my mind to the extent that I could accept myself for what I was, and this is not to say that I thought myself better than I was, or more capable than I had been, only that I was not particularly worried about other people's estimation of me. From this point on is where my personal advancement took place for I did not have to focus my attention in impressing my employers, business associates and relatives. This impression-making may sound like a small thing and I know from my own experience that when one is involved in this type of life that one is not aware that any other attitude is available. This attitude begins in school with students doing school work not because they are interested in it but to impress the teacher and get passing grades. It carries on into the business world with trying to impress the boss. One would think that a person doing this sort of thing would feel degraded and like a prostitute. However, at least their conscious mind believes that that is what life is all about. The important thing about this attitude is that it manifests itself into one not doing anything or thinking about anything unless it has some impression or status value in relation to the group one wishes to impress. The only understanding of others that is done is in order that one may use the understanding for their own personal gain. The friends one makes under this attitude are not true friends, but are only tools which one uses to advance up one's self-made ladder of success. For me, marijuana was useful in relaxing my mind to the point where I could realize who was a REAL person and who was a PHONY person. This, I suppose, was the major benefit which I had from marijuana. However, another interesting and somewhat beneficial aspect of the drug is this. The mind operates at a much faster speed resulting in conversations which to a straight person sound incoherent but to another person equally as high is perfectly understandable. As we know, the mind works considerably ahead of the words being spoken. With marijuana both the speaker and the listener are thinking so much ahead of the conversation that this thinking graduates to a point of conclusion maybe sentences ahead of the speaker. At this point the speaker usually stops talking as the talking has no more value. Doing this often enough can probably increase one's telepathic perception. Another benefit of this quick thinking is the vast amount of thinking one can do in say, one night in relation to what the same person could do if he were not high. Quite often I have been amazed that only half an hour has passed when I could have sworn two hours had passed. This is because I had covered the same amount of thinking in this short time as I normally covered in the longer period. The good thing about any of these things I have mentioned is that these qualities after extended usage of marijuana become part of you not because any of the drug remains in your system, but because you recognize this type of thought as existing and beneficial.

I have smoked a good deal of hashish over the past year and have found its effects to be almost identical to marijuana. I think one of the main differences between the two is the form hashish is in and the manner in which it must be smoked. It is much more difficult to attain the same degree of communion between participants as marijuana. It is difficult to keep it lit when smoking it in a pipe and if you hold a match to it, the substance burns rapidly. This usually because of the cost of it, causes the pipe to be passed around in such a hurry as to distract from the calm atmosphere which would be present with marijuana. Smoking it from the tip of a cigarette, while alleviating the problem of it not burning steadily, means that people must be jumping up and down for their toke. It is obvious to see why this atmosphere is not conducive to any degree of conversation. Smoking a drug in this fashion starts one feeling like a dope addict who is taking a drug just to get high. This is an immediate hangup which one must rid one's self of before anything constructive can get started.

Mescaline, I found to be more interesting rather than really helpful. It increased the intensity of my visual perception. Colours were distinct and sometimes brighter. Through this increased visual perception I could become involved with the artistic beauty of practically everything I saw. Having no artistic ability beforehand, I discovered upon sitting down before a piece of paper that I could imagine an image on that paper and draw that image. It has always been impossible to be angry with anyone while I was stoned, not because I didn't realize that I was entitled to be angry, but because I understood that the person was doing or saying something because of a hurt or a hangup they had. The only difficulty I encountered, and which I encountered each time I took mescaline was an intense paranoia of the police.

I have suffered no physically or mentally harmful effects from my usage of these drugs, to the contrary, I returned to night school last year and again this year and have never before received the grades I am now achieving. Last year I got straight "As" in English where previously I had "Cs" and "Ds" and this year I am at the top of my class in first year university English. I have also taken up music by learning how to play the guitar and frequently get together with other musicians for jam sessions which I enjoy immensely. I hold down a full-time job which I have been employed at for the last five years. I keep this job only because I am in debt from my past years of trying to keep up with the Jones's. I will be out of debt by the end of next summer and will be starting full-time at University. I plan to become a social worker.

I believe that all drugs should be available through government controlled outlets. A standard quality and potency would then be able to be controlled and would put the syndicates out of the drug business. I say all drugs, not because I think all drugs are safe or even useful, but only because of the fact that people are going to use these drugs whether they buy them from the government or from the syndicate. If they buy it from the latter it is (1) financing a criminal organization (2) not controllable as to quality (3) not able to keep statistics as to the number using it (4) if an addictive drug, not able to control cost which would of course skyrocket and cause criminal addicts. I believe that an intensive education system must be developed to accompany this freedom of the individual in deciding for himself whether or not he will take a drug. This education or information must be strictly scientific, medical and objective with no moral judgements placed upon the individual for these judgements are what have caused the distrust towards authorities' findings in the past. The final responsibility must be placed on the individual. There should be "trip centres" where a person could take drugs in pleasant surroundings for a small fee to cover the cost of a "guide" or an attendant who is familiar with these drugs.

I believe there should definitely be an age limit of eighteen years old for hard drugs and no age limit for marijuana and hashish. I also believe that each person should be held legally responsible for actions detrimental to others while under the influence of these drugs for he would be informed that he may well do something he wouldn't normally under some of these drugs.

I am not trying to make a moral judgement on drug taking for I personally would like to see man utilize his brain power without the use of drugs. However, I firmly believe that this decision should be left to the individual to decide, for only when he accepts the responsibility for his own action, will he be able to really think for himself if the dangers are worth the results for some drugs are dangerous, very dangerous. If our society is or is not to be a drug society it will not be decided by legislation, but by the people. Let's not forget, "The government that governs least governs best." '

From a 51-year-old male professional living in a Canadian city:

'About two years ago I was introduced to marijuana by some young friends who were concerned over my tensions and heavy drinking at that time. I now smoke about 3 or 4 joints a week, either alone or with friends. I must exercise great caution for obvious reasons, but will continue to "break the law" because I consider it unreal, unjust and unfounded on facts.

I have nothing but positive facts to give you. My drinking has reduced itself to wine before dinner (I can no longer "tolerate" hard liquor). I sleep well and have found two psychosomatic symptoms of tension (psoriasis and neurasthenia) have all but disappeared. I have "re-discovered" music. I find my creative interests and abilities enhanced. A waning sexual capacity has reversed itself, particularly when I use the drug in making love with my wife. I have had little paranoia – and only that when not sure of the identity of my smoking companions. I seem to have a quieter, deeper understanding of my children (two boys, 6 and 10) and other children and have not physically punished my boys for over a year.

I am particularly impressed with the effect of cannabis on sensory awareness with nature – and of course my work constantly takes me into this area. I find no habit-forming characteristics in the drug and go for weeks at a time without its use. If there is any psychic dependence it is probably no more or less than that felt for Bach or sunshine.

I feel marijuana should be legalized but controlled by Government and restricted to 18 years and older.'

From a 26-year-old skilled tradesman who says he and his wife, also regularly employed, have been regular users of marijuana since 1967:

'Our use of marijuana has not affected our ability to fulfil our employment obligation, nor is there any problem with our functioning in society the way this ridiculous assumption has been played up in local newspapers.

Before I started using pot, I was basically an aggressive person who perhaps drank a little too much. I was basically lazy with no ambition other than having a good time at any expense, with little or no respect for the opposite sex, nor did I feel any obligation in any form of religion and followed no moral code whatsoever.

I feel the use of marijuana has broadened my outlook on life and caused me to take stock of myself and my future. Marijuana can be used in whatever way the user desires. It caused me to think of my future, and changed me from an irresponsible, rather uncultured individual into one with responsibility. It provided me with a desire to get ahead. It gave me compassion for other people as well as all living things. It has caused me to appreciate the small things in life, something I never before gave any thought to.

I realize I have to contribute a lot of this change that has come over me to growing up and maturing, as well as the love of a wonderful girl who shares all my views, but I know my own mind, and marijuana at the least has played a small but important role in the evolution of myself.

I do not use alcohol anymore, because I find it causes nothing but aggressiveness and arguments and sometimes fights between the people using it. Give the same group marijuana and the aggressiveness is gone. The loudmouth trouble-maker does not exist. People tend to communicate with their fellow man and an atmosphere of friendliness and consideration is enjoyed by most. It would be ridiculous to say it is automatic Utopia for all, but it is definitely an improvement in social behaviour for most.'

From a senior student of languages at a Canadian University:

'The point I want to draw to the attention of the Commissioners today is that while alcohol kills enough brain cells to temporarily cloud the mind and its memory function while generally fuzzing the sensibilities, with marijuana the effect is OPPOSITE. Let me say that during the past two and one half years I've used marijuana three times; most recently in April of this year. And I should say also that

I carry no brief for drugs in general. I come from a family so ornery about human intake of artificial compounds that as a matter of course we use neither aspirins nor monosodium glutamate nor cyclamates – and brew our own wine, beer and cider, out of distaste for chemically-aged alcohol and respect for dissident Irish ancestors.'

From a teacher living in one of Canada's larger cities who signs himself 'A middle-class dope fiend':

'I am 30 years old, married, with three children and one dog. We live in a three-bedroom house in the suburbs purchased three years ago, about the time my wife and I began smoking marijuana. Our children attend the public school system, where their performance is substantially better than average. They also attend Sunday school, though my wife and I have rather fallen away from the strong Catholicism of our upbringing. We own two cars, two TVs, a barbecue and a large mortgage by the standard valuations, we are typical, responsible citizens. We usually vote Liberal, visit the dentist twice a year and have never been in jail. At least not yet.

But for the past three years we have courted economic and social ruin by having in our possession, usually, small quantities of marijuana, LSD and mescaline. Why take such a risk, which to a non-user probably seems disproportionately great? Simply because we feel we have the personal right to determine the ways in which our own consciousness will be altered. Psychedelic chemicals have become a part of the kind of lives we are attempting to lead, as much as television or beer fit into the life-styles of others in our society.

By now you are undoubtedly familiar with the reasons people give for using psychedelics, so I will merely say that marijuana provides us with a useful means of relaxing out of the tensions of everyday, while LSD offers an occasional break with "reality" not unlike a religious retreat in its therapeutic effects. My wife and I have used marijuana about three times a week and LSD perhaps five times a year over the last three years, with no apparent physical, mental or psychological ill effects.

I am a teacher, and have found it convenient to conceal my use of drugs from my students and colleagues. Nevertheless, it is obvious from my vantage point that a large proportion of students – larger by far than the usual estimates of principals and other "experts" – are using soft drugs regularly. I have never advocated the use of drugs to my students; nor can I in conscience recommend to them the unjust and inconsistent laws which govern the use of drugs, including alcohol, in this country. I have observed that the very illegality of marijuana often inclines students to try hard drugs, on the theory that they have nothing to lose, since they're already breaking the law by smoking grass. It is also difficult to persuade a student who *knows* that marijuana is harmless, that society is not lying when it says that heroin too, is bad for him.

I have a large circle of friends, about half of whom are professionals – teachers, lawyers, doctors, etc. – and half belong to the drug-youth sub-culture of artists, hippies and students. Of perhaps 200 acquaintances who use drugs regularly, none to my knowledge has ever had a serious problem resulting from the use of drugs, though some will overdo it, by, for example, staying on LSD for several weeks. It appears to me that serious difficulties arise in those who have personal problems which precede the use of drugs. Stable, "respectable", mature people tend to remain stable after the drug experience. Others, myself included, are able to use psychedelics therapeutically to assist their personal growth.

Self-therapy is at best risky, however, and I would much prefer to have taken LSD for the first time in a medically and psychologically safe environment where pure drugs would be administered to prepared people in ideal surroundings. Such a centre, which might be governmentally licensed, would be used for such powerful drugs as LSD, MDA, psilocybin, STP and mescaline. The innocuous marijuana requires no such elaborate trappings, of course.

May I propose my "ideal" drug laws?

1. Marijuana would be available in much the same way as tobacco is now, preferably marketed by the federal government; parents would likely be about as successful in controlling its use as they now are regarding tobacco (i.e. entirely, if they are adequate parents, not at all if they are not);
2. LSD, psilocybin *et al*, would be available on doctor's prescription, after the "patient" had been introduced to the drug in a Hollywood Hospital (New Westminster, B.C.) type of establishment;
3. The "speed" group of drugs would be available by prescription only, and a massive *true* programme of drug education instituted;
4. The British example with regard to narcotics would be followed.

The easy availability of any drug in a free society suggests that education, not laws are the only reasonable response to the problem. But every day the present laws are perpetrated on the young people of the country, the cause of those who argue that only revolution can bring about necessary change is furthered. The youth of Canada are watching you to either prove or disprove this theory. You have an urgent responsibility in justice, to see that these laws are changed for the better, as soon as possible. Godspeed.'

From a middle-aged mother of three who is a professional writer married to a scientist:

'In his bid to solve the "generation-gap" our middle son brought a packet of marijuana to us for a Christmas present a year ago. I was slightly horrified because I hoped, like most other parents, that my children were not using it. I was not prepared to try it then. However, with the same sort of persuasion that had previously won him the permission to keep a live garter snake, paint his room in odd colours, and study art instead of mathematics, I tried it as did his father, brother and sister.

Not too much happened the first time, except that a kind of mellowness settled over the family. We smiled a lot and listened to music that seemed somehow less forbidding than when the kids played the records previously. The next night we smoked the rest of it, and the place started swinging. It was really marvellous. Everyone managed to talk together, about trivialities mainly, there was no tendency to put down anyone. Opportunities to complain or dig at the lack of academic diligence that was always part of the previous conversations with this boy were ignored, and father in particular listened to some of his ideas with a semblance of civility. That alone made the experience worthwhile. The family that night was closer together than anytime I can recall. I was greatly surprised to see that what had seemed to be many hours was only an hour and a half. We were all very happy together, and went off to our rooms feeling as if we loved each other for the human beings we were, not for mere points on a scale of achievement.

For the first time in years my husband and I talked for an hour or more about work, plans, memories, problems and possible solutions – all things we never discussed with each other because of the old scientist/humanist conflict and the rivalries that develop between people in conflicting fields of interest. The miracle is that he seemed also to be a human being, and not only a work machine that ignored people, and particularly his family. I must have seemed somewhat more reasonable to him too, as he did not try to depreciate my interests.

The real miracle followed when we had intercourse. Instead of the dull, perfunctory act it had become, usually indulged in on my part because it made it possible to get out of it the next night, sex was something splendid. All the old routine thrust and counter thrust to get it over with as soon as possible disappeared. The sensation was extraordinary, each second was a kind of new adventure, each movement an experience, and the climaxes beautiful beyond description. It was far more beautiful than the first weeks of marriage, and the glow of fulfilment lasted throughout the next day. It was both a physical and intellectual rediscovery between two people who knew each other too well for too long.

I sincerely wish it were possible to share this discovery with some of my friends who find their own marriages as stupidly dull as I had done, but the legal restrictions make it unwise to offer this information. It seems to me that the wise prescription of marijuana by marriage counsellors and/or physicians might be helpful in "unblocking" the hang-ups that develop over years of marriage. I would think its therapeutic use in their field alone could contribute to the solution of many problems in our society. Also, the ability to forget old differences and communicate with the grown children in a more genuine manner is also socially significant.

The effect is exactly opposite (to me) to alcohol. Drinking with my husband alone is always a depressing situation, and I do not like the idea of drinking with my children other than wine with dinner. Unlike alcohol, I have not seen in the dozen or so times I've tried marijuana, anyone become hostile or aggressive, or obnoxious for that matter. People do withdraw into themselves to listen to music or explore their own thoughts, but it is not a negative kind of withdrawal. During a couple of sessions I wrote down snatches of conversation which seemed particularly entertaining or brilliant, and when I looked at them later (sober?) they were still valid points to note. Some fascinating flights of fancy have taken place during which a subject was discussed and elaborated upon, and projected into more complex levels, and at least three of these hold the basis for some good research ideas. As a writer, I can compare it to those rare moments when the creative process is at work and ideas flow into some kind of form that can be expanded with the aid of diligent research.

Another phenomenon which interests me is the change in the time/space ratio that one experiences with marijuana. Five minutes can seem like an hour under some circumstances, and awareness of all things present is greatly heightened. Textures are obvious, colours brighter, sounds much more intense, etc., as expressed in the pot poetry of the young. I wish someone would study this phenomenon and see if this expanded awareness is conducive to greater and more rapid learning. Can you shove more information into a five minute period that seems like an hour than you can in a non-pot five minute period? In my own experience I've learned more about music in 12 pot sessions than in the previous 40 years, and even find that I can both speak and understand more French than normally. If this is not due to the time/space phenomenon, maybe it helps establish the role of inhibitions in the learning process. I'm not recommending a joint before every language class, but am suggesting that there are things to be learned from research into the effects of marijuana that might have positive implications in human conditioning.

It is only honest to report that I have experienced one "bad trip". I was very depressed about a variety of matters and my husband suggested a smoke. It was a poor idea, as the depression magnified and on that occasion it was impossible to substitute good experiences for the ideas that were already disturbing me. It is much more fun in a group than with only two people, possibly because there is more opportunity to interact. All the major sorts of discretion and codes of conduct seem to remain intact. I doubt if people do things under marijuana that they would not normally do. There has been no tendency to group sex, orgies, obscenity, etc. in my experience. Among people who are less up-tight about such things, it is probably a normal part of it, but one doesn't have to do things that are against his value system unless he wants to. What it does do is make people feel kindly to one another. It permits a discarding of those preconceptions and prejudices that we hold to one another. It may be valid to extrapolate this further by saying that one holds prejudices as a kind of self-protection. If one drops the prejudice and admits the equality of another, he is in a sense dropping his guard, leaving his ego undefended. If, under marijuana, one does not need this big ego protection, then it is reasonable to regard others in their essential humanity. Applying this concept to the behaviour of the younger generation, one begins to understand why differences in class, race, social position, affluence, etc., hold little interest and are not the source of conflict among them. If this could be proven, I might as a sociologist, recommend that we put pot in the metrecal of the Pentagon and Kremlin, and a few other places too.

Thank you for listening. You have my permission to use this information in any way you wish, since I think the names of the guilty have been changed sufficiently to protect the innocent. May I also commend your committee on the genuine, considerate and intelligent manner in which you have conducted the hearings. I am truly impressed by your approach, and am prepared to respect your conclusions.'

From a 25-year-old male university graduate:

"I have been using grass and hash for four years and feel it should be legalized immediately. Grass and hash are two beautiful gifts to man from mother nature, and have made my life fuller. To think those two substances are classified together with such hard drugs as heroin is absolutely absurd. I have never used heroin and don't intend to.

I hope your task has a happy conclusion in the legalization of marijuana and hashish.

Love and peace.'

From the mother of three children, living in a medium-sized Canadian town:

'I wasn't able to attend any of your hearings so thought I would write our experience and opinions to you. I understand I could write anonymously but I will use our names. I don't mind what you do with what I write about but I would appreciate it if our names were not publized.

We have a family of three – our oldest daughter, aged 21, is married since last May. Our son who is 18 is in first year Science. Our youngest daughter who was 17 in October is also in her first year of an Arts course.

We are comfortable financially, (I would say in the above-average income group locally).

We enjoyed a happy home. In bringing up our children we weren't stuffy about unimportant things but put our stress on the basic values of life – honesty, etc. We think we were good parents (by this we are not saying we didn't make any mistakes). Our children tell us we are good parents and their teachers have said we are good parents. We brought them up to express their own opinions, even though it may not always have been the most popular opinion, in class discussions they contributed a lot and yet their good sense of values in the Humanities showed through.

There was no communication gap in our home. We discussed everything and no subject was taboo.

In spite of all the above mentioned we have just gone through two years or so of our own private hell in our own family life because our youngest daughter decided to experiment with drugs.

I should mention that all three of our children are very intelligent (above average) so it wasn't a case that she was ignorant of the facts. She didn't put us into any danger as far as the law goes as she never brought any home, just the results.

When I hear drug users, in defence of drugs, say teenagers should be allowed to use them because it is their own life, they are messing up – no one else's – this is not true. When you love the member of your family as we all did, and see the change in attitude and personality before you, there are no words to describe the agony the rest of the family goes through and how it does disrupt normal family life.

Our younger daughter was a brilliant student and excelled in sports and had many friends who were always welcome in our home. She was very close to her brother as they shared many common interests and friends.

About three years ago, after seeing TV programmes on drugs (mind expanding), mostly pro, like Timothy O'Leary she asked me if she could try LSD. I said I couldn't give my permission because there are too many unknowns as far as I could tell and since she was only fourteen I couldn't stand the idea that she could destroy her brilliant mind. It was too much of a gamble.

Against our wishes and without our knowledge – she tried it. I became suspicious when we noticed a great change in her attitude and personality and she was frightened to sleep in her own room, as a matter of fact, she got so she couldn't sleep and we were concerned for her sanity. She herself became worried that she was losing her mind, so I encouraged her to see her pediatrician at our clinic. Unfortunately, he was of no help to her and she lost faith in doctors. She gradually dropped all her friends (some loyal friends since kindergarten) and associated exclusively with drop-outs, marijuana users and pushers and American draft dodgers were her exclusive social life now. Most of them were five or six years her senior. Her marks slipped at school (but she never failed a grade). She still was interested in sports but in her own words she couldn't hack it because she wasn't physically fit enough. Relations between her and her brother became strained and to make a long story short she was a horrible child that only a mother could love, and even for the mother it took some doing.

Her sister was away at University so missed out on a lot of the hassle that went on but my husband, son and I discussed it with great concern and decided since we could not seem to get her to see what she was doing to herself (her only answer was that it was harmless), we would show her that we love her which we truly did, regardless of what she said or did to hurt us. We did this for a year without any results (as a matter of fact, she came home stoned more frequently than ever). We never knew what combination of junk she had had because she herself didn't always know. I don't think she took heroin although she tried to assure me that you couldn't become addicted to heroin by skin popping heroin. One of her drug pusher friends told her so and it seemed what he told her was gospel truth.

As much as we tried we found no one that could really help us – a minister was no use because she had given up believing in God. If there is information available we weren't able to find any that was useful to us.

We were beginning to have doubts as to whether we were using the right approach so we decided to contact the R.C.M.P. constable that was working with the schools in the drug field. We have never told our daughter about this and perhaps we will never tell her if there is nothing to be gained from it. We told him some of our friends were advising us to get tough and tell her to quit drugs or pack her bags, but he said: "No, smother her with love." We were glad he said that because we never could have rested had we put her out.

To shorten the story the stress and strain and worry became a lot worse, off and on and about the only time we got a little relief was when the pusher got busted and there was no stuff available. Several of her close friends got busted for possession and it was during one of these periods when she had time to clear the cobwebs from her mixed up brain that we started noticing a marked improvement in her attitude and she started to admit how harmful it had been and how psychologically dependent she had become on marijuana. She realizes that she has lost the power to concentrate for longer periods of time, she has trouble sleeping at times and has days of depression, but after being off it for four, five months now we are hopeful that she has licked it and will not fall prey to it again. She said she gets it offered frequently on campus but so far has been able to say "no thank you" to all the offers.

When she was home for Thanksgiving week-end I asked her if she thought marijuana should be legalized and she said "no, it shouldn't". She has discovered around town that the users start at a younger age than she did (and she was plenty young) so she feels it would be far too dangerous. She also feels there should not be so much publicity about it describing exactly how to glue sniff, etc. because she said if kids haven't thought about trying it before, it just makes them curious enough to try it. She said she never would have tried drugs if it hadn't been for hearing Tim O'Leary tell about it on TV and the programme didn't have a good enough balance telling the bad sides of it. She did feel kids shouldn't get sent to jail or have a criminal record if they are caught with it because she said they learn worse things in jail from hardened criminal types. I am inclined to go along with that. She feels kids that try it, a good many of them, have some mental quirk to start with and should be given psychiatric treatment instead.

You have no idea how happy we all are to have this monstrous problem behind us and to be a happy family again.

Hope this will help you in a small way in your decisions.'

From a 21-year-old electronics technician:

'I have been smoking marijuana regularly for about two years now. During this time I have been working and studying and at no time has this interfered with either. I am definitely in favour of legalizing pot at this time. I would definitely not attribute any gains to my use of pot but it has in no way been a liability to me. I have quite a few friends who also use pot and also fall in the same category. My hopes are that this Inquiry may be instrumental in reversing this law.'

From a 31-year-old father of three who calls himself an 'average Joe' earning $9,500 a year, and who has experimented with cannabis, mescaline and LSD:

'Now, to be logical and realistic – how on earth can we condone the use of alcohol and tobacco and saturate ourselves daily with these substances while at the same time hanging criminal records on people who dare to touch marijuana and hashish – substances that have yet to be proven even equally as harmful?

To me this would represent the height of hypocrisy and is an obvious blatant evidence of a sick society!

Do we stop to realize that with every day that the existing legislation continues, the gap of our young people's confidence in our government and our legal system widens? Need we even enumerate here the ultimate consequences of such a state of affairs?

When I think of our government, or any government putting young people away to rot for years with hardened criminals in penitentiary – for such things as smoking "grass" or "hash", I cannot help but be reminded of what the Communists did to political prisoners in Siberia! I would like to think that we are part of a slightly more enlightened society.

There is no denying that the Government of Canada is faced here with a difficult and serious task and all consequences of a change in legislation must be carefully weighed.

The following are my suggestions and I feel certain that most knowledgeable people would concur with them and I am confident that something along these lines will eventually come to pass:

1. Marijuana and hashish to be legalized and manufactured under government control with supervision of quality and distribution, and the application of excise tax etc.
Alternatively, each citizen can grow cannabis for the use of his own household only (much like wine can be made now) with continued ban on the sale of such substances.
This should certainly detract from the use of such harmful substances as speed, heroin, etc.
2. LSD and mescaline to be responsibly manufactured and distributed to certain people by pharmacists on a doctor's recommendation or prescription only. When I say "certain people" I mean people who have satisfied a doctor that they are responsible and sane. Why not let the medical men decide who can use these beautiful and in many cases useful (alcoholism) substances?
3. Heroin must be legally prohibited – I doubt that Heroin can ever do anyone any good.
4. The use of speed, amphetamines, bennies, diet pills, etc., should be discouraged by appropriate educational campaigns supported by the government. Most people already know that these things are harmful. The government might also have a look at some of our food dyes and artificial flavours, sweeteners, etc.

Most marijuana that large percentage of users have come in contact with has been of an inferior grade and cut with various possibly harmful substances or impurities. I am sure that many kids have tried this "garbage" and shrugged it off as ineffective and uninteresting and have consequently, in order to obtain the alleged "kick", turned to methedrine and amphetamines, thereby doing themselves untold damage.

This hazard could in all probability be largely eliminated by legalization and quality control of real marijuana and hashish. (It would also be pointless to legalize "grass" only and continue to condemn "hash".)

In my humble opinion, the discovery of LSD-25 and its possible use in psychotherapy and medicine is a twentieth-century achievement of far greater importance and beneficence to man than walking on the moon. Taking a small dose of LSD can be a very beautiful and enriching experience indeed.

The only problem with "acid" is that in order to benefit from it and really have a good "trip", it requires that the individual make a certain effort to be aware of himself while under its influence, to concentrate a bit or meditate, if you will. If this is not done, you have a 50/50 chance of getting "lost" in the corners of your mind or in your imagination alone, and this can be terrifying to say the least. *A good trip conductor* should be present for anyone trying it for the first time or for anyone who has had previous difficulties under it. It should never be arbitrarily given to anyone who already has an unbalanced emotional-mental make-up or who is paranoid, has strong guilt complexes, etc.

It is easy enough to see that anyone who has latent suicide tendencies could go off the deep end under acid. On the other side of the coin, I happen to know a married couple who had been bickering for years and were on the verge of a break-up who, after an acid trip together, re-discovered their original love for each other and are now living in model marital bliss. And it is great for those who want to have a glimpse or an inkling of what "God" is; what creation is all about. Of course it will not transform overnight a real criminal into a model citizen, but in certain cases, with proper guidance it could probably go a long way in this direction. For anyone in doubt, it can show that needless killing is a sin or that insincerity is a form of sin. Also, it is almost useless to try and describe it to anyone who has not tried it.

I would recommend that all serious members of the Commission go on a conducted acid trip prior to further research or probing, and it goes without saying that anyone conducting research on grass should know first-hand what grass is all about. Otherwise, it would be like studying swimming by watching swimmers.'

From an instructor at a Canadian university:

'Recently I was unable to purchase marijuana and when a friend offered me some "MDA" I thought it would be interesting to try this drug. The first "trip" was a good one where I experienced all the usual symptoms, euphoria, etc., but the second one had disastrous consequences. After a brief period of euphoria I went into a state of extreme depression in which my only concern was to end my misery by any means possible, including suicide. Luckily, the friend with me pulled me out of my depression by making me walk

394

and talk. (The "MDA" I believe had some stimulant in it as we walked for six hours and felt "strange" whenever we were standing still.) The worst part of the trip came later when I noticed that every inanimate object was hostile towards me. Everything had the power to destroy me. A candlestick could club me, shoes could trample me, the fireplace could devour me, etc. I wrote my thoughts down hoping that setting them out would make me see how ridiculous they were. I wrote, "It's like going insane and knowing every minute of it." Needless to say, I was terrified. Fortunately the paranoia did not last and I believe I have fully recovered now, about one week after my "bad trip".

I have told you this story hoping you would come to the same decision about drugs that I have reached. I felt safer (legally) taking MDA than marijuana because I had previously found out that although possession of this drug was illegal, prosecutions were rare and conviction did not carry such harsh penalties as those imposed on marijuana users. Also, since all these drugs were illegal and I knew marijuana was harmless, I was not about to reject the drug on the grounds that it was forbidden. The law concerning marijuana was stupid, therefore, in my opinion, so were all laws about all drugs.

I urge you to recommend the legalization of marijuana. Perhaps young people, then, will regain respect for the law. Perhaps they will use marijuana (if they must use something) and reject destructive and dangerous amphetamines. I will allow my children to use marijuana and at the same time I will try and convince them of the dangers in these unknown drugs. Further, I will give them marijuana if doing so will protect them from the experience I had. Do you see that I must be sensible and just, to win their respect and obedience? Do you also see that legislators must exercise the same reason before they can expect cooperation from the people?'

From a 23-year-old graduate student in engineering, male, who smokes marijuana and hashish 'socially' and finds that it does not affect his studies:

'I think the law on soft drugs must be changed. Marijuana, hashish and mescaline should be legalized. Marijuana should be treated exactly as tobacco is treated presently. Mescaline is a more tricky case, all I can say is that the federal government should control it so that quality would be ensured and pushers would be eliminated. I do not think age restrictions would work any better than the age restrictions we have on tobacco which mean only a slap on the wrist for an offender. The present laws have totally alienated young people. Policemen are "pigs", MLAs are "pigs" in their eyes. Can you blame them? People who have never tried a "joint" are telling kids they cannot smoke because of countless harmful effects. Take a walk along Hastings Street in downtown Vancouver (Gastown) and see what alcohol, the adult poison, has done to what were once human beings. The type of kids who get busted for smoking are the ones who go to the street dances to dance with and entertain all those pitiful alcoholics. I've been there so I'm not making it up.

Make marijuana legal and the kids will believe that heroin and speed kill when told by the lawmakers. They do *not* when all the illegals are lumped together.

LSD? I have not tried it, so no opinion. I can say that many of my friends have, with no bad trips or noticeable lasting personality changes. I'm not sure, though, and don't want to try it, especially with the quality being sold now.

Another danger with present laws is that we could have the situation which exists in the United States where a Black Panther can be conveniently put away for thirty years for possessing a "joint". We have no Black Panthers? How about separatists, radical students, dirty long hairs, future Indian rebels.

Want to know how easy it is to get grass or hash? I have three sources of hash and can pick up a gram at any time. I usually buy a gram every few weeks or else smoke some of my friends'. I have to admit that good grass is rare because it is becoming much riskier to smuggle or sell due to its bulkiness. During the summer there is lots more particularly on the west coast. Much is locally grown. In any case I've never been short in three years. All one has to do to get some is to make friends who know a few people, etc. People talk about it. There is very little paranoia.'

From a female school-teacher in a medium sized Canadian town:

'Both my husband and I smoke marijuana and hashish and have not found it the least bit detrimental to our health — physical or mental. Marijuana has been an encouraging factor in our marriage and partnership to tie our union closer together as we can explore and discover ourselves and our environment with an open and free mind.

Because of my profession, a school-teacher, and my husband's job we have to be extremely cautious and careful, limiting our enjoyment of smoking marijuana in our basement behind locked doors.

Many of our friends join us and unite with us in our plea to the Canadian Government to reconsider the "marijuana laws". May I say now, that I exclude other mood-changing drugs such as LSD.

Smoking marijuana and hashish has not affected my teaching in a destructive way, but rather, helped it. I teach primary children and find it much easier now to communicate with the children at their level and meet their demands in a more satisfying way.

The people who have made the laws against marijuana (government) and the people who administer the laws (policemen) have most probably never lit a marijuana cigarette and never will. Some changes and improvements in these laws should be done in the near future.

It is ironic that our present marijuana laws are upheld chiefly by the older generation and condemned by the young generation. For it is the senior generation that should understand the issue most clearly, having lived through the era of alcohol prohibition.'

From a female school-teacher:

'My husband and I are 25 years of age, middle class, school-teachers and heads. On week-ends we break the existing law by smoking pot or hashish. We break the law with many other respectable young men and women such as accountants, guidance counsellors and teachers. We have been committing this crime for three years and are quite paranoic about it. You see, if we are busted, besides the fine or sentence, we would surely lose our jobs because we would not be fit to teach the nation's young.

Why do we take the chance?

The effect of the plant is delightful but I don't think that warrants taking such a risk. I believe partially I'm taking a stand. I believe in individual freedom as long as no harm comes to another human. I don't feel the government has the right to forbid me from smoking just as they have no right to tell me with whom to sleep. Pierre E. Trudeau agrees with me on the latter point. It is like a strict parent compelling a child not to do something without proof of any danger to the child.

About the effect, that depends upon the environment. Usually one's paranoia never leaves so it is never as relaxing as it could be. One feels happy, giggly, hungry, sometimes friendly and other times alone. I can bring myself down if I have to although I am aware that my sense of timing is off.

We have not increased the amount we smoke therefore I can not agree that it is addictive. During the summer we don't smoke because we are usually travelling and it is not safe to carry it with you. We don't suffer any symptoms during that time.

We have never tried LSD or any other chemical substances, use few drugs, do not believe in sleeping pills or stimulants. Several of our friends have used LSD frequently. We are afraid for our future children although I think the chances are slim. My cousin has also used LSD. He's a psychiatrist and used it for medical research.

About the gossip that it leads to hard drugs – nonsense, the statistics are turned around to make it reach such a conclusion. It is most inaccurate. I have never had the slightest desire to try harder stuff, sniff in glue or banana peels.

I smoke in the same circumstances as people drink, at social gatherings. I don't come home from school, grab a bottle or take a smoke. I can face life without it although I don't always want to. It is not a crutch to me.

I don't believe the law should make me into a subversive person. The law must try to keep up-to-date. Pot must be legalized and perhaps an age limit of sixteen should be imposed. You must become informed as to its effects so teenagers will know what they can and cannot do under the influence.'

From a young man employed in the broadcasting industry:

'I have used drugs for these reasons: In the beginning, I was experimenting. I bought some marijuana, and forgot to ask how much you were supposed to smoke . . . went home and smoked what I have come to realize is about twice as much as is normally consumed, or five cigarettes thereof, without looking up. At that time, I was living right beside the sea. I went to the window after smoking the dope, noting as I went that there was an unaccountable but very pleasant grin spreading across my visage, and looked out.

Before my very own eyes was a magnificent sight . . . the yachting school was having a course of instruction in sailing, and there was a race between about thirty little sailboats in progress, their sails coloured like easter eggs, so bright in the beautiful sun. "Easter Sails" I thought, and promptly went outside to sit in the sun on the beach, and watch the miracle of wind play its tricks on a group of fairly doubtful sailors, some of whom got pretty wet in the proceedings, and a fantastic time was had by all, and (I felt) especially me.

That did it. From that day forth I was a drug-freak, and over the next two years experimented with, enjoyed, and learned from, all the soft drugs on the market . . . pot, hash, mescaline and acid.'

From a 19-year-old university student, male, who says it is time the government 'stopped protecting individuals from themselves':

'My experience of drugs! I've tried both grass and hash for roughly two years. I really enjoyed the high that I got and it got me off the drinking kick that every high school kid gets into. And now that I have begun to realize that life itself is the best kick possible, I have watered down my own smoking. But it's still fun to drink a few beers or smoke a few joints every now and then. If anything, I think marijuana has helped to slow me down and appreciate life through my senses instead of drinking myself into a fun thing at parties! I went to a Hallowe'en party last night sober and it was fun. Especially the costumes.'

From a student nurse who says it is 'high time that a well-qualified, dispassionate and objective commission review the drug question':

'I am a student nurse and although I do not smoke marijuana now (due to its legal hazards and my hopes for a career), prior to this time I smoked it for about four years. I suffered no harmful effects, either temporary or long-term, from its use and observed none in others, whom I know smoked it on a regular basis. I might add that some of these people were older (30–40 years) and engaged in various skilled professions. I found that, while under its influence, peoples' social behaviour did not degenerate into belligerence or numb stupor as it often does under alcohol, nor that their sexual inhibitions were in any way affected by it.

Personally, I found it made contemplation, constructive intro-spection, the fulfilling of creative potential (I was painting quite seriously at the time), and appreciation of subleties in music and art much easier due to heightened perceptions and increased sensitivity. I certainly disagree with those people who say it leads *per se* to apathy.

Granted, there will always be people who will abuse (i.e. over-indulge in) any beneficial thing that comes along – by this I mean they will make the mistake of centring their life's activities around it – alcohol is a prime example of this. However, I feel that the majority of people have the good sense to use moderation. Prohibition tried to make the *many* suffer for the indiscretions of the *few* and I feel the present marijuana laws present a parallel. They are equally as unenforceable, I think. Over this issue in particular, I feel, young people have lost respect for law due to its hard-headed, antiquated and unreasonable approach to the matter.

I have sat in courtrooms here in this city and watched fresh-faced young people, charged with possession of marijuana, forming a part of the regular courtroom parade of prostitutes, petty criminals and hard-core drug addicts (those to whom heroin, for example, has become a way of life). I must say that the contrast is remarkable and I feel that if these young people, whose minds are still developing and whose educations are not yet completed, are put in jail at such a critical period, as their attitudes are still forming, will rapidly become cynical and disillusioned with a society which enforces such a severe penalty for a (to them) non-existent crime.

I truly feel, from my experience, that the insights I gained with this, a very natural drug, have stayed with me and helped me to appreciate more freely the wonder of the universe and the sacredness of life. I think that if most (and/or even any) people can gain this from the use of marijuana then it certainly has a useful place in a society with as many problems both spiritual (mental illness due to loss of faith, lack of contact with nature, etc.) and physical (overpopulation, pollution, etc.) as ours has in 1969. Anything which can help (especially the younger generation) to gain insights on how to solve these problems should be made use of, rather than be forbidden by law.

I think LSD holds the same potentials for individual self-development, but I feel that it should be government controlled to maintain purity. I believe many of the disastrous effects experienced by people are due to the impurities contained in the "bath tub" varieties made by amateur chemists. I believe strychnine is found in some lots sold on the streets. I think there should be places where, after some psychological investigation as to fitness, people should be allowed to take it in pleasant surroundings with, perhaps, a psychiatrist available, if needed. The person should be allowed to have friends around him at this time. This, of course, is a hypothetical suggestion for the future – I offer it because a problem exists now. Publicity has aroused curiosity in many people who want now to take it themselves, and will, sooner or later, find a source. The trouble is that what they find may be so impure as to have catastrophic effects. Also, perhaps there are people who never should take it, due to severe psychic conflicts. But I do feel that the situation as it exists now will *not* be resolved simply by legal suppression. I more than feel it, I *know* it. Since this is a more complex problem than marijuana (and hashish) I offer merely a suggestion.

However, in regards to marijuana, I think that time (a short time, too) and the growing number of people using it – both young and not-so-young, will make it mandatory that marijuana become legalized. The only question is – how many more people will have to suffer the stigma (and worse) of a criminal record before this ban is removed? Surely the search for truth and the wish to evolve is the natural prerogative of mankind and youth in particular.'

From a university professor in Eastern Canada:

'I have enjoyed smoking marijuana and hashish several times, and I feel that if they are made legal, we have far more to gain than to lose. I think they can easily be incorporated with our way of life in Canada without eroding any but purely materialistic or exploitive values. Marijuana does not provide an escape from reality any more than alcohol, sex or a drive in the country: we know we cannot be high all the time; we enjoy taking a trip (in both senses of the word) and we remember it with pleasure, but we know that we have to come back home again and go to work, and continue our everyday life. I have so often heard the argument that pot or hashish lead to hard drugs. For the vast majority of pot smokers, this is rubbish. It is the argument that temperance societies use against alcohol: social drinking leads to alcoholism. I have never had the slightest desire to shoot anything into my arm, nor do I want to try speed in any of its forms. There will always be a few disturbed people in our world, and I don't think that laws should be made for that tiny minority.

What are the benefits of marijuana? Some people talk about a feeling of euphoria as though a state of bliss was somehow unnatural and depraved because they think it will lead to an escape from reality. Actually, the opposite is true: getting high lets you appreciate reality in much more of its complexity than you normally would. Music becomes unquestionably clearer when you are high, even quite complex music, from Bach to electronic productions – you perceive more than you ordinarily would and this perception is not lost afterwards: it becomes part of you. Food – particularly good food – tastes better. Conversation, especially if you are with close friends, becomes more meaningful than the frivolous chit-chat of everyday communication. You get beneath surfaces and appearances and penetrate to a clearer vision of reality, because you realize that every word you say is important: words count: they're not the pastimes or instruments of manipulation. They explore and describe reality. And finally, love-making. Pot, as almost everyone knows, is not an aphrodisiac in the way alcohol is. It doesn't make you want to pounce on the person you happen to be next to. But if you are with someone you love, and you're both high and want to make love (and I must repeat that pot does not break down barriers you don't want broken down), making love on pot is a beautiful experience. Every sensual reaction is enlarged and prolonged, including of course the climax. You may say that this sounds like a floodgate of sensuality, but I must point out that pot does not reinforce sensuality to the detriment of the mind. If you want it to be an enrichment of intellectual experience, it will be. Habitual smokers are very correctly called "heads", because pot helps you to reconcile emotions and intellect – you don't see them as contradictory but as partners. I am not saying that you can perform feats of intellect when high. For serious, concentrated thinking you need to be sober, but pot acts on your mind in somewhat the same fashion as inspiration touches a poet. He sees something illuminating; he dashes off a first impression and then comes back and works on it again in the cold light of dawn. That is what happens with pot, and I find I come back again to this idea of perception; pot helps you perceive the world and yourself, while allowing your mental faculties to investigate the ideas later. You don't black out or forget, as you do with large amounts of alcohol. It helps you reconcile an instinctive with a cerebral perception of the world if you want to.

I wrote to John Turner last winter deploring the persecution of young long-hairs by the police and the R.C.M.P. As many people have observed, this leads not to a lessening of pot and hash smoking, but to a disrespect for the police. I would like to see the force more respected, because, as we all know, police need public support and sympathy in order to perform efficiently. What sympathy can they expect when they disguise themselves as hippies in order to infiltrate and arrest them? Hippies are not communists *circa* 1947, and this police tactic only degrades the officer who undertakes it, as well as the force in general. The hippies feel that the R.C.M.P. is acting out of ignorance and fear; they believe that pot-smoking is good, and there is no reason why they should change their minds: they are working from experience, and R.C.M.P. actions no matter how "legal", spring from institutionalized paranoia.

I am not underestimating the temporary upheaval which legalizing marijuana and hashish might cause in certain sectors – police, puritans, all those who wish to force their own limits of freedom and pleasure on the country as a whole. I think we should have the right to choose for ourselves whether we want to smoke or not. I think we have far more to gain than to lose in legalizing pot and that in a few years, once people have tried and accepted them for what they are – neither instruments of destruction, nor passports to paradise, but simply pleasurable adjuncts to everyday life (and, I believe, a richer life) – we will see what a false problem the whole thing was, and will, I hope, spend more of our energies and public time and funds coping with more pressing problems facing mankind.'

COMMISSIONERS AND STAFF

Chairman Gerald Le Dain, Q.C., Dean of Law, Osgoode Hall Law School, York University, Toronto.

Commissioners Marie-Andrée Bertrand, Associate Professor of Criminology, University of Montreal, Montreal.
Ian L. Campbell, Dean of Arts, Sir George Williams University, Montreal.
Heinz E. Lehmann, M.D., Clinical Director, Douglas Hospital, Montreal.
Peter Stein, Social Worker, Vancouver.

Executive Secretary James J. Moore

Commission Counsel John Bowlby, Q.C.

Research and Administrative Staff C. W. Doylend
Dr C. G. Farmilo
Melvyn Green
B. R. Hemmings
Mrs Vivian Luscombe
J. K. Macbeth
N. T. G. Martin
Dr R. D. Miller

NOTE: Professor André Lussier, an original member of the Commission, resigned June 25, 1969, following which Professor Bertrand was appointed.

SOME SURVEYS OF DRUG USE AMONG CANADIAN HIGH SCHOOL AND UNIVERSITY STUDENTS

Reference has been made in Chapter Three of the interim report to studies carried out in Canada during 1968 and 1969 on the estimated extent and some patterns of use of various drugs by some high school and university students. The authors of the studies will be found in the list of references.

Estimated Extent of Use of Alcohol by High School Students

Location	Date	Sample	% Using[1]	Conducted by
Toronto	1968	6,447	46·3[2]	A.R.F. (Smart & Jackson)
London	1968	11,454	M–73[3] F– 63	A.R.F. (Stennett *et al*)
Montreal	1969	4,504	48·1[4]	O.P.T.A.T. (Laforest)
Halifax	1969	1,606	39·9[5]	Whitehead
National	1969	2,249	88·5	C.H.S. & P.T.F.
North Vancouver	1969	207	44·4	Rush
British Columbia[6]	1969	3,340	46·2	N.A.F. (Russell)

[1]At least once within previous six months.
[2]By Grade: VII – 22·9%; IX – 41·6%; XI – 59·7%; XIII – 70·9%.
[3]Frequent drinkers: Males – 20%; Females – 11%.
[4]By Grade: VIII – 23·8%; X – 53·0%; XII – 67·2%; XIV – 77·8%.
[5]By Grade: VII – 21·1%; IX – 37·8%; XI – 57·4%; XII – 54·8%.
[6]Six school districts.

Estimated Extent of Use of Alcohol by McGill University Students in 1969[1]

Faculty	Sample Size	% Total Use	% Used Before Attending McGill	% Commenced Use After Attending McGill
Science	721	82·4	61·2	21·2
Arts	713	89·7	85·0	4·7
Medicine	202	91·2	79·8	11·4
Law	118	89·0	80·5	8·5

[1]Conducted by Brophy and Propas.

Estimated Extent of Use of Barbiturates by High School Students

Location	Date	Sample	% Using[1]	Conducted by
Toronto	1968	6,447	3·3[2]	A.R.F.
London	1968	11,454	1·5	A.R.F.
Montreal	1969	4,504	2·7[3]	O.P.T.A.T.
Halifax	1969	1,606	3·0[4]	Whitehead

[1]At least once within previous six months.
[2]By Grade: VII – 1·3%; IX – 3·9%; XI – 4·4%; XIII – 3·8%.
[3]By Grade: VIII – 1·4%; X – 4·5%; XII – 2·1%; XIV – 1·9%.
[4]By Grade: VII – 1·4%; IX – 2·9%; XI – 5·1%; XII – 3·1%.

Estimated Extent of Use of Tranquillizers by High School Students

Location	Date	Sample	% Using[1]	Conducted by
Toronto	1968	6,447	9·5[2]	A.R.F.
London	1968	11,454	9·0	A.R.F.
Montreal	1969	4,504	9·8[3]	O.P.T.A.T.
Halifax	1969	1,606	5·9[4]	Whitehead
B.C.[5]	1969	3,430	27·3	N.A.F.

[1]At least once within previous six months, with or without prescription.
[2]By Grade: VII – 4·8%; IX – 11·4%; XI – 11·6%; XIII – 14·6%.
By Sex: Females – 10·4%; Males – 8·1%.
[3]By Grade: VIII – 5·0%; X – 9·2%; XII – 8·7%; XIV – 11·1%.
By Sex: Females – 9·6%; Males 6·3%.
[4]By Grade: VII – 2·4%; IX – 6·6%; XI – 8·4%; XII – 8·2%.
By Sex: Females – 6·6%; Males – 5·4%.
[5]Six school districts.

Extimated Extent of Use of Amphetamines (Stimulants) by High School Students

Location	Date	Sample	% Using[1]	Conducted By
Toronto	1968	6,447	7·3	A.R.F.
London	1968	11,454	5·6	A.R.F.
Fort William	1968	214	4·2	Hayashi
Port Arthur	1968	101	5·0	Hayashi
Province of Quebec	1968	8,500	9·7	Radouco-Thomas *et al*
Halifax	1968	1,606	6·4	Whitehead
Montreal	1969	4,504	5·8	O.P.T.A.T.
National	1969	2,249	3·6	C.H.S. & P.T.F.
B.C.[2]	1969	3,430	3·7	N.A.F.

[1]At least once within previous six months.
[2]Six school districts.

Estimated Extent of Use of LSD by High School Students

Location	Date	Sample	% Using[1]	Conducted By
Toronto	1968	6,447	2·5	A.R.F.
London	1968	11,454	M– 1·9	A.R.F.
			F– 0·6	
Fort William	1968	214	0·5	Hayashi
Port Arthur	1968	101	1·0	Hayashi
Montreal	1969	4,504	3·0	O.P.T.A.T.
Halifax	1969	1,606	2·4	Whitehead
National	1969	2,249	2·2	C.H.S. & P.T.F.
British Columbia[2]	1969	3,430	6·6	N.A.F.
Regina	1969	216	11·5	King *et al*

[1]At least once within previous six months.
[2]Six school districts.

Estimated Extent of Use of LSD by University and College Students

University or College	Location	Date	Sample	% Using[1]	Conducted By
Loyola	Montreal	1968	700	1·6	Menard
Bishop's	Lennoxville	1968†	619	0·7	Campbell
Bishop's	Lennoxville	1969†	609	3·1	Campbell
McGill[2]	Montreal	1969	1,745	6·0	Brophy & Propas
Sir George Williams	Montreal	1969	137	10·0	Axelrod & Rubinstein
Saskatchewan	Regina	1969	850	10·4	King *et al*

[1]At least once within previous six months.
[2]By Faculty:

	Science	Arts	Medicine	Law
LSD	5·3%	9·7	3·9	6·0
Mescaline	3·7	8·4	3·9	5·0

†Surveys carried out in fall and spring terms of the same academic year.

Estimated Extent of Use of Cannabis by High School Students

Location	Date	Sample	% Using[1]	Conducted By
Toronto	1968	6,447	6·7	A.R.F.
London	1968	11,454	M– 7·9 F– 3·6	A.R.F.
Fort William	1968	214	8·9	Hayashi
Port Arthur	1968	101	13·0	Hayashi
North Vancouver	1968	208	24·2	Rush
Montreal	1969	4,504	8·5	O.P.T.A.T.
Halifax	1969	1,606	6·6	Whitehead
Province of Quebec	1969	8,500	9·7	Radouco-Thomas *et al*
Pembroke-Renfrew	1969	2,083	5·9	Renfrew County Sch. Bd.
Regina	1969	216	23·6	King *et al*
British Columbia[2]	1969	3,430	19·7	N.A.F.

[1]At least once within previous six months.
[2]Six school districts.

Estimated Extent of Use of Cannabis by University and College
Students

University or College	Location	Date	Sample	% Using[1]	Conducted By
Loyola	Montreal	1968	700	M–15·0 F– 7·0	Menard
Bishop's	Lennoxville	1968†	619	19·6	Campbell
Bishop's	Lennoxville	1969†	609	27·3	Campbell
McGill	Montreal	1969	1,745	34·6 (marijuana) 29·3 (hashish)	Brophy & Propas
Sir George Williams	Montreal	1969	137	32·6	Axelrod & Rubinstein
Saskatchewan	Regina	1969	850	30·5	King *et al*
B.C.	Vancouver	1969	434	44·5	Linde

[1]At least once within previous six months.
†Surveys carried out in fall and spring terms of the same academic year.

Estimated Extent of Use of Solvents (Glue) by High School Students

Location	Date	Sample	% Using[1]	Conducted By
Toronto	1968	6,447	5·7	A.R.F.
London	1968	11,454	10·2	A.R.F.
Fort William	1968	214	8·0	Hayashi
Port Arthur	1968	101	12·0	Hayashi
Halifax	1968	1,606	3·1[2]	Whitehead
Montreal	1969	4,504	1·9[3]	O.P.T.A.T.
National	1969	2,249	6·0	C.H.S. & P.T.F.
British Columbia[4]	1969	3,430	12·4	N.A.F.

[1]At least once within previous six months.
[2]By Grade: VII – 3·6%; IX – 5·2%; XI – 1·9%; XII – 0·0%.
[3]By Grade: VIII – 2·3%; X – 2·6%; XII – ·8%; XIV – 1·0%.
[4]Six school districts.

REFERENCES

1. Axelrod, C., and Rubinstein, S. Research study: 'Recreational drugs'. Sir George Williams University, Montreal, 1969.

2. Brophy, J., and Propas, S. McGill drug survey. Montreal, 1969.

3. Campbell, I. Marijuana use at Bishop's University. (A preliminary statistical report). 1969.

4. Campbell, I. Marijuana use at Bishop's University. (A second preliminary statistical report). 1969.

5. Canadian Home and School and Parent-Teacher Federation. Progress report: Use of drugs and alcohol by young people. National Family Life Committee, Canadian Home and School and Parent-Teacher Federation, 1969.

6. Hayashi, T. The nature and prevalence of drug and alcohol usage in the Port Arthur Board of Education Summer School. Fort William, Addiction Research Foundation, 1968.

7. Hayashi, T. The nature and prevalence of drug and alcohol usage in Fort William schools. Fort William, Addiction Research Foundation, 1968.

8. King, J., McDonald, D., and Salloum, H. A survey of the use of marijuana and LSD in the University of Saskatchewan, Regina Campus, and in Regina High Schools. 1969.

9. Laforest, L. *La consommation de drogues chez les étudiants du secondaire et de collégial de l'Ile de Montréal.* Québec Office de la Prévention et du Traitement de l'Alcoolisme et des Autres Toxicomanies, 1969. (O.P.T.A.T.)

10. Linde, W. C. Brief on extent of use and opinions regarding marijuana submitted to the Commission of Inquiry into the Non-Medical Use of Drugs, Vancouver, 1969.

11. Menard, L. C. In *Loyola Conference on Student Use and Abuse of Drugs.* Montreal: Canadian Student Affairs Association, 1968.

12. Radouco-Thomas, S., Villeneuve, A., Hudon, M., Monnier, M., Tanguay, C., Tessier, L., Lajeunesse, N., Gendron C., et Radouco-Thomas, C. Enquête sur l'usage des psychodysleptiques (hallucinogènes) dans les collèges et universités de la province de Québec, Partie 1. *Laval Médical,* 1968, *39,* 817–33.

13. Radouco-Thomas, S., Villeneuve, A., Hudson, M., Tanguay C., Monnier, D. Gendron, C., et Radouco-Thomas, C. Enquête sur l'usage des psychodysleptiques (hallucinogènes) dans les collèges et universités de la province de Québec, Partie II. *Laval Médical*, 1969, *40*, 103–7.

14. Renfrew County School Board, Pembroke Police Department, and Pembroke R.C.M. Police Department. Secondary school drug survey. 1969.

15. Rush, G. B. A brief on marijuana use and school leavers presented to the Commission of Inquiry into the Non-Medical Use of Drugs, 1969.

16. Russell, J. *Survey of drug use in selected British Columbia school districts.* Vancouver: Narcotic Addiction Foundation of British Columbia, 1970.

17. Smart, R. G., and Jackson, D. J. *A preliminary report on the attitudes and behaviour of Toronto students in relation to drugs.* Toronto: Addiction Research Foundation, 1969.

18. Stennett, R. G., Feenstra, H. J., and Aharan, C. H. *Tobacco, alcohol and drug use reported by London Secondary Schools.* London: Addiction Research Foundation and London Board of Education, 1969.

19. Whitehead, P. C. The incidence of drug use among Halifax adolescents. 1969.

CURRENT RESEARCH ON CANNABIS AND OTHER DRUGS

The Commission is aware of a number of research projects underway in Canada and the United States which are intended to provide scientific information on cannabis and other psychotropic drugs. In the short time allotted to it, the Commission has attempted to survey the current state of some of this research.

General Problems of Research. Research on certain psychotropic drugs is controlled by governmental regulations and policies. The Food and Drug Directorate (F.D.D.), Department of National Health and Welfare (N.H. & W.), Ottawa, and the United States National Institute of Mental Health (N.I.M.H.), the United States Food and Drug Administration (F.D.A.), and the United Nations Narcotic Commission on Drugs are among the organizations which administer regulations respecting the exchange of certain psychotropic drugs among scientists and institutions. The Commission invites scientists interested in drug research to comment on these protocols and regulations which may affect their research and planning of new projects.

Reference Standards. Research on cannabis is still hindered in Canada by a very short supply of chemically pure cannabinols, particularly delta -1-, and delta-1(6)-tetrahydrocannabinols. Consideration should be given to production of these and other cannabinols in Canada, at an adequate laboratory scale. Controlled cultivation of cannabis and production of purified natural resin cannabinols has been undertaken at relatively low cost from time to time in the past by F.D.D. In addition, studies of cannabis seized by police, and the extraction of active constituents of these materials had been carried on in Canada up until 1964. Only limited research of this type has been carried on since that time but could be easily expanded. This work should be directed towards the development of standards and methods of analyses of cannabis. Such effort would be essential to the development of a cannabis research programme.

Research Projects. The Commission is compiling lists of research projects which have been approved by appropriate authorities in Canada. Some of these projects will be supported by grants from agencies such as the Narcotic Addiction Foundation of British Columbia, the Addiction Research Foundation of Ontario, and l'Office de la Prévention et du Traitement de l'Alcoolisme et des Autres Toxicomanies of Quebec City. Later in this report we refer to a number of Canadian and American studies presently underway or being considered.

The following are the nine major areas of research: I – Epidemiology; II – Legal Aspects; III – Drug Effects on Human Behaviour; IV – Drug Effects on Animal Behaviour and Metabolism; V – Chemistry and Biochemistry; VI – Applied Biochemistry (e.g., Determination of Drugs in Body Fluids); VII – Clinical Research; VIII – Prevention and Education; IX – Documentation Research.

I – Epidemiology

Three studies of selected samples of (1) The Canadian population as a whole; (2) High School students and (3) College and University students are being sponsored by the Commission to determine the social characteristics of drug users and their patterns and frequency of use. Information is also being sought on factors predisposing to, precipitating and perpetuating non-medical drug use in Canada. A number of recently completed Canadian surveys are referred to in Chapter Three and reported in Appendix E. Other studies are underway in Canadian universities.

Twenty-three studies of patterns of drug use in student, college and other young adult populations are shown in the N.I.M.H. marijuana research programme list. Another survey of subjective effects of cannabis as reported by questionnaire respondents is underway in the United States.

II – Legal Aspects

Two major reviews of the laws and regulations controlling marijuana and other drugs are under way in California. A study of the genesis of the present drug laws including examination of the sociological factors has been completed by the Department of Sociology at the University of Toronto. A detailed study of the Canadian criminal justice system and its effect on the drug offender is being sponsored by the Commission. A study of the criminal law processes on those apprehended for drug offences, including any 'criminalizing' consequences is also being conducted. By these means the Commission is endeavouring to measure the social costs of the pre-

413

sent methods of drug control, and to assess the efficiency of the control system.

III – Drug Effects on Human Behaviour

Mention has been made of a proposed study by the Addiction Research Foundation of Ontario of effects of administration of cannabis on humans. The study is being planned in three phases – physiological effects of cannabis; social behaviour under chronic use; micro methods for detection of cannabis in human tissues.

Marijuana studies on humans are listed by the United States N.I.M.H. Center for Studies on Narcotics and Drug Abuse (C.N.D.A.). The following are among the projects which have been approved in the United States; studies of cannabis effects on perceptual and cognitive functioning; time sense, self-concept, depersonalization during THC intoxication; mechanism of action of marijuana including biological and behavioural aspects; mechanism of conditioning and drug action of marijuana; study of effects of marijuana (crude) in human volunteers on various psychological and physiological inputs; clinical research employing EEG profile analysis in humans under the influence of THC, and Synhexyl*; study of marijuana users' reports of their experiences while under the influence of the drug.

Two United States research projects deal with the effects of marijuana on driving and attention.

IV – Drug Effects on Animal Behaviour and Metabolism

Five Canadian investigators have received authorization from the F.D.D. to acquire marijuana or THC for animal research; two at the Addiction Research Foundation of Ontario, and one each at the Departments of Pharmacology at Dalhousie University and Ottawa University, and one at a Montreal private research laboratory.

Similar studies on the neuropharmacology of central nervous system stimulating agents, including THCs, are proceeding at the University School of Medicine, Nashville. At the University of Rochester, a study of specific behavioural processes which are related to the neuropharmacological actions of THC isomers (added to cigarettes) in monkeys is continuing. Research is being carried out at the University of Oregon on the behavioural effects resulting from the administration of cannabis, THC and other psychotropic drugs.

Various branches of the National Institute of Mental Health are conducting several related studies, including: determination of the effects of marijuana on heart and circulatory systems of anaesthetized dogs; the development of procedures for evaluating behavioural dependence liability of non-narcotic drugs, and the exploration of environmental factors controlling such behavioural dependence in male albino rats and monkeys dependent on LSD, THC, amphetamines, barbiturates, chlordiazepoxide, and some other tranquillizers.

V – Chemistry and Biochemistry

The Canadian Food and Drug Directorate has undertaken analytical chemical studies of cannabis, and other plants containing psychotropic substances, for law enforcement purposes. Cannabis is being studied along with homologues of amphetamine (MDA, MMDA) for the development of standards and methods of analysis for similar purposes. A project to synthesize THC and label the molecule is also being planned.

The United States Center for Studies on Narcotics and Drug Abuse and other branches of the National Institute of Mental Health report a number of studies in this category, including: extraction of cannabinol mixtures from seized and cultivated plant materials; synthesis of pure THC isomers and development of industrial pilot plant production procedures for THC; study of kinetics of *in vivo* transportation following inhalation of THC as a vapour; examination of the toxicological potential of cannabinols on mammalian reproductive systems; examination of pregnant rats, hamsters, mice and rabbits for teratogenic reactions to marijuana resin; and a study of the effects of two marijuana-active substances on the central nervous system and on the biochemical interactions of enzyme systems and biogenic amines.

VI – Applied Biochemistry (e.g., Determination of Drugs in Body Fluids)

The Department of Pharmacology, University of Toronto (and the Addiction Research Foundation) are jointly continuing an animal study of behavioural pharmacological properties of THC, which includes a study of sensitive, rapid methods of detection of THC in urine, blood and saliva of rats and charting the route of metabolic transformation. A similar study is under way in the United States. The analytical service laboratory at the Addiction Research Foundation is also planning to carry out human biological assay of cannabinols.

The Center for Studies on Narcotics and Drug Abuse of N.I.M.H. in the United States is supporting four projects to develop new methods for the detection of narcotics, barbiturates, amphetamines, phenothiazines, marijuana and hallucinogens for use in the study of behavioural pharmacological problems and their relationship to levels of these drugs in body fluids.

VII – Clinical Research

No Canadian experimental research on the effects of cannabis in humans is currently under way to our knowledge. However, sixteen clinical research programmes with LSD are mentioned in the Food and Drug Directorate lists. Marijuana research supported by various N.I.M.H. programmes in the United States which may be active during 1970 includes clinical screening of psychotropic drugs (e.g. LSD, mescaline, THC and Synhexyl*) in schizophrenics and non-psychiatric subjects.

VIII – Prevention and Education

There are several programmes of drug education under way by various agencies in Canada. Critical evaluation of major drug education programmes will be undertaken by the Commission.

Five projects are supported by the Center for Studies of Narcotics and Drug Abuse which relate to the prevention of non-medical drug use by means of education. An advertising agency is providing consultative services to N.I.M.H. on the use of mass media for public education in narcotics and drug use, including development of national advertising campaigns using television and radio commercials, newspaper and poster advertisements and brochures, etc. The American Association for Health, Physical Education and Recreation is developing guidelines for teacher education and instructional materials to be used in schools. A number of American studies are testing newly developed health education materials and evaluating teacher-student responses to them.

IX – Documentation Research

The Commission is studying the problems of collecting, storing, sorting and retrieving annotated and abstracted scientific and technical information on the subject of psychotropic drugs. It is planned to consult with experts in Canada and abroad to attempt to identify the centres of information, to assist in providing an information network in order to make recommendations for further activities in this area.

INNOVATIVE SERVICES

A. INTRODUCTION

Innovative Services are social and welfare agencies that are conceived of, and staffed and directed by persons indigenous to the youth communities they serve. These agencies represent a responsible attempt to provide, through innovative means, social, material, or professional assistance for young people in need.

Few of these services are concerned exclusively with drug use. Some are not primarily oriented towards adolescent or bohemian sub-cultures. However, all of these agencies have developed institutionally atypical or experimental methods of dealing with drug related problems that constantly come to their attention.

These Innovative Services utilize a direct, personal, empathetic and immediate approach to the needs of those whom they serve. This is an approach that the Commission has been told is particularly productive in eliciting the voluntary cooperation of those in need of help.

During the course of the Commission's hearings, we have been approached in all parts of Canada by representatives of these youth agencies. They describe their organizations as a human response to the social problems directly associated with the various life styles embraced by large numbers of Canadian youth. Some characteristics of this style are: a desire to travel, a disinterest in material things in and for themselves, less than usual concern with conventional standards of health and sanitation, and sexual and drug experimentation. This way of life has given rise to a host of social problems that range from the need for temporary accommodation and food, to the need for a variety of medical services to deal with such things as malnutrition and 'freak outs' produced by drug use.

The Commission has attempted to understand why young people have set up their own agencies to handle these problems. In grappling with this question, much can be learned about the general problem of value conflict that presently exists between the youth and adult populations. Established social service agencies such as the Welfare Department, the Y.M.C.A., Children's Aid, and the like, are described by members of the youth agencies as being too rigid, impersonal, detached and often too committed to traditional values to respond to the unique problems of their generation. There is a feeling that these agencies are characterized by punitive and condescending attitudes and excessive professionalism. Bureaucratic and formal procedures are seen as dehumanizing, and there is resentment at the unwillingness of many agencies to be available at all times of the day or night. Some established agencies are accused of lecturing and moralizing to the young people who have, for the time being, tended to drop out of the so-called 'straight' society.

Further, these youths express their disinclination to accept help from agencies which, they feel, embrace what they consider to be the conventional middle-class morality that affirms the compulsive observation of such values as the work ethic, sexual propriety, cleanliness, and moderation.

Whether in fact the established agencies do operate in a paternalistic fashion and do demand from the young person a commitment from him to change his transient, unemployed status before he will be able to receive services, is not the important point. The fact is that many young people believe that this is true. Some also fear that the established agencies may not respect the confidential character of information regarding their drug use history, and that revelations to authorities may result in the apprehension for drug or drug related offences.

B. *Organizational and operating characteristics of Innovative Services*

They tend to be very informal. Some are closely identified with a charismatic personality around whom the programme and facilities evolve.

Most of the agencies operate in a relatively non-bureaucratic fashion. This means that they have limited records. Their requirements for staff have little to do with formal educational and training programmes. The result of this departure from the traditional agency's way of seeking staff is to raise questions regarding the criteria to be used to assess both the competence of staff and the products of their endeavours. Further complicating this are very real value-conflicts with conventional conceptions of the 'right life'. Some of the criteria accepted by the staff of the Innovative Services will be referred to in the discussion of funding problems.

Most Innovative Services have advisory councils or boards of directors which are composed of respected members of the established community. Their functions include giving the service visible approval and thereby helping to attract funds for its continued operation. The board members are also *partners* in the decision-making processes of the agency. They act as a sounding board on policy matters. The traditional hierarchical structure in which a board of directors sets policy and hands down directives is viewed as objectionable and inconsistent with the value systems of the young people who have set up these agencies.

C. *The kinds of service generally provided*

Innovative Services make available, usually on a short-term basis, facilities for both eating and sleeping for transient youth who are often in towns other than their own. In some instances these services are only provided during the busy summer season.

They are sources of information regarding the existing social services available in a community. Referrals are often made to welfare or medical agencies that they believe can be 'trusted' or with which a working agreement has been established.

There is a real difficulty facing the Innovative Services when an underage minor presents himself at the door as a runaway. Child Protection Statutes in most provinces generally require that Law Enforcement authorities be contacted immediately in such circumstances. The police may try and return the child to his home or place him with the Children's Aid Society. We have been told, however, that if a runaway suspects that he will be turned over to these legal authorities, he may not seek help at all.

In some provinces, the Innovative Services have been strongly urging the Children's Aid Agencies to consider their residential setting at least as a recognized and official temporary alternative during the initial planning period for the runaway. These youth agencies, although often different in appearance and milieu to the transitional foster homes and group homes, are an important addition to the range of placements available to today's teenage runaway.

They provide a setting within which young people can talk to one another about their travels and experiences. One of the major criticisms of these organizations is that the young people have only their own age and attitudinal group to talk with, and therefore they are cut off from any challenges to their viewpoints. Though this may be a valid point, the fact remains that the youth have expressed a need and a desire to have drop-in centres in which they can openly discuss those matters which concern them.

The Innovative Service is often viewed as a 'cool' setting, relatively free of the police 'hassling' that is said to characterize living on the street. This security is partly a function of the apparently universal 'no drugs on the premises' rule, and partly a consequence of the partial and perhaps growing acceptance by the community of most Innovative Services. Some drop-in locations, however, have suffered repeated police raids, although the lack of actual arrests in many cases suggests that the purpose may often be harrassment rather than serious law enforcement.

Innovative Services often operate as emergency crisis centres. In most cases, members of their staff are accessible 24 hours a day, seven days a week, to talk to youngsters who are in a state of panic as a result of drug experiences. There is access in some communities to doctors who can be summoned quickly. Medical care is often required for a variety of conditions, including malnutrition, pregnancy and venereal disease. The staff is also generally familiar with the most appropriate means of treating adverse reactions to various drugs, and with the procedures required to obtain emergency admission to hospitals.

The very existence of these Innovative Services appears to operate, in a general way, as a gadfly to the more traditional social welfare services. They are continually confronting the established community services and insisting that they become more humanly relevant and more responsive to the changing nature of social problems that the youthful life style reflects. Some youth services have accused the established services of treating young people as though they were helpless and infantile and have suggested they should perceive them as more responsible and self-sufficient.

Another way in which this is stated is the request that the established agencies work *with* their clients as co-partners, rather than *for* them. Thus, the definition of the human problem and its alternative solutions should come from a *shared* exploration, rather than as a result of a decision made by a professional social worker, who assesses the individual requesting help and then tells him what he ought to do with his life.

D. *Reasons for involvement of the Innovative Services in the problems of non-medical drug use*

There is a greater amount of experimentation in illicit drug use among the clients of these services than among the clients of other agencies.

Established agencies are unfamiliar with the drug phenomenon and, in some cases, they are unwilling to deal with it because they view it as a criminal problem.

Many youths have told the Commission that they go to the Innovative Services because of the age of the staff and the staff's nonmoralizing orientation towards drug use in general. Stated simply, they find a more sympathetic and knowledgeable awareness of their drug problems and a more congenial setting.

Young people have also stated that Innovative Services are more cognizant than established agencies of the fact that when a young person is having difficulties with drugs, the drug use itself is likely only symptomatic of underlying emotional or physiological difficulties that warrant attention.

E. *Drug use problems dealt with by Innovative Services*

Legal. Although legal aid is available in some provinces, Innovative Service staff often experience difficulty in locating adequate legal aid for young persons in the community. The youth in need of these services are often extremely naïve regarding their legal rights. Legal services may be sought for any number of reasons, including violations of drug laws.

Medical. Youths in a drug-induced state of panic are often afraid to seek out hospitals or doctors because of a fear that they will be treated in a hostile or punitive way or reported to the police. The staff of an Innovative Service assist in neutralizing the panic reaction that may occur, and they also help the person to obtain the needed medical assistance. The staff may also act to neutralize the hostile and punitive attitudes that may be found in medical facilities and thereby increase the likelihood of effective post-crisis treatment.

Educational. The general ignorance on the part of the public and mass media concerning the effects of various illegal and legal drugs presently used by youth has led to what some Innovative Service staff call an 'information gap'. Most of these organizations are therefore committed to informing youth *and adults* about various drugs and their effects. Some agencies, for example, have developed specific educational programmes to convey to young people the very real physical dangers that can result from excessive use of amphetamines.

Since impurities are often found in 'street' drugs, some Innovative Services have attempted to obtain an analysis of the chemicals young people are using in order to alert them to the potential danger of 'bad trips' from poor quality drugs. Established drug foundations have been wary of seeking out this information, because they are not anxious to be accused of appearing to encourage youthful 'illegal' drug use and because of the necessity of authorization to possess drugs for purposes of analysis.

F. *Funding*

The high visibility of these organizations means that any mistakes become glaringly evident to the public. Because of the nature of the problems with which they attempt to deal, they are prone to evoke strong emotional responses in their local communities. The degree to which these youth services are able to function with any effectiveness depends to a large extent on their capacity to gain trust in the community. The opening of some of those agencies has been greeted by organized community protests which have taken the form of petitions to city hall requesting strict enforcement of zoning by-laws to force the closure of 'overcrowded' and allegedly 'unsanitary' hostels.

In the first months of their existence, the Innovative Services have the problem of being unable to demonstrate in a bureaucratically convincing way just exactly what their programmes will involve. Money from private foundations or 'Red Feather' community service grants are often unavailable to new social agencies until they have demonstrated that the service is viable over a period of one or two years.

The very nature of the problems being dealt with by these services causes suspicion from some adult critics. Such critics claim that the existence of these services encourages young people to use drugs or to run away from home. Innovative Service staff reply that this claim is a gross over-simplification. They insist that the services are a response to the social problems resulting from new youth life styles that are evolving out of a host of social, political and economic factors. The representatives of these agencies suggest that some adults use the agencies as scapegoats rather than giving serious consideration to the social issues on which young people have focused.

Reference was made earlier to the problem of developing criteria that can be used to assess these services. One general criterion that has been accepted by all of the Innovative Services that have come to the Commission's attention is the strict compliance with the law on the premises of the services. This is obviously a prerequisite for remaining open since the community could not allow such services to function in defiance of the law. A further criterion is some form of fiscal accountability which will permit public knowledge of the manner in which money is spent. Thus, the staff must be willing to engage openly with the community in an examination of the agency's methods and processes. This task is welcomed by most Innovative Services.

A variety of funding arrangements are made by Innovative Services, including donations from private individuals and foundations and grants from federal, provincial and municipal governments. A number of youth agency staff have expressed appreciation of the awareness and flexibility that they have found to characterize the welfare grant policy of the federal Department of National Health and Welfare. In general, there is an apparent desire on the part of most Innovative Services to receive funds from a wide variety of public and private sources so as to not become dependent on any particular source in the community.

G. *Summary*

The Commission believes that the development of Innovative Services represents, on the whole, a positive attempt to deal with the problems faced by a growing number of Canadian youth. Increased cooperation and understanding are required by the public in order to assist these Innovative Services to continue their efforts to overcome information and communication gaps in our communities.

The existence of innovative and youth services provides an example of a structure towards which some of our social institutions may be evolving. Here are agencies which have developed in response to a new set of value priorities emerging among young people. These values stress human relationships over bureaucratic excellence. They develop programmes in a cooperative policy-making fashion, utilizing clientele, staff, and board members as co-equals. They provide an outlet for meaningful social service at a time when many young persons are cynical about committing themselves in traditional ways to working for the improvement of society.

H. *Some examples of Innovative Services*

Despite the basic similarities in their approaches to drug related problems, each of the Innovative Services remains an independent agency. Their working-philosophies, self-conceptions, and financial sources, reflect, in each case, their unique circumstances and the influence of varying personalities and schools of thought. The following cases serve as a few illustrations of the nature and ideological range of these agencies. The information has been gathered from conversations with agency staff and clientele, concerned citizens, and formal agency briefs.

The Trailer Project is designed, primarily, to serve the needs of those young persons who inhabit the Yorkville area of Toronto, where it is situated. The principles which underlie the Trailer's entire operation are probably best expressed in the following extract from their November, 1969 Report:

> In order to serve any group of people, it is essential to attempt to understand emotionally and intellectually their environment. This understanding develops if we are directly involved in that environment – thus, 'be where the action is'. Young people have the right to have needed services available if they wish to change their life style or need a crisis response. Non-professional young people are able to serve other young people in an environment with which they are familiar. It is important to have professional people working in a back-up capacity.
>
> Young people are demanding changes within society. Many of their demands are absolutely essential to our society's adaptive survival. The Trailer concept then must also be a vehicle for educating the established community, to facilitate these changes . . .
>
> Thus the Trailer was born in an effort to bridge the gap between the unchanged institutions and the changing young people who need those institutions to become alive, relevant, and aware of their needs.

The Trailer Project is sponsored by the Jewish Family and Child Service of Metropolitan Toronto.

COOL-AID – Victoria

Cool-Aid was originally founded as a working committee of the Victoria Youth Council on June 10, 1968. It was established as the result of an analysis of the 'extent and facilities available to young people in the Greater Victoria Area', conducted by the Victoria Youth Council in April and May of that year. The Victoria Youth Council's conclusion was that there was a great need for youth-run and youth-oriented organizations in the City of Victoria.

Initially Cool-Aid billeted transients in private homes across the city. But as demands on its facilities became greater the private resources were unable to meet the growing need and so Cool-Aid decided to seek public support. In March of 1969, it published a budget asking for six months' support in the amount of $6,120 for two houses in the City of Victoria. In April, 1969 both the City of Victoria and the provincial Department of Social Welfare agreed to provide the requested financial support. Cool-Aid opened its first house on May 1, 1969. Essentially, the staff make all final decisions including how all monies are to be handled.

Cool-Aid sees itself as a multi-purpose organization dedicated to a number of ends: (1) providing 'housing on a temporary basis for transient or displaced young people', (2) making professional medical services (medical, dental, and psychiatric) available, (3) providing professional legal services, (4) making counselling services available (for runaways, families, drug freak-outs, attempted suicides), (5) finding jobs for young people and (6) providing 'information about and liaison with other community service organizations'.

Cool-Aid sees itself as a 'group of kids learning, trying to help other kids. It is kids, in a very peculiar way, trying to be their brothers' keepers. People helping people. Cool-Aid is for kids who can't be helped in any other way'. Its success, like the success of any drop-in centre across Canada, depends on its 'credibility', on its proven trustworthiness: 'Kids often will turn to us for help just because we are ourselves kids. This has been, and continues to be, the secret of Cool-Aid's success.'

CRYPT – Winnipeg

(Committee Representing Youth Problems Today)

CRYPT was founded in May, 1968 to deal, at first, with the problem of transient youth. This remains its primary function and orientation. It was given financial assistance by both the Manitoba government and local private donors. There is a staff of 60 volunteers to help youths with medical, legal, housing, counselling and employment problems. CRYPT operates as an intermediary between more professionalized assistance and young persons who are either ignorant of where to go for help or who fear that help may have a punitive approach or involve detention.

CRYPT has been the object of severe local anti-drug criticism. Thus, it claims to go to some length to dissociate itself from the promotion of drug use.

CRYPT believes the function of a drop-in centre is to provide 'a neighbourhood-based focus for youth activities and projects, and allow the problems of youth ... to be aired, understood, intercepted and resolved before a damaging crisis point, such as dropping out of school or running away from home, is reached'.

One of its reports on the difficulties encountered by youths when they attempt to obtain help for their drug problems stated that – 'A previously accepted policy of reporting drug abuse cases to the police made the hospitals the last place a young person sick with drugs wanted to go.' As a result of consultation with hospitals, the policy changed. The policy of reporting drug abuse to the police was replaced by a policy of treating those who suffer in one way or another from the effects of drug use in the same way that any patient would be treated for any other 'disease'.

CRYPT is defined in one of its publications as:

A diverse collection of people, reflecting varied backgrounds of education, experience and occupation united in a consensus of concern for alienated young people in society. This concern stems from the inability or unwillingness of existing social services and agencies to provide effective, constructive and immediate assistance to those in need. The volunteer staff are prepared to help any person find their own best solution to any problem.

THE YOUTH CLINIC – Montreal

The Youth Clinic was originally developed as part of the Youth Emergency Services programme established by the Y.M.C.A. and the Montreal Council's social agencies in the summer of 1968. This support ended in September of 1968, but it was decided to maintain the Clinic.

The Youth Clinic is primarily a medical-social service agency serving the needs of young people in Montreal. The needs of youth, it says, can best be met if these services are 'planned by young people, or those empathetic to the needs of young people'.

The stated functions of the Youth Clinic are threefold: 1. to provide medical and professional services for needy young persons who would otherwise not receive these services; 2. 'to act as a referral and/or liaison link with the appropriate services in the wider community', 3. 'to place indigenous, detached youth workers in the clinic and on the street, for counselling and referrals'.

The Youth Clinic, which is open nearly every night of the week, provides, as well as it can, comprehensive medical attention. Among major medical problems treated at the Youth Clinic are venereal disease, chronic chest disease, malnutrition, psychological or emotional problems (for which a psychiatric clinic is provided), and problems connected with drug use, including 'drug-induced acute anxiety states (freak-outs)'.

YOUTH COMMUNICATION SOCIETY – *Halifax*

Motivated by a lack of facilities for transient youth during the summer of 1968, a group of young people, with the assistance of the Nova Scotia Provincial Youth Agency, rented a house and opened it as a demonstration project during the summer of 1969.

Salaries for the director and for part-time workers were provided for by the Provincial government. Additional funds to meet operating costs were also raised by young people through dances.

The house was used as a hostel for transients, and as a comfortable place for young people to get together and talk. A medical clinic, staffed by voluntary doctors, was available one night a week. Youth with non-medical problems were referred to other agencies. The project closed at the end of summer when the house was returned to its owners.

The organizing group has carried on during the fall and spring of 1969–70 without a residence. They have informed the Commission that they have an urgent need for funds if they are to continue this programme the year round.

X-KALAY – *Vancouver*

X-KALAY is an Innovative Service of a type rather different than those services described in this Appendix in that they focus on older drug users who have been in prison. Furthermore, their treatment philosophy is based on complete abstinence.

The idea of X-KALAY was initiated by a number of Indian recidivists in a British Columbia prison about the year 1966. These men felt that they needed a self-run half-way house in the Vancouver area to enable them to break out of the recidivists' circle (i.e. leave jail, spend your $10 for alcohol or heroin the first night, and go back to jail the next day).

With the exception of a member of the Company of Young Canadians' staff who became involved in assisting with the formation of this project, the original organizers were all Indians. Thus, it was at first called the Indian Post-Release Centre. The primary techniques employed were T-group sessions, confrontation approaches, and marathon therapy, along with general 'hard hitting' methods of rehabilitation.

In 1968 the name was changed to X-KALAY and the Company of Young Canadians assisted with financial support for one full-time staff member and two paid volunteers. Other funds came from occasional private grants, real estate transactions, and other business ventures, including a service station franchise.

Most of X-KALAY's clientele are men and women who have been heavy users of hard drugs. However, X-KALAY representatives stress that they are more interested in general rehabilitation than in drug problems. As X-KALAY's founder explained at the Vancouver hearings: 'X-KALAY is a totally self-disciplined, self-supportive type of venture. We operate a service station, own apartments and so on. Through work, play, learning, talk ... through a number of different kinds of group processes, as well as a simple community process of living your life and putting food into your mouth and so, we demonstrate that it is possible to live without drugs.'

GLOSSARY OF SCIENTIFIC AND
TECHNICAL TERMS

Abstinence Syndrome
See *withdrawal syndrome* and *physical dependence*.

Acute
Of short duration and usually of relatively high intensity.

Addiction (*drug*)
An ambiguous term with various meanings in different situations. The concept usually implies a strong *psychological dependence* (or compulsion to use) and/or *physical dependence* (*withdrawal symptoms* in abstinence) and, often, a tendency to increase dose (*tolerance*).

Administration (*drug*)
The process of introducing a drug into the body (e.g., swallowed, inhaled, injected).

Adverse Reaction
A drug reaction which is unpleasant or harmful psychologically and/or physiologically.

Analgesic
Pain relieving.

Anaesthesia
The loss of feeling or sensation, and may imply (with general anaesthetics) a loss of consciousness.

Antagonist (*drug*)
A drug which blocks or counteracts certain effects of another drug.

Aphrodisiac
Sex-drive stimulating.

Biology
The scientific study of life and living things in general.

Blood Alcohol Level
The concentration of alcohol in the blood (usually represented in per cent by weight).

Cardiovascular
Pertaining to the heart and blood vessels.

Central Nervous System (*CNS*)
That portion of the nervous system consisting of the brain and spinal cord.

Chromosomes

Thread-like materials in the nucleus of a cell which contain the genes (i.e., the factors responsible for hereditary transmission).

Chronic

Persisting over a long period of time.

CNS

Central nervous system (brain and spinal cord).

Cognitive

Psychological processes involved in perception, thinking, reasoning, etc.

Control Group

A group of subjects as similar as possible to the experimental subjects (and exposed to all the conditions of the investigation) except for the experimental variable or treatment being studied. (Compare *experimental group*.)

Cross-Dependence

A condition in which one drug can prevent the *withdrawal symptoms* associated with *physical dependence* on a different drug.

Cross-Tolerance

A condition in which *tolerance* developed to one drug results in a lessened response to another drug, as well.

Delirium

A condition (usually of relatively short duration) characterized by excitement, confusion, incoherence, *illusions, delusions* and, sometimes, *hallucinations*.

Delusion

A belief which exists in spite of contrary reason or evidence which would normally be considered sufficient to change it.

Dependence (drug)

A state of *psychological* and/or *physical dependence* on a drug following periodic or continued use of the drug. Specific characteristics of dependence usually vary depending on the particular drug in question.

Dependent (drug)

An individual who has developed *dependence* (*physical* and/or *psychological*) on a drug or group of drugs.

Depersonalization

A state in which a person's sense of his own (or his body's) 'reality' or existence is weakened or lost.

Depressant

A drug which depresses or decreases bodily activity. Depressants may be classified according to the organ or system upon which they act. The terms 'CNS depressant' and 'sedative' are often used interchangeably.

Dose (or *Dosage*)
The amount or quantity of drug administered.

Double Blind
A term used to describe an experiment in which neither the subject nor the researcher knows which particular treatment (e.g., the identity or dose of a drug or a *placebo*) is being given at the time of the study. This procedure may reduce the influence of *placebo* effects and other kinds of subject and scientist bias. (Compare *single blind, placebo*.)

Drug
Any substance that by its chemical nature alters structure or function in the living organism.

Electroencephalogram (EEG)
The graphic record of wavelike changes in electrical potential (voltage) obtained when electrodes are placed on the scalp or on (or in) the exposed brain.

Experimental Group
Those subjects who are exposed to the experimental (or treatment) variable (e.g., a drug) and whose behaviour or condition is considered to reflect the influence, if any, of that variable. This influence may be revealed by comparing the experimental subjects with a matched *control group*.

Extrapolate
To make estimates or inferences about a variable or factor in relatively unknown circumstances on the basis of what is known from studied situations.

Foetus (*Fetus*)
The unborn offspring developing in pregnancy.

Gastro-intestinal
Pertaining to the stomach and intestines.

Habit-Forming (*drug*)
A drug which may produce *dependence* (usually psychological) in certain users in certain circumstances. (Compare *habituation*.)

Habituation (*drug*)
Usually implies (1) a desire (but not a compulsion) to continue drug use, (2) little or no tolerance, (3) no physical dependence.

Hallucination
A sensory perception which is not based on an external physical stimulus. *Pseudo-* and *true hallucinations* are often distinguished:

A true hallucination includes the belief that the abnormal perception is physically real, while a pseudo-hallucination is recognized as being 'unreal' or a distortion of normal perception (compare *illusion*). Hallucinogenic drugs usually produce pseudo-hallucinations rather than true hallucinations, although in acute psychotic drug reactions 'reality contact' may be lost.

Hypnotic
Sleep inducing.

Illusion
A false or misinterpreted sensory impression. The individual is usually aware of the 'unreal' qualities of the perception. (Compare *delusion, hallucination.*)

Intravenous (*Injection*)
The injection of a drug directly into a blood vein (usually with a hypodermic syringe).

Latency
The period of inactivity between stimulation and the response or reaction to that stimulus.

Non-Medical Use of Drugs
Use which is not indicated (or justified) for generally accepted medical reasons, whether under medical supervision or not.

Overdose (*drug*)
The administration of a quantity of drug larger than that desired or normally taken. Usually implies some adverse or toxic reaction.

Paranoia
A condition characterized by *delusions* of persecution and/or grandeur. In severe instances paranoia may be considered a sign of *psychosis* (e.g., paranoid *schizophrenia*).

Pharmacology
The scientific study of the effect of drugs on the living organism.

Physical Dependence
A physiological state of adaptation to continuous use of a drug (normally occurring after the development of *tolerance*) which results in a characteristic set of *withdrawal symptoms* (often called the *abstinence syndrome*) when administration of the drug is stopped.

Physiology
The scientific study of biological functions in the living organism.

Placebo

A substance without relevant pharmacological activity which is used in drug research to determine and control for the influence of the subject's motivation, expectations, etc. (e.g., his psychological *set*). A placebo effect is a reaction entirely due to the subject's *set* and *setting* rather than the pharmacological properties of the substance.

Poison

A drug in a quantity which exceeds the amount which the body can tolerate without damage or injury. Any drug can be poisonous if the dose is high enough. (Compare *toxic*.)

Potentiation

An overall effect of two drugs taken together which is greater than the sum of the effects of each drug taken alone.

Psychoactive

See *psychotropic*.

Psychological (or *Psychic*) *Dependence*

A condition in which a person depends upon something (e.g., a drug) for satisfaction or a feeling of well-being. Psychological dependence on a drug may vary in intensity from a mild preference to a strong craving or compulsion to use the drug. In severe cases, unpleasant psychological symptoms may develop if continued administration of the drug is stopped. (Compare *physical dependence, habituation*.)

Psychology

The scientific study of behaviour and the mind.

Psychomotor

Pertaining to muscular activity or behaviour associated with certain psychological functions. Psychomotor tests usually measure such things as muscular coordination, behavioural skills, etc.

Psychopharmacology

The scientific study of the (interaction) effect of drugs on psychological and behavioural activity.

Psychosis (*Psychotic*)

An ambiguous term with a variety of meanings. It has often been used to refer to any severe mental or behavioural disorder, although more specific applications usually also imply the presence of *delusions* or *hallucinations* and a general inability to test or evaluate external 'reality'. There is often considerable disagreement among authorities as to what exactly constitutes a psychotic state; the diagnosis is often highly subjective and may vary greatly among observers.

Psychotropic (or Psychoactive) Drugs

Those drugs which alter sensation, mood, consciousness or other psychological or behavioural functions.

Reverse-Tolerance

A condition in which the response to a certain dose of a drug increases with repeated use. (Compare *tolerance*.)

Schizophrenia

A group of naturally occurring psychotic disorders generally becoming manifest in late adolescence or early adulthood. (Contrary to popular belief this term does not refer to 'split'- or 'dual-personality').

Set

The psychological state or disposition of an individual which affects his subsequent drug experience. Such factors as the person's expectations, motivations and attitudes may be important factors in determining drug effects. (Compare *setting*.)

Setting

The circumstances or environment in which the drug experience occurs. It is usually a significant factor in determining drug effects. (Compare *set*.)

Single Blind

An experiment in which the subject does not know which particular treatment (e.g., the identity or dose of a drug, or a *placebo*) is being given. The researcher is aware of these experimental factors at the time of the test in a single blind design. (Compare *double blind*.)

Statistically Significant

A measurement or score which is highly unlikely to have occurred by chance alone and might therefore be attributed to some specific non-random factor (e.g., an experimental treatment or selection variable).

Teratogenic

Producing physical defects or abnormalities in the offspring (*foetus*) during pregnancy.

Tolerance

A condition in which the response to a certain dose of a drug decreases with repeated use.

Toxic

A damaging or disrupting drug effect (often used to describe symptoms of poisoning). All drugs have toxic effects if the dose is high enough. (Compare *poison*.)

Withdrawal Syndrome (or Symptoms)

A characteristic set of adverse physiological (and psychological) symptoms which occur, after the development of *physical dependence*, when the regular administration of the drug is stopped (or its effect inhibited by an *antagonist*). Also called the *abstinence syndrome*. The characteristics of withdrawal vary with different drugs and with the individual patterns of use associated with the *dependent*. In severe instances the withdrawal symptoms may be fatal.

INDEX

References are to page numbers throughout. Only those names which appear in the text of the report are listed in the index. The index does not include the references and footnotes for each chapter or the individuals and organizations listed in Appendix A. The relation of one topic to another is shown by using the second as a subheading under the first; thus in most cases the subheadings also appear as index entries.

438

441

443

444

447